MEDIATION REPRESENTATION

NATIONAL INSTITUTE FOR TRIAL ADVOCACY

MEDIATION REPRESENTATION
ADVOCATING IN A PROBLEM-SOLVING PROCESS

HAROLD I. ABRAMSON
TOURO LAW CENTER

Please send your feedback to habramson@tourolaw.edu.
All comments will be welcomed and much appreciated.

Anthony J. Bocchino, NITA Editor in Chief
Temple University Beasley School of Law

Zelda Harris, NITA Associate Editor
University of Arizona College of Law

ISBN 978-1-55681-821-9

Abramson, Harold I., *Mediation Representation: Advocating in a Problem-Solving Process* (NITA 2004)

Library of Congress Cataloging-in-Publication Data

Abramson, Harold I.
    Mediation representation : advocating in a problem-solving process / Harold I. Abramson.
        p. cm.
    Includes bibliographical references and index.
    ISBN 978-1-55681-821-9
        Mediation--United States. 2. Dispute resolution (Law)--United States. 3. Attorney and client--United States. 4. Negotiation. I. Title

KF9084.A915 2004
347.73'9–dc22   2003071025

10   09   08   07   5   4   3

To my mother and father
who continue to inspire me by the way they live.

—

To my children Todd and Elizabeth
who have made my life so rich.

Summary of Contents

TABLE OF CONTENTS

Appendixes

ACKNOWLEDGMENTS

This book culminates a decade of researching, developing, and testing approaches to mediation representation in a variety of demanding settings inside the classroom, in continuing legal education and training programs, as well as in mediations. These settings were filled with inquiring students, seasoned and sometimes cynical litigators, and experienced and talented mediation advocates. I owe all these anonymous teachers a deep debt of gratitude for permitting me to learn from them.

My mediation representation journey began in January 1994, when Norman Itzkoff, Cathy Cronin-Harris, Steve Younger, and I got together to design a program on mediation representation for the annual meeting of the New York State Bar Association. Planning this program with these thoughtful colleagues impelled me to prepare my first public thoughts on the subject and propelled me to focus on it in depth.

Thereafter, I began researching, interviewing experienced attorneys, and evaluating approaches to effective advocacy in mediation. I initially turned to the law students in the course I teach on dispute resolution. These students became involuntary subjects for testing concepts, ideas, and materials. As I experimented on my students, I was fortunate to be offered many opportunities in continuing legal education programs to present ideas to academics and practicing attorneys and to learn from their reactions. These programs included a workshop, sponsored by the Association of American Law Schools' 2002 conference, for law faculty on how to teach mediation representation, and two intensive half-day training programs that I was asked to design, one for the Commercial and Federal Litigation Section and Corporate Counsel Section of the NYS Bar Association in 1999 and another for the Nassau County Bar Association in 2001. I also observed numerous advocates in the legal cases that I mediated.

As I continued my research, I was helped along the way by many people whom I want to specially acknowledge and thank.

Scott Hughes and Andrea Schneider, the organizers of the ABA Mediation Representation Competition, gave me an unexpected and welcomed gift when they asked me to chair a new Mediation Representation Rules Committee. I had just finished hosting the first New

York regional competition for the ABA Spring 1999 Competition. They wanted to form a committee to examine the criteria for evaluating participants in the competition and to consider whether the criteria that were being utilized needed to be revised or replaced.

They gave me the opportunity to participate in a bedazzling one-year seminar with many of the leading thinkers in the field. The committee included Beryl Blaustone, Jim Coben, Eric Galton, John Lande, Lisa Lance, Jackie Nolan-Haley, as well as Scott Hughes and Andrea Schneider. During 2000–2001, we debated and explored what were good mediation representation practices and drafted a completely new set of judging criteria based on a problem-solving approach to representation, the approach that informs this book. The new criteria have been used since 2001 in the national mediation representation competitions that continue to grow. In 2003, the competition took place in nine regions, attracting teams from almost fifty law schools throughout the United States, leading to a national final competition at the annual meeting of the ABA Section of Dispute Resolution.

Lela Love asked me to team-teach a course with her on mediation representation at Cardozo Law School. I had previously developed a substantial mediation representation segment for my ADR course at Touro. She now presented the opportunity to delve deeper into the subject by collaborating on designing a separate mediation representation course. Since January 2001, Cardozo has offered our course as an alternative to the semester break intensive trial advocacy course.

Gerald Lepp, ADR Administrator, and Magistrate Judge Robert Levy, the judge overseeing the ADR programs in the U.S. District Court, Eastern District of New York, invited me to informally counsel the court-annexed mediation program on training advocates and mediators. Their invitation offered me a rich opportunity to learn from and test approaches with an exceptionally demanding audience—New York litigators. I designed and conducted a one-day training program in 2001 for about 150 experienced litigators turned mediators on how to convert adversarial advocates in the mediation into problem-solvers. I also designed and conducted several half-day and full-day training programs for the litigators in the NYC Department of Law, a frequent participant in federal court mediations.

A number of people contributed their precious time and considerable expertise to commenting on segments of the book. I received valuable feedback on sections from James Coben, Ken Fox, Dwight Golann, Elayne Greenberg, Russell Korobkin, John Lande, Jackie Nolan-Haley, Christopher Moore, Andrea Schneider, and Barbara Swartz.

Wayne Outten, an outstanding and active mediation advocate who has thought deeply and reflectively on what constitutes good representation practices, generously reviewed and commented on a number of chapters.

It is through this rigorous and, at times, brutal screening of ideas and approaches that this book has survived, a book that develops a coherent approach to representing clients in mediation as a problem-solving process. Of course, I remain solely responsible for the final product.

This book would never have come to fruition without the essential and generous support from Touro Law Center, especially from Dean Howard Glickstein, who gave me sabbatical time, summer research grants, and flexibility in course scheduling to work on this project. I also appreciated the support given by Vice Deans Eileen Kaufman and Gary Shaw.

I benefited greatly from our all-purpose Associate Dean Ken Rosenblum, who reviewed chapters for clarity from the point of view of an attorney with no formal training and experience in mediation, and who was able to quickly locate talented law students for me whenever I needed assistance.

And finally, this project benefited from the valuable assistance of a number of particularly dedicated Touro law students, including Jonathan Kirchner, Maryam Jadali, and Jianhua Zhong, as well as Nichoel Forrett who so professionally and efficiently edited and formatted all the footnotes.

This book was brought to conclusion by the wonderful and professional staff of NITA. I am thankful for the careful, patient, and thoughtful editing of Ashley Smith and the creative design and marketing expertise of Kathy Pitts, Jeanne Philotoff, and Jude Phillips.

ABOUT THE AUTHOR

Professor Harold Abramson has been deeply involved in the development and practice of dispute resolution methods for over eighteen years of his almost thirty years in the legal profession.

Professor Abramson is a full-time faculty member at Touro Law Center, located on Long Island, New York, where he served for nine years as vice dean responsible for academic programs, faculty development, and international programs. At Touro, he teaches courses on methods of dispute resolution, administrative law, business organizations, remedies, sales, and international business and trade. Prior to joining the Touro faculty, he worked in both private practice and government, where he helped formulate regulatory policies and litigated contract disputes and complex regulatory cases.

Hal Abramson has published extensively, lectured widely, and taught numerous courses on domestic and international negotiations and mediations, public policy negotiations, alternative methods of resolving disputes, and the representation of clients in mediations. He has lectured or taught courses throughout the United States, Hungary, Italy, India, and Russia.

Hal Abramson's domestic and international dispute resolution practice includes mediating, facilitating, and arbitrating business, organizational, and public policy disputes. He has mediated trademark infringement claims and claims for breach of licensing agreements, employment contracts, distribution contracts, purchase contracts, and service contracts. He has mediated international business disputes that have involved parties from China, Colombia, Egypt, Guinea, India, Israel, Hong Kong, Russia, Taiwan, South Korea, and Venezuela. He also has facilitated the feasibility stage of a "negotiated rule-making" process and long-term planning processes at law schools.

Hal Abramson serves on various neutral panels, including the Mediation Panels of the U.S. District Court for the Eastern District Court of New York, the American Arbitration Association, and the CPR Institute for Dispute Resolution, the Commercial Arbitration Panel of the American Arbitration Association, and the Facilitation Panel of the Association of American Law Schools.

He is a member of numerous local and national dispute resolution organizations, including the ABA Section on Dispute Resolution, the ADR Committee of the NYS Bar Association (former Chair), and the Association for Conflict Resolution (formerly SPIDR—Society of Professionals in Dispute Resolution.)

Hal Abramson began concentrating on the subject of mediation representation in January 1994, after teaching dispute resolution courses since 1986 from the point of view of a neutral and realizing that there were so few employment opportunities for graduates and lawyers as neutrals. At that time, he began researching and lecturing on mediation representation and developing teaching materials for his basic dispute resolution course. In fall 2000, he jointly developed a mediation representation course that he now team-teaches at Cardozo Law School every January. He also has been training lawyers and lecturing on the subject regularly in continuing legal education programs.

He hosted at Touro the inaugural regional Mediation Representation Competition for the New York City-area law schools in March 1999, for the ABA Section of Dispute Resolution and then chaired the committee that developed a new set of national competition rules based on the problem-solving approach to representation, the same approach reflected in this book. At the Annual Meeting of the ABA Section of Dispute Resolution in April 2002, he received an award for his distinguished work chairing the rules committee.

His other publications in the area of mediation representation include: "Representing Clients in International Mediations" in *Practitioner's Guide to International Arbitration and Mediation* (Editors—Chernick, Kolkey, Rhoades, 2002) and "Representing Clients in Business Mediations," *The Touro Lawyer* (Alumni Magazine) (December 1999).

He also writes in the area of private international dispute resolution. His publications include "International Dispute Resolution" in Rau, Sherman, and Peppet, *Processes of Dispute Resolution* (3th edition 2002)(law school textbook); "International Mediation Basics" in *Practitioner's Guide to International Arbitration and Mediation* (Editors—Chernick, Kolkey, Rhoades, 2002); "Protocols for International Arbitrators Who Dare to Settle Cases", 10 *American Review of International Arbitration* 1 (1999); "Time to Try Mediation of International Commercial Disputes", 4 ILSA J. of Intl. & Comp. L. 323 (1998), and

"Transnational Litigation: International Arbitration and Alternatives, Opportunities and Pitfalls", 10 *International Law Practicum* 74, 84 (International Law and Practice Section, NYS Bar Association, 1997) (transcript of simulated negotiation of ADR Clause). He is currently co-authoring a law school textbook on international public and private conflict resolution.

His other articles in the field of dispute resolution include "Comparing Settlement Conferences and Mediations," Videotape and Instructors Manual, co-author (NYS Bar Association, 1999); "A Primer on Resolving Disputes: Lessons From Alternative Dispute Resolution", 64 *NYS Bar Journal* 48 (March/April, 1992) and "Regulatory Negotiation: An Opportunity for State Agencies" in *Attorneys General and New Methods of Dispute Resolution* 109 (co-author) (American Bar Association and National Association of Attorneys General, 1990).

Hal Abramson's academic degrees are in business administration (BBA, University of Michigan), public administration (MPA, Harvard University), and law (JD, Syracuse University, and LL.M., Harvard University).

Introduction

Topics in this chapter include:

1. Different Approach to Representation
2. The Mediation Representation Formula
3. Answers to Essential Representation Questions
4. Coverage of the Book
5. Three Special Features of the Book

1. Different Approach to Representation

This book is inspired by one overarching goal—to provide a comprehensive guide on how to advocate as a problem-solver in mediation. Much has been written about how mediators can create a problem-solving process[1] and many mediators have been trained to use a problem-solving approach,[2] but surprisingly little has been written on how to represent clients in such a process.

The mediation process is indisputably different from other dispute resolution processes. Therefore, the strategies and techniques that have proven so effective in settlement conferences, arbitrations, and judicial trials do not work optimally in mediation. You need a different representation approach, one tailored to realize the full benefits of this

---

1. *See e.g.*, Golann, MEDIATING LEGAL DISPUTES 14–26 (1996); Moore, THE MEDIATION PROCESS 18–19, 55–56 (2nd Ed. 1996); and Folberg and Taylor, MEDIATION 7–9, 38–72 (1994).

2. Even though I could not find a rigorous study of the approaches taught in mediation training programs, I came across ample anecdotal evidence that suggests that many, if not most, training programs teach mediators the interest-based or problem-solving approach. This approach seems to be taught to mediators in many court-connected programs, by numerous private trainers, and at Harvard Law School (where Professors Fisher, Sander, and Mnookin train negotiators and mediators from around the world). Although a significant number of mediators are trained in the transformative approach, a number of them also seemed to have been trained in problem-solving.

1

burgeoning and increasingly preferred[3] forum for resolving disputes. Instead of advocating as a zealous adversary, you should consider advocating as a zealous problem-solver.[4]

This book develops an approach to representing clients for a dispute resolution process[5] that offers you access to a neutral third party, a mediator, who is likely to be trained in facilitating problem-solving negotiations. The mediator's sole purpose is to assist the disputing clients and their attorneys in resolving the dispute. The mediator knows how to help people resolve disputes. The mediator knows how to structure a process that can provide your client and the other side an opportunity to fashion enduring and, when at all feasible, inventive solutions. The mediator knows how to involve clients constructively and to use various dispute resolution techniques at propitious moments in the mediation session.

The familiar adversarial strategy of presenting the strongest partisan arguments and aggressively attacking the other side's case may be effective in court where each side is trying to convince a judge to make a favorable decision. But, in mediation, there is no third-party decision-maker, only a third-party facilitator. The third party is not even the primary audience. The primary audience is the other side, who is surely not neutral and can often be quite hostile. In this different representational setting, the adversarial approach is less effective if not self-defeating.

---

3. *See* Galanter, "The Vanishing Trial: An Examination of Trials and Related Matters in Federal and State Courts" (Preliminary Version, October 24, 2003, prepared for Symposium on The Vanishing Trial Sponsored by the Litigation Section of the American Bar Association, December, 2003)(In this study sponsored by the Litigation Section, the author has preliminarily documented that while the number of federal lawsuits filed has increased, the number of trials has decreased, from 11 percent in 1962 to 1.8 percent in 2002, with comparable trends in the state courts. One of the documented replacements for trials is mediation.) and Lande, *Getting the Faith: Why Business Lawyers and Executives Believe in Mediation,* 5 HARV. NEG. L. REV. 137 (2000).

4. *See* Schneider, *Shattering Negotiation Myths: Empirical Evidence on the Effectiveness of Negotiation Style*, 7 HARV. NEG.L.R. 143, 196 (2002) (In an extensive study of negotiation styles, 75 percent of true problem-solving negotiators were considered effective as compared with less than 50 percent of adversarial bargainers, a percentage that shrunk to 25 percent when examining adversarial bargainers who were unethical); Mnookin, Peppet & Tulumello, BEYOND WINNING: NEGOTIATING TO CREATE VALUE IN DEALS AND DISPUTES 321–322 (2000)(Authors concluded that clients are usually better off when a lawyer adopts a problem-solving approach over an adversarial one.);and Shell, BARGAINING FOR ADVANTAGE 12–14 (1999)(Other studies are cited that suggest that cooperative negotiators are more effective than competitive ones.).

5. For a more complete definition of mediation as well as an explanation of the process, see Chapter 2, "Familiarizing Yourself with Mediation."

Many sophisticated and experienced litigators realize that mediation calls for a different approach, but they still muddle through the mediation sessions. They are learning on the job. Even though many attorneys prefer a problem-solving-type approach to negotiations,[6] attorneys are still in the early stages of figuring out how to do it in mediations. Many attorneys went to law school before courses on dispute resolution were offered, and the dispute resolution courses that have shown up in law schools during the last twenty-five years have been largely limited to teaching students to be mediators, not advocates.[7] Continuing legal education programs are only beginning to focus on teaching representation skills, with many programs limited to sharing anecdotal experiences and idiosyncratic advice. This book provides you a coherent approach to representing clients—an approach suitable for mediation, an approach that applies from your first client phone call until the mediation process is concluded.

This representation approach will be labeled throughout this book as creative problem-solving. As a problem-solver that is creative,[8] you do more than just try to settle the dispute. You creatively search for solutions that go beyond the traditional ones based on rights, obligations,

---

6. *See* Heumann & Hyman, *Negotiation Methods and Litigation Settlement Methods in New Jersey: 'You Can't Always Get What You Want,'* 12 OHIO ST. J. ON DISP. RES. 253, 309 (1997) ("While 61% of the lawyers would like to see more problem-solving negotiation methods, about 71% of negotiations are carried out with positional methods instead.").

7. *See* Schmitz, *What Should We Teach in ADR Courses: Concepts and Skills for Lawyers Representing Clients in Mediation,* 6 HARV. NEG. L. REV.189 (2001).

8. *See, e.g.,* Symposium, *Conceiving the Lawyer As Creative Problem Solver,* 34 CAL. W. L. REV. (1998); Thomas Barton, *Creative Problem Solving: Purpose, Meaning, and Values,* 34 CAL. W. L. REV. 273 (1998); Paul Brest & Linda Hamilton Krieger, *New Roles: Problem Solving Lawyers As Problem Solvers,* 72 TEMPLE L. REV. 811 (1999); Seamus Dunn, *Case Study: The Northern Ireland Experience: Possibilities For Cross-Fertilization Learning,* 19 CPR INST. FOR DISP. RESOL., June 2001, at 153; Carrie Menkel-Meadow, *Aha? Is Creativity Possible In Legal Problem Solving and Teachable In Legal Education,* 6 HARV. NEG. L. REV. 98 (2001); Carrie Menkel-Meadows, *When Winning Isn't Everything: The Lawyer As Problem Solver,* 28 HOFSTRA L. REV. 905 (2000); Carrie Menkel-Meadow, *The Lawyer As Problem Solver and Third Party Neutral: Creativity and Non-Partisanship In Lawyering,* 72 TEMPLE L. REV. 785 (1999); Carrie Menkel-Meadows, *Toward Another View Of Legal Negotiation: The Structure Of Problem Solving,* 21 UCLA L. REV. 754 (1984); Linda Morton, *Teaching Creative Problem Solving: A Paradigmatic Approach,* 34 CAL. W. L. REV. 375 (1998); and Janet Reno, *Lawyers As Problem-Solvers: Keynote Address To The AALS,* 49 J. LEGAL EDUC. 5 (1999). *See also,* California Western School of Law, Center For Creative Problem Solving (2003), *at* http://www.cwsl.edu.

and precedent. Rather than settling for win-lose outcomes, you search for solutions that can benefit both sides.[9] To creatively problem-solve in mediation, you develop a collaborative relationship with the other side and the mediator, and participate throughout the mediation process in a way that is likely to result in solutions that are enduring as well as inventive. Solutions are likely to be enduring because both sides work together to fashion nuanced solutions that each side fully understands, can live with, and knows how to implement. Solutions are likely to be inventive because you advocate your client's interests instead of legal positions;[10] use suitable techniques for overcoming impediments; search expansively for multiple options; and evaluate and package options imaginatively to meet the various interests of all parties. And solutions are likely to be found because you advocated as a creative problem-solver.

In this pitch for a problem-solving approach, I do not blindly claim that it is the only one that results in settlements. Attorneys frequently cite success stories when they use unvarnished adversarial tactics or a hybrid of adversarial and problem-solving strategies.[11] The hybrid supporters claim that the best approach is a flexible one, a philosophy that surely is advisable in life as well as in legal negotiations. But, flexibility should not be confused with inconsistency. Shifting between adversarial and problem-solving tactics during the course of mediation can undercut the problem-solving approach. A consistent adherence to problem-solving will more likely produce the best results for clients.

---

9. Instead of referring to "win-win" solutions, I suggest searching for solutions that can benefit both sides. I avoid using the more familiar, if not overused, "win-win" jargon because that jargon carries baggage that can blind people to the underlying valuable point that still retains considerable vitality. The "win-win" attitude can be sharply contrasted with the opposite one of "win-lose." These contrary attitudes neatly capture a fundamental difference between the problem-solving and adversarial approaches.

Many lawyers consider the idea that both sides can secure benefits as naïve, not anchored in reality. However, the notion that both sides might be able to gain something in negotiations reflects an optimistic attitude that can open the mind to creative searches. The liklihood of finding such gains in negotiations is greater than in court. In negotiations, for instance, even the defendant who agrees to pay considerable damages may gain other benefits, such as no publicity, no precedent, and a continuing business relationship—benefits that are usually unavailable in court.

10. For a full discussion of how to identify client's interests as opposed to positions, *see*, Chapter 3.2(a).

11. In the hybrid approach, attorneys switch between adversarial and problem-solving tactics, depending on how the mediation is unfolding.

For problem-solving advocacy to be effective in practice, engage proactively in problem-solving strategies at every stage of representation. The sort of practical problem-solving moves that are illustrated throughout this book should be used from the moment you interview your client and adhered to when calling the other attorney about trying out mediation, selecting the mediator, preparing any pre-mediation submissions, participating in pre-mediation conferences, presenting opening statements, and participating in joint sessions and caucuses.

You should be a constant problem-solver. It is relatively easy to engage in simple problem-solving moves such as responding to a demand with the question "why?" in order to bring to the surface the other party's interests. But it is much more difficult to stick to this approach throughout the mediation process, especially when faced with an adversarial, positional opponent. Trust the problem-solving approach. And, when the other side engages in adversarial tactics—a frequent occurrence in practice, you should react with problem-solving responses, responses that might even convert the other side into a problem-solver.[12]

Also strive to create a problem-solving process when your mediator does not. Your mediator may fail to follow a problem-solving approach (even though she professes to foster one) because she lacks the depth of experience or training to tenaciously maintain a consistent approach throughout the mediation process. Or, your mediator may candidly disclose her practice of deliberately switching tactics based on the needs of the parties—a philosophy that I have already suggested undermines the problem-solving approach.

Finally, for the skeptics who think that problem-solving does not work for most legal cases because they are primarily about money, I offer three responses.

First, the endless debate about whether or not legal disputes are primarily about money is distracting. Whether a dispute is largely about

---

12. *See* Chapter 1.5 on "Converting Adversarial Negotiations into Problem-Solving."

money varies from case to case.[13] You have little chance of discovering whether your client's dispute is about more than money if you approach the dispute as if it is only about money.[14] Such a preconceived view backed by a narrowly focused adversarial strategy will likely blind you to other parties' needs and inventive solutions. You are more likely to discover comprehensive and creative solutions if you approach the dispute with an open mind and a problem-solving orientation.

Second, if the dispute or any remaining issues at the end of the day turn out to be predominately about money, then at least you followed a representation approach that may have created a hospitable environment for dealing with the money issues. A hospitable environment can even be beneficial when there is no expectation of a continuing relationship between the disputing parties.

Third, the problem-solving approach provides a framework for resolving money issues. These types of disputes can sometimes be resolved by resorting to the usual problem-solving initiatives discussed throughout this book.[15] If they fail, you then might turn to adversarial

---

13. *See* Golann, *Is Legal Mediation a Process of Repair—or Separation? An Empirical Study and Its Implications,* 7 HARV. NEG. L.R. 301, 334 (2002)(In the only empirical study on the subject, the author found that "almost two-thirds of all [mediated] settlements were integrative in nature....The results suggest that both mediators and advocates should consider making a search for integrative outcomes an important aspect of their mediation strategy.")

At least one category of disputes is usually primarily about money. The classic personal injury dispute between strangers who will never deal with each other again can be only about money and therefore not open to creative resolutions other than a tailored payment scheme. But, even in these disputes, one side may occasionally want more than money such as vindication, fair treatment, etc.

14. In a recent case that I mediated, the parties arrived with extreme monetary claims on the table and a long history of failed negotiations. After more than three hours of mediation, the parties and attorneys negotiated a written apology signed by the defendant and a written introduction to future buyers signed by the plaintiff. The monetary issues were then resolved in less than a minute! The parties were apparently already on the same page for settling the money claims but were not ready to settle until some non-monetary needs were met.

15. *See* Chapter 1.3(a)(iii) on "Manage Remaining Distributive Conflicts" where the text considers how to use problem-solving moves to resolve easy distributive issues.

strategies, strategies that have been tempered and modified for a problem-solving process.[16]

In short, the problem-solving approach provides a comprehensive and coherent approach to representation that can guide you throughout the mediation process. By sticking to this approach, you will be prepared to deal with the myriad of unanticipated challenges that inevitably arise as the mediation unfolds.

2. The Mediation Representation Formula

The problem-solving approach in mediation can be encapsulated in a succinct mediation representation formula:

In mediation, you should negotiate using a *creative problem-solving approach* to achieve the two goals of meeting your client's *interests*[17] and overcoming any *impediments* to settlement. Your negotiation strategy should take specific advantage of the *presence of a mediator* at each of the six *key junctures* in the mediation process.

Packed in this slender formula is an enormous amount of knowledge and skills that effective advocates should possess. Please focus on the five italicized concepts as they arise throughout this book. Because mediation is simply the continuation of the negotiations, you should know how to negotiate as a *creative problem-solver* in the mediation.[18] You need to understand the fundamental idea of *interests*[19] and how to learn about them from your client.[20] You need to know how to diagnose *impediments* and how to fashion ways to hurdle them.[21] You should be familiar with what a mediator does and how a mediator can contribute

---

16. *See* Chapter 1.3(a)(iii) on "Manage Remaining Distributive Conflicts" where the text considers how to resolve difficult distributive issues by using tempered adversarial strategies. For example, you would omit the traditional tricks and extreme threats when engaging in the negotiation dance of offers and counteroffers.

17. This goal of meeting interests is different from the goals in what has become known as "transformative mediation" in which mediators focus on "empowerment" of parties and parties' "recognition" of each other. *See*, ROBERT A. BARUCH BUSH AND JOSEPH P. FOLGER, THE PROMISE OF MEDIATION-RESPONDING TO CONFLICT THROUGH EMPOWERMENT AND RECOGNITION (1994).

18. *See* Ch. 1.3.

19. *Id.*

20. *See* Ch. 3.2.

21. *See* Ch. 3.2 and Ch. 5.1(d)(h).

to resolving a dispute so that you can develop a representation plan that takes advantage of the *mediator's presence*.[22] And, you should understand the mediation process so that you can implement your plan to take advantage of the mediator's presence at each of the six *key junctures* in the mediation.[23]

3. Answers to Essential Representation Questions

This representation approach offers answers to the numerous, persistent, and strategic questions that inevitably arise when representing clients in mediations. The answers to the following essential questions are proffered throughout the book.

What types of cases are suitable for mediation?

How do you approach the other attorney about using mediation without looking weak or desperate?

What should you include in an agreement to mediate?

What credentials and experience should you look for when selecting a mediator?

What should you include in a pre-mediation submission?

What do you want to accomplish in a pre-mediation conference?

---

22. *See* Ch. 2 and Ch. 5.1(e) and (f).

23. *See* Chs. 5.1(g) and 7.

The term "junctures" is used to identify points in the process of representation when you should focus on staying in a problem-solving mode. Junctures are not the same as stages in the mediation process in that stages identify the sequential steps in the mediation process. Junctures and stages, however, do overlap.

Three of the six key junctures arise before the first mediation session when (1) selecting a mediator, (2) preparing pre-mediation submissions, and (3) participating in a pre-mediation conference. The other three junctures arise in the mediation session when (4) presenting opening statements, (5) participating in joint sessions, and (6) participating in caucuses.

The mediation representation formula also applies during other junctures in mediation representation. You should engage in problem-solving to advance interests and overcome impediments in a way that takes advantage of the availability of a mediator when (1) initially interviewing your client, (2) approaching the other attorney about the use of mediation, (3) preparing your case for mediation, (4) preparing your client, and (5) drafting a settlement agreement or developing an exit plan from an unsuccessful mediation.

How do you prepare a mediation representation plan for a problem-solving process?

How do you prepare your client for the mediation session?

How do you use the mediation process to overcome any impasses and to advance your client's interests?

How can you enlist the mediator to help you resolve your client's dispute?

How do you learn the other side's bottom line?

How do you evaluate your client's legal case using a decision-tree analysis?

How can you convert an adversarial adversary into a problem-solving one?

How do you deal with issues that are only about money?

4. Coverage of the Book

This book covers negotiation techniques, the mediation process, your role at each stage of your mediation representation, and alternative processes to mediation if the mediation is not fully successful. In particular:

Chapter 1 considers the foundational subject of how to negotiate in mediations. You should give special attention to negotiation techniques, realizing that mediation is simply a continuation of the negotiation process. The same skills needed for preparing and participating in a negotiation apply to mediation. If you use problem-solving strategies in negotiations, you will engage in the same strategies when representing clients throughout the mediation process. The more familiar adversarial approach to negotiations is compared with the preferred problem-solving approach in chapter 1. If you do not already have a strong foundation in problem-solving negotiations, read this chapter with care because its main points are built upon and developed throughout the entire book.

Chapter 2 explores the mediation process from the vantage point of an advocate. You should understand how the mediation process works, just as you would understand how any forum works in which you represent clients. When representing clients in court, for instance, you must understand the procedures and norms of settlement conferences, court appearances, and judicial decision-making. Similarly, you should know the mediation process, including its different stages, the function of opening statements, the use of joint sessions and caucuses, and the various approaches and techniques of mediators.

Chapters 3–7 cover the distinctive knowledge and skills that you should grasp to effectively perform four specific roles in mediation representation. Your roles include: (1) advising your clients about the mediation option (chapter 3); (2) negotiating an agreement to mediate with other attorneys (chapter 4); (3) preparing cases and clients for the mediation session (chapters 5 and 6); and (4) appearing in the mediation in pre-mediation conferences, mediation sessions, and post-sessions (chapter 7).

Chapter 8 prepares you for the possibility that the mediation may not result in settling all the issues. Just in case you reach an impasse that cannot be overcome in the mediation, you should be familiar with alternative processes for resolving any remaining issues. Alternative processes will likely be suggested by skilled mediators. These alternatives may include the use of mini-trials, summary jury trials, and less conventional forms of arbitration such as final-offer arbitration. You should be prepared to assess which alternatives make sense to try next. In chapter 8, a number of needs that may not be met in mediation are described and a glossary of alternative process solutions is furnished along with some guidelines on how to select the right one.

5. Three Special Features of the Book

Three special features have been added to the book to make the materials more accessible.

I highlighted in boxes "critical junctures" and "differing views." Each "critical juncture" box signals that the subject or moment in representation is especially vital or particularly vexing. At each critical juncture box, pause to give extra thought to the boxed topic. The "differing views" boxes recognize that even among those who subscribe to a problem-solving approach, there is no single view of how to do it. This subject is indeed a work in progress. Differing opinions would be expected, and some of the more substantial ones are recognized throughout the book. For each view, I suggest the advantages and disadvantages.

However, you are not left rudderless. I also make recommendations. By making the choices transparent, you can independently determine whether to adopt or modify the recommendations.

Second, I used footnotes extensively to cross-reference sections where key concepts were developed. If you skipped the section where a concept was initially presented or if you need to review a key concept, be sure to look for the appropriate cross-reference.

Key concepts are used repeatedly throughout the book because concepts presented early are applied and further developed as you progress through the different stages of client representation. Instead of repetitively explaining concepts, I selected one discrete section of the book for developing each basic concept and then when it became relevant in different parts of the book, a fuller explanation of the concept was cross-referenced. For example, while the need to identify your client's interests arose many times throughout the book, the definition of interests and how to identify them are primarily discussed in chapter 3.2(a) on interviewing your client about interests. Whenever the subject of interests is mentioned elsewhere in the book, the section of the book where it was primarily presented is cross-referenced in a footnote.

Third, at the end of most of the chapters, I added convenient checklists. The checklists are designed to be copied and used as portable reference tools to help you keep track of what you are doing and what needs to be done.

CHAPTER ONE

NEGOTIATING IN MEDIATIONS

"…what is needed are more problem solvers who care, not just about winning, but about really solving the problems."

Carrie J. Menkel-Meadow[1]

Topics in this chapter include:

1. Mediation as a Continuation of the Negotiation Process
2. Adversarial Approach
3. Problem-Solving Approach
4. Differences Between Adversarial and Problem-Solving Negotiations
5. Converting Adversarial Negotiations into Problem-Solving
6. Advancing Problem-Solving with the Assistance of a Mediator
7. Checklist

---

1. Mediation as a Continuation of the Negotiation Process

If you are a competent negotiator, you possess the basic skills to be a competent advocate in mediation. Remember that the mediation process is simply a negotiation process with the added assistance of a third party. This chapter examines the structure and details of two negotiation approaches— the more common adversarial approach and the preferred problem-solving approach.

The negotiations examined in this book involve the settlement of legal cases that are in court or moving toward court. Any litigator is familiar with how negotiations are an integral part of the litigation process. Litigators live the negotiation routine. Before initiating a court case, litigators typically try to negotiate a settlement. After initiating the court case, both sides customarily try again to settle the dispute. After

---

1. Carrie Menkel-Meadow, *When Winning Isn't Everything: The Lawyer as Problem Sovlver*, 28 HOFSTRA L.R. 905, 923 (2000).

some discovery, the sides are likely to try again, and to keep trying right up to the doorsteps of the courthouse. (See the table on the next page.)

Negotiations are so enmeshed in the litigation process that colorful descriptions of the intimate relationship between negotiations and adjudication have been coined. One thoughtful observer conjured up the illuminating image of "bargaining in the shadow of the law."[2] Another astute observer suggested that instead of viewing litigation and negotiation as separate processes, they should be viewed as a single process of disputing called "litgotiation," He defined litgotiation as "the strategic pursuit of a settlement through mobilizing the court process."[3] In these legal negotiations, attorneys frequently try to demonstrate that they are likely to win in court and then use the predicted outcome as the reference point for forming settlement proposals and compromises. As a result, attorneys involved in litigation negotiate like litigators. But, to realize the full potential of mediation, attorneys should negotiate differently. They should negotiate like problem-solvers.[4]

This chapter first examines the typical litigator's approach to negotiations, better known as the adversarial or positional approach, and then compares it with the preferred problem-solving approach.[5] The next section discusses techniques for converting an adversarial negotiator into a problem-solving one. The last section explores how mediators can contribute to advancing problem-solving negotiations.

---

2. *See* Robert H. Mnookin & Lewis Kornhauser, *Bargaining in the Shadow of the Law: The Case of Divorce*, 88 YALE L.J. 950 (1979).

3. Marc Galanter, *Worlds of Deals: Using Negotiation to Teach about Legal Process*, 34 J. LEGAL EDUC. 268, 268 (1984).

4. *See* Schneider, *Shattering Negotiation Myths: Empirical Evidence on the Effectiveness of Negotiation Style*, 7 HARV. NEG.L.R. 143, 196 (2002). (In an extensive study of negotiation styles, 75 percent of true problem-solving negotiators were considered effective as compared with less than 50 percent of adversarial bargainers, a percentage that shrunk to 25 percent when examining adversarial bargainers who are unethical.)

5. *See generally*, ROBERT H. MNOOKIN ET AL., BEYOND WINNING—NEGOTIATING TO CREATE VALUE IN DEAL AND DISPUTES (2000); ROGER FISHER ET AL., GETTING TO YES—NEGOTIATING AGREEMENT WITHOUT GIVING IN (2d ed. 1991); Carrie Menkel-Meadow, *Toward Another View of Legal Negotiation: The Structure of Problem Solving*, 31 UCLA L. REV. 754 (1984).

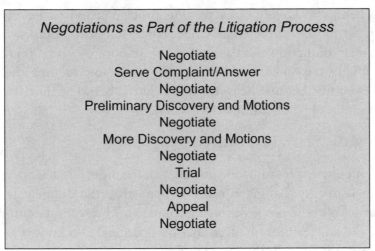

Negotiations as Part of the Litigation Process

Negotiate
Serve Complaint/Answer
Negotiate
Preliminary Discovery and Motions
Negotiate
More Discovery and Motions
Negotiate
Trial
Negotiate
Appeal
Negotiate

Hypothetical

Throughout this chapter, the following employment dispute will be used to demonstrate the two basic approaches to negotiations.

Stephen Saleson founded, owns, and runs a small company called *Shirts for You*. The company sells several major brand name shirts to retail outlets and is staffed by two support people and one other salesperson, Philip Upton. When Stephen hired Philip several years ago, Philip signed an employment contract in which he agreed that if he leaves his position, he would not compete against *Shirts for You* within the city of Buffalo for three years.

During the first year of employment, Stephen spent considerable time teaching Philip the "secrets" of good salesmanship. Under Stephen's tutelage, Philip quickly learned the job and did superlative work solidifying and maintaining existing customers in Buffalo. Unfortunately, the personal relationship between Philip and Stephen soured during their third year together. Philip felt that Stephen was stifling Philip's professional development by preventing him from developing new customers. Stephen reserved those opportunities for himself. So, even though Philip continued to admire Stephen's sales skills and welcome his mentoring, he quit the sales position and went into his own business selling a different brand of shirts. Because Philip had become such an excellent salesman, he was able to secure a group of retail customers in Buffalo that Stephen had never solicited for sales.

Stephen, who is very upset that his protégé abandoned him, sued Philip for breach of the employment contract not to compete and is seeking an injunction and damages in the amount of $100,000 for lost sales. Philip responded by claiming that he is not violating the non-compete clause because he is selling a different brand of shirts to a different group of retail customers in Buffalo.

2. Adversarial Approach

You should first re-acquaint yourself with the more familiar adversarial approach to negotiations in order to appreciate the different features and benefits of the problem-solving approach. This section examines in detail the key features of adversarial negotiations, also known as positional negotiations. At the end of this section, the reasons why attorneys prefer this approach are suggested.

a. Key Features

In adversarial negotiations,[6] each negotiator generally starts with firm, extreme, and opposite positions and then makes calibrated concessions until the negotiators are close enough to either split the difference or adopt one of the last offers on the table. In particular, each party prepares for the negotiations by first establishing in his own mind the parameters of the negotiation dance which usually means forming a target goal, bottom line, and a specific opening offer strategy. Then, at the table each party implements his opening offer strategy and engages in a negotiation dance of offers, counteroffers, compromises, and concessions. The dance consists of the carefully orchestrated movement of information, played to the battle music of partisan arguments, clever tactics, and sharp threats.

This section initially describes the various orientations that attorneys (and their clients) are likely to bring to the negotiations. Then, it considers how adversarial attorneys prepare for the negotiations and what strategies they are likely to take at the negotiation table. For a summary of the key features, see table "Key Features of Adversarial Negotiations."

---

6. *See, e.g.*, Goodpaster, *A Primer on Competitive Bargaining*, 1996 J. Disp. Resol. 325 (1996).

Key Features of
Adversarial Negotiations

Orientation

View Dispute as a Distributive Problem or Zero-Sum Gain
View Strategy as Win-Lose
View Dispute as Only One Issue, so No Opportunity for Trades
View Resources as Fixed and Valued Equally by Both Sides
  (Fixed Pie)
View Problem Narrowly
Approach Other Side as Adversaries
Advocate for Client's Position
Claim One Right Solution—My Client's Solution
Disinterested in Other Side's Case
View Strategically the Use of Information
Compete for Larger Piece of Pie

Preparation (with Client)

Establish Client's Target Goal, Based on Legal Rights and
  Monetary Solutions
Evaluate Client's BATNA (Best Alternative to a Negotiated
  Agreement)
Establish Client's Reservation Value (Bottom Line)
Surmise Other Side's Reservation Value and BATNA
Plan Strategy for Use of Information
Develop Strategy for Opening Offers
Prepare Opening Offer in Anticipation of Making Compromises

Strategies at the Table

Implement Opening Offer Strategy
Present Extreme First Offer (Initial Position)
Emphasize Positions
Emphasize Legal Case (BATNA)
Propose Solutions Based on Likely Court Outcome and
  Compromises
Engage in Negotiation Dance of Offers, Counteroffers,
  Compromises, Concessions
Use Information Strategically
Make Adversarial Arguments
Employ Tricks and Threats
Solve Narrow Presenting Problem
Move Toward Compromise Solution

i.   Orientation

The adversarial attorney is oriented in a particular way toward the negotiation process. This orientation influences how the attorney prepares for and participates in the negotiation sessions.

View Dispute as a Distributive Problem or a Zero-Sum Game
View Strategy as Win-Lose
View Dispute as One Issue, so No Opportunity for Trades
View Resources as Fixed and Valued Equally by Both Sides (Fixed Pie)
View Problem Narrowly

An adversarial negotiator frequently views his dispute as primarily distributive, as a contest over who gets the targeted resource. One side wins at the expense of the other. In the employment contract dispute, Stephen views the dispute to be about money: How will he recover the money he lost because of the customers stolen by Philip? Stephen either wins by recovering money for lost sales or loses by getting nothing or only a nominal recovery. The dispute is framed narrowly: Did Philip breach the employment contract? The parties do not look for multiple issues or opportunities for mutually beneficial trades.

Approach Other Side as Adversaries
Advocate for Client's Position
Claim One Right Solution—My Client's Solution
Disinterested in Other Side's Case

An adversarial negotiator views the other side as an antagonist who is competing to win the negotiation contest. The attorney's role is to advocate for his client's position. His client's position is the one right solution to resolve the dispute. When consumed by this adversarial mind-set, the attorney has little interest in understanding the other side's case. Stephen no longer sees Philip as a friend and protégé. Instead, he sees Philip as an adversary. Stephen expects his attorney to forcefully advocate his position that he should be paid $100,000. In this environment, Stephen has difficulty seeing see any merit in Philip's view that he is not competing when he sells a different brand of shirts to different customers.

View Strategically the Use of Information

An adversarial negotiator views manipulating information as central to his negotiation strategy. The negotiator realizes that information is power and hides and engineers it to gain advantages. The negotiator uses information strategically to mislead the other party about his reservation value, his alternatives to settlements, potentially harmful facts, and even his interests.

Compete for Larger Piece of Pie

In an adversarial environment in which the dispute appears distributive, the negotiator competes to win the largest piece of the fixed pie. Stephen sees a sales pie of $100,000 that Philip stole from him. The negotiation is over how to split the $100,000 pie, and Stephen, of course, wants the whole pie.

ii.   Preparation (with Client)

In preparing for the negotiation, the attorney formulates parameters for the negotiation sessions. The attorney establishes his client's target goal, assesses his alternatives to settlement (BATNA: Best Alternative To a Negotiated Agreement),[7] fixes a reservation value (bottom line), and surmises the other side's reservation value and BATNA. Then, in view of these parameters, the attorney develops a strategy for presenting an opening offer and engaging in the highly stylized negotiation dance.

Establish Client's Target Goal, Based on Legal Rights and Monetary Solutions

The attorney helps his client formulate a target or aspirational goal. The goal is highly optimistic but not so extreme that it would drive the other party away from the negotiation table. The target goal is affected by the attorney's opinion of the strength of his client's legal rights and the likely judicial remedies. In other words, the goal is framed in the shadow of the law. Because Stephen has not done any discovery, he may not have the necessary data for calculating lost sales. But, based on some sense of what might have been lost and a very optimistic judicial result, he will likely establish a target goal less than the $100,000 demanded in court papers. The target goal will likely be less than the amount in the papers because the demand in the papers is usually exceptionally extreme in order to protect the client from understating the damages before discovery and to get the other side's attention. As will be discussed below on preparing an opening offer, the opening offer is usually inflated above the target goal in order to leave ample room for "compromises."

---

7. BATNA (Best Alternative To a Negotiated Agreement) is a term coined by Roger Fisher and Willima Ury in Fisher et al., Getting to Yes 100 (2d ed.1991). It refers to the best option that is available to the party if he leaves the negotiating table.

An attorney usually translates his client's grievance into a monetary equivalent because that is what courts customarily do. Except in the most unusual cases, courts do not order creative, tailor-made remedies. Courts fit grievances into preexisting legal categories and then select remedies that are easy and practical to implement. The most practical remedy is one framed in monetary terms. While Stephen may be upset about losing his protégé—a valued employee—his judicial remedies would be typically limited to enjoining him from selling in Buffalo and money damages.

Evaluate Client's BATNA (Best Alternative To a Negotiated Agreement) Establish Client's Reservation Value (Bottom Line[8])

The attorney also prepares a trip wire that when crossed would trigger the attorney and his client to leave the negotiation table. This trip wire, sometimes known as the bottom line and more precisely called the reservation value, is derived from the client's BATNA—the best alternative to settlement.

A client's *reservation value* is the value that the settlement offer must meet or improve upon for the party to accept. A plaintiff's reservation value is the minimum benefit that the party must secure to settle. A defendant's reservation value is the maximum cost that the party is willing to incur to settle. Although reservation value is related to the BATNA, the BATNA offers a very different perspective on the negotiation. Instead of focusing on what a client needs in the negotiation to settle, the BATNA focuses on what the client will do after leaving the table. While reservation value and BATNA are different concepts, the value of each is usually the same when a client accounts for all of the public and personal costs and benefits of opting for the BATNA.[9]

---

8. *See* Russell Korobkin, Negotiation Theory and Strategy, 37–51 (2002).

9. *See id.* at 43–50 (Describes seven factors that can affect the reservation value: the party's no-agreement alternative, a party's particular preferences for reaching an agreement, his probability estimates of future events, his ability to tolerate risk, the value of time, transaction costs, and the opportunities for future relationships.)

For example, a BATNA that consists of going to court can be calculated by using a decision-tree analysis[10] that factors in the risk of losing to compute the monetary benefit or cost of litigating. But, this calculation of the public BATNA fails to explicitly factor in such personal costs of litigating as inconvenience, aggravation, and uncertainty over not knowing what will happen. It also does not factor in such personal benefits of litigating as creating precedent or feeling vindicated. A client tries to approximate a composite value of these personal costs and benefits and then adds or deducts the value from the public BATNA value. The total comprises of a fully analyzed net benefit or cost of exercising a client's BATNA, a calculation that becomes the reservation value that must be met or beat in the negotiations.

Stephen, as the plaintiff, needs to develop a list of possible alternatives to settlement. Stephen could do nothing, could complain to Philip's new customers about Philip, could solicit Philip's new customers, or could sue Philip for breach of his employment contract not to compete. Of these options, Stephen might decide that his most attractive alternative to settlement is going to court, a public BATNA.

Stephen's attorney would research thoroughly the strengths and weaknesses of the court case and then predict the likely court outcome and the likelihood of winning.[11] His attorney may predict a likely favorable jury verdict of $80,000 and then deduct his estimated attorney fees and other litigation costs of $20,000 for a net benefit of $60,000. By multiplying his net benefit of $60,000 by his attorney's predicted 60 percent chance of winning, Stephen would arrive at a positive value of $36,000.

Next, Stephen needs to incorporate the risk of losing. If Stephen loses, Stephen would still have to pay his attorney fees and other litigation costs of $20,000. By multiplying the $20,000 by his 40 percent chance

---

10. For a full explanation of the use of decision trees for calculating the value of the BATNA, including an explanation of what is an expected value and the differences between a public BATNA and a personal one, *see* Appendix A.

Attorneys can assess the court alternative through the use of decision-tree analysis, a process that involves estimating the probability of key events and the likely outcome for each event. *See* AARON & HOFFER, DECISION ANALYSIS AS A METHOD OF EVALUATING THE TRIAL ALTERNATIVE IN MEDIATING LEGAL DISPUTES 307–334 (Dwight Golaan ed., 1996).

11. Stephen faces a risk of losing the court case because it is not clear whether Philip has breached the covenant to not compete when Philip is selling a different brand of shirts to a different group of customers in Buffalo.

of losing, Stephen would calculate a negative value of $8,000. Finally by subtracting the negative value of $8,000 from the $36,000 positive value, Steven would arrive at the expected value of his public BATNA in the amount of $28,000.

Stephen's public BATNA value needs to be adjusted for a number of personal benefits and costs in order to arrive at his reservation value in the negotiations. Personal costs might include spending time preparing for the case, suffering the emotional angst of being consumed by litigation, and living with the 40 percent chance of losing. Stephen needs to make a rough and subjective estimate of what he is willing to give up to avoid suffering these costs. He may decide that he is willing to sacrifice up to $10,000. By deducting the $10,000 from the value of his public BATNA of $28,000, Stephen would calculate his fully analyzed BATNA, a reservation value of $18,000.

Thus, if Stephen cannot secure at least $18,000 at the negotiation table, a settlement that would result in him avoiding his personal costs of litigating, Stephen should leave the table to take a chance of securing the positive value of his public BATNA, the likely litigated net outcome of $28,000.

Philip also needs to identify and assess his alternatives to settlement. Phillip, as the defendant, does not have too many options once the suit is commenced. Philip can do nothing and risk a default judgment. Philip could ask his former customers, the ones still serviced by Stephen, to lobby him to drop the lawsuit. Or, Philip could defend by trying to win the jury trial. Of these options, Philip might decide that the most attractive alternative to settlement is defending himself in court, his public BATNA.

Philip's attorney would research thoroughly the strengths and weaknesses of the court case and then predict the likely court outcome and the chances of winning.[12] His attorney may predict that if a jury verdict holds Philip liable, he would likely be liable for $80,000. Philip's attorney also might predict that attorney fees and other litigation costs would be $20,000 for a total loss of $100,000. Then, by multiplying

---

12. Stephen faces a risk of losing the court case because it is not clear whether Philip has breached the covenant to not compete when Philip is selling a different brand of shirts to a different group of customers in Buffalo.

the $100,000 by his attorney's predicted 40 percent chance of losing, Philip would calculate a negative value of $40,000.

Next, Philip needs to incorporate the advantages of winning. If Philip wins, he would still have to pay his attorney fees and other litigation costs of $20,000. By multiplying the $20,000 by his 60 percent chance of winning, Philip would calculate a negative value of $12,000. Finally by adding together the negative $12,000 of winning and the negative $40,000 of losing, Philip would arrive at the expected value of his public BATNA in the amount of $52,000.

Now, Philip's BATNA needs to be more fully analyzed and adjusted to account for a number of personal factors in order to arrive at his reservation value in the negotiations. By going to court, Philip may incur a number of personal costs and benefits. Philip may incur the costs of spending time preparing for the case and suffering the emotional stress of litigation. But, these costs may be exceeded by two possible benefits of litigating. Philip may welcome the 60 percent chance of winning and paying nothing, a risk-taking propensity common among defendants as a group, and he may want to try to exonerate himself in court so he can freely pursue his lucrative business in Buffalo. Philip may estimate that the personal benefits of his BATNA are worth roughly $10,000 more than the personal costs.[13] Philip would deduct this positive $10,000 benefit from the negative public BATNA of $52,000 to arrive at a fully analyzed BATNA, a reservation value of $42,000.

Thus, if settlement possibilities involve Philip paying more than $42,000, Philip should leave the table to litigate where he may pay nothing but his attorney fees or risk losing on the average $52,000.

Surmise Other Side's Reservation Value and BATNA

The attorney gathers information on the other party's BATNA and his reservation value. He needs to know this information so that he is

---

13. It is not unusual for repeat defendant players to attach a positive value to litigating for the purpose of scaring off future potential plaintiffs. This personal benefit can be incorporated into the reservation value by the defendant estimating the positive value of litigating to send a message and then *deducting* that amount from any expected loss. If the defendant estimates the expected loss to be $40,000 and benefit to be $10,000, then the defendant's fully analyzed BATNA or reservation value would be $30,000. The defendant would be willing to pay no more than $30,000. Otherwise, the defendant would turn to his public BATNA of an expected average loss of $40,000.

aware how far he can push the other side before the other side will leave the table.

Plan Strategy for Use of Information

The attorney collects critical information and devises a plan for strategically using it during the negotiations, as described in the next section on "Strategies at the Table."

Develop Strategy for Opening Offers

The attorney develops a strategy for introducing the first offer. Should the attorney put the first offer on the table or induce the other side to present the first offer?

Many articles have been written about this strategic moment in the negotiations. The first offer communicates valuable information that impacts directly on how the negotiations will unfold. The first offer locks in the outer range of settlement. When Stephen puts an offer of $100,000 on the table, he knows he has foreclosed any chance of getting more.[14] The offer also anchors the other side's view of the settlement value. Philip might not know his exposure until Stephen presents his $100,000 offer, which anchors Philip's thinking about the range of settlement. A realistic first offer reveals that the offeror prepared for and is serious about settling the dispute. A too extreme or conservative offer suggests that the offeror has not done his homework or may have made some faulty assumptions. A too extreme offer also could mean that the offeror has adopted a highly competitive strategy, a strategy that might provoke the other side to abandon the negotiations.

Some recommend engaging in tactics to enlist the other party to present the first offer in order to benefit from the other party's miscalculation.[15] Philip will be relieved that Stephen's initial offer is only $100,000 if Philip had made several hundred thousand dollars and feels vulnerable in court. He will benefit from Stephen's error. He has now learned about the bargaining range of the other side.

---

14. However, this upper range could be exceeded if during the negotiations it becomes evident that a court might award damages greater than the $100,000.

15. *See* Harry Edwards & James J. White, The Lawyer as a Negotiator 115–116 (1977).

Others recommend presenting the first offer in order to benefit from the other party's inadequate preparation. The first offer can anchor the other party's thinking about the range of settlement and establish a favorable midpoint. The extreme offer can draw the other party's offer in a favorable direction and even influence his view of his reservation value.[16]

Prepare Opening Offer in Anticipation of Making Compromises

The adversarial attorney usually prepares an extreme first offer or counteroffer in order to fix a wide range for settlement discussions.[17] The attorney either inflates or deflates his target goal in anticipation of the negotiation dance of offers, counteroffers and compromises. The attorney wants ample space to dance. The initial offer is set higher than the target goal with an eye on an advantageous midpoint between each side's initial offers. If the offer is too extreme, however, the offer can chase the other side away. Stephen purposely asks for the upper limit of $100,000 in order to leave room for the inevitable concessions and compromises.

iii.   Strategies at the Table

At the negotiating table, the attorney implements his opening offer strategy, a strategy that includes stressing his settlement positions and legal case. Initial positions and compromises are related to the likely court outcome. The opening offers induce a negotiation dance of counteroffers, compromises, and concessions. Positions are supported by the strategic use of information channeled through adversarial arguments, tricks, and threats. And, the terms of settlement are usually limited to resolving the narrow presenting problem.

Implement Opening Offer Strategy
Present Extreme First Offer (Initial Position)

The adversarial attorney typically begins by orchestrating the first offer. Depending on the selected strategy, the attorney tries to induce the other side to present the first offer or tries to present the first offer. As

---

16. *See* DAVID LAX & JAMES SEBENIUS, THE MANAGER AS NEGOTIATOR 132–134 (1986); HOWARD RAIFFA, THE ART & SCIENCE OF NEGOTIATION 127–128 (1982).

17. For an analysis of whether the first offer should be moderate or extreme, *see* Korobkin & Guthrie, *Opening Offers and Out-of-Court Settlement: A Little Moderation May Not Go a Long Way*, 10 OHIO ST. J. OF DISP. RES. 1 (1994).

already discussed under "Preparation," the first offer is likely to be extreme in order to establish an ample bargaining range.

Emphasize Positions
Emphasize Legal Case (BATNA)
Propose Solutions Based on Likely Court Outcome or Compromises

The attorney presents the first offer emphatically as his client's position backed by his strong legal case. The legal case becomes the omnipresent reference point that dominates the unfolding negotiations including shaping the framing of offers, counteroffers, and compromises. Stephen firmly presents his $100,000 offer, emphasizes that this is what he will likely secure in court, and then considers proposals that are shaped by the likely court outcome.

Engage in Negotiation Dance of Offers, Counteroffers, Compromises, and Concessions

The negotiation follows the combative dance routine of initial extreme offers and swirling rounds of calibrated compromises and concessions.

Use Information Strategically
Make Adversarial Arguments
Engage in Tricks and Threats

The offers and counteroffers are backed by carefully orchestrated use of information that surfaces in the form of arguments, tricks, and threats. The negotiator embellishes flamboyant arguments so that they are more rhetoric than substance. He exploits clever or transparent tricks[18] such as pressing false demands[19] and appearing with limited settlement authority. And, he makes aggressive threats about dragging the other side through lengthy and expensive court proceedings. The strategic use of information permeates every move. The negotiator may deviously disclose partisan information to either pressure or trick the other side in making key concessions. He may hide vital information because of the fear that disclosure will result in sacrificing advantages at

---

18. For a catalogue of negotiating tactics, *see* CHARLES B. CRAVER, EFFECTIVE LEGAL NEGOTIATION AND SETTLEMENT 181–224 (3d ed. 1997).

19. A false demand is when a negotiator presents a demand as vital when it is not. As a tactic, the negotiator then gives up this "false" demand for something vital from the other side.

trial or exploitation by the other side in the negotiations.[20] For instance, Stephen may be reluctant to disclose his interest in working with Philip in the future. Instead of seeing this disclosure as an opportunity for designing a better solution, Stephen fears that Philip might exploit this disclosure by exacting a reduction in the damage claim in return for working with Stephen again.

Solve Narrow Presenting Problem
Move Toward Compromise Solution

The negotiation dance focuses on solving the narrow presenting problem that was framed in the legal papers. And as the bargaining session rushes to closure, clients are under great pressure to compromise, including pressure to split any remaining differences and make last-minute concessions.

Stephen and Philip confine themselves to the narrow presenting problem framed by Stephen's legal claim of damages for breach of the non-compete covenant. They ignore other issues such as the potential for a future working relationship. They limit themselves to rounds of concessions over money damages and the familiar formula of splitting the difference between the last two offers. Stephen initially offers $100,000 and Philip counteroffers with $5,000 in order to get rid of the nuisance claim. Stephen counteroffers with $90,000 and the dance continues until Stephen asks for $40,000 and Philip offers $20,000. At the end of the day, they feel compelled to split the difference and settle for $30,000.

b.   Lawyers Favor Adversarial Negotiations

Why do many lawyers adopt an adversarial approach to negotiations? The simple and glib answer is that lawyers are preoccupied with litigating. As suggested in this chapter's introduction, negotiations are so enmeshed in the litigation process that negotiations and litigation have become an integrated, single process of dispute resolution. Thus, lawyers are likely to approach the negotiated settlement of a court case with a litigators' mind-set.[21] This mind-set is molded by an intensely adversarial legal culture and reinforced by attorney fee arrangements.

---

20. *See* Menkel-Meadow, *supra* note 5, at 780–782. (Professor Menkel-Meadow points out that fear of disclosure may be displaced in this era of discovery and that disclosure of preferences in negotiations is not the same thing as disclosing "evidence.")

21. Mnookin, *supra* note 5, at 108–118, 167–172.

Many clients crave and many lawyers relish a fiercely combative approach to legal representation. Overly optimistic clients want to be protected by aggressive hired guns. They are not very receptive to reality checks and can become uneasy with lawyers who may not appear faithful to the cause when they flag legal risks and inquire about the other side's perspective and needs.

Legal training and experience teach lawyers to view legal disputes as zero-sum or distributive conflicts about money in which one party wins and the other one loses. The very function of courts is to declare winners and losers. And, they prefer the winners winning monetary awards over such equitable relief as specific performance and inventive injunctions. Based on the well-established maxim that "equitable relief is not available to one who has an adequate remedy at law," courts award creative equitable relief only when legal remedies, primarily damages, are inadequate. Before awarding equitable relief, a party must demonstrate that he would otherwise suffer irreparable harm and that the nature of the equitable relief would be practical, convenient, and not sap judicial resources.[22]

The litigator's mind-set is also molded by the only too familiar routine for pursuing litigation. First, a litigator's conception of the dispute is shaped by the way he converts the dispute into a legal case. When drafting the complaint or answer, the attorney sculpts and fits the dispute into recognized legal categories and then reinforces this conception of the dispute with supporting partisan arguments. The attorney then engages in various strategies to bolster the legal case because the perceived likely court outcome will impact on the settlement value of the case. In addition to using old-fashioned puffery and bluffing, the attorney typically turns to various litigation strategies. By pursuing more discovery and a motion for summary judgment, for instance, the attorney pursues the chance that more disclosure or a successful motion will strengthen the court case and its settlement value. The attorney may further press the other party to settle by resorting to litigation strategies that increase the other party's cost of staying in the litigation. By demanding voluminous discovery, for example, the attorney can increase the other party's costs of not settling. As the attorneys and parties become consumed by these litigation tactics, the litigation and corresponding negotiation strategy quickly become sharply adversarial.

---

22. *See* Dan Dobbs, Dobbs—Law of Remedies §2.5 (2d ed. 1993).

These litigation strategies can be fueled by the fee arrangements between attorneys and their clients, arrangements that can encourage unethical professional conduct. Obviously, an hourly rate arrangement can
motivate attorneys to engage in adversarial strategies that prolong the
litigation. And, it takes only one attorney with the hourly rate incentive
to prolong the litigation. Even though the alternative of a contingency
fee arrangement may motivate early settlement (by working less hours,
the attorney can make more), it can discourage problem-solving searches for value-creating trades. A settlement that includes a new car instead
of money damages, for instance, produces a settlement that cannot be
neatly split into one-third for the attorney.

These litigation strategies are unconstrained by any incentive for a
party to disclose weaknesses in his own court case. Neither party wants
to be the first person to blink. Each party wants to avoid any appearance
of self-doubt that might empower the other party to intensify the litigation until the blinking party capitulates.

In short, when the litigator's mind-set is adapted to legal negotiations,
his approach is bound to be adversarial.[23] This adversarial approach to
negotiations has been long-standing, despite the finding of at least one
prominent study that lawyers would prefer problem-solving strategies.[24]
The study of New Jersey litigators suggested that lawyers may negotiate
adversarially out of habitual social practice that is less costly and more
easily routinized than problem-solving.[25]

---

23. One creative solution for changing the litigator's mind-set is to change the attorney who tries to settle the case. Instead of the litigator pursuing both the litigation and
the negotiations, the litigator only litigates. Any negotiations would be handled by a
separate settlement counsel who is committed to a problem-solving approach. For a
thoughtful development of this solution, *see* Coyne, *The Case for Settlement Counsel*,
OHIO ST. J. ON DISP. RES. 367 (1999). The author concluded that "...the mind-set
needed to do effective problem-solving is incompatible with the mind-set needed to
pursue litigation whole-heartedly." *Id.* at 393.

24. *See* Heumann & Hyman, *Negotiation Methods and Litigation Settlement Methods
in New Jersey: 'You Can't Always Get What You Want,'* 12 OHIO ST. J. ON DISP. RES.
253, 309 (1997) ("While 61% of the lawyers would like to see more problem-solving negotiation methods, about 71% of negotiations are carried out with positional
methods instead.").

25. *Id.* at 295–309.

3. Problem-Solving Approach

This section first examines in detail the key features of problem-solving negotiations, also know as interest-based or principled negotiations. Then, these key features are translated into fourteen distinct stages of negotiation.

a. Key Features

The starting point and structure of problem-solving negotiations are radically different than adversarial negotiations. Instead of executing clever opening offer strategies, problem-solving negotiators begin by gathering information about each other's interests and BATNAs (alternatives to settlement). Instead of engaging in the ritualistic negotiation dance, problem-solvers brainstorm options and select and shape a solution that satisfies parties' interests and objective standards. A central difference between the two is how information is managed. Instead of manipulating and withholding information, the problem-solver shares information judiciously. Observe carefully how information is managed in a problem-solving process.

This section initially describes the different orientation that problem-solving attorneys and their clients bring to the negotiations. Then, this section considers how problem-solving attorneys prepare for negotiations by identifying each party's interests and BATNA, and thinking about sources of value and inventive options for solutions. This section ends by describing strategies that attorneys and clients are likely to take at the negotiation table. Parties and their attorneys solidify their understanding of the parties' interests and BATNAs, identify issues for resolution, brainstorm multiple options for mutual gain, and assess and select options based on the criteria of meeting parties' interests and satisfying objective standards. If any issues are still unresolved, the parties may either engage in a tempered negotiation dance or turn to another method of dispute resolution. For a summary of the key features, see table "Key Features of Problem-Solving Negotiations."

Key Features of
Problem-Solving Negotiations

Orientation

View Problem Broadly to Encompass Underlying Interests and Needs
View as Shared Problem
View Dispute as an Integrative Opportunity, Not a Distributive Problem
View Dispute as Search for "Win-Win" and Pareto Optimal Solutions
Think Creatively Outside of the Legal Box
Search for Increase Value
Promote Effective Communications and Exchange of Information
No Early Opening Offer Strategy
Value Relationship
Be Open to Other Side's Views and Interests
Approach Search for Solutions with an Open Mind

Preparation (with deep client involvement)

Investigate Facts
Identify Client's Interests
Surmise Other Party's Interests
Identify Issues for Resolution
Investigate and Improve Client's Total BATNA
Surmise Other Party's Total BATNA
Gather Information on Reservation Value
Identify Sources of Objective Criteria and Value to Bring to Table
Engage Client in Imagining Inventive Solutions
Plan to Share Information Judiclously

Strategies at the Table

Establish Rapport and Open Communclations
Share Information Judiciously about Interests
Educate Other Party About Party's Interests
Learn More About Other Party's Interests
Advocate for Client's Interests
Understand Each Other's Total BATNA
De-emphasize Legal Case (Public BATNA)
Identify and Overcome any Impediments
Identify Issues for Resolution
Jointly Generate Multiple Options for Mutual Gain
Search for Non-Monetary Solutions
Search for Objective Criteria and Opportunities to Expand Value for
    Trades
Search for Inventive Solutions that are Unavailable in Court
Formulate Reservation Value
Assess and Select Options Based on Interests and Objective
    Standards
Use Reasoned Explanations and Principled Justifications
Formulate Settlement Proposals/First Offers
Convert Emerging Settlement Proposals into Monetary Equivalents
Compare Settlement Proposals with Reservations Value
Manage Remaining Distributive Conflicts

i.   Orientation

The problem-solving attorney is likely to bring to the negotiating table a distinctive orientation toward the negotiation process. This orientation influences how the attorney prepares for and participates in the negotiation sessions.

View Problem Broadly to Encompass Underlying Interests and Needs
View as Shared Problem
View Dispute as an Integrative Opportunity, Not a Distributive Problem
View Dispute as Search for "Win-Win" and Pareto Optimal Solutions

Central to the problem-solving enterprise is the lens through which the negotiator views the dispute. By viewing the dispute broadly, the problem-solving negotiator searches beyond the issues specifically raised in the court case. He does not feel confined to resolving the legally defined dispute. He does not view the dispute as a limited distributive problem over how to divide a fixed resource. He does not approach the other side as arch adversaries, but instead as collaborators trying to resolve a shared problem. By uncovering the underlying interests and needs of both sides, the negotiator engages in a search for integrative opportunities to increase the resources (also known as "value") for resolving the dispute. He is looking for ways that both sides can gain or ways one side can gain without making the other side worst off. He is looking for the often-repeated "win-win"[26] and Pareto optimal solutions.[27]

---

26. In case you missed this explanation of the "win-win" terminology in the introductory chapter, I am repeating it here. I think the overused "win-win" terminology still retains utility because of the contrast that it makes with the opposite attitude of "win-lose." These contrasting attitudes neatly capture the fundamental differences between problem-solving and adversarial approaches. However, for many lawyers, the idea that both sides can win something seems naïve and not anchored in reality. Instead, lawyers should consider the idea that both sides might be able to gain something in negotiations reflects an optimistic attitude that can open the mind to creative searches. Moreover, the possibilities of a gain in negotiations are greater than in court. In negotiations, even the defendant who has to pay considerable damages may gain other benefits such as no publicity, no precedent, and maybe even a continuing business relationship.

27. Pareto optimal solutions are reached by parties making a series of Pareto superior moves until they reach the point where there are no more improvements that can make one party better off without making the other party worst off. A Pareto superior move is simply when an improvement for one party does not make the other party worst off. *See* Raiffa, *supra* note 16, at 139.

Stephen does not view the dispute as a narrow breach of contract claim but instead views it more broadly about the break down in the employment relationship between Stephen as teacher and Philip as protégé. He approaches the break down as a shared problem that Stephen and Philip could work together to resolve in a way that both might gain something or the harm to one side would be none or minimal.

Think Creatively Outside of the Legal Box
Search for Increased Value

Through the problem-solving lens, the negotiator searches for solutions outside the legal box of legal rights, legal obligations, and precedent. By not viewing the dispute as limited to dividing up a fixed resource, the negotiator looks for solutions that are more inventive than the simple payment of money from one person to another. The negotiation presents an opportunity to expand resources and increase value that might be available to help the parties creatively resolve the dispute. (For a fuller discussion, see section 1.3 on how to "Identify Sources of Value to Bring to Table.")

Promote Effective Communications and Exchange of Information

The problem-solving negotiator is committed to opening up communications between the parties and exchanging information. In contrast with an adversarial negotiator, a problem-solving one appreciates the benefits of forthrightly exchanging accurate information about key issues, interests, BATNAs, potential resources and value, and options for settlement.

No Early Opening Offer Strategy

In a problem-solving process, the negotiator does not prepare an early opening offer strategy to launch the negotiations. Instead, the negotiator focuses on jointly developing proposals through a discussion of each other's interests and a process of generating options and selecting options based on interests and objective standards. Out of this process, the negotiator constructs a first offer to put on the table.[28]

Value Relationship

In contrast with adversarial negotiations where relationships can be subject to great stress and even destroyed, problem-solving negotiators approach relationships with respect and with an eye toward improving them.

---

28. *See* Fisher, *supra* note 5, at 169–170.

Be Open to Other Side's Views and Interests

The negotiator is interested in learning about the other side's perspective, needs, and priorities. As discussed below under "Preparation," this information is valuable for developing a solution that meets the interests of both sides, a solution that will more likely be adopted by both sides.

Approach Search for Solutions with an Open Mind

The negotiator does not enter the negotiations with a pre-conceived view of the right solution. Instead, the negotiator approaches the negotiations with an open mind that is ready to learn about the other party's interests and to engage in a process of generating monetary and non-monetary options and searching for opportunities to trade value. Stephen would not enter the negotiations convinced that the right solution is Philip paying him $100,000. Even though Stephen would arrive with an understanding of his alternative to settlement as a trip wire, Stephen would approach the initial negotiations as an opportunity to learn more about Philip's interests and to engage in a process of generating options for resolution.

ii. Preparation (with deep client involvement)

Investigate Facts
Identify Client's Interests
Surmise Other Party's Interests

CRITICAL JUNCTURE

When preparing, the attorney gives intensive attention to the essential question that forms the foundation of a problem-solving negotiation: What are the needs and interests of her client?

> "Interests motivate people; they are the silent movers behind the hubbub of positions. Your position is something you have decided upon. Your interests are what caused you to so decide."[29]

The attorney searches for the interests that lie beneath his client's demands (positions) by posing the simple and penetrating question of "why." By bringing to the surface the underlying interests of his client

---

29. *See id.* at 41.

and surmising the interests of the other party, the attorney is no longer preparing for a contest over competing positions, a contest that usually produces a narrow legal solution. Discovering interests is much harder than it appears. Techniques for interviewing clients to uncover interests are examined in detail in chapter 3.2.

Stephen is demanding damages in the amount of $100,000. But when asked "why" he wants the money, he may answer that he wants to be compensated for stolen business opportunities and recognition for providing Philip good training and mentoring. A little more questioning may reveal that Stephen's interests are in making money and in being recognized for how he helped Philip get started as a salesperson. The damage claim is only one way (or position) for satisfying these interests. Later on, it will be shown how understanding these interests can light the way toward other options for satisfying Stephen's interests.

Identify Issues for Resolution

Out of the massive facts, the attorney will develop tentative issues for resolution. For the *Shirts for You* dispute, one obvious issue to propose is: Are there any options for Stephen and Philip to work together in the future? Another more subtle framing of the issue might be: Are there any ways that Philip might be helpful to Stephen in the future?

Investigate and Improve Client's BATNA
Surmise Other Party's BATNA

The attorney thoroughly researches his client's best alternative to settling the dispute, known as the BATNA (Best Alternative To a Negotiated Agreement).[30] For attorneys representing clients in court cases, the BATNA will typically but not always be[31] litigating the dispute. By the attorney advising his client about the likely court outcome as an alternative to settlement, the client will enter the negotiations knowing what would happen if he leaves the negotiating table. The court alternative becomes a standard against which the client can evaluate whether to accept or reject emerging settlement packages.

---

30. *See id.* at 97–106.

31. For example. sometimes the most attractive alternative to settling a court case might be filing for bankruptcy, doing nothing, or publicizing the dispute. In one case that I mediated, the defendant spent most of the mediation session trying to convince the plaintiff that if he does not accept the defendant's offer, the defendant will be forced to file for bankruptcy and the plaintiff will get nothing.

The attorney also surmises the other party's BATNA in order to learn when the other party is likely to leave the table. His alternative may be different. This information provides the negotiator a valuable reference point for understanding what is possible to achieve in the negotiations. The negotiator cannot expect the other party to agree to something that is less attractive than his alternative to a negotiated agreement. However, if the negotiator thinks the other party has an unrealistically optimistic view of his BATNA, the negotiator will prepare a plan for educating the other party.

Neither Stephen nor Philip can be confident about winning in court. Stephen risks losing the court case because it is not clear whether Philip has breached his covenant to not compete when Philip sells a different brand of shirts to a different group of customers in Buffalo. Philip risks losing because Philip is competing in the same market as Stephen—selling shirts to retail outlets in Buffalo. These mutually uncertain BATNAs should motivate the parties to try to settle the dispute.

Gather Information on Reservation Value

The attorney and client begin gathering information on the client's likely reservation value, the client's trip wire in the negotiations.[32] They need to do the essential preliminary work of researching and calculating a fully analyzed BATNA that considers the less tangible and hard to quantify factors that impact on the resulting reservation value. But, the client avoids prematurely formulating a firm reservation value when participating in a problem-solving negotiation. If he formulates specific terms of settlement too early, he may cripple his ability to approach the negotiation with the flexibility necessary for thinking creatively as the negotiation unfolds.

Identify Sources of Objective Criteria and Value to Bring to Table

The attorney begins prodding his client to think broadly, creatively, and outside of the traditional legal box for possible sources of objective criteria as well as sources of value that could be part of a creative, tailor-made resolution.

---

32. For a full discussion of how to calculate the reservation value—a fully developed BATNA—*see* subsection 2(a)(ii) on establishing a client's reservation value in an adversarial negotiation.

Objective criteria[33] comprise of neutral standards that are either substantive or procedural that can be used as a fair basis for decision-making between the parties. Objective criteria can be derived from practice, custom, precedent, scientific findings, mathematical and econometric models, expert opinion, and simply autonomous sources. The criteria are independent and cannot be influenced or modified by any of the parties at the table. They also are perceived to be legitimate and practical to use. Examples of substantive standards include the average price of all four-bedroom houses in a particular neighborhood and the cost-of-living index of the U.S. Department of Commerce. Examples of procedural standards include the familiar formulae of splitting the difference or taking turns and such procedures as asking an expert to make a decision. Stephen and Philip might agree to select a new sales commission rate for Philip based on the average rate for salespeople in the Buffalo area with more than ten years of experience.[34] This rate would be derived from independent sources, making it an objective criterion.

Value can be found by tapping common interests, exploiting economies of scale, and taking advantage of differences between the parties.[35]

Common Interests That Do Not Conflict. When parties have common interests, parties may find ways to work together for securing joint benefits. Both Stephen and Philip may have a common interest in a continuing relationship that will make both of them more money. Instead of competing with each other, they may approach their common interest as non-conflicting and as an opportunity to work together selling shirts.

Economies of Scale. Parties can work together to create value. By sharing costs, they can gain scale economies and lower their overall costs. Both Stephen and Philip need a back office to support their sales effort. By joining together, Stephen and Philip could maintain one back office more efficiently by sharing their fixed costs. Their fixed costs, costs, which will be incurred regardless whether they work together or separately, include the cost of rent, office equipment, and minimum support staff.

---

33. For a full discussion of objective criteria, *see* Fisher, *supra* note 5, at 81–94.

34. This proposal assumes that there are no antitrust risks compiling this information.

35. See Mnookin, supra note 5, at 12–17, 25–27; Fisher, supra note 5, at 70–76.

Differences. Differences between parties can be a source of value for enlarging the pie and for trades that can benefit the parties.

Different Interests That Do Not Conflict. A party can bring value to the table by finding ways to satisfy the interests of the other party without hurting his own interests. At no cost to himself, Philip may be able to satisfy Stephen's interest in being recognized for providing good training and mentoring. In addition to thanking him, Philip may further express his appreciation by sending Stephen a sales order for brand name shirts that Philip does not stock.

Different Resources to Trade. Each party may have something different to contribute. By trading, the parties can increase value at the table. Stephen has business relationships with many retail outlets and several major brand name shirts. Philip now has business relationships with a number of new retail outlets and a different brand of shirts. The parties can trade by giving each other access to selling his brand names in the other's retail outlets.

Different Relative Valuations. Each party may value the same contribution differently. The contributing party can contribute something that cost the contributor relatively little but that provides a greater benefit to the receiving party. At little cost, Stephen may be able to provide Philip a better opportunity to grow professionally than if Philip worked alone. Stephen could provide Philip access to new customers, support staff, and his experience and wisdom. For Philip, this access could be worth a lot. For Stephen, he would continue to do a little more of what he was already doing—provide leads, supervision, and support staff.

Different Forecasts. Each party may predict different futures. These differences can be used as a basis for constructing a resolution that is tied to the different forecasts. Although Stephen is impressed by Philip's salesmanship, he thinks Philip needs more maturing. Stephen is not as optimistic as Philip about his ability to recruit new retail customers over the next couple years. Therefore, when Philip asks for 10 percent ownership in *Shirts for You* because he predicts he will increase the number of retail outlets by 10 percent, Stephen may suggest tying increased ownership to the actual increase in number of retail outlets. By doing this, they are constructing a resolution that takes account of each party's different forecast. This resolution gives Philip what he wants, 10 percent ownership interest. If his forecast is correct, he will secure the maximum ownership interest in a couple years; if Stephen's forecast is correct, he will get the maximum interest much later.

Different Risk Preferences. Even if both parties believe in identical forecasts, they may tolerate differently the risks of being wrong. Different risk preferences open the door for trading: the risk-averse party can pay money or other things of value to the more risk-tolerant party to assume the risk. While both Stephen and Philip project the same 10 percent increase in new retail outlets that Philip will enlist for *Shirts for You*, Stephen is less willing to assume the risk of an error than Philip. Stephen may be willing to pay Philip to assume the risk. When Philip achieves the 10 percent increase in the number of retail outlets for the company, Stephen will give him a 2 percent bonus for a total of 12 percent ownership interest.

Different Time Preferences. Each party may value the timing of events differently. One party may need something today; the other party may prefer something later or has more flexibility. The party that needs something today may be willing to pay the other party money or other value to get it today. Philip may need money today because he is getting married and plans to buy a new house. Therefore, he may be willing to accept a lower sales commission in exchange for advances on his commissions.

Engage Client in Imagining Inventive Solutions

CRITICAL JUNCTURE

Engage Client in Creative Thinking about Solutions

The client can be a vital source of original and inventive ideas for solutions.

When the attorney initiates a discussion of objective criteria and value sources with his client, the attorney inevitably enters into a discussion about solutions. Developing objective criteria and value is about devising options for solutions. While the positional negotiator views solutions in terms of legal rights and remedies, a problem-solving one views solutions more broadly and imaginatively.

In preparing for the negotiation, the attorney tries to stimulate his client's creative juices. The client can be a vital source of original and inventive ideas that the client can live with. At this juncture, the attorney's goal is not to formulate firm proposals; his goal is only to prod his client to think broadly, imaginatively, and outside of the legal box. When asking Stephen to think more broadly about his dispute, Stephen may begin to imagine other ways to make money than recovering damages for lost sales. He might consider making even more money by Stephen and Philip working together again. Options for working together could be explored at the negotiation table.

Plan to Share Information Judiciously

The problem-solving negotiator's most vexing question is: What information should be disclosed? Disclosure offers benefits and poses risks because of the clash of two fundamental goals in negotiations.[36] To maximize the creation of joint value, the negotiator should disclose full and accurate information about interests, priorities, issues, and potential resources and value. But, to maximize his personal benefits, in other words to claim the largest possible share of the pie, he may want to strategically conceal and misrepresent his interests, priorities, and resources/value. The negotiator does not want information that he discloses during the creation efforts to disadvantage him when claiming value.

For example, if Philip really disliked working by himself and wants to work again with Stephen, he should find a way to disclose that interest when trying to create value. By sharing that information, the parties would know to focus their energy on creating options that include re-hiring Philip. But, Philip may fear that Stephen will exploit this information by trying to extract a concession such as a lower sales commission until Philip pays him back for the lost sales. Philip also would lose some leverage for gaining a higher commission by not feigning any interest in working again with Stephen—assuming Stephen wants to rehire him.

Because of these risks of exploitation or lost leverage, many attorneys tend to play it safe and withhold information. This instinctive reaction should be guarded against and tested against the three exacting questions in the box.

---

36. *See* ROBERT H. MNOOKIN & LEE ROSS, *Barriers to Conflict Resolution: Introduction* in BARRIERS TO COFNLICT RESOLUTION 7–8 (Arrow et al. eds., 1995).

> **CRITICAL JUNCTURE**
>
> *What Information to Disclose?*
> *The Creating/Claiming Dilemma*
>
> Three Questions
>
> 1. What information should you disclose to expand value (the pie)?
>
> 2. What are the risks?
>
>   What is the risk of withholding the information? What is the risk of disclosing when you shift to claiming value?
>
> 3. How can you disclose the information in a way that will promote expanding value and minimize the risk of exploitation or lost leverage?[37]

These three questions can be collapsed into one: How do you disclose the information that needs to be shared in a way that will minimize the risk of exploitation or lost leverage? Philip can indicate that he might consider returning if the terms were sufficiently attractive. This indeterminate, non-committal answer puts his interest on the table for discussion while reducing his exposure to exploitation. And, Philip can still try to leverage favorable re-hiring terms by pointing out his impressive sales record when he was on his own. In short, it is not about withholding information. It is about disclosing information judiciously.

iii.   Strategies at the Table

Establish Rapport and Open Communications

At the outset, a problem-solving negotiator tries to establish a comfortable rapport and working relationship with the other side in order to open effective communications. The negotiator approaches the other side respectfully and cordially, formulates carefully framed questions, and uses passive and active listening techniques.[38] He presents points in a way that are likely to be heard by the other side. Instead of posturing and making contentious positional arguments, the negotiator presents points with reasoned explanations supported by principled justifications.

---

37. How to share your bottom line in mediations is discussed in Chapter 7.2(c)(i).

38. These techniques, commonly used by mediators, are discussed in Chapter 1.(4) on the Mediation Process.

Instead of Stephen and Philip approaching each other as archenemies, they approach each other as parties who want to meet, talk, and communicate with each other (actually understand each other's perspective). Rather than Philip attacking Stephen for interfering with Philip's professional growth, Philip explains that he left because he was running out of opportunities to grow. As a young salesperson, he wanted new and challenging professional opportunities. This reasoned explanation leaves the door open for Stephen to pick up where Philip left off and explore how working again at *Shirts for You* might be an attractive professional opportunity.

Share Information Judiciously about Interests
Educate Other Party About Client's Interests
Learn More About Other Party's Interests

As already emphasized in the section on "Preparation," the interests of the parties form the starting point in problem-solving negotiations. Interests include not only the interests behind the legal positions but also interests that go beyond those raised in the legal case. Now is the occasion for the attorney to be sure that his client's interests are understood by the other party. Now is the occasion for the attorney and his client to solidify their understanding of the other party's interests. How to share this information judiciously was considered under "Preparation." With an understanding of each other's interests, the parties are ready to develop proposals.

Advocate for Client's Interests

Instead of advocating narrow legal positions, a problem-solving attorney advocates zealously for his client's interests. For example, Stephen's attorney would not advocate Stephen's legal position that he be paid $100,000 in damages. Getting $100,000 is not a statement of Stephen's interest. It is only one way to meet his interests. Stephen's interests are likely to include getting recognition for providing good training and mentoring and making money. There are a number of ways that Stephen could make money including securing damages as well as re-hiring his successful protégé, Philip.

Understand Each Other's BATNA
De-emphasize Legal Case (BATNA)

Because each party's BATNA (the alternative of returning to court) casts a dark shadow over the negotiations, parties usually allocate some time to discussing how attractive it is to return to court. Remember that the more attractive a litigated outcome is, the less motivated the party will be to find a resolution at the table. Therefore, parties need to understand each other's BATNA. In contrast with an adversarial negotiator, a problem-solving one engages in less posturing and a more realistic assessment of each other's BATNA. But, the evaluation task should not be given too much attention in order to guard against the parties stumbling into a positional debate that can easily escalate out of control and back into court.

Because both Stephen and Philip are facing uncertain results in court and attractive options for settlement, they are likely to acknowledge that neither side has a sure win in court and will proceed to negotiate diligently.

Identify and Overcome any Impediments[39]

As the negotiations unfold, parties might stumble due to an impediment. For example, parties may trip because of their different views of critical facts or a deeply fractured relationship. Parties need to find ways to overcome any impediments. Stephen may not be able to negotiate with Philip until he explains why he left to start up his own business. After Stephen gets this information and understands the reasons, he may be able to move forward in the negotiations.

Identify Issues for Resolution

After sharing facts, learning about each other's interests and BATNAs, and dealing with any impediments, negotiators formulate the issues to be resolved in the negotiations.

Jointly Generate Multiple Options for Mutual Gain
Search for Non-Monetary Solutions
Search for Objective Criteria and Opportunities to Expand Value for Trades
Search for Inventive Solutions that are Unavailable in Court

At the negotiating table, parties search for inventive solutions. One common method relies on a structure in which the process of generating ideas is kept rigidly separate from the process of evaluating and selecting them. Parties partake in brainstorming in order to compile a list of uncensored ideas. For brainstorming to succeed, parties agree to

---

39. For a fuller discussion of obstacles to settlement, *see* Chapter 5.1(d) on preparing the case for mediation; Chapter 8 on breaking impasses.

not evaluate any ideas when voiced or expect the person voicing the idea to defend it. Producing an options list is one of the distinctive benefits of a problem-solving process. By abandoning a positional strategy based on legal rights, parties search for solutions outside of the constraining judicial practice of converting parties' needs into monetary equivalents. They can discover useful objective criteria and creative ways to increase value for trades.

Through brainstorming, Stephen and Philip may develop a list of options for working together in the future. The uncensored list might include merging businesses, rehiring Philip, Philip buying Stephen's business and keeping Stephen as a consultant, no future business relationship, and so on.

Formulate Reservation Value

The client should formulate the critical trip wire for marking when to leave the negotiation based on what is learned during the negotiation.[40] The trip wire or reservation value is developed as settlement options are being developed and assessed. These two basic tasks are very separate but need to be done simultaneously. A party cannot reach the best settlement possible without both a clear understanding of his reservation value and a suitable opportunity to generate and assess settlement options.

Assess and Select Options Based on Interests and Objective Standards
Use Reasoned Explanations and Principled Justifications
Formulate Settlement Proposals/First Offers

The list of uncensored options is evaluated. Instead of selecting options based on brute exercise of power, parties assess and select options based on specific reasons and principled justifications. Parties may appraise options based on the criteria of which ones further the interests of both parties, further one party's interests while not making the other party worse off, or minimize harm to one party. Parties also may judge options against agreed-upon objective standards. The advantages of parties articulating specific reasons are many:

---

40. The seven factors that influence the reservation value can be a source of questions for investigation during the negotiation. *See* Korobkin, *supra* note 8, at 43–50 (Describes six factors in addition to the BATNA that can affect the reservation value: a party's particular preferences for reaching an agreement, his probability estimates of future events, his ability to tolerate risk, the value of time, transaction costs, and the opportunities for future relationships.)

In the process of considering possibilities, the problem solver articulates reasons why a particular solution is acceptable or unacceptable, rather than simply rejecting an offer or making a concession. Articulating reasons during the negotiation facilitates agreement in a number of ways. First, it establishes standards for judging whether a particular solution is sensible and should be accepted. If the reason is focused on the parties' underlying needs, the negotiator can consider whether the proposal is satisfactory to the parties. She need not be concerned with such conventional evaluation as "Is this the most I can get? Or its counterpart, "Is this the least I can get away with?" Second, principled proposals focus attention on solving the problem by meeting the parties' needs, rather than winning an argument. Furthermore, continuously focusing justification on the parties' needs may cause negotiators to see still other solutions, rather than simply to respond with arguments about particular offers. The use of principled proposals can decrease the likelihood that unjustified and unnecessary concessions will be made simply to move toward agreement. Finally, the use of principled proposals causes the parties to share information about their preferences that they might otherwise be reluctant to reveal.[41]

Out of this discussion, parties jointly develop options that become settlement proposals. But, this approach does not always avoid the need for one party to put forward a "first offer" in the form of a settlement option to consider. At this advanced point in the negotiations, the offer is one based on transparent, principled justifications. The offer can be further discussed and refined by the parties.

Convert Emerging Settlement Proposals into Monetary Equivalents
Compare Settlement Proposals with Reservation Value

The attorney and client may need to translate any emerging settlement proposals into terms that can be meaningfully compared with the client's reservation value. In contrast with adversarial negotiations in which the legal case in court, the dispute in negotiations, and the likely settlement are usually defined in monetary terms, the negotiated result in a problem-solving process may include difficult to quantify

---

41. *See* Menkel-Meadow, *supra* note 5, at 825.

non-monetary features. The emerging negotiated result may need to be converted into a monetary equivalent so that it can be readily compared with the reservation value for the purpose of determining whether an emerging settlement is equal to or better than the reservation value.

For example, Philip may have difficulty comparing his reservation value of $42,000[42] with an unexpected two-part proposal in which he would pay $45,000 and would be freed to develop his business fully in Buffalo. Philip will need to translate this proposal into a total value that can be meaningfully compared with his reservation value.

Philip will have to confront the difficult question of what it is worth to him to secure a negotiated release. The personal benefit of securing the release in litigation was already incorporated in his reservation value when Philip estimated the personal benefits of $10,000 that included the release he would secure if he wins in court. But the emerging settlement proposal is offering an unexpected, not easily quantifiable equivalent benefit—a negotiated release that would give him the freedom to pursue his business in Buffalo.

This release is worth something to Philip. He should try to estimate its worth. If it is worth more than $3,000 to him—the difference between his reservation value of $42,000, the most he is willing to pay, and the $45,000 settlement offer that includes the benefits of a release, Philip should accept the offer. If Philip estimates the release to be worth

---

42. In subsection 2(a)(ii), Philip's reservation value of $42,000 was calculated as follows: His attorney predicted a 40 percent chance of a jury verdict holding Philip liable for $80,000 plus litigation costs of $20,000 for a negative of $40,000. If Philip wins, he would still have to pay his attorney fees and other litigation costs of $20,000. By multiplying the $20,000 by his 60 percent chance of winning, Philip calculated a negative value of $12,000 and then added it to the negative $40,000 for a public BATNA in the amount of $52,000.

Next, he adjusted Philip's public BATNA value to account for a number of private costs and benefits in order to arrive at his reservation value. By going to court, Philip faced the private costs of spending time preparing for the case and suffering the emotional stress of litigation. But, these costs were offset by two possible private benefits of litigating. Philip welcomed the 60 percent chance of winning and paying nothing, and he wanted to try to exonerate himself in court so he could freely pursue his lucrative business in Buffalo. Philip estimated that the private benefits of his BATNA are worth roughly $10,000 more than the private costs. Therefore, Philip's public BATNA value was decreased by $10,000 to produce a fully analyzed BATNA or reservation value of $42,000. Thus, if settlement possibilities involve Philip paying more that $42,000, Philip would leave the table to litigate where he would be at risk of paying $52,000 and at risk of experiencing the various private costs and benefits.

$5,000, the settlement offer will only cost him $40,000. Philip will pay $45,000, reduced by the benefit of a $5,000 release. This $40,000 cost is less than his reservation value of $42,000. By accepting the offer, Philip avoids the judicial risk of losing $52,000 and failing to secure the release in court.

Manage Remaining Distributive Conflicts

CRITICAL JUNCTURE

Resolving Distributive Conflicts

The most challenging point in a negotiation arises when parties must face the distributive issues in their dispute. At this moment, it appears that any resolution will benefit one party at the expense of the other. Distributive moments can be divided into two types:

1. Easy Distributive Issues that can be resolved through the use of objective standards, procedural solutions, and trades.

2. Difficult Distributive Issues that may require the use of adversarial tactics.

Parties may still face conflicting interests that result in distributive obstacles even after exhausting all possibilities for increasing value (the pie) and meeting parties' interests. There is some good news, however. If the parties have followed problem-solving strategies up to this point in the negotiations, they would have created a hospitable environment for dealing with these remaining stubborn issues.

Easy Distributive Issues. When parties are assessing and selecting options, they may see distributive conflicts rise to the surface. It is at this juncture that objective standards and procedural solutions[43] as well as trading can be especially useful.

For example, in a discrimination case in which the employer agrees to reinstate an employee, the employer and employee may still need to calculate the amount of back pay for the five years of discrimination. The two parties might have been able to resolve every other aspect of

---

43. A familiar procedural solution is the overused, last-resort formula of splitting the difference between the last two offers. For a fuller discussion of options, *see* Korobkin, *A Positive Theory of Legal Negotiation*, 88 GEORGETOWN L.J. 1789, 1821–1829 (2000).

the financial package. This remaining issue presents a distributive conflict because every dollar increase in back pay will result in a gain for the employee at the expense of the employer. Instead of hard adversarial bargaining, they could negotiate the details of a neutral formula based on the average salary increases of employees in his job category during the five relevant years. This is an objective formula because neither party can readily manipulate or influence the formula's results.[44]

In view of their common interests in making money, Stephen and Philip may select the option of joining forces and working together. They may resolve the distributive issue of how to share profits by adopting the objective and facially fair standard of splitting profits based on the percentage of business each person brings to the partnership each year.

Trading means each party searching for opportunities to trade something of relatively low value for something of relatively high value. Or stated more plainly, each party gives up something of less value for something of more value. This trading formula helps parties avoid stark distributive conflicts by folding them into a set of trades and then trading the distributive conflicts away.

If Stephen and Philip are trying to negotiate the amount of damages for lost sales—a classically distributive negotiation, Stephen might offer to give up part of his damage claim in return for Philip working again with *Shirts for You*. Stephen essentially agrees to trade giving up some money for securing a great salesman. Philip may like this trade because he gets to pay less and he gets his old job back, presumably with more favorable terms now that he has a proven sales record and his own business contacts.

Difficult Distributive Issues. Not all distributive conflicts can be easily resolved through use of objective standards, procedural solutions, and trades. This moment can be the most arduous one in any negotiation. Then, what? Do negotiators now turn to adversarial tactics? Yes, as a last resort. But what adversarial tactics should be used?

---

44. There might be some areas of discretion when compiling the historic salary data; however, any different views can be isolated, narrowed, and resolved by using techniques already familiar to lawyers.

DIFFERING VIEWS

How to Resolve Difficult Distributive Issues
How to Claim Value

Options:[45]

1. Resort to classical adversarial negotiations (see section 1.2 on Adversarial Negotiations). [The Combative Dance]

2. Resort to adversarial techniques that have been adapted for a problem-solving process. [The Collaborative Dance]

Recommendations:[46]

Adapt adversarial techniques: The Collaborative Dance

• Engage in a tempered opening offer strategy consisting of a gentle negotiation dance of offers, counteroffers, compromises, and concessions.

• Eliminate such harsh moves as aggressive tone, clever tricks, belligerent threats, and deviously and purposefully misleading disclosure of information.

• Justify each offer, counteroffer, compromise, or concession with reasoned explanations and principled justifications.

• Add or emphasize such problem-solving moves as cultivating a relationship with the other side, learning the other side's interests and perspective, promoting effective communications, sharing information in a way that reduces exploitation risk, and acknowledging that both sides are claiming value.

• Employ the BATNA consistently with a problem-solving approach by using it as a guide for the negotiation dance, avoiding theatrical posturing and threats, and assessing realistically both side's BATNAs.

---

45. Mediators' techniques that can be especially valuable when facing intractable distributive conflicts are considered in Chapter 7.2(d) on methods for inducing parties to move toward their bottom lines. That section considers methods that can be used when parties are stuck over how much money to be paid and are reluctant to disclose their bottom lines to each other. The section suggests several safe ways for parties to find out whether their bottom lines put them in a settlement range.

46. This section suggests one approach to claiming in a problem-solving process. This subject needs more empirical research and creative thought. At a program of the Association of American Law Schools in January 2001, another law professor and I were featured speakers on presenting competing views on how to teach mediation representation in law schools. I was surprised by how little thought that I, along with the dispute resolution scholars in attendance, had given to how to adapt claiming strategies to a problem-solving process. It is too easy of an answer for us to advise attorneys to resolve intractable distributive conflicts by resorting to the traditional techniques of an adversarial negotiator, an answer that is likely to cripple the problem-solving process. We need to come up with better ways to deal with difficult distributive disputes in a problem-solving process. We are only beginning to develop the better ways.

If a court holds that Philip violated the non-compete clause, the parties need to calculate the amount of sales lost by Stephen. He claims he lost sales in the amount of $100,000. Philip knows that he will have to pay something based on his realistic assessment of his BATNA. Both parties realize how difficult it will be to arrive at an objectively proven amount and do not want to expend large fees on experts

Instead of belligerently threatening protracted and expensive litigation, Philip says:

"I think we are stuck over how much I will pay you. You seem to agree that it is just too difficult to calculate with confidence what you would have sold if I did not start selling shirts on my own in Buffalo. We have tried to calculate lost sales from each of our sales records without spending time and money on selecting and using outside experts to estimate lost sales. What do you think of us exchanging realistic offers for settlement that are based on the use of the sales records?"

Stephen answers: "Sounds good to me. Let's use each of our audited sales records for the last twelve months."

Philip continues: "Okay. Let me take a fresh look at those audited records and present an offer." (He takes time to study the sales records.)

"Instead of my starting with the traditional and unproductive offer of paying nothing or only a nominal amount, I offer to pay you $10,000. This amount is based on the assumption that the most that you lost was 10 percent of what I sold because you did not have the time to cultivate a significant number of new customers while still maintaining your existing customer base." (Philip is testing the good faith of Stephen by seeing how he responds.)

Stephen responds: "I want to thank you for a serious although inadequate offer. I undoubtedly lost more than $10,000 in sales due to your breach of the non-compete clause. I expended considerable time trying to solicit new customers. I spent about 25 percent of my time on the road contacting new prospects and was specifically told by at least three prospects that they were not interested because they were being served by you. After reviewing your audited sales records, I learned that I had solicited six of your customers to whom you sold a total of $75,000 of shirts. Let us see if we can settle this for around the $75,000, the amount of sales that would have otherwise gone to me."

Thus, the collaborative negotiation dance of offers, counteroffers, compromises, and concessions is commenced.

b.   Stages of Problem-Solving Negotiations

If you view linear schemes to be a useful way to map routes, you may find it helpful to view problem-solving negotiations as consisting of a number of predictable stages. (See table below.) The stages map a pathway toward settlement, with each stage providing a signpost to guide you. By understanding negotiations as a route with a destination, you acquire a diagnostic tool that you can use to figure out where the negotiation is and where it still needs to go.

Are both parties ready to move forward to the next stage? If one party is still at the gathering information stage, for instance, then that party is not ready to go to the next stage of identifying issues and interests.

Are both parties at the same stage of the negotiation? If one party is trying to formulate an agenda while the other party is trying to understand the parties' interests, then the parties are at different stages. The party working on interests is not ready to participate in the next stage of formulating an agenda.

Is one party regressing? If both parties have moved forward to formulate an agenda and one party starts to introduce new issues, then that party has regressed to the issue identification stage and possibly the information gathering stage. That party needs more time to identify issues before the party is ready to focus on developing an agenda.

Do both parties need to regress? As issues are being identified, for instance, some issues might seem unclear and confusing so the parties need to return to the stage of gathering information.

Stages of Problem-Solving Negotiations

1. Prepare for Negotiation
2. Rhetoric
3. Relationship Building
4. Negotiate a Problem-Solving Process
5. Venting, Being Heard, and Information Gathering for Specific Purposes
6. Identify Issues, Interests, BATNA, and Impediments
7. Agenda Formulation—Issues to Resolve and Impediments to Overcome
8. Overcome Impediments to Settlement
9. Generate Options for Each Issue
10. Assess and Select Options
11. Manage Any Remaining Distributive Conflicts
12. Broad Outline of Settlement
13. Final Agreement in Writing
14. Post-Agreement Tasks

Negotiation is a dynamic process. Even though this description of the stages projects a linear approach to negotiations, negotiations are not so neat and compartmentalized in practice. Negotiations naturally move forward and backward, sometimes called cycling among the stages. Negotiators even can be at several stages at the same time. For instance, negotiators can engage simultaneously in relationship building, negotiating the negotiation process, and venting.

1. Prepare for Negotiation

How to prepare for a problem-solving negotiation has already been discussed in detail in subsection 3(a)(ii). The attorney investigates the facts, law, and client's BATNA and begins to identify issues, client's interests as well as the other party's interests and BATNA. The attorney also prods his client to begin identifying sources of value, objective standards, and inventive solutions.

2. Rhetoric

If the other party has adversarial propensities, the other party is likely to exude much rhetoric. Rhetoric usually takes the form of extreme posturing about demands and may include threats. The posturing may be designed to anchor the thinking of others about what is possible in the negotiations. The rhetoric may take place in the media, pre-negotiation meetings, and even the negotiation sessions. It is ignored and never copied by a problem-solving negotiator.

3. Relationship Building

Negotiators work together more effectively when they have a positive relationship. To cultivate a positive relationship, negotiators engage in small talk during which they become acquainted with each other, if not friendly with each other. They may even discover they have common views of current topics or shared experiences involving matters unrelated to the dispute. This early relationship building can help lubricate the negotiation process. Parties may become more forthcoming with information and more committed to the demanding task of collaboratively formulating creative solutions.

4. Negotiate a Problem-Solving Process[47]

A negotiator may need to take some time to negotiate the process of negotiation. This stage is essential if the other party has put down the positional gauntlet. Instead of responding in kind or trying to unilaterally impose a problem-solving process, the negotiator opens a discussion about the negotiation process. The negotiator asks problem-solving questions that involve the other side in considering alternative ways to negotiate. By asking questions, the negotiator initiates a collaborative process:

> Is there an alternative to the conventional approach of my counteroffering and our haggling until we are at the point where we can split the difference? Do you have any thoughts on how we might first explore our clients' interests—that is, what they would like out of these negotiations?

As the substantive negotiations continue, the negotiator asks process questions about ways to generate options, increase value, and assess and select options.

Even though parties might try to resolve early the sort of negotiation process that they will follow, deviations and relapses are likely to occur as the negotiations proceed. When evaluating options, for example, the other party may instinctively push positionally for a particular option instead of testing it against interests or objective standards. Therefore,

---

47. *See* Mnookin, *supra* note 5, 62–63, 121–125, 207–211.

the negotiator may sporadically revisit and renegotiate the process throughout the negotiations.[48]

5. Venting, Being Heard, and Information Gathering for Specific Purposes

Clients and even attorneys may need to vent their frustrations or anger before they can negotiate productively. Each party also may need to tell his story about what happened. Only after "being heard" can each party move forward. Venting and being heard have considerable value all by themselves. But, when parties vent and tell their story, they also convey valuable information during this stage of gathering information. Additionally, each side poses many questions that are designed to enlist specific information about interests, issues, BATNAs, and impediments to settlement.

6. Identify Issues, Interests, BATNA, and Impediments

Based on the garnered information, the negotiators formulate issues for resolution, learn about each other's interests and BATNAs, and isolate any impediments to settlement.

7. Agenda Formulation—Issues to Resolve and Impediments to Overcome

In complex cases, parties negotiate the order in which issues and impediments will be considered. Should parties progress from the easiest to most difficult issues, or the reverse? Should parties progress from the most important issues to the least, or the reverse?

8. Overcome Impediments to Settlement

Negotiate a resolution to any impediments that are blocking the negotiations.[49] If a conflict over access to vital data is blocking the negotiations, for instance, then the parties would negotiate a process for providing equal access to the data.

---

48. *See* Chapter 1.5 on how to transform adversarial negotiations into problem-solving ones

49. *See* Chapter 5.1(d) on dealing with impediments to settlements.

9. Generate Options for Each Issue

As explained earlier, negotiators engage in brainstorming in which parties invent ideas for creating value and expanding the pie.[50]

10. Assess and Select Options

As explained earlier, negotiators assess and select options based on the interests of all the parties and objective standards.[51]

11. Manage Any Remaining Distributive Conflicts

Even after engaging in a thorough brainstorming session, fully assessing multiple options based on interests and making trades, the negotiator may not be able to resolve the entire dispute. As already examined, the negotiators may be stuck with a surviving distributive conflict such as a claim for damages. For these stubborn conflicts in which one party would clearly gain at the expense of the other, negotiators turn to the specialized techniques for easy and difficult distributive conflicts.[52]

12. Broad Outline of Settlement

As key elements of the settlement emerge, attorneys outline areas of agreement. The areas could involve specific matters such as the dollar amount of damages to be paid or general principles that can guide the resolution of the dispute such as agreeing that the resolution will not imply who was responsible for the problem.

13. Final Agreement in Writing

Within the bounds of the outline, attorneys reduce to writing the nitty-gritty details of the agreement.

14. Post-Agreement Tasks

After the agreement is signed, the attorneys' work is not quite finished. Depending on the details and intricacy of the agreement, the attorneys may need to monitor or execute its implementation. Post-agreement tasks may be as straightforward as the payment of one lump sum or more intricate such as the exchange of goods for services over several years.

---

50. *See* Chapter 1.3(a)(iii) on "Strategies at the Table."

51. *Id.*

52. *Id.*

4. Differences Between Adversarial and Problem-Solving Negotiations

The following chart highlights differences between adversarial and problem-solving negotiations by pairing contrasting characteristics.[53]

Differences Between Adversarial and Problem-Solving Negotiations	
Adversarial	**Problem-Solving**
Act as Adversaries	Act as Problem-Solvers
Competitive	Collaborative
Advocate for Rights-Based Positions	Advocate for Client's Interests
Put Positions on Table	Put Interests on Table
Opening Offer Strategy	Explore Parties' Interests
Win-Lose	Win-Win
Distributive Dispute	Integrative Dispute
Fixed Pie	Create Value and Expand Pie
Hard Positional Bargaining (that blind parties to value-creating opportunities)	Search for Value to Trade
Compromise Between Positions	Reconciling Interests
Emphasize Monetary Solution	Search for Non-Monetary Solutions
Propose Solutions Based on Legal Rights or Compromise of Rights	Search for Inventive, Creative Solutions Based on Interests
Emphasize Legal Case (BATNA)	De-emphasize Legal Case (BATNA)
Manipulate Information	Use Information Forthrightly
Engage in Tricks and Threats	Establish Rapport and Be Open to Reason
Make Adversarial Arguments	Make Reasoned Points
Be Blinded to Other Side's Case	Be Open to Other Side's Reasoned Points
Yield to Pressure	Yield to Reason
Decide Based on Pressure	Decide Based on Principled, Objective Standards
Limit Exchange of Information	More Freely Exchange Information (Especially About Interests)
Contest over Competing Positions	Generate Options for Mutual Gain
Solve Narrow Presenting Problem	Solve Broader Interest-Based Problem
Less Client Involvement	Greater Client Involvement

---

53. For another interesting comparison, *see* CHARLES B. CRAVER, EFFECTIVE LEGAL NEGOTIATION AND SETTLEMENT 21–27 (1997) (compares cooperative/problem-solving lawyering style with competitive/adversarial lawyering style).

5. Converting Adversarial Negotiations into Problem-Solving

> **CRITICAL JUNCTURE**
>
> *Converting the Other Side into a Problem-Solver*
>
> 1. Recognize adversarial tactics.
> 2. Respond with initiatives to convert.

Much has been written about how you can transform the other side into a problem-solver.[54] This section gives you an overview of various proactive responses that you can use when the other side engages in adversarial tactics.

After reading this negotiation chapter, you should be able to spot a negotiator who is engaging in hard adversarial bargaining. When the other side is making extreme demands, presenting take-it-or-leave-it proposals, hurling threats, or belittling your offers, the other side presents you with a critical choice: Should you adopt the other side's adversarial approach or try to convert the other side into a problem-solver? It is too easy to slip into the adversarial cycle. It is too easy for you to respond to the other side's extreme demand with your own extreme counteroffer. It is too easy for you to respond to the other side's threats with your own threats. The more the other side pushes you, the more entrenched you and your client can become. The more you respond in kind, the more entrenched the other side becomes. Both sides can quickly lock into an adversarial negotiation that can spin out of control. Here are some suggestions of how to avoid the adversarial trap, stay in a problem-solving mode, and even convert the other side.

Engage Proactively in Problem-Solving. By engaging persistently in a problem-solving approach, you can avoid slippage and even change the other side's approach. At the negotiating table, you can start by sharing your client's interests and asking what the other party wants to achieve in the negotiation and why. By educating the other side about your client's interests and inviting a discussion of what the other side wants to accomplish, you will have initiated a problem-solving approach. The

---

54. *See* Mnookin, *supra* note 5, at 211–221; William Ury, Getting Past No—Negotiating Your Way From Confrontation to Cooperation 76–104 (1993); Fisher, *supra* note 5, at 107–112.

more you persevere, the more likely the other side will follow suit, not because of a deliberate decision to do so, but because of the party's natural response to your questions and your modeling of problem-solving behavior.

Use the Other Side's Tactic as an Opportunity. Use each adversarial tactic of the other side as an opening for you to introduce the problem-solving approach.

In their classic book, *Getting to Yes*, Roger Fisher, William Ury, and Bruce Patton offer this valuable advice.

> How can you prevent the cycle of action and reaction? *Do not push back.* When they assert their positions, do not reject them. When they attack you, don't counterattack. Break the vicious cycle by refusing to react. Instead of pushing back, sidestep their attack and deflect it against the problem. As in the oriental martial arts of judo and jujitsu, avoid pitting your strength against theirs directly; instead, use your skill to set aside and turn their strength to your ends. Rather than resisting their force, channel it into exploring interests, inventing options for mutual gain, and searching for independent standards (emphasis in original).[55]

In his later book, *Getting Past No*,[56] William Ury explains how a negotiator can change the game by reframing the negotiation to redirect it into a problem-solving process. Instead of responding with positions, the negotiator responds with questions that focus "attention on the interests of each side, the options for satisfying them, and the standards of fairness for resolving differences."[57]

Rather than respond to Stephen's demand for $100,000 in damages with a counteroffer (do not push back), Philip would treat the demand as one proposal (treat proposal as one option), suggest developing multiple options (brainstorming), and ask for the rationale behind his proposal (invite search for independent standards to guide selection of options).

---

55. Fisher, *supra* note 54, at 108.

56. *See supra* note 54 (explains strategy for "changing the game" through problem-solving questions and methods for reframing tactics and exposing tricks.).

57. *See id.* at 80–89 (discussion of various types of open-ended problem-solving questions—Why? Why Not? What if? What advice? and What makes that fair?). *Also see* Schneider, *Effective Responses to Offensive Comments*, NEG. J.107 (April 1994).

Name the Negotiation Tactic. By labeling their tactic as adversarial, you can put on the table for discussion the negotiating approach that both sides would like to follow. In response to Stephen saying "either pay me $100,000 or see you in court," Philip could put on the table for discussion whether he should put down a counteroffer of zero with a threat to go to court or try another approach to settling the dispute. This response could lead to a negotiation over how to negotiate: Should they engage in a process of offers and counteroffers or a process commencing with a discussion of interests followed by brainstorming and assessing options?[58]

Change Participants at Table. If the other attorney, his client, or his client representative cannot be converted, you might consider how to bring to the table replacement people or additional people. This solution requires you to exercise considerable diplomatic skills. For example, if Stephen's attorney seems to be the obstacle, Philip's attorney could suggest that each side bring their clients to the negotiation meeting. If Stephen seems to be the obstacle and his company was a larger organization, Stephen could be asked to bring any other people who will need to approve the settlement.[59]

Bring in a Mediator. As suggested in the next section on "Advancing Problem-Solving in Mediations" a mediator can be especially effective in helping parties transform an adversarial negotiation into a problem-solving one.

6. Advancing Problem-Solving with the Assistance of a Mediator

If you like the potential benefits of the problem-solving approach, you will love the opportunities for achieving this potential in mediations. In cases in which you can not achieve the benefits of problem-solving on your own, you may benefit from the assistance of an outside party, a mediator. In disputes that involve a particularly hostile client, intensely bad relationships, a patently unskilled attorney, or a variety of other intractable difficulties, a mediator can bring not only his training in problem-solving methods, but also his enormously valuable asset of neutrality. Without a vested interest in the outcome, a mediator can

---

58. *See* Mnookin, *supra* note 5, at 217–218.

59. *See id.* at 218–220.

focus credibly on facilitating a productive process so that both sides can focus primarily on resolving the substantive conflict.

At the outset, the mediator can help both sides design a process that will facilitate problem-solving. During a pre-mediation conference with the attorneys, for instance, the mediator can raise for discussion the process that the clients want to use to resolve the dispute. Even if all sides agreed to follow a problem-solving approach, one or more participants may be inexperienced problem-solvers. The mediator can educate and even coach the participants. The mediator, for example, can suggest that the attorneys prepare for the first mediation session by discussing with their clients their interests (what they want out of the mediation) and ways to expand value and package inventive solutions.

The mediator can create a constructive environment in which clients vent, improve their communications, and develop rapport. By giving the clients a forum where their interests can be voiced and then acknowledged, clients may be more apt to work together to resolve their dispute. The mediator can improve communications through skillful questioning, active listening, and framing and re-framing of statements. This improved negotiating environment can increase the flow of information, information that each side can use to identify the issues to be resolved, the interests of each client, the BATNAs, and any impediments to settling the dispute. The mediator also can help both sides use the information to formulate an orderly and productive agenda.

The mediator can provide each side access to a caucus, which is simply a private meeting with the mediator. In the caucus, you can safely do things that you might not dare do in a joint session. In the caucus, you can share confidential, damaging, and inflammatory information; engage in a candid assessment of the court case and settlement options; and seek advice on how to package proposals and guard against reactive devaluation and bargaining against your own proposal.[60] For example, if your client wants particular information kept confidential for business reasons or out of fear of being exploited by the other party, you and your client can request a caucus with the mediator. In the caucus, your client might share the information confidentially with the mediator who then can gain a fuller picture of the dispute, see fresh possibilities for resolution, and explore options for safely using the information.

---

60. *See* Chapter 5.11 (Joint Sessions versus Caucuses).

The mediator can help both sides identify impediments and ways to overcome them. When both sides, for instance, reach the common impasse caused by conflicting views of the legal case, the mediator can provide a constructive forum for evaluating the court alternative to settlement. In order to guard against this highly charged subject trumping everything else in the mediation sessions, the mediator can organize and skillfully manage a safe format of joint sessions and caucuses in which both sides rigorously evaluate each of their BATNAs.

The mediator can assist both sides in formulating inventive solutions. The mediator can guide you, your client, and the other side through a problem-solving structure in which the stage of generating options is segregated from the stage of evaluating and selecting options. In order to stimulate a search for more options, the mediator can conduct a formal brainstorming session that abides by the two rules of no evaluation and no attribution of ideas. After brainstorming, the mediator can help both sides evaluate the options against the criteria of meeting interests and satisfying objective standards.

If you reach a difficult distributive moment, the mediator can facilitate a more amicable and productive negotiation dance that avoids the use of tricks, threats, and misleading disclosure of information. The mediator can help each side behave more like problem-solvers by helping them communicate with each other and understand each other's interests. The mediator also can aid both sides in gaining a realistic assessment of each other's BATNA that can shed light on the sort of offers and counteroffers each side should reasonably exchange.

If your client or the other side slips backward into an adversarial approach, the mediator can coax the regressing person back into a problem-solving mode. The mediator can do this by posing carefully crafted questions. If the other side starts the mediation with an opening offer strategy of an extreme proposal, for example, the mediator can ask whether all proposals could be deferred until after the parties gather more information, including sharing information about each other's interests. If the other party insists on ten million dollars in damages, the mediator may search behind the party's position by asking for a reasoned explanation of the level of damages. If the other side approaches the problem as a narrow legal dispute, the mediator may ask whether other issues should be addressed in the mediation. If the other party treats the dispute as distributive—one gains at the expense of the other, the mediator may ask integrative-oriented questions about the party's interests and opportunities to increase value and expand the pie. These reactive moves by the mediator can temper your need to react. Instead, you can defer to the mediator's moves to prod the adversarial person into a problem-solving mode.

This myriad of mediator's initiatives can help you, your client, and the other side stay in a problem-solving mode, and as a result help both sides maximize the benefits of mediation.

Of course, problem-solving is not the only way to achieve settlements in mediations; you can procure settlements using the adversarial approach. By taking strong and extreme positions and participating in the negotiation dance of offers, counteroffers, and compromises, you can secure settlements in mediations just like you can secure settlements in negotiations. The difference is that in mediations a third party helps you navigate the bumps and overcome any obstacles in the adversarial negotiation.[61] If a hostile relationship between the parties is preventing you from even engaging in the negotiation dance, a mediator can help you and your client dance with the other side by shuttling positional proposals between sides. If the parties are at an impasse due to each side's firm belief in conflicting views of their BATNAs, the mediator can offer his opinion on the strength of the legal case. If each party has presented his "final" proposal, the mediator can try breaking the impasse by recommending a compromise proposal. In short, a mediator can facilitate an adversarial negotiation that can produce familiar, compromise resolutions. But, you and your client are losing the opportunity to achieve more creative, customized, and enduring solutions.

---

61. For a description of one approach that a mediator might take, *see* DWIGHT GOLAAN, MEDIATING LEGAL DISPUTES—EFFECTIVE STRATEGIES FOR LAWYERS AND MEDIATORS 164–167 (1996).

7. Checklist: Problem-Solving Negotiations

Consider Your Orientation
❐ View problem broadly to encompass underlying interests and
    needs.
❐ View as shared problem.
❐ View dispute as an integrative opportunity, not a distributive
    problem.
❐ View dispute as search for "win-win" and Pareto optimal
    solutions.

❐ Think creatively outside of the legal box.
❐ Search for increased value.

❐ Promote effective communications and exchange of
    information.
❐ Eliminate opening offer strategy.

❐ Value relationship.

❐ Be open to other side's views and interests.
❐ Approach search for solutions with an open mind.

Preparation (with deep client involvement)
❐ 1. Investigate facts.
❐ 2. Identify client's interests and needs.
❐ 3. Surmise other party's interests.

❒   4.   Identify issues for resolution.

❒   5.   Investigate and improve client's BATNA.
❒   6.   Surmise other party's BATNA

❒   7.   Identify sources of objective criteria and value to bring to
         table.
         ❒   Common interests that do not conflict.
         ❒   Economies of scale.
         ❒   Different interests that do not conflict.
         ❒   Different resources to trade.
         ❒   Different relative valuations.
         ❒   Different forecasts.
         ❒   Different risk preferences.
         ❒   Different time preferences.

❒   8.   Engage client in imagining inventive solutions.
❒   9.   Plan to share information judiciously.

Strategies at the Table
❒   1.   Establish rapport and open up communications.

❒   2.   Share information judiciously about interests.
❒   3.   Educate other party about party's interests.
❒   4.   Learn more about other party's interests.

❒   5.   Advocate for client's interests.

❒ 6. Understand each other's BATNA.
❒ 7. De-emphasize legal case (BATNA).

❒ 8. Identify and overcome any impediments

❒ 9. Identify issues for resolution.

❒ 10. Jointly generate multiple options for mutual gain.
❒ 11. Search for non-monetary solutions.
❒ 12. Search for objective criteria and opportunities to expand value for trades.
❒ 13. Search for inventive solutions that are unavailable in court.

❒ 14. Assess and select options based on interests and objective standards.
❒ 15. Use reasoned explanations and principled justifications.
❒ 16. Make trades that include distributive issues.

❒ 17. Manage remaining distributive conflicts.

Chapter Two

Familiarizing Yourself with Mediation

> Topics in this chapter include:
>
> 1. Mediation Definition
> 2. Mediators and Their Approaches
> 3. Stages of Mediation
> 4. Techniques of Mediators

You cannot be an effective mediation advocate unless you understand the nuances of the mediation forum. You should be familiar with how the mediation process operates as well as how mediators carry out their job. The uninitiated should read this chapter with care. Even the initiated, who have been trained as mediators or have some experience as advocates in mediation, should still skim this chapter because it presents familiar concepts and information from the less explored perspective of an advocate.

This chapter[1] defines mediation and its distinguishing features, introduces various approaches of mediators, describes the stages of mediation, and explains some commonly used techniques of mediators.

1. Mediation Definition

Mediation is simply a negotiation conducted with the assistance of a third party. This generic definition should fit any process that can be legitimately classified as mediation.[2] There has been much debate

---

1. This chapter is only a primer, intended to provide a basic overview and understanding of the mediation process. For a fuller and deeper understanding of the mediation process and the role of mediators, you should read one of a number of excellent books on the subject. Examples include Kimberlee K. Kovach, Mediation—Principles and Practice (2d ed. 2000); Dwight Golann, Mediating Legal Disputes—Effective Strategies for Lawyers and Mediators, chs. 2 & 3 (1996); Christopher W. Moore, The Mediation Process—Practical Strategies for Resolving Conflict 63–68 (2d ed. 1996); and Jay Folger & Allison Taylor, Mediation—A Comprehensive Guide to Resolving Disputes Without Litigation 7 (1984).

2. *See generally*, Kovach, *supra* note 1, at 23–25; Golann, *supra* note 1; Moore, *supra* note 1, at 63–68; Folger, *supra* note 1.

over what processes can be rightfully called mediation. After reading and listening to much of the thoughtful debate and observing how loosely the term is used by such diverse sources as judges, the media, and the United Nations, the final clincher in my intellectual travels occurred when I encountered an oven advertisement on television. The manufacturer's salesman was presented as a "great mediator."[3] I think it is just too late to justify a favored, circumscribed definition of mediation. It is more productive to focus on defining the adjective in front of mediation. Is the mediation facilitative, evaluative, transformative, bias, power, problem-solving, or whatever? This book focuses on one particular adjective—problem-solving.

In problem-solving mediation, the specially trained and neutral mediator skillfully structures a process that provides disputing parties an opportunity to fashion enduring and inventive solutions that can go beyond what a court might be willing to do. In contrast with the more familiar settlement conference before a judge,[4] the mediator has no decision-making power, maintains strict confidentiality, and involves clients deeply in the settlement process.

The mediation process is a separate and self-contained one that is informal and yet still follows predictable stages[5] with a beginning, middle, and end. The mediator serves as the guide by managing a structured discussion that includes gathering specific information, identifying issues, interests, and impediments, and generating, assessing, and selecting options for settlement.

The mediator employs a mix of refined techniques that are designed to encourage client involvement, to explore clients' interests, and to create a collaborative environment for settling the dispute.[6] The mediator

---

3. Maytag Corporation ran nationally a television advertisement that it called "The Great Mediator (pizza or casserole)." In the advertisement, the Maytag Man appears as "a great mediator" who has the answer to the question that has "aroused fierce passions for centuries: What's for dinner." The mediator presents a new range that can "cook two different foods, at two different temperatures, for one complete meal." The advertisement ran from August 1999 to December 1999. Interview with Nicole Kaczmarek, LB Works, Operations Manager, Advertising Agency for Maytag Corporation (July 2003).

4. ABRAMSON & CRONIN-HARRIS, NYS BAR ASSOCIATION, COMPARING SETTLEMENT CONFERENCES AND MEDIATIONS (Videotape and Instruction Manual) (1999).

5. *See* Section 3 on "Stages of Mediation."

6. *See* Section 4 on "Techniques of Mediators."

poses open-ended and focused questions, reframes issues, conducts brainstorming sessions, and uses strategies for defusing tensions and overcoming impasses. The mediator may use private caucuses to gain confidential information and specialized methods for helping participants evaluate the strengths and weaknesses of their legal case. If the dispute does not settle, the mediator may help the participants design an alternative process for ultimately resolving the conflict.

2. Mediators and Their Approaches

You should be familiar with the professional standards that guide a mediator because they can give you valuable insight into how the mediator is likely to behave in the mediation process. You should inquire what professional standards that your mediator follows. One set of widely used professional standards focuses on three standards of performance.[7]

First, the mediator should conduct the process with a high regard for the principle of party "self-determination." Parties should be given an opportunity to reach a "*voluntary, uncoerced* agreement."[8] As a result, the mediator should encourage clients to participate actively in discussions throughout the mediation process to ensure that the clients make a volitional and informed decision to settle.

Second, the mediator should conduct the process in an impartial and evenhanded manner. If the mediator thinks she has any potential conflicts of interest, she should disclose them and only serve if the parties still consent.[9]

Third, the mediator should honor parties' expectations that what happens in the mediation will be held in confidence.[10]

Even though many mediators may be guided by common professional standards, they do not adhere to a uniform approach to conducting mediations. They can embrace a varying mix of mediation approaches. First and foremost, mediators adopt one of several possible approaches

---

7. *See* American Arbitration Association, American Bar Association, & Society of Professionals in Dispute Resolution, Model Standards of Conduct for Mediators (1995). (Although these standards are not binding, they provide a widely recognized general framework for the practice of mediation.) *See* Appendix M.

8. *See id.* at Standards I & VI.

9. *See id.* at Standards II and III.

10. *See id.* at Standard V.

on how to manage the overall mediation process. The three most prominent adjectives used are facilitative, evaluative, and transformative. Mediators also adopt a mix of approaches to three specific issues: how to define the problem, what is the role of the clients, and when to use caucuses.

a.   Facilitative, Evaluative, and Transformative Mediation

Mediators are likely to practice a predominately facilitative approach, a predominately evaluative one, a facilitative/evaluative hybrid, or a transformative approach. Because the choice impacts significantly on how you should represent your client, the differences will be explained in detail in chapter 4.2(b) on negotiating an agreement to mediate and will be followed up in chapter 5.1(e) on how the approaches impact on your mediation representation plan. This section provides only the basic definitions of facilitative, evaluative, and transformative mediation.

The central distinguishing feature between facilitation and evaluation is how the mediator helps each side evaluate the merits of the legal case, the consequences of failure to settle, and any settlement proposals.

Facilitative:[11] A facilitative mediator creates an environment in which parties work together collaboratively as problem-solvers. The mediator uses techniques that place full responsibility for resolving the dispute on the shoulders of the participants. The facilitative mediator gives special attention to improving the rapport and communications between the parties, and assists the attorneys and parties in identifying both sides' interests, in generating options for settlement, and in shaping their own creative resolution of the dispute. Using techniques consistent with the facilitative approach, the neutral helps the parties conduct an evaluation if one would be useful. The neutral poses evenhanded, probing questions to the participants, such as asking precisely why a settlement proposal is unattractive. The mediator may also introduce the use of decision-tree analysis by asking participants to formulate the branches

---

11. A distinctively different form of facilitation is the transformative model of mediation, an approach that its advocates believe qualifies as a separate category. The transformative model has been receiving much attention, with a growing number of mediators identifying themselves as "transformative." Instead of focusing on settlement, transformative mediators focus on "empowering" the parties and the parties "recognizing" each other. Then, it is up to the parties to decide what to do. *See* ROBERT A. BARUCH BUSH & JOSEPH P. FOLGER, THE PROMISE OF MEDIATION—RESPONDING TO CONFLICT THROUGH EMPOWERMENT AND RECOGNITION (1994).

and to suggest the key data for analysis.[12] But, the neutral will *not* give an opinion regarding the merits of the dispute, the consequences of failure to settle, or the merits of any particular settlement terms.

Evaluative: An evaluative mediator assists the participants in breaking impasses by contributing her views of the merits of the legal case, the consequences of failure to settle, and the benefits of particular settlement proposals. For instance, if each side has strongly conflicting views of the legal merits, the neutral might try to break the impasse by giving an evaluation of the merits of the dispute. By predicting the likely outcome in the adjudicatory forum, the neutral gives the participants a basis against which to assess the attractiveness of emerging options for settlement. If the case is not settling, the neutral might suggest how failure would impact on the interests of each party. If each side has strongly conflicting views of the benefits of a particular settlement proposal, the neutral might give an assessment of how the proposal benefits each side. The neutral might even present a proposal for adoption by the participants (sometimes known as the "mediator's proposal"). The neutral may present these assessments gently for consideration or may aggressively advocate their adoption.

A mediator who engages in evaluation is no longer engaging in a predominately facilitative, problem-solving approach to the mediation process. The mediator is engaging in a mixed approach or a predominately evaluative one.

Transformative:[13] A transformative mediator engages in a mediation practice based on communication and relational theory. Instead of promoting the goal of settlement for the parties, the transformative mediator allows the parties to determine their own direction and supports the parties' own opportunities for perspective-taking, deliberation, and decision-making. The mediator focuses on the parties' interactions and supports their shifts from destructive and alienating interactions to

---

12. *See* Appendix M. *Also see*, e.g., Marjorie Corman Aaron & David P. Hoffer, *Decision Analysis as a Method of Evaluating the Trial Alternative*, in DWIGHT GOLANN, MEDIATING LEGAL DISPUTES—EFFECTIVE STRATEGIES FOR LAWYERS & MEDIATORS ch. 11 (1996) (In decision-tree analysis, parties identify adjudicatory paths for resolution, estimate the probability of success of proceeding down each path (branch), and approximate the likely substantive outcome and the cost of getting to the end of each adjudicatory path.)

13. *See* Bush, *supra* note 11. For an extensive resource list, see www.transformative mediation.org.

more constructive and open interactions (referred to as empowerment and recognition shifts). In this model, parties are likely to be able to make positive changes in their interactions with each other and, consequently, find acceptable resolutions for themselves, where such terms genuinely exist.

b.   Narrow or Broad View of Problem[14]

Mediators may approach the dispute narrowly or broadly. When approaching it narrowly, the mediator accepts the parties' "positions," typically legal positions, as the basis of the dispute and as the parameters for discussion and resolution. However, many mediators prefer to approach problems broadly—to go beyond the presenting problems by delving deeper into the dispute. The mediator probes the broader interests of parties by posing variations of the basic question: Why? Why does the person want the claimed damages? By getting behind the positions, the mediator tries to bring to the surface what parties really want, which can lead to imaginative solutions that go beyond what an adjudicatory body can do or is likely to do. The complaining party in a trademark case, for instance, can be limited to suing for damages and seeking to enjoin the defendant from using that particular trademark. An answer to the "why" questions may reveal that the complaining party is mostly concerned about the colors used in the defendant's trademark. This complaint could be addressed more responsively in a negotiation where the parties explore different ways to modify the defendant's trademark. Which approach to the problem is preferable depends on the needs of your client, a subject that is covered in more detail in chapter 4.2(b) on mediator's approaches.

c.   Limited or Active Client Participation

Mediators hold different views on how clients should participate in the mediation session. Some mediators view client participation skeptically and prefer to rely on the attorneys to speak in the session. The attorneys are the advocacy experts; they are in the best position to be sure that parties' interests are fully articulated and protected. Other mediators view active client participation as vital to the success of the mediation process, especially a problem-solving one. They believe that the parties who must live with the results have much to contribute because the parties are experts on the problem and possible solutions. In chapter

---

14. *See* L. Riskin *Understanding Mediators' Orientations, Strategies, and Techniques: A Grid for the Perplexed*, 1 Harv. Neg. L.R. 7, 18–23 (1996).

5, I not only recommend that clients be present but that they also participate actively. My reasons are elaborated in chapter 5.5(b) on "Should Clients be Present and Active?", chapter 5.6 on "Divide Responsibilities Between Attorney and Client," and chapter 5.10 on "Prepare Preliminarily the Opening Statements."

d. Primarily, Selective, or No Caucuses

After the mediator's opening statement, many mediators move the participants back and forth between joint sessions and caucuses. Joint sessions are simply when the mediator and all participants meet together, that is "jointly." Caucuses are when the mediator meets privately with only one side, usually with both the attorney and client.[15] Whether to use caucuses and when to use them are much debated topics in the field of mediation.

The mediator's mix of joint sessions and caucuses depends very much on the preferred approach of the mediator. Many mediators prefer to hold most meetings in joint sessions in order to promote communications and joint problem-solving between the parties. These mediators limit the use of caucuses to accomplishing very specific purposes that they believe can only be accomplished in private meetings. They may use caucuses to obtain confidential or highly sensitive information, for instance. Other mediators conduct mediations primarily through caucuses; the parties only meet with each other at the beginning of the mediation and when signing the settlement agreement. By using caucuses, the mediator can insulate hostile parties from each other. The mediator also can carefully screen and tightly manage the flow of information and framing of proposals. At the other extreme, another group of mediators opposes the use of any caucusing. They believe that private meetings with one side can taint the neutrality of the mediator, cut off communications between the parties, create undue reliance on the mediator to screen communications and carry messages between the sides, and undermine the opportunity for parties to resolve their own problems. They choose to conduct the entire mediation process in joint sessions.

For a fuller discussion of the three approaches to caucusing, see chapter 5.11 on caucusing. In that section, I recommend that caucuses be avoided or limited to selective, specific purposes.

---

15. Occasionally, mediators may hold lawyer caucuses—that is, caucuses with both lawyers or the lawyer of one of the parties. *See* Ch. 7 on lawyer caucuses.

3. Stages of Mediation

Stages of Mediation Process

a. Initiation of the Mediation Process

b. Pre-Mediation Submissions

c. Pre-Mediation Conference

d. Mediation Session

    i.   Begin with Mediator's Opening Statement

    ii.   Vent and Gather Information for Specific Purposes—Issues, Interests, and Impediments [opening statements of participants, first joint sessions, and first caucus]

    iii.   Identify Issues, Interests, and Impediments

    iv.   Formulate Agenda—Issues to Resolve and Impediments

    v.   Overcome Impediments to Settlement

    vi.   Generate Options for Settlement [inventing stage]

    vii.   Assess and Select Options for Settlement [deciding stage]

    viii.   Conclude Session—Agreement or Exit Plan

e. Post-Session Tasks

Each stage of the mediation process serves functional purposes. The mediator wants to accomplish specific goals at each stage. You should be aware that as the mediation progresses, the mediator's goals change. As the goals change, so do the stages of the mediation. Each stage calls for different strategies for representing clients, a subject that is covered in detail in later chapters. Identifying the stages, as some do, by opening statements, joint sessions, and caucuses, do not reveal what is ultimately valuable to an advocate because this classification ignores what the mediator is trying to accomplish.

The stages are not followed rigidly. (See chart above.) Because mediation is a dynamic and unpredictable process, mediators must respond flexibly and intelligently, not mechanically, to whatever unfolds in the mediation. The stages in practice are not tidy and discrete. One stage is not necessarily finished before the next one begins. The mediation may be in more than one stage at the same time. For example, the mediator may simultaneously collect information and preliminarily identify issues. Even when a stage is finished, such as information gathering or issue identification, new information may surface in later stages that may result in regressing to gather more information or to reconsider the definition of issues. Finally, these stages are not uniformly followed; different mediators may adopt variations of these stages.[16]

Even though the stages do not operate uniformly and in sequential lockstep, this description of stages should provide a useful guide regarding what to expect as well as insights into how to represent your clients as the mediation progresses.

a. Initiation of the Mediation Process

The mediation process can be initiated in one of several ways. The mediation process may be initiated pursuant to the terms of a mediation clause in a pre-dispute agreement or in an agreement to mediate entered into after the dispute arose. The mediation process also may be triggered by a judge or court administrator referring the case to a court-connected mediation program. The agreement or court-connected program will provide procedures for selecting the mediator.[17]

Goals: A suitable mediator will be selected, and the mediator or organization administering the mediation will usually commence educating the participants about the mediation process and how the mediator will approach the mediation. At this stage, you will learn about the mediator's orientations, whether any pre-mediation submissions are due, whether a pre-mediation conference will be held, and the scheduling dates for the pre-mediation conference and mediation session.

b. Pre-Mediation Submissions[18]

Not all mediators request pre-mediation submissions. They are frequently solicited in business disputes.

---

16. For other descriptions of stages, *see* Kovach, *supra* note 1, at 31–34; Moore, *supra* note 1, at 66–67.

In the transformative mediation model, the stages are not a variation but are different because the purpose of the process is different. Instead of promoting settlement, the transformative model promotes a party-centered process in which the parties are empowered and give recognition to each other so that the parties become capable of producing whatever result they want—which could be settlement or no settlement. As a result, the stages consist of early, midstage, and late-stage opportunities for empowerment and recognition. *See* Bush, *supra* note 11, at Ch. 7, Figure 7.1 & Table 7.1.

17. For a discussion of how to select a mediator, *see* Chapter 4.2.

18. For a discussion of further discussion of pre-mediation submissions, *see* Chapter 5.3.

Goals: The purpose of these submissions can vary depending on the mediator's approaches to the mediation. Some mediators only want enough information to become acquainted with the substance of the dispute and its legal history. Other mediators may request settlement-related information that is designed to begin engaging the attorneys and clients in the problem-solving process. For example, the mediator may ask why the dispute has not settled and what new ideas might provide a framework for a settlement discussion. A more evaluative neutral may request most of the papers in the legal case, including any legal briefs.

c.   Pre-Mediation Conference[19]

Not all mediators hold pre-mediation conferences. They are frequently used in business disputes, especially complex ones.

Goals: The mediator's goal may be limited to only touching base with the attorneys before the first mediation session in order to answer any questions and verify that the right clients will be participating in the session. Or, the goals could be more ambitious, including educating the attorneys about the mediator's mix of approaches, resolving any discovery disputes in advance of the mediation session, or feeling out reasons for impasse and settlement possibilities.

d.   Mediation Session

The initial stages of the mediation session are clear and stable as the mediation progresses from the mediator's opening statement to the gathering of information through the opening statements of the participants, the joint sessions, and the first caucus. After that, the mediation can become turbulent and swift as the mediator moves back and forth between joint sessions and caucuses as the mediation moves forward, slips backwards, and moves forward again through the various mediation stages.

i.   Begin with Mediator's Opening Statement

Goals: The mediator wants the parties and attorneys to feel secure participating openly and taking risks in the mediation session. Thus, the mediator is likely to make a number of deliberate points in her opening statement. Because she wants to demystify the process and help everyone become comfortable with its informal, collaborative atmosphere,

---

19. For a discussion of how to represent a client in the pre-mediation conference, *see* Chapters 5.4, and 7.1.

she usually explains the process and offers to answer any questions. She wants to be sure that everyone has a common understanding of what to expect during the course of the session. In explaining the process, she strives to establish an optimistic and friendly tone. The mediator commonly emphasizes her role as a neutral facilitator who is not a decision-maker. The mediator typically explains the use of caucuses and reviews any ground rules such as no interrupting the other party. And, the mediator routinely highlights the confidentiality of the process, especially measures taken to ensure that what happens in the mediation cannot be used in related legal proceedings.

ii.　Vent and Gather Information for Specific Purposes (Opening Statements of Participants, First Joint Sessions, and First Caucus)

Goals: At this early stage, the mediator wants to give participants an opportunity to do two important things: vent and gather information relevant to resolving the dispute.

Venting is a recognized feature of mediation in which the mediator provides each party a safe place to express her frustrations, anger, and other emotions.[20] The mediator customarily imposes some limits on venting that are designed to prevent it from escalating out of control. The mediator may establish and enforce such basic ground rules as no threats and name-calling. Venting can be beneficial because it can "clear the air." Equally important, valuable information can be buried in the venting .

Throughout this stage, information is collected for specific purposes—to help the participants develop a full picture of the dispute and to answer several basic questions: What are the interests of each party? What are the issues? And, what are the impediments to settlement?

The venting and information gathering will likely surface in the opening statements of the participants, joint sessions in which the participants engage in a discussion guided by the mediator, and in private caucuses between the mediator and one side.

Throughout each of the remaining stages, the mediator may move back and forth between joint sessions and caucuses to accomplish the goals of each stage.

---

20. *See* Kovach, *supra* note 1, at 48–49.

iii. Identify Interests, Issues, and Impediments

Goals: By using the information gathered in the previous stage, the mediator helps the participants identify the specific interests of each party and each issue for resolution. The mediator also assists the parties in pinpointing any impediments to settlement. If there was not an impediment, the parties would not be in mediation. They would have settled the dispute on their own.

iv. Formulate Agenda

Goals: The mediator focuses on forming an agenda or order in which issues and impediments will be discussed and resolved. Each issue will likely be coupled with an impediment to settlement. For instance, when the issue is whether the defendant breached the contract, the issue may be linked to an impediment due to a factual dispute regarding what the defendant did.

In relatively uncomplicated cases, the mediator may formulate the agenda and disclose it incrementally by selecting the first issue for discussion, then the second one, and so forth. In more complex cases, the mediator may formulate the agenda openly by inviting the participants into a discussion of what should be included in the agenda. The mediator may suggest one of a number of options for formulating an agenda.[21] The mediator may propose starting with the easiest or most difficult issue, beginning with the issues of greatest importance, selecting an overarching principle that could be used as a basis for selecting issues such as those that relate to saving the business relationship, or soliciting the parties to suggest how issues could be grouped.

v. Overcome Impediments to Settlement

Goals: The mediator focuses the discussion on ways to overcome the impediments. In court cases, parties frequently reach an impasse due to their clashing views regarding who has the stronger legal case.[22] The mediator might help participants to overcome this impediment by asking

---

21. *See* Kovach, *supra* note 1, at 141–144; Moore, *supra* note 1, at 223–227.

22. Assessing how attractive the alternative is to settlement (going to court) has become known as assessing the BATNA or the Best Alternative to a Negotiated Agreement. *See* Roger Fisher Et Al., Getting to Yes—Negotiating Agreement Without Giving In Ch. 6 (2d ed.1991).

probing questions about the strengths and weaknesses of the case in a caucus and introducing the use of decision-tree analysis.[23]

vi.   Generate Options for Settlement (inventing stage)

Goals: At this critical juncture, the mediator moves the participants into the creative stage of inventing settlement options, including ones that might not be possible to secure in court.[24]

The mediator focuses participants on methods for expanding the pie (known as creating value). In doing so, the mediator tries to manage the distorting "negotiator's dilemma."[25] Negotiators typically experience a tension between daring to collaborate to create value and the need to compete for as much of the expanded value as possible. The mediator tries to manage this tension by separating sharply the inventing stage from the deciding stage, and then creates an atmosphere that encourages participants to invent, that is, to be imaginative and take risks. The mediator prods participants to generate a list of many options without regard to whether the options are practical or even acceptable. Determining what is practical and acceptable is deferred to the next stage.

The mediator may employ one of a number of methods for encouraging participants to generate options.[26] The best known technique, brainstorming, frees parties to generate a list of wide-ranging ideas without each party feeling constrained by the imminent critique of the other participants.[27] For example, in a suit claiming that the defendant infringed the plaintiff's trademark consisting of a flying horse painted in red, white, and blue, a brainstorming session with all the participants might produce an uncensored list of a dozen options for the defendant to modify its trademark. In a suit for employment discrimination, a brainstorming session might produce a list of a half dozen ways to

---

23. For a detailed discussion of impediments and how to overcome them in mediations, *see* Chapters 3.2(b) and 5.1(f).

24. *See* Moore, *supra* note 1, at 244–266; Golann, *supra* note 12, at Sec. 9.5.2.

25. *See* DAVID A. LAX & JAMES K. SEBENIUS, THE MANAGER AS NEGOTIATOR 29–41(1986).

26. *See* Moore, *supra* note 1, at 250–261 (Examples of techniques for generating options include "open discussion," "plausible hypothetical scenarios," and "single text negotiating document.").

27. For a description of brainstorming, *see* Subsection 4(e) of this chapter.

compensate the plaintiff for damages due to lost opportunities for promotion.

vii. Assess and Select Options for Settlement (deciding stage)

Goals: The mediator invites parties to assess the list of options to determine which one best meets the interests of the parties and satisfies recognized standards of fairness or objectivity. Objective standards may be drawn from such sources as industry custom or widely accepted expert opinion. This moment in the mediation can be the most formidable one because it is the moment for the parties to make unambiguously final and frequently painful decisions.

The mediator may resort to one or more techniques for conducting this final round of negotiations.[28]

The mediator may facilitate the development and implementation of a settlement formula consisting of agreed-upon criteria. The mediator may assist the participants in formulating the settlement criteria and applying them to the list of options. Then, the mediator may help the participants clarify and refine the most appealing options. Lastly, the mediator may facilitate further negotiations toward selecting an option from the prime list. For example, in the trademark infringement dispute, the mediator may facilitate developing settlement criteria consisting of meeting the needs of both parties and not offending any group, not risking infringing someone else's mark, and not including the combined colors of red, white, and blue. The parties may select for further refinement the three most appealing options for modifying the use of the defendant's mark and then further evaluate them against the settlement criteria.

The mediator may assist the parties in formulating and making gradual concessions that lead to incremental convergence and agreement. For example, the parties could converge on an agreement by first assessing and selecting a number of acceptable colors that could be used in the defendant's mark, then assessing and selecting an acceptable style of lettering, and finally assessing and selecting acceptable variations of a horse's image.

---

28. For a detailed discussion of these final bargaining techniques, *see* Moore, *supra* note 1, at 280–291.

Or, the mediator may suggest a leap-to agreement based on settlement criteria, in which a party packages a proposal that is an unmistakable leap forward that will induce the other party to jump to a final agreement. For example, the plaintiff could propose to drop the infringing lawsuit if the defendant would not use any combined shades of red, white, and blue and agree to include a small notation below its trademark that the defendant company is not associated with the plaintiff company. This bold proposal might induce the defendant to respond with an equally daring proposal to resolve the dispute.

viii.   Conclude Session—Agreement or Clear Exit Plan

Goals: If the mediation is moving toward agreement, the mediator may try to bring closure in two steps: first the mediator may help participants reach a final agreement on critical terms and then help them work out the remaining substantive and implementation details. For instance, the parties may first resolve the most contentious issue of the specific dollar damages and then settle the payment schedule, due dates, and terms of any releases.

If the parties reached a specific impasse, the mediator may moderate a discussion of alternative dispute resolution processes for overcoming it. For example, parties may agree to use a suitable alternative process for overcoming an impasse due to a factual dispute. Then, the process, such as conventional arbitration or a fact-finding process, may be implemented under the auspices of the mediator or after the mediation ends.[29]

At the end of the mediation session, the mediator usually sums up the progress made in the mediation and what needs to be done next. Even if all the issues were not settled in the mediation, it is likely that the mediation resulted in clarifying the unresolved issues, securing agreement on some central facts, and illuminating, if not developing, another pathway out of the dispute.

e.   Post-Session[30]

Goals: After the last mediation session, the mediator may offer to oversee finalizing and implementing the agreement.

---

29. For a discussion of alternative dispute resolution processes, *see* Chapter 8—Breaking Impasses with Other Dispute Resolution Processes—Alternatives to Mediation (ATM).

30. For a fuller discussion, *see* Chapter 7.3.

If the details of the agreement are incomplete, the mediator may offer to assist the attorneys with finishing the drafting of the agreement. The mediator also may oversee the implementation of critical terms, such as the payment of money and delivery of assets. The mediator may engage in post-session activities in conference calls, telephone calls, letters, and e-mails.

4.   Techniques of Mediators

Mediators are trained to use a variety of specific techniques at suitable moments during the course of the mediation process. They have at their disposal specialized techniques for improving communications, defusing tensions, breaking impasses, and generating options for solutions. This section catalogues and describes some of the more widely used techniques. By acquainting yourself with them, you will be better able to respond appropriately in the mediation session and to advise your client what to do.

a.   Facilitating the Negotiation of a Problem-Solving Process

By suggesting that the parties consider how they will negotiate in the mediation, the mediator can shift potential adversarial strategies to problem-solving ones. If the parties are starting to engage in the negotiation dance of offers and counteroffers, for instance, the mediator may ask whether they want to pause and consider another approach to the negotiations.

The mediator also might respond with problem-solving initiatives. If a party is pursuing a narrow legal position, for example, the mediator may inquire about the party's broader interests.

b.   Promoting Communications

Throughout the mediation process, the mediator may employ various techniques to promote improved and robust communications between the sides. The mediator uses these techniques to induce a full exchange of information about the dispute, the interests of the parties, and possibilities for settlement.

i.   Questioning Techniques

The mediator carefully phrases questions to serve the goals of improving communications and eliciting valuable information. She selects the appropriate form of question to meet whatever may be her need of the moment.[31] In order to maintain her appearance of neutrality, the mediator carefully frames questions neutrally (as well as reacts to answers neutrally.)

Mediators frequently use the very question form that you have been indoctrinated to never pose in court unless you confidently know the witness' answer: the *open-ended question*. It is widely used in mediation because it invites broad, unfettered answers. The mediator wants to bring to the surface as much information as possible. The mediator may pose simple open-ended questions such as "What happened?" or progressively more focused open-ended questions such as "What happened on the day that you first met each other?" The mediator also may ask *clarifying questions* such as "Can you further explain what happened?"

When the mediator needs to solidify a specific point, usually toward the end of the questioning, the mediator uses the type of *closed question* that is most familiar to attorneys and least used in mediation—the quintessential lawyer question known as the *leading question*: "Is it not true that....?" The wording of the question suggests the answer. This question form is infrequently used because it discourages open, full answers. In addition to occasionally using *leading questions*, the mediator may pose other *closed questions* such as ones that call for a specific answer, a yes/no answer, or an answer in which the party selects one of the choices posed in the question.

ii.   Listening Techniques

The mediator may use passive and active listening techniques to promote improved communications between sides and the exchange of information.[32] The judicious use of these techniques can coax parties to talk frankly and fully.

The mediator may use passive listening techniques that entail conveying nonverbal and verbal signals of her interest in what your client is saying. She may use nonverbal signals such as simply nodding her head and making eye contact with the speaker. She may use verbal signals such as posing short, open-ended questions or voicing one-word prompts like "oh" and "interesting." The mediator may even deliberately become

---

31. *See* Kovach, *supra* note 1, at 116–119; DAVID A. BINDER ET AL., LAWYERS AS COUNSELORS: A CLIENT-CENTERED APPROACH 69–81 (1991).

32. *See* Binder, *supra* note 31, at 46–68; ROBERT BOLTON, PEOPLE SKILLS 32–33, 40, 50 (1979).

silent in order to give the speaker the space to think and talk or to induce the speaker to fill in the silence by talking.

The mediator also may employ active listening techniques such as reframing and reflecting in which she encourages talking by explicitly demonstrating to the speaker that she is being heard and understood (not necessarily agreed with). The mediator may carefully paraphrase the content of what the speaker just said or verbally acknowledge it, as well as acknowledge the feelings or emotional reactions of the speaker. For instance, the mediator might say: "I understand that you are very distressed."

c.   Managing Emotions[33]

Upset and angry parties are usually welcomed in mediation. Many mediators realize that addressing the emotional dimension of a dispute can be an essential prerequisite for resolving it. The emotional obstacle may not always be obvious, however. You should be sensitive to subtle clues that can be found in the tone of voice, facial expressions, and body movements of your client or the other side. You, as the person who has had longer contact with the dispute than the mediator, should alert the mediator to any emotionally charged issues or parties.

The mediator may fashion a strategy for helping the parties overcome any emotional obstacles to settlement.

The mediator might encourage the emotionally charged party to vent. The party may need to vent as a psychological or physiological release— to get it off her chest or to be simply heard. In joint sessions, the mediator may establish some ground rules, such as no direct personal attacks, in order to contain the risk that the venting might escalate the conflict. In caucus, the mediator may suggest ways that the party can vent in a less volatile manner when the party returns to the joint sessions.

The mediator may diagnose the substantive reason for the heightened emotions and look for ways to remove or temper the cause. For instance, in a case where the defendant is intensely angry because she is convinced the lawsuit is totally frivolous, the defendant's attorney may be counseled by the mediator to consider securing an evaluation from a former judge. If the evaluation indicates that the case is not totally

---

33. This section summarizes Christopher Moore's recommended strategies for managing emotions. *See* Moore, supra note 1, at 164–169.

frivolous, then the defendant's anger is likely to be diminished. If the evaluation supports the defendant's belief, then the evaluation can be used in the mediation to try to convince the other party that she has a weak case.

In some extremely hostile situations or when the mediator is not comfortable dealing with intense emotions, the mediator may try to circumvent any emotional obstacles. The mediator might resort to the extreme measure of cutting off communications between the parties and requiring them to communicate through the mediator. The mediator might separate the sides into different rooms and then shuttle between the two rooms.

d.   Framing and Reframing of Statements and Issues[34]

The mediator frequently listens for any crucial statements or questions that are provocatively slanted or blatantly hostile and then restates them, using neutral words while omitting judgmental, accusatory, positional, or biased words. The mediator may try to reframe them in a way that makes the statements or questions minimally acceptable to all the people at the table. This framing and reframing technique is used to temper partisan statements and questions and defuse hostile ones so that the statements and questions do not further escalate the conflict.

The mediator also may use this technique of framing and reframing when issues are being defined and refined. Each side tends to define issues in terms unabashedly favorable to its side, a practice that is commonly done when lawyers draft legal briefs for court. The mediator may remove language that is toxic and reframe each issue more broadly to be acceptable to all the parties while still trying to capture the essence of what is vital to each side. The mediator also might try restating an issue in more general terms in order to increase the number of available options for settlement.

For example, in heated disputes, the party framing the issues tends to incorporate her partisan and agitated perspective in the case. "The issue is whether the defendant was racist when she gave me the smallest pay increase in the department." The mediator might cull from this statement a neutral and broader way for framing the issue. "I understand that you are concerned that you were not given a higher pay increase because

---

34. *See*, Kovach, *supra* note 1, at 138–140; Moore, *supra* note 1, at 217–223.

you are an African-American. Would it be accurate to say that you think the issue is whether salary increases were given based on merit?"

You should listen attentively to be sure that the framing and reframing captures the essential substantive points and perspective of your client.

e.   Generating Options for Settlement: Brainstorming

The mediator may employ various techniques for spurring the parties to generate fresh, original, and creative settlement ideas. The mediator has available a number of tested techniques[35] of which the best-known one is brainstorming.

Brainstorming[36] is a highly structured process. The mediator and participants frame an issue as a question that might be answered by the participants brainstorming for options. Participants react simultaneously to the question by rapidly suggesting any and all options that come to mind. They are invited to imagine options that might meet the interests of all the parties. They are encouraged to build on or modify each side's ideas so long as the changes move in the direction of meeting everyone's interests. Brainstorming is conducted in accordance with two basic rules that are designed to promote the free flow of ideas: First, parties should not interrupt each other, including not making any verbal or nonverbal judgments regarding the practicality or acceptability of any of the ideas. Second, parties will not be held accountable for what they say. The ideas will not be judged and evaluated until after the brainstorming is completed.

f.   Methods for Structuring the Inventing and Deciding of Settlement Options

Mediators may use various schemes for sequencing and designing the process of generating settlement options and the process of assessing and selecting which ones to adopt. Here is a description of three possible schemes:

---

35. *See* Moore, *supra* note 1, at 256–261 (The author describes the techniques of brainstorming, nominal group process, discussion subgroups, hypothetical scenarios, single text negotiating document, and using outside resources.).

36. *See id.* at 257–258.

In the building-block approach or bottom-up approach,[37] the mediator assists the parties in "fractionalizing" the issues by dividing them into smaller, more manageable blocks or subissues. For each subissue, parties generate options and assess them. Then through a sequential resolution of each subissue, the parties move toward a resolution of the full dispute.

In the discrimination claim, the broad issue may be whether the defendant gave salary increases based on merit. This broad issue may be divided into a series of subissues: What were the formal procedures for evaluation? How were those procedures applied in practice? How were those procedures applied to the plaintiff? For each subissue, the participants can generate possible answers, assess which ones to pursue, and then resolve the subissue. For the first subissue, for example, the participants could generate a list of sources for the formal procedures. It might include an employee handbook, supervisor handbook, separately published notices, the settlement from a prior lawsuit, etc. When assessing each option, participants may realize that the procedures for each source are somewhat different and that the one the company expected to be used was the one published in the most recently dated memorandum. Next, participants move to the issue regarding whether this procedure was used in practice. After generating and investigating possible answers and resolving that these procedures were used consistently throughout the company for the past three years, participants turn to the third issue of how the procedures were applied to the plaintiff and so on. As each subissue is resolved, parties progress closer to a settlement.

In the agreement in principle approach or top-down approach,[38] the mediator assists the parties in identifying and fashioning principles that can be incorporated into a bargaining formula. Then the formula becomes the guiding structure for generating options and assessing them. If the parties in a divorce case agree that the overarching principle is to do what serves the best interests of their children, then this principle would guide them when they are generating and assessing options for resolving the visitation arrangements or level of child support.

---

37. *See id.* at 248–249. This technique is a more elaborate version of the gradual concession method that was described in the stage of mediation when options are assessed and selected. *See* subsection 3(d)(vii).

38. *See id.* at 249–250. This technique is similar to the settlement formula method that was described in the stage of mediation when options are assessed and selected. *See* subsection 3(d)(vii).

In the single text negotiating approach,[39] the mediator invites the participants into a discussion of their interests and issues and then presents a single text in which the mediator identifies their likely interests and suggests a responsive settlement proposal. The single text draft may be put in writing on a flip chart or a handout. Each party is encouraged to offer comments and suggest revisions that might better meet the needs of all the parties. These incremental revisions can lead to a single text acceptable to all the parties. Note how this approach can change the dynamics among the parties. Instead of each side reacting and criticizing the ideas of the other side, each side is reacting to and criticizing the ideas in the single text. The single text approach can be especially effective if not essential in multiparty disputes.

In a breach of contract dispute where the only issue is the remedy, the technique might work as follows. Instead of each side presenting proposals for damages and future business relationships, each side comments and suggests modifications to a single text presented by the mediator after she had an opportunity to clarify the parties' interests and conduct a brainstorming session.

g.   Dealing with Power Inequalities

Mediators are acutely aware of how unequal bargaining power can both fairly and unfairly impact on the substantive negotiated outcome. The mediator may try to temper some bargaining power inequalities between the parties by promoting procedural equality, not substantive equality. For instance, if the defendant's weak negotiating position is due to the party's weak legal case—she clearly breached a contract to pay for purchased goods and lacks any legal defense—the mediator should do nothing to improve the defendant's substantive bargaining power.[40] But, the mediator still might promote procedural equality by encouraging each party to review any draft agreement with her attorney to be sure that each party is fully informed of her obligations before signing it. In promoting procedural equality, many mediators do not give legal advice because to do so could compromise their neutrality.

---

39. *See id.* at 260.

40. The party may have little power, but not necessarily no power. The party may have the power of a good relationship with the other side, the power of a continuing relationship, the power of being judgment-proof, or the power to cause harm to the other side by forcing the other side to spend time and money on the dispute.

Mediators might promote such forms of procedural equality[41] as equal access to data, professional advice, and personal support, as well as equal understanding of facts and law. But, mediators may recognize different needs of parties that can warrant adjusting procedures to accommodate one side. For instance, giving both parties the same amount of time to review drafts or weigh options may appear facially equal but if it will rush one party who needs more time, the procedure would not be fair and would be adjusted.

In the legal mediations covered in these materials, parties are usually assured of procedural equality because they are represented by attorneys who are knowledgeable in the law, experienced in negotiations, and trained to protect procedural fairness. But, these assumptions about attorneys are not always reliable. An attorney may be blindly partisan, misinformed on the law, or an unskilled negotiator. As a result, the mediator might suggest some procedures to assure equality. For instance, when an attorney for one side has not adequately examined a key statute, the mediator might suggest that the statute be parsed in a joint session with the other side. When suggesting procedures, the mediator must be careful to maintain her neutrality by avoiding any appearance of becoming an advocate for the interests of one side.

Even though most mediators are not likely to address substantive power inequalities, you should be aware that mediators have debated for years whether they should be concerned about the fairness of the substantive result. Despite the process meeting every imaginable procedural standard of equality, parties might move toward an agreement that in the view of the mediator is unfair or might not be upheld in court due to its unconscionability. Many mediators believe that they should not impose their own view of fairness on the parties; if the parties agree, then the agreement should be respected. Some other mediators believe that the integrity of the mediation process depends on mediators assertively ensuring a fair, substantive result.

h. Overcoming Impediments to Settlement

As noted in the section on mediation stages, the mediator may help parties identify impediments to settlement as well as ways to overcome them. The mediator will pose probing questions designed to uncover why the negotiation has reached an impasse. Possible impediments as

---

41. *See* Moore, *supra* note 1, at 335–337.

well as corresponding impasse-breaking strategies are examined in chapter 3.2 on interviewing clients, chapter 5.1 on developing a representation plan, and chapter 8 on breaking impasses by using other dispute resolution processes.

i. Overcoming a Chronic Impediment: Clashing Views of the Court Outcome (BATNA)

Parties frequently reach an impasse because each party has an equally optimistic view of what will happen if the dispute does not settle in the mediation. Both sides cannot be right. The mediator realizes that what each side believes will happen to them outside the mediation influences what each side does in the mediation.[42] Therefore, the mediator wants to be sure that both sides realistically assesses how attractive their alternative to settling in the mediation is, which in legal cases will usually be the litigated outcome. Only then will parties know whether they are better off litigating or settling.

This impasse can arise for a number of reasons. One or both sides failed to undertake a thorough and objective analysis of the likely court outcome. The legal assessment of one of the lawyers was not shared with or understood by her client who may cling to an unrealistic view of what a court might do. One of the sides assumed in good faith an incorrect assumption about whether a critical fact can be proven or how a court will interpret a dispositive statute.

The mediator may use various techniques to help both sides more intelligently "bargain in the shadow of the law."[43] The mediator may pose a series of even-handed, probing questions about what each side thinks will be the likely court outcome and why. The mediator may focus the discussion on parsing critical statutes or cases. To encourage more rigor, the mediator may introduce a decision-tree methodology.[44] The mediator may ask each side to map their litigation pathway, estimate the probability of success at each fork, approximate the financial cost of reaching

---

42. Marjorie C. Aaron, *Evaluation in Mediation*, in Dwight Golaan, Mediating Legal Disputes—Effective Strategies for Lawyers and Mediators Ch. 10 (1996).

43. Robert H. Mnookin & Lewis Kornhauser, *Bargaining in the Shadow of the Law: The Case of Divorce* 88 Yale L.J. 950 (1979).

44. For a full discussion of the use of decision trees, *see* Appendix A on Decision-Tree Plus Analysis and Marjorie C. Aaron & David P. Hoffer, *Decision Analysis as a Method of Evaluating the Trial Alternative*, in Dwight Golaan, Mediating Legal Disputes-Effective Strategies for Lawyers and Mediators Ch. 11 (1996).

each juncture, and predict the likely judicial outcome. Through this sort of mathematical analysis, the mediator assists each side in calculating the "expected value" of litigating that can then be compared with the "expected value" of any settlement proposals. If the expected value of litigating is less than settling for the defendant, then the defendant knows to settle. The mediator also may suggest testing key assumptions by changing them and re-running the decision-tree analysis to see how much the result is changed. For example, if the probability estimate of winning is reduced from 80 percent to 60 percent, will litigating still be more attractive than settling?

The mediator may suggest analyzing the court option in a joint sessions so that each side can hear and react to the other side's assessment. Or, the mediator may prefer using a caucus in order to reduce the pressure on each side to posture in front of the other side, which may increase the likelihood of candid responses. In caucus, the mediator also can ask pointed questions without worrying that her questions may be interpreted by the other side as favoring one side or the other.

j.   Closing the Final Gap: "Mediator's Proposal" and Other Techniques

After various creative methods for finding a resolution have been exhausted, a gap may still need bridging. The gap-closing technique in a classically positional negotiation is only too familiar: After a string of offers, counteroffers, and compromises, the parties are still $50,000 apart. The parties either have gone as far as they can or will turn to the often-used and exceedingly uncreative formula of splitting the difference. As an alternative, some mediators may offer to use one of various devices for closing the last gap. The mediator may offer to present a "mediator's proposal," evaluate the merits of the legal case, package various trades, or employ a scheme designed to induce each side to use their "bottom lines."

The "Mediator's Proposal"[45]

The mediator offers to formulate a settlement proposal that she would recommend for adoption by both sides. The scheme works as follows: The mediator develops a settlement proposal based on her understanding of the dispute, the progress in the mediation session, and her view

---

45. See DWIGHT GOLAAN, MEDIATING LEGAL DISPUTES-EFFECTIVE STRATEGIES FOR LAWYERS AND MEDIATORS SECTION 2.16 (1996).

of what is "fair," the "correct result," or acceptable to both sides. Each side is asked whether they could live with the proposal if the other side would accept it. If both sides confidentially accept the proposal, the mediator informs the parties that the dispute is settled. If one or both sides veto the proposal, the mediator advises the parties that the proposal has been rejected without indicating whether either side had accepted it. This arrangement gives each side the ability to agree to the proposal without revealing to the other side that they were willing to make further concessions. While this technique is suitable for bridging money gaps, it also can be used to bridge gaps that involve more complex settlement terms.

Parties should weigh the benefits and risks of using a mediator's proposal. "Disputants like the fact that they will only have to make the concession if it brings about a settlement, and that if the effort fails, their adversary will never know they were willing to compromise."[46] The scheme also eliminates the risk that one side will reactively devalue a proposal because it is presented by the other side. The proposal is presented by the mediator. However, the scheme can impact negatively on the dynamics of the mediation process, which is why the technique should be used only at the end. It can shift the problem-solving responsibility from the parties to the mediator who crafts the proposal; it can harden the position of the party who likes the proposal; and it risks compromising the neutrality of the mediator who would now appear partial to a particular solution.

If you approve of the mediator formulating a mediator's proposal, you should ask for an opportunity to offer some input, including comments on provisions that the mediator is considering incorporating.

Evaluation of Legal Case and Proposals

At the very end of the session, a mediator may offer to give her own evaluation of the legal case or settlement proposals when such an evaluation seems essential for breaking a last impasse. An evaluation should be done only with the specific approval of both sides. A mediator's opinion is very risky because it can undermine your confidence in the mediator's neutrality and can be unfairly influenced by information that you candidly disclosed in the name of problem-solving or that the other side

---

46. *Id.* at 58.

might have strategically disclosed. Legal evaluations should usually be done by an independent substantive expert.[47]

Packaging of Trades

When the mediator has a good sense of the dispute, she might begin negotiating directly with each side to package a set of trades that may be acceptable to both sides. The mediator might suggest to one party that she reduce her demand by $10,000 if the other party would agree to pay immediately in cash instead of over time with a mix of cash and stock options. Then, the mediator would suggest to the other side that she pay $10,000 less and then pay the remaining lump sum immediately in cash. Under this approach, the parties are negotiating a settlement package with the mediator as well as with each other.

Other Ways to Induce Use of "Bottom Line"

Mediators have at their disposal a number of other schemes to induce parties to use their bottom lines. These schemes give parties the confidence to either move toward their bottom lines or to disclose them to the mediator who would use the information responsibly and adeptly to close any remaining gaps. A number of schemes are described in another chapter on methods for reducing the risks of using your client's bottom line in the mediation session.[48] The methods include the use of final-offer arbitration, hypothetical testing, confidential disclosure of bottom lines, confidential disclosure of settlement numbers, and the safety deposit box.

---

47. The subject of evaluations and how to safely secure them in mediation are discussed in detail in Chapter 4.2(b)(i).

48. *See* Chapter 7.2(d).

CHAPTER THREE
COUNSELING YOUR CLIENT ABOUT MEDIATION

Topics in this chapter include:

1. Professional Obligation
2. Client Interviewing Techniques-Interests and Impediments
3. Disputes Suitable for Mediation
4. Disputes Less Suitable for Mediation
5. Disputes Ripe for Mediation
6. Presenting Mediation Option to Your Client
7. Checklist

You begin your mediation representation as a problem-solver when you first meet your client who is entangled in a dispute. This chapter considers how to fruitfully interview your client about the dispute. It discusses the importance of and techniques for inquiring into your client's interests and possible settlement obstacles. Then, it examines which disputes are suitable for mediation, when a dispute is ripe for mediation, and finally how to approach a client who is unfamiliar with or reluctant about using mediation.

1. Professional Obligation

In the first client interview, it is simply good lawyering to educate your client about alternative processes for resolving his case, and presumably many attorneys do. Attorneys may even have a professional obligation to do so. There is an argument gaining broader support that attorneys are obligated to explain the advantages and drawbacks of various alternative processes such as mediation, neutral evaluation, court, and so forth. This counseling would help clients intelligently select a suitable dispute resolution forum. It has been argued that this professional obligation may be derived from the ABA Model Rules of Professional Conduct and may be necessary to avoid liability for malpractice.[1]

Proposals have been made to modify the Model Rules to specifically mandate attorneys to advise clients about ADR, and a number of state professional rules have adopted such requirements.[2] The Colorado rule, for instance, states that:

> In a matter involving or expected to involve litigation, a lawyer should advise the client of alternative forms of dispute resolution which might reasonably be pursued to attempt to resolve the legal dispute or to reach the legal objective sought. Colorado Court Rules, Rules of Professional Conduct, Rule 2.1 Advisor (effective January 1, 1993)

2. Client Interviewing Techniques

CRITICAL JUNCTURE

Interview Your Client

Interview your client about the interests of both sides and impediments to settlement.

---

1. *See* NANCY H. ROGERS & CRAIG A. MCEWEN , MEDIATION LAW, POLICY, AND PRACTICE, SECTION 4:03 DUTY TO ADVISE CLIENTS ABOUT SETTLEMENT AND DISPUTE RESOLUTION ALTERNATIVES (2d ed. 1994 & Supp. 1996); Warmbrod, *Could an Attorney Face Disciplinary Actions or Even Legal Liability for Failure to Inform Clients of Alternative Dispute Resolution?*, 27 CUMB.L.R.791 (1996–97); Stuart M. Widman, *Attorneys' Ethical Duties to Know and Advise Clients About Alternative Dispute Resolution*, THE PROFESSIONAL LAWYER, 1993, at18; Robert F. Cochran, Jr., *Legal Representation and the Next Steps Toward Client Control: Attorney Malpractice for the Failure to Allow the Client to Control Negotiation and Pursue Alternatives to Litigation*, 47 WASH.& LEE L.REV. 819 (1990); Moberly, *Ethical Standards for Court-Appointed Mediators and Florida's Mandatory Mediation Experiment*, 21 FLA. ST. U.L.REV. 701, 723–26 (1994); Sander & Prigoff, *At Issue: Professional Responsibility: Should There Be a Duty to Advise of ADR Options?* ABA J., Nov. 1990, at 50.

2. *See* Rogers, *supra* note 1; Breger, *Should an Attorney be Required to Advise a Client of ADR Options*,13 BRO.J. LEGAL ETHICS 427 (2000)(Appendix I consists of a fifty-state survey of which states have rules on attorneys advising clients about ADR.); Cochran, *ADR, the ABA, and Client Control: A Proposal that the Model Rules Require Lawyers to Present ADR Options to Clients*, 41 S.TEX.L.R. 183 (1999); Dauer & McNeill, *New Rules on ADR: Professional Ethics, Shotguns and Fish*, 21 COLORADO LAWYER, Sept. 1992, at 1877.

Much has been written about what you should accomplish in your initial client interview and the techniques for doing so.[3] In addition to the conventional goals of developing a rapport with your client, gathering information about your client's story and legal case, and signing a retainer, you should begin gathering information relevant to assessing whether to use mediation and to representing your client in mediation. You should inquire about the interests of your client and the other side as well as the likely impediments to a negotiated resolution. You will recall that the goals in mediation representation are to advance the interests of your client and to overcome any impediments that get in the way, two key features of the mediation representation formula.[4]

The interviewing techniques that are vital to the success of any client interview apply when you are inquiring about interests and impediments. You should meticulously frame your questions and use effective listening methods.[5]

In one questioning technique that has been labeled as the T-funnel method,[6] you pose *open-ended* questions to encourage your client to share information and then follow up with more open-ended questions to jog your client's memory and stimulate more in-depth answers. When your open-ended questions no longer trigger further responses, you follow up with *closed* questions that are designed to solidify and refine the information that your client is sharing.[7] These questioning techniques will be demonstrated below.

Effective listening methods encourage your client to not only share information but also develop fuller and more thoughtful responses.

---

3. *See, e.g.*, ROBERT F. COCHRAN, JR. ET AL., THE COUNSELOR-AT-LAW: A COLLABORATIVE APPROACH TO CLIENT INTERVIEWING AND COUNSELING (1999); STEFAN H. KRIEGER AND RICHARD K. NEUMANN, JR. , ESSENTIAL LAWYERING SKILLS—INTERVIEWING, COUNSELING, NEGOTIATION, AND PERSUASIVE FACT ANALYSIS (1999); DAVID A. BINDER ET AL., LAWYERS AS COUNSELORS: A CLIENT-CENTERED APPROACH (1991); ROBERT M. BASTRESS & JOSEPH D. HARBAUGH, INTERVIEWING, COUNSELING, AND NEGOTIATING—SKILLS FOR EFFECTIVE REPRESENTATION (1990).

4. *See* explanation of mediation representation formula in the introductory chapter.

5. These two techniques were introduced in Chapter 2.4 on "Techniques of Mediators."

6. *See* Binder, *supra* note 3, at 171–179.

7. Open-ended questions give your client substantial latitude for responding. Closed questions restrict your client's response. *See* Chapter 2.4 on "Techniques of Mediators" for examples and variations for framing questions.

"Listening is a skill of paramount importance, and one which few lawyers employ successfully. Most lawyers are too busy asking questions and giving advice to take the time to listen."[8] Effective listening involves more than listening attentively. It entails using passive and active listening techniques[9] such as verbal and nonverbal signals as well as reframing responses in various ways to stimulate sharing of information.

a.   Interests

You should artfully inquire about the substantive interests of your client. Deciphering your client's interests can be much harder than it appears. Interests capture an idea that is easy to talk about but difficult to identify in practice. Interests as defined by Roger Fisher and William Ury are what "motivate people; they are the silent movers behind the hubbub of positions. Your position is something you have decided upon. Your interests are what caused you to so decide."[10] The difficulties unmasking the interests behind positions also were succinctly expressed by Fisher and Ury: "A position is likely to be concrete and explicit; the interests underlying it may well be unexpressed, intangible, and perhaps inconsistent."[11]

With more than fifteen years of teaching the subject, I have frequently seen the difficulties that attorneys and law students experience deciphering clients' interests as opposed to their more familiar positions. Positions tend to be what clients first blurt out based on a lifetime of telling others what they want—whether they want to see a particular movie on Saturday night, pizza for dinner, or money to compensate them for lost wages. We have too much experience answering questions with solutions and little experience voicing what motivates us to want these solutions. We may want to see a particular movie because of our underlying interest in seeing an action movie or a romantic comedy. We may want pizza for dinner because we are looking for something quick and simple. We may want money because we are so accustomed to habitually translating what we want into money equivalents when in fact we want financial security.

---

8. *See* Binder, *supra* note 3.

9. The techniques are described in Chapter 2.4 on "Techniques of Mediators."

10. *See* Roger Fisher Et al., Getting to Yes—Negotiating Agreement Without Giving In, 41 (2d ed. 1991).

11. *Id.*at 44.

You may find it difficult to identify your client's interests due to your professional training and experiences that reinforce a positional, win-lose view of problems. The litigator's mind-set that includes a narrow view of legal disputes is shaped by your legal education, the way the common law evolves, the pervasive, adversarial legal culture, the all too familiar routine for pursuing litigation, and traditional fee arrangements.[12] As a result, you may be professionally blinded to your client's interests. You may need to conquer your blind spot.

Your client may welcome your help in spelling out what he really wants, his broader interests—interests that have the potential of being met in a number of ways. You should formulate appropriate questions along with suitable follow-up ones. The single most penetrating and revealing question turns out to be a simple one—"Why?" "Why do you want that?" By bringing to the surface your client's underlying interests and surmising the interests of the other party, you can free the parties from the traditional contest over competing positions, a contest that usually produces a narrow legal solution. By doing this, you will have taken the first step in preparing for a problem-solving approach to representation.

In addition to culling your client's substantive interests, you should uncover your client's interests in a dispute resolution process. Process interests can vary considerably.[13] Your client may have an interest in a process that:

- Gives him the opportunity to retain control over the outcome of his dispute,

- Provides a forum that will address all issues, legal and non-legal,

- Preserves or improves a continuing relationship with the other side,

- Avoids or sets a precedent,

- Leads to creative remedies that go beyond what a court is likely to do,

---

12. The basis for the litigator's mind-set is discussed in Chapter 1.2(b) on "Why Lawyers Prefer Adversarial Negotiations."

13. These process interests are elaborated in the next sections on "Interests and Impediments Suitable for Mediation" and "Interests and Impediments Less Suitable for Mediation."

- Produces an enduring settlement,
- Maintains confidentiality,
- Saves time and money,
- "Cleans up" the case,
- Vindicates him,
- Permits him to avoid compromising a principle,
- Deters future, baseless litigation by others, or
- Opens the door to the possibility of a large jackpot.

The distinction between process and substantive interests can seem murky because your client's substantive interests and his interests in the process can be the same. This overlap occurs because your client's substantive interests can be advanced, if not met, by selecting a suitable process. For instance, your client's substantive interest in confidentiality can be met by selecting a process that is likely to preserve confidentiality. Your client's substantive interest in preserving a relationship with the other side can be advanced in a process that is suitable for preserving relationships. Your client's substantive interest in vindication may be achieved in a process that can vindicate your client by producing a decision that declares your client is right. And, your client's substantive interest in securing compensation can be advanced in most processes.

Example

Here is an example of how to use open-ended and closed questions as well as effective listening techniques for bringing to the surface your client's substantive interests for advancing in the dispute resolution process as well your client's procedural interests in selecting a particular dispute resolution option.

Client: (Explains that he has a dispute with a new car dealership where he purchased a car six months ago. The car has not worked right since the day he drove it out of the dealership parking lot.)

Attorney: (After learning the basic chronology of events, the attorney begins to pose questions about his client's interests.) What do you want out of this dispute? *[open-ended question]*

Client: I want to be paid for all my aggravation and inconvenience. *[position]*
              I have taken the car to the dealer six times, and it is still not working right—the car keeps stalling at red lights and makes all kinds of strange rattling noises when going over bumps.

Attorney: Six times to the dealer... *[paraphrasing]*
              You must be very upset. *[reflective framing]*
              Is there anything else you want out of this? *[open-ended question]*

Client: I am *very* upset. And what I want is a new car. *[position]*

Attorney: Humm, hum. *[verbal prompts]*
              Is there anything else you want? *[open-ended question]*

Client: I also want the manager fired for doing such an incompetent job. *[position]*

Attorney: You must be angry at him because the car was not fixed. *[reflective framing]*
              Is there anything else that you want to achieve? *[open-ended question]*
              Take some time to think about this. *[silently wait for several minutes]*

Client: I don't think so.

Attorney: Do you have any thoughts on the process you want to use for resolving this dispute? *[open-ended question about procedural interests]*

Client: Yes. I don't know very much about going to court or other alternatives, but I don't want to spend a lot of money on this. I need a way that will resolve this as quickly as possible because I need a reliable car now. As we already discussed, I also want more than the dealer just fixing the car. And, I suspect the dealer does not want to go to court in order to avoid any bad publicity.

Attorney: Let me follow up on some of your answers.

Attorney: Were there any expenses incurred due to the aggravation and inconvenience you had with the car? *[follow-up clarifying question]*

Client: Yes, I had to miss work to drop off the car and pick it up. I used six hours for the six times that I took the car to the dealer. I should be compensated for this. *[The client is expressing an interest in some sort of compensation for the uncompensated six office hours, but the client did not take a position on the form of compensation.]*

Attorney: Why do you want the manager fired? *[follow-up focused, open-ended "why" question]*

Client: He treated me horribly. Every time I called, he seemed to avoid talking with me. And when he did, he was curt and discourteous, implying that the problem was me, not the car. *[The client seems to be suggesting an interest in some recognition that the client was treated badly.]*

Attorney: Is getting him fired the only way to satisfy you? *[follow-up focused, open-ended question]*

Client: No. I just want to be sure that he does not get away with the way he treated me. *[The follow-up question clarified the client's interest in some recognition for being treated badly, not in getting the manager fired.]*

Attorney: Why do you want a new car? *[follow-up focused, open-ended "why" question]*

Client: I need a car that I can count on. I cannot count on the car that they sold me. *[Client is expressing an interest in a reliable car; getting a new car is just one possible way to meet this interest.]*

Attorney: Let me summarize what I think you are saying. Let me know whether I understand correctly your goals. Your interests are to get a reliable car, to be compensated for lost time, and to be sure that the dealership does something about how badly you were treated. *[follow-up closed question]*

Client: Yes, except that my primary interest is getting a reliable car. *[Client makes it clear that all interests are not of equal importance.]*

Next, you would ask questions about what your client thinks might be the substantive and process interests of the other side. Then, you might further discuss the process options for resolving the dispute.

Attorney: Let's discuss different processes for resolving this dispute. You have indicated an interest in a process that minimizes the dispute resolution costs, resolves the dispute quickly, and can result in solutions that involve more than just paying money. You also think that the dealer wants to avoid any bad publicity.

I would like to suggest some of the benefits and drawbacks of two very different options: court and mediation. If we go to court, you will participate in a public process that can be quite acrimonious and costly, but that will result in a decisive resolution in which you win and get a new car, or lose and get nothing. In mediation, we meet around a table, and with the assistance of a mediator, try to negotiate a tailored resolution. Mediation is likely to cost less than going to court and will be quicker. The dealer may find mediation appealing because the results are not publicized. But, if the mediation does not succeed, we then may have to incur the costs of returning to court for a final resolution. Do you have any questions about these two options? How would you like to proceed?

[This is a short and simple explanation that is designed to give you a flavor of how a discussion of process interests might be approached. In an actual interview, you would go into more detail to clarify your client's process interests as well as to explore the advantages and disadvantages of each option. You also would answer any client questions before sorting out which process option to pursue.]

Caveat: At this early interview, your client may be unsure of his substantive and process interests and incapable of fully articulating them. Your client may be able to express only vague notions of what he wants. You may need to patiently follow up with open-ended and closed questions and view the information on interests (and impediments in the next section) as only preliminary. Then, you should revisit these questions again when you prepare your client for the mediation sessions at which time new information might have surfaced since your initial interview, the personal circumstances of your client might have changed, your client has had time to mull over what he wants to accomplish, and your client will be sharply focused on the upcoming mediation session.[14]

b. Impediments

When you interview your client about the dispute and interests, you should inquire about any specific obstacles that might be impeding a negotiated resolution. This inquiry can be especially illuminating when you base your questions on an approach developed by one of a number of distinguished authors that have helped to demystify the murky world of impasse breaking.[15]

My personal favorite, developed by Dr. Christopher Moore,[16] relies on taking three discrete steps that can produce a tailor-made strategy for overcoming impasses. His approach is built around his critical observation that impasses can be divided into five conflict categories that he labels as *relationship, data, value, interest, and structural.* Under his approach, you first inquire about the cause of the impasse; then you

---

14. *See* Chapter 6.3 on re-interviewing your client. For a thoughtful explanation of the difficulties in getting full information at the initial client interview, *see also* the discussion on how to preliminarily identify your client's problem in David A. Binder Et Al., Lawyers as Counselors: A Client-Centered Approach 88–104 (1991).

15. *See* Jean R. Sternlight, *Lawyers' Representation of Clients in Mediation: Using Economics and Psychology to Structure Advocacy in a Nonadversarial Setting*, 14 Ohio St. J. on Disp. Res. 269, 297–331 (1999) (identifies barriers to negotiations based on economists' insights, psychologists' insights, flaws in rationality assumption, and principal/agent conflicts); Christopher W. Moore, The Mediation Process—Practical Strategies for Resolving Conflicts 60–61 (2d ed. 1996)(identifies five causes of conflicts—data conflicts, interest conflicts, structural conflicts, relationship conflicts, and value conflicts); Dwight Golann, Mediating Legal Disputes—Effective Strategies for Lawyers and Mediators chps 6–8 (1996)(identifies three categories of impasses—process, psychological, and merits); and Frank E.A. Sander & Stephen B. Goldberg, *Fitting the For m to the Fuss: A User-Friendly Guide to Selecting an ADR Procedure*, 10 Negotiation J., Jan. 1994, at 54–59 (identifies ten impediments to settlement).

16. *See* Moore, *supra* note 15, at 60–61 (Author presents Circle of Conflict in which five sources of conflicts are identified along with possible strategies for intervention).

classify the cause in one of the five impasse categories; and finally you devise a suitable intervention for overcoming the impasse.

For instance, if parties are at an impasse because they have calculated different seller's lost profits that resulted from the buyer breaching a sales contract, you first would diagnose its cause, which may be different sales assumptions over the next twelve months. You would then classify the cause, which in this case, would be a data conflict. These first two steps enable you to get behind the impasse to the root of the conflict— conflicting views of a key assumption. This conclusion would give you the basis for devising a suitable intervention. In this case, you might simply focus your inquiry on the reasons for the different assumptions and ways to reconcile the differences.

This section explains Moore's five impasse categories[17] as well as a few of his suggestions for how mediators might intervene. (*See* Moore's Pie Chart.) The details of what you might do are deferred to a later chapter[18] that covers how to formulate a representation plan that takes advantage of the opportunities for overcoming impediments to mediation.

Here are the five categories:

Relationship conflicts can arise when parties are deeply upset with each other, cling to destructive misperceptions or stereotypes of each other, or suffer from poor communications.

The mediator can help parties identify the particular causes and help them classify the conflict as a relationship one. Then, the mediator can assist the parties in implementing a suitable intervention. The mediator might help the parties constructively explain to each other why they are upset, assist them in clarifying their perceptions of each other, focus on other ways to improve their communications, and cultivate their problem-solving attitudes. Relationship conflicts are common in disputes where parties distrust each other and are occupied with hurling threats.

---

17. In a training program that I attended in June 2000, Dr. Moore suggested that a mediator should first deal with relationship, data, and interest conflicts. Then, when these conflicts have been diminished or overcome, parties will be more receptive to dealing with any remaining structural or value conflicts.

18. *See* Chapter 5.1 on how to prepare a mediation representation plan,

Data conflicts can be caused by inadequate, inaccurate, or untrustworthy information. Or they can be caused by different views of what is relevant information or different interpretations of relevant data.

The mediator can help the parties identify the specific causes and aid them in classifying the conflict as a data one. The mediator might intervene by helping the parties resolve what data are important, negotiate a process for collecting reliable data, or develop common criteria that can be used to assess the data. Data conflicts are common in court cases where parties may hold conflicting views of what happened, what might happen in court, or what is an appropriate interpretation of decisive data such as financial statements.

Interest conflicts can arise when parties' substantive, procedural, or psychological/relationship wants conflict with each other.[19] Interest conflicts cover the classical positional conflict inherent in adversarial negotiations. They can be caused by parties wanting the same thing (such as property), wanting different amounts of the same thing (such as time), wanting different things that another is not prepared to give (such as one party wanting a precedent that the other party opposes), or even wanting something that another is not even aware of (such as an acknowledgment or an apology). Although many interest conflicts may be distributive, they can be integrative in nature, depending upon how the conflict is framed.

After clarifying the causes of the conflict and classifying it, the mediator can help parties pinpoint shared or non-conflicting wants, identify objective criteria for overcoming conflicting wants, and search for increased value and productive trades.[20] Court cases typically present conflicting substantive wants because of the nature of the litigation process in which plaintiffs' attorneys draft complaints bursting with demands and defendants' attorneys draft answers that righteously reject almost everything.

---

19. In a problem-solving process in which the concept of "interests" performs such a vital and pervasive role, Moore's narrow and distinctive use of "interest" conflicts can be confusing. I prefer referring to wants or desire conflicts. Parties may reach an impasse because their substantive, procedural, or psychological wants or desires are in conflict with each other.

20. These techniques are covered in Chapter 1.3, "Problem-Solving Negotiations"; Chapter 1.5, "Converting Adversarial Negotiations into Problem-Solving"; Chapter 1.6, "Advancing Problem-Solving in Mediations."

Structural conflicts often overlap with relationship conflicts and can be the murkiest to identify. The two most common, as well as easiest, structural obstacles to spot are impasses due to unequal bargaining power or impasses due to conflicting goals of attorneys and their clients, known as principal-agent conflicts. Other structural conflicts can be more subtle such as ones caused by no deadline, time constraints facing one side, missing key party, a party without sufficient settlement authority, geographical or technological limitations that impact disproportionally on one side, and unequal control of resources for resolving the conflict. Because structural conflicts frequently overlap with relationship conflicts, it can be difficult deciphering the nature of the conflict.

For example, an attorney-client conflict can be due to the structure of the relationship, a bad relationship between the attorney and client, or both. The mediator can help a side overcome an attorney-client conflict by exploring the details of the conflict. If it has arisen because the attorney thinks his client should settle while his client wants to pursue the litigation, for instance, the mediator can facilitate a discussion of the different views and ways for bridging possible differences. If the reason that the client wants to litigate is because he does not trust his attorney's advice, a reaction that suggests a relationship problem is impeding progress, the mediator might engage in initiatives to help mend the fractured attorney-client relationship.

A competent mediator will not do anything to neutralize a structural conflict due to a fair advantage of one party. When one side has greater bargaining power due to a stronger legal case, for instance, the mediator may help the disadvantaged party develop a realistic understanding of his legal options and then help the parties negotiate a resolution that recognizes the structural advantage of one side. When doing this, the mediator must be careful to avoid any appearance of siding with one party.

Value conflicts can be the most intractable ones because they implicate a party's core personal or moral values. This narrow category can embrace matters of principle, ideology, or religion. A grassroots environmental group, for instance, may have difficulty settling with a housing developer because to do so might compromise the group's ideology to preserve all large tracts of open space.

The mediator may first help the parties clarify their core values because sometimes they might discover that their core values are not at stake or that both sides possess similar values, and as a result, are not in conflict. Otherwise, the mediator may try to help parties work around their personal beliefs because compromise is usually unacceptable. The mediator can help parties search for an overarching shared goal, ways to avoid defining the problem in terms of a particular value, or solutions that do not compromise the value. Or, the mediator might assist parties in reaching an agreement to disagree. If the value conflict can be overcome by modifying the value, then, by definition, the conflict does not implicate a value. It is a conflict that fits within one of the other impasse categories.

Value conflicts can be difficult to recognize in court cases because values can be masked by all too familiar legal categories, arguments, and remedies. When a party wants to win in court, for example, the party may be motivated by the need for a clear victory to preserve a personal value—his personal integrity. A mediator might intervene by inquiring whether the party's personal integrity could be preserved in another process such as mediation.

Sphere of Conflict—Causes and Interventions[21]

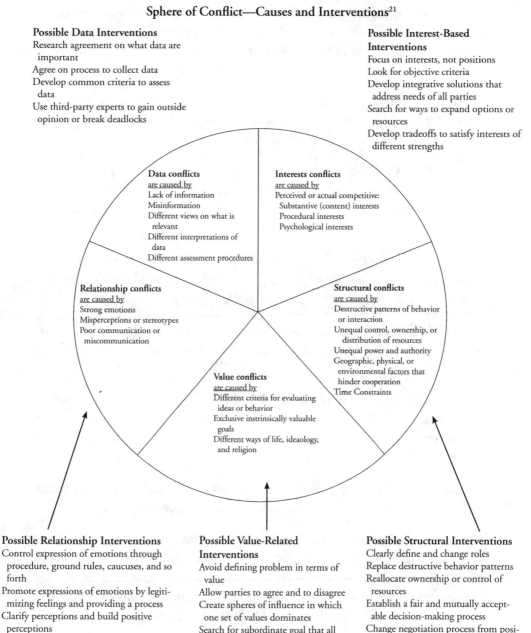

Possible Data Interventions
Research agreement on what data are important
Agree on process to collect data
Develop common criteria to assess data
Use third-party experts to gain outside opinion or break deadlocks

Possible Interest-Based Interventions
Focus on interests, not positions
Look for objective criteria
Develop integrative solutions that address needs of all parties
Search for ways to expand options or resources
Develop tradeoffs to satisfy interests of different strengths

Data conflicts
are caused by
Lack of information
Misinformation
Different views on what is relevant
Different interpretations of data
Different assessment procedures

Interests conflicts
are caused by
Perceived or actual competitive:
   Substantive (content) interests
   Procedural interests
   Psychological interests

Relationship conflicts
are caused by
Strong emotions
Misperceptions or stereotypes
Poor communication or miscommunication

Structural conflicts
are caused by
Destructive patterns of behavior or interaction
Unequal control, ownership, or distribution of resources
Unequal power and authority
Geographic, physical, or environmental factors that hinder cooperation
Time Constraints

Value conflicts
are caused by
Different criteria for evaluating ideas or behavior
Exclusive instrinsically valuable goals
Different ways of life, ideaology, and religion

Possible Relationship Interventions
Control expression of emotions through procedure, ground rules, caucuses, and so forth
Promote expressions of emotions by legitimizing feelings and providing a process
Clarify perceptions and build positive perceptions
Improve quality and quantity of communication
Block negative repetitive behavior by changing structures
Encourage positive problem-solving attitudes

Possible Value-Related Interventions
Avoid defining problem in terms of value
Allow parties to agree and to disagree
Create spheres of influence in which one set of values dominates
Search for subordinate goal that all parties share

Possible Structural Interventions
Clearly define and change roles
Replace destructive behavior patterns
Reallocate ownership or control of resources
Establish a fair and mutually acceptable decision-making process
Change negotiation process from positional to interest-based bargaining
Modify means of influence used by parties (less coercion, more persuasion)
Change physical and environmental relationships of parties (closeness and distance)
Modify external pressures on parties
Change time constraints (more or less time)

---

21. CHRISTOPHER W. MOORE, THE MEDIATION PROCESS—PRACTICAL STRATEGIES FOR RESOLVING CONFLICTS 60–61 (2d ed., Jossey-Bass 1996). This material is used by permission of John Wiley & Sons, Inc.

Other distinguished authors have developed impasse breaking approaches that focus specifically on legal disputes. Their classification categories should be familiar to lawyers, and as result, may resonate with you.

In one approach, Professors Sander and Goldberg identify ten common causes of impasses.[22] In brackets, I suggest how each cause might be classified under the Moore approach.

1.   Poor Communications [relationship conflict]. Due to a poor relationship between the parties and/or their attorneys, the sides cannot communicate effectively with each other. This poor communication is interfering with productive settlement discussions.

2.   Need to Express Emotions [relationship conflict]. A party needs to vent (express his views, disappointment and even anger) plus feel heard by the other party before the party is ready to settle.

3.   Different View of Facts [data conflict]. Conflicting views of critical facts in the case make it difficult for parties to even agree on the problem that needs to be resolved.

4.   Different Views of Legal Outcome if Settlement is Not Reached [data conflict]. Because each party is optimistic about a favorable court outcome, at least one side has unrealistic expectations about what he can lever out of the mediation.

5.   Issue of Principle [value conflict]. A party cannot agree to terms that might compromise a "fundamental" principle or value.

6.   Constituency Pressure [structural or substantive interest conflict]. A party at the table is influenced by people who are not at the table and as a result, settlement discussions are being hampered. The outside pressure may be due to the diverse interests of constituents or due to the party representative having staked his future with others on achieving a particular result in the mediation.

7.   Linkage to Other Disputes [structural or interest (substantive or procedural) conflict]. Other disputes between the parties may contaminate settlement discussions because the other disputes are linked to the dispute in settlement discussions.

---

22. See Sander, *supra* note 15 (identifies ten impediments to settlement).

8.   Multiple Parties [structural or substantive interest conflict]. Multiple parties with diverse interests in the mediation can hinder settlement efforts in a way that is similar to impediments caused by diverse constituencies and issue linkages.

9.   Different Lawyer/Client Interests [procedural or substantive interest conflict]. The attitudes and interests of lawyers can conflict with the attitudes and interests of their clients, resulting in a breakdown of settlement efforts. For example, the attorney may be interested in litigating an issue while the client may be interested in disposing of the dispute quickly and quietly.

10. The "Jackpot" Syndrome [interest conflict]. A side may be unwilling to settle because a party or attorney may be tempted by the small chance of a huge jackpot such as a runaway jury verdict.

In an in-depth analysis of impasse breaking in legal disputes, Professor Golann classifies impediments into three general categories: process obstacles, psychological barriers, and merits conflicts.[23] For each general category, he identifies a number of possible obstacles and then suggests detailed strategies that a mediator might use to help parties overcome each obstacle. Under process obstacles, Professor Golann lists such examples as absent parties, the lack of a settlement event, failure of the positional negotiations process, and a party without sufficient bargaining authority. Under psychological barriers, he offers such examples as strong emotions, selective perceptions and reactive devaluation, and uncompromising moral and symbolic principles. Under merit conflicts, he cites such examples as lack of information, misevaluation of likely judicial outcome, and a party's need for a precedent.

Professor Golann recommends to mediators a number of practical and ample strategies for overcoming each impasse, strategies that you as an advocate could enlist your mediator to do.[24] For example, if you think the disputants are at an impasse due to the process obstacle of a lack of a settlement deadline (a Moore structural conflict), you could ask the mediator in a caucus to help create a deadline that will motivate the parties to focus their energies now on making the hard decisions

---

23. *See* DWIGHT GOLAN, MEDIATING LEGAL DISPUTES—EFFECTIVE STRATEGIES FOR LAWYERS AND MEDIATORS chps 6–8 (1996).

24. *Id.*

essential to resolving the dispute.[25] If you think the case is at an impasse due to the psychological barrier resulting from the other side devaluating any proposals suggested by your client (a Moore data conflict), you could ask the mediator in a caucus to present your client's proposal hypothetically to the other side.[26]

Each of these three approaches for identifying and overcoming impediments provides a somewhat different way for reaching the same goal. Each approach provides a stand-alone methodology. Together, they present a full and rich picture of impasse breaking. In this book, I demonstrate how to use the Moore approach.

Example

Here is an example of how to use open-ended and closed questions and the Moore impasse classification system for identifying possible impediments to a negotiated settlement. This example is a continuation of the client interview about the new car problem.

Attorney: Can you explain how you tried to resolve this dispute directly with the manager of the dealership? *[focused, open-ended question]*

Client: Yes, I had one aggravating and worthless telephone call with the manger, Mr. Servin. I called him several times before he would even return one of my calls. When we finally talked, or more accurately, when he talked—he would not let me talk—Mr. Servin kept blaming me for all the problems with the car. I tried to point out to him that the problems are all covered by the new car warranty. He would not listen. He is the most arrogant person that I have met. *[Relationship conflict—The client could not communicate with Mr. Servin and is obviously angry at him. The dispute has become personal.]*

Attorney: Did Mr. Servin think that the problems were covered by the warranty? *[closed question]*

Client: No, Mr. Servin claims that the warranty was voided because I took the car to an unauthorized dealership. I did ask my

---

25. *Id.* at 154–162.

26. *Id.* at 201–202.

neighborhood mechanic to look at the car to see what was wrong because I wasn't getting any help from the dealership. But, the mechanic did not do any work on the car so the warranty should still be valid. *[Data conflict—The two sides agree that the client took his car to the neighborhood mechanic. But, they may be disagreeing about what happened next and its implications. What did the neighborhood mechanic do? Did his work invalidate the new car warranty?]*

Attorney: Did you tell Mr. Servin what you wanted him to do? *[closed question]*

Client: Yes. I told him that I wanted my car replaced with a new one. He said no way. He said that the service department did fix the car but once someone else worked on it, they had no further obligations. The dealership and manufacturer will not spend any more money investigating my complaints. *[Interest conflict—The parties have conflicting wants. The client's position that he wants a new car conflicts with the dealership's position that it will not spend any more money on the complaint.]*

Attorney: There seem to be at least three impediments that are getting in the way of your settling this dispute with the manager. You have a bad relationship with the manager because you feel he treated you so badly. Critical facts are in dispute about your complaints and what your mechanic did. And, what you want conflicts with what the manager wants. First, we should try to overcome these obstacles in our negotiations with the dealership. If we are successful, you and the manager may be able to arrive at a solution that each of you can live with. If not, you may want to consider using mediation.

A mediator can help structure a discussion where you can share your frustrations directly with the manager and hear his views. You might learn something new, and getting together may open up useful communications. A mediator also can help us clarify critical information about the warranty's terms, what your mechanic actually did, and whether what your mechanic did impacted on your legal rights. Finally, a mediator can help you and the manager exchange information about each of your interests and then provide a setting for trying to develop options for resolving the dispute. *[After analyzing the causes of the impasses and classifying them, the attorney suggests a few intervention strategies that mediators might use to overcome the impasses.]*

3. Disputes Suitable for Mediation[27]

Whether your client will find mediation appealing does not depend on the substantive dispute; it depends on whether your client's process interests can be met in mediation. When interviewing your client, you will learn much about his process interests,[28] including his interest in a process that will help him overcome particular impasses.[29] Some mediation opportunities may not otherwise be available to your client such as the opportunity to share information confidentially with a neutral third party. Other opportunities may not be as easily available to your client such as the opportunity to design creative solutions. Your client should weigh these benefits against the benefits offered by other dispute resolution options. (See section below on "Interests and Impediments Less Suitable for Mediation.") As the following list of process interests suggests, your client can gain much and risk little by trying mediation.

Process Interests That Can Be Met in Mediation (Other than Overcoming Impediments)

Your client may want a process where he can meet his interest in:

1. **Resolving Own Dispute.** Your client may want to retain control over the outcome of the dispute. Instead of risking an imposed decision by a judge or arbitrator, your client may prefer a non-binding settlement process in which the third party empowers the participants

---

27. *See, e.g.,* JOHN W. COOLEY, MEDIATION ADVOCACY 36–37 (1996); Sander, *supra* note 15, at 49 (Using a scale of 0–3, authors rate the likelihood of a process such as mediation overcoming a particular impediment to settlement.). *See also,* NANCY H. ROGERS & CRAIG A. MCEWEN , MEDIATION LAW, POLICY, PRACTICE, SECTION 4:06 WHEN TO INITIATE THE PROCESS (2d ed. 1994 & Supp. 1996).

28. For a full discussion of role of interests and ways to identify them, *see* Chapter 1.3(a)(ii), "Critical Juncture (Table)—Identify Interests," and Chapter 3.2, "Client Interviewing Techniques."

29. For a more in-depth discussion of impediments and how to overcome them, *see* Chapter 5.1.

to control and shape the outcome. Especially in a facilitative process, mediation reinforces client self-determination. If your client thinks that the mediation is not producing a resolution that reflects the strength of his case, your client can choose to leave the mediation.

2. Selecting Forum for All Issues—Legal and Non-Legal. Your client may want to resolve more than the narrow legal issues that brought the parties to court. The legal solutions alone may leave parties festering and leave non-legal issues unresolved. In mediation, all the issues can be put on the table so that any resolution can be global. Furthermore, the additional issues may open the door to more advantageous and enduring solutions. For example, in a suit for breach of a contract to deliver computers, a mediated solution may go beyond the legal dispute about past orders and also solidify the delivery terms of future orders.

3. Preserving or Improving Continuing Relationships. Your client may want to preserve or even improve his relationship with the other client. Relationships are more likely to be bolstered in a collaborative and informal mediation than in an acrimonious, adversarial trial. This benefit can be significant when continuing relationships are important such as in business dealings when parties expect to or would like to continue to work together.

4. Avoiding Precedent. Your client may want a forum that lacks the power to establish a binding judicial precedent. In mediation, as in most settlement processes, parties resolve their dispute privately. For instance, your client may not want an agreement about a non-infringing use of his trademark to become a precedent.

5. Developing Creative Remedies. Your client may prefer remedies that are not restricted to what an arbitrator or judge is likely to order. Under the guidance of a skilled mediator, participants can devise creative, tailor-made settlement terms that might include inventive monetary and non-monetary solutions unavailable in an adjudicatory forum. Rather than being limited to judicial remedies of reinstatement and back pay in an employment discrimination lawsuit, for instance, your client may prefer a forum where non-legal solutions are possible such as securing good references, assistance in finding a new job, or even an apology.

6. Forming Enduring Settlement. Your client may desire a process that increases the likelihood that any settlement agreement would be

implemented. Especially for an agreement that might include more intricate and inventive terms than the immediate payment of money, mediation can be attractive. Due to the collaborative nature of the process, clients are more likely to understand the nuances of the settlement terms and be committed to implementing them.

7. Maintaining Confidentiality. Your client may want a process that assures confidentiality before sharing critical information and settlement ideas with the other side. Under well-settled law, nothing said in the mediation sessions can usually be used against any party if the case returns to court or arbitration.[30] Based on local laws or the terms of a signed confidentiality agreement, what happens in mediation also might be hidden from others, including competitors, customers, and suppliers.

8. Saving Time and Money. Your client may want a process that produces a resolution relatively quickly in order to save time and money. In mediations, parties may not need to complete expensive, extensive discovery, and typical mediation sessions do not last as long as trials. In simple cases, mediation sessions may last less than a day. In more complex cases, multiple sessions may be required, but usually only a few sessions. Much of the preparation for the mediation can be recycled if the case does not settle because a lot of the work is of the sort that must be done if the case goes to trial.

9. "Cleaning up" the Case. Your client may want a process to clean up the case, even when you do not expect the case to settle fully in the mediation. At least, your client will gain a better understanding of his interests, will clarify what issues need to be resolved, may dispose of some issues, might solidify a discovery schedule, and will probably develop a plan for resolving any remaining issues.

Process Interests in Overcoming Impediments That Can Be Met in Mediation

Your client may want a process that is capable of meeting his interest in overcoming particular impediments. Disputing parties may welcome the assistance of a mediator who has specialized training in diagnosing impasses and developing intervention strategies. Parties can reach an impasse for a variety of reasons, several of which are described here

---

30. For a more in-depth discussion of how much confidentiality you can count on, *see* Chapter 5.13.

along with what mediators might do. Each impasse has been classified under the Moore approach, as noted in brackets.

1.   Conflicting Views of the Facts or Law [data conflict]. Your client may need a forum that provides participants an opportunity to examine and discuss conflicting views of the facts or law. This assessment can be done under the guidance of a skilled neutral who can help your client and the other side gain a shared understanding of the case's strengths and weaknesses. A facilitative neutral may use an approach in which each side evaluates the case or an evaluative neutral may offer his independent case evaluation. This realistic preview of what might happen in court can make it easier for the party with the weaker case to concede key points and spare everyone the cost of litigation. This preview also can provide a valuable reference point for parties who are trying to assess whether to accept a proposal on the table or to continue litigating.

2.   Parties Need to Vent [relationship conflict]. Your client or the other client may need a forum where the person can constructively discharge any built-up anger. Parties also may crave the feeling of being heard by the other side. Under the guidance of a mediator, parties can safely tell each other directly what each one is really thinking. Venting can be an essential first step before parties can work productively to resolve their dispute.

3.   Communications Problems Between Participants [relationship conflict]. Clients, the other attorney, and even you may need help communicating with the other participants involved with resolving the dispute. Mediation can provide a forum in which participants can improve communications with each other and, consequently, their relationship with each other. By using various techniques, the mediator can facilitate communications among participants so that each person can understand the viewpoints of the other participants. This improved communications between the sides can open the door to new opportunities for settlement.

4.   Unskilled Negotiators [structural or relationship conflict]. Participants may have difficulty initiating the negotiations or one or more participants may be handicapped with limited negotiation skills. The mediator can help parties negotiate more productively by the way he structures the mediation process and the type of questions he poses.

5.   Conflicts Between Attorney and Client [structural conflict]. If there is a conflict between you and your client or the other attorney and his client, mediation can be helpful. For example, you and your client may have divergent views of reasonable settlement terms or the other attorney may want to litigate while his client wants to settle. Cognizant of these sorts of settlement obstacles, mediators can select suitable strategies for overcoming them while still respecting attorney-client relationships.

4.   Disputes Less Suitable for Mediation

Some party's process interests are less suitable for mediation. Although these less suitable interests can occasionally be met in mediation, they usually are more meaningfully satisfied in other forums such as court or possibly arbitration.

Mediation may be less suitable for your client's interest in:

1.   Establishing Precedent. Your client may need a process that will establish legal precedent to guide future conduct. Although courts surely serve this interest well, mediation can occasionally contribute by leading to a settlement in which parties control the outcome and agree to publicize their settlement terms as a guide for future conduct.

2.   Deterring Future Litigation. Your client needs to litigate the case in order to establish a reputation that he will not capitulate to threats of baseless lawsuits. Although a vigorous and even unsuccessful defense has been know to discourage other lawsuits, a favorable mediated agreement can sometimes serve the same ends if it can be procured and publicized widely.

3.   Securing Vindication. Your client may need a process that will give him the opportunity to exonerate himself, prove himself, or protect himself from criticism by winning before a neutral third party. Your client may need the authoritative decision to convince a constituency such as superiors, family members, or a union membership. A clear win in court can certainly vindicate your client. But, sometimes mediation can help vindicate your client if the other party is willing to make a key concession or apologize. This might be enough when your client is trying to clear his name of discrimination charges but may be insufficient when your client needs to prove that he correctly interpreted the law.

4.   Going for Jackpot. Your client or the other side may be tempted by the possibility of a big win before a jury, judge, or arbitrator. Even though a mediator can focus a session on providing a reality check, the prospect of the big jackpot elsewhere can sometimes be just too enticing.

5.   Overcoming Particular Impediments. Some impediments can be especially difficult to overcome in mediation. Here are a few examples.

a.   Preserving Principle [value conflict]. Your client may be unwilling to agree to any settlement in which he must compromise a personal principle or value. Conflicts that implicate personal principles are among the most difficult ones to settle. Rather than consenting to a compromise, a party may prefer taking the risk of a court forcing him to compromise the principle. Nevertheless, sometimes a mediator can help a party craft an agreement that avoids jeopardizing his principle.

b.   Party Inadequately Represented [structural conflict]. The other party cannot effectively represent his interests in mediation and will not be represented by counsel.

c.   Critical Party Not Participating [structural conflict]. A party that is essential to a productive mediation will not participate in the sessions despite the efforts of the mediator to be sure the right people attend.

d.   Bad Faith Negotiations [structural conflict]. The other party has a history of acting in bad faith including engaging in a strategy of delay.

5.   Disputes Ripe for Mediation

When is the best point in the adjudicatory process to opt into mediation? In other words, when is a case suitable for mediation ready for mediation? There are no hard-and-fast rules. At an early stage, parties may be ready for a settlement process because they may not be too wedded to their positions and their relationship may not be too fractured by the litigation process. At a later stage, parties also may be ready to participate in a settlement process because discovery is mostly done, issues have been narrowed through motions to dismiss or summary judgment motions, and parties feel more knowledgeable about the likely court outcome and litigation costs.

"The appropriate time to mediate, considering all these factors [outlined below], is the *earliest practical time* at which the parties are in a position to evaluate their case,"[31] (emphasis in original) has been recommended by Eric Galton, a highly experienced mediator. He suggests that the following factors weigh in favor of early mediation:[32]

Subjective Reasons for Early Mediation

1.   Parties are more flexible and oriented towards resolution earlier in the dispute. Ideas and opinions about a party's position harden over time and re-evaluation becomes more difficult as time progresses.

2.   Parties become more committed to 'the case' itself as time progresses. The attitude becomes "I've gone this far, why not go all the way to trial?"

3.   Parties are more likely to settle their dispute and obtain closure the farther away trial and final resolution appears to be. People have a natural and innate desire to resolve their problems. As the trial moves closer, many litigants see the trial itself as providing closure.

4.   In many instances, the litigation process itself breeds distrust and creates close-mindedness. On occasion, a party may grow to dislike opposing counsel, and this may create a new layer of rigidity.

Objective Reasons for Early Mediation

1.   Cost containment is the most compelling factor. In some instances, the litigation costs incurred can become an impediment to settlement. Monetary savings through early resolution is an incentive towards settlement.

2.   Attorneys' fees are less of a factor at the front end of the litigation process. The claimed attorneys' fees themselves may become an additional obstruction to resolution. Lawyers may be more willing to discount or re-adjust their fees earlier in the litigation.

---

31. Eric Galton, Representing Clients in Mediation 7 (1994).

32. *Id.* at 6–7.

3. Court dockets don't always move as quickly as we may hope. A party may have a specific, objective need for an early resolution.

It is not easy to identify the earliest optimum moment for entering mediation. You are ready when you know enough about the dispute to engage in a productive mediation session. That point is usually after you have completed enough discovery to adequately, but not necessarily thoroughly, evaluate the merits of the legal case—the best alternative to settlement.[33]

The good news is that a wrong-timing decision will not seriously harm your client's case. If you enter mediation too early, too late, or with an unsuitable case, you are just less likely to settle the entire case. You are still likely to benefit from the mediation cleaning up the case.[34] As suggested earlier, parties can gain a better understanding of their interests, issues can be clarified, some issues might be settled, a discovery schedule may be developed, and what remains to be done to resolve the case will usually be illuminated, if not mapped out.

6. Presenting Mediation Option to Your Client

You can introduce the mediation option to your clients at four different stages of representation:

a.   When Retained

Whenever a client brings a dispute to you, you have an opportunity to educate your client about the various process options for resolving it. One of those options might be mediation. Suggesting mediation does not mean to suggest that mediation makes sense for resolving every dispute. But, you should at least analyze each dispute resolution process with an eye toward "fitting the forum to the fuss."[35]

---

33. For further discussion of discovery in mediations, *see* Chapter 5.12.

34. *See* Cooley, *supra* note 27, at 22–31 (detailed discussion of reasons other than complete settlement for using mediation).

35. *See* Sander, *supra* note 15, at 49 (develops a method for selecting ADR options based on an understanding of client objectives and the impediments to settlement). *See also*, H. Abramson, *A Primer on Resolving Disputes: Lessons From Alternative Dispute Resolution*, 64 NYS Bar J. 48 (1992) (develops method for selecting options based on an understanding of issues, interests, and characteristics of dispute).

Review Subsections 3 and 4 on "Disputes Suitable for Mediation," and "Disputes Less Suitable for Mediation."

Your client may initially resist discussing alternatives to a day in court. Your client may have come to your office looking for total vindication in the courtroom and an aggressive attorney to ensure that it happens. When you start talking about the gentler options of settlement, you risk driving your client away. Therefore, you should artfully and gingerly present any alternatives in a way that your client will hear you and can appreciate each of their advantages and risks.

You can first ask your client more about his substantive goals and procedural interests. You then can engage your client in a candid assessment of how these goals and interests can be served by each dispute resolution process including mediation and court. When discussing mediation, you may want to highlight the various benefits of mediation including how mediation might offer greater flexibility in fashioning a settlement at less cost and less stress on personal and business relationships

b.   When Negotiating a Contract

Whenever one of your clients seeks assistance in negotiating a contract, your client can be counseled about whether to include a dispute resolution clause in the contract. Regardless of how well-intended the parties are and how thorough the contract is, something is likely to go wrong after signing the contract. You can present to your client these unpleasant possibilities as well as the options for dealing with them. One of those options may be a clause that requires parties to try mediation before turning to an adjudicatory process. This type of dispute resolution clause can be especially attractive when drafting licensing agreements, setting up closely held corporations, and negotiating joint-venture agreements.

You can present the mediation option as a natural final step in finalizing the contract. You can emphasize the benefits of mediation. You may point out that it is easier to negotiate a mediation clause when everyone is optimistic about the future, getting along with each other, and still in a decision-making mode.

c.   When Case Ripe for Mediation

As a case progresses through the adjudicatory process, you should be alert for spotting when the case may become ripe for mediation. This moment could arise very early such as right after the complaint has been filed but before the answer is served or very late such as the day before the scheduled trial. You, of course, should explain to your client why his case might be suitable and ripe for mediation. Sometimes, you may be compelled to introduce mediation to your client because the judge either "encouraged" you to try mediation or formally referred your case into a court-connected mediation program.

d.   When Finalizing a Settlement Agreement

When you are negotiating settling a dispute, you might consider including in the settlement agreement a dispute resolution clause that contains a mediation provision. The dispute resolution clause would provide a mechanism for resolving any disputes that might arise when implementing the settlement.

In a mediated case, it would be ironic for you to omit a mediation provision in the settlement agreement. As will be described later,[36] it is easy for this sensible idea to get lost in the rush to settle the dispute at the end of a hectic mediation session. Before leaving the mediation session, you could inquire whether the participants would prefer trying to avoid the default dispute resolution process of court by including in the settlement agreement the efficient and cost-effective preliminary step of mediation.

---

36. For more discussion, *see* Chapter 7.2.

7. Checklist: Client Interview

Interview Client
☐ 1. Learn client's substantive and process interests.

☐ 2. Learn substantive and process interests of other side.

☐ 3. Identify possible impediments.
  ☐ a. Relationship conflicts.
  ☐ b. Data conflicts.
  ☐ c. Interest conflicts.
  ☐ d. Structural conflicts.
  ☐ e. Value conflicts.

Assess Case for Mediation
☐ 1. Party's process interests suitable for mediation.

☐ 2. Party's process interests less suitable for mediation.

☐ 3. Suitable case ripe for mediation (sufficient evaluation of legal case).

Consider When and How to Present Mediation Option to Client
☐ 1. When retained.

☐ 2. When negotiating a contract.

☐   3.   When case ripe for mediation.

☐   4.   When finalizing a settlement agreement.

CHAPTER FOUR

NEGOTIATING AN AGREEMENT TO MEDIATE

> Topics in this chapter include:
>
> 1. Procuring Agreement to Mediate
> 2. Negotiating Agreement to Mediate—Selecting Mediator
> 3. Negotiating Agreement to Mediate—Other Provisions
> 4. Selecting the Mediator
> 5. Checklist

After your client agrees to try mediation, you next need to contact the other party's attorney. This step warrants careful thought. You should be prepared to explore why the dispute may be suitable for mediation and to negotiate the details of an agreement to use mediation.

1. Procuring Agreement to Mediate

Attorneys commonly feel reluctant to call other attorneys about using mediation. The very act of calling might imply that you have a weak case. If it was so strong, why are you not pursuing total victory in court? You need a strategy for dealing with this myth. Here are three approaches.

> **CRITICAL JUNCTURE**
>
> *Contacting the Other Attorney*
> *Overcoming the Myth*
>
> 1. Activating Mediation Agreements and Pledges
> 2. Using Third Parties to Procure Agreement
> 3. Persuading Directly the Other Side

a. Activating Mediation Agreements and Pledges

You can circumvent the myth all together if the parties have previously entered into an agreement or pledge to use mediation. You should be so lucky! And, sometimes you are. The parties might have entered into a business contract that contained a provision to use mediation, in which case you can call the other attorney to activate the contractual obligation. Or, you or your client may have signed a "pledge" to explore the use of ADR whenever a dispute arises.[1] Even though the pledge may not be legally binding, you can call the other side to advise them about your practice of routinely observing the pledge, suggest some of the possible benefits of mediation, and ask whether they might be willing to try mediation. If the other side also had signed a pledge, the other side is likely to be receptive to your call and might even feel obliged to try mediation.

b.   Using Third Parties to Procure an Agreement

You also can circumvent the myth by enlisting a neutral, third party to help funnel the case into mediation. You may contact an ADR provider about whether the case is suitable for mediation. The provider, as a neutral facilitator, can call the other attorney and assist both you and the other attorney to assess whether to use mediation. Alternatively, you could seek advice from a judge in a pretrial conference. Then the judge can assist you and the other attorney in assessing the case for mediation or the judge may make the decision for you by referring the case into mediation.

c.   Persuading Directly the Other Side

When you do not have handy one of these triggering options, you can overcome the myth by inviting the other attorney into a discussion of the opportunities in mediation even for the party with a strong case. You can point out that entering into mediation does not obligate her or her client to compromise a strong, sure-win case. Instead, mediation provides an opportunity for her client to educate your client. It also provides an opportunity for the other side to become educated about your views of the legal case, your client's perspective on what happened, and possibilities for settlement that might not be apparent from the narrowly framed legal claims.

---

1. The CPR Institute for Dispute Resolution offers pledges for law firms and companies to sign. In the pledges, a law firm agrees to "discuss with the client the availability of ADR procedures" and a company agrees to "explore" with the other party the use of ADR techniques "before pursuing full-scale litigation." As of June 2003, pledges have been signed by about 1,500 law firms and 4,000 operating companies.

You can suggest other benefits that may become evident after you have learned more about the process interests of the other side and possible impediments to settlement. You should emphasize how those specific interests might be served in a mediation process as well as how mediation might help overcome particular obstacles to settlement.[2] For instance, if it appears that the other party does not want a public airing of the dispute, you should emphasize the confidentiality of the process. If the other attorney wants a forum to show how her client has been wronged, you should emphasize how her client will have an opportunity to convey this in her opening statement at the mediation session. As the clincher, you should remind the other attorney that if her client is unhappy with the direction of the mediation, her client can always walk away; it is a nonbinding process.

You might consider two very different tactics for approaching the other attorney. You could make a forthright pitch, emphasizing the benefits of mediation, including why mediation makes sense in this case, that the process is nonbinding, and that her client has little to lose and much to gain. As an alternative, you could try a less direct approach designed to invite the other attorney into a discussion of alternative pathways for resolving the conflict. Instead of calling to recommend mediation, you call to discuss multiple options including ones suggested by the other attorney. As the discussion unfolds, you can introduce the option of mediation. When the discussion turns to mediation, you can emphasize its various benefits in this case.

2. Negotiating Agreement to Mediate—Selecting Mediator

After agreeing to use mediation or after a court refers your case to mediation, you and the other attorney may need to negotiate the details of an agreement to mediate. A number of specific issues should be resolved in the agreement.[3]

a. Credentials of Mediator

i. Training and Experience

In your agreement, you should give careful attention to the quality of a mediator's training and experience. Just because someone is trained

---

2. *See* Chapter 3.3, "Cases Suitable for Mediation."

3. *See* Sample Agreements to Mediate, which incorporate the suggestions in this chapter, in Appendix G.

as an attorney or judge does not mean the person is qualified to serve as a problem-solving mediator. A former judge, for instance, can successfully advance settlements by bringing to bear her vast experience in evaluating and deciding cases. But, only a person formally trained in problem-solving mediation knows the nuanced structure of the mediation process and the refined techniques of mediators and, as a result, can give participants the full benefits of an authentic problem-solving process.

Mediator candidates may be certified by a governmental agency or serve as a member of a mediation roster administered by a court-connected program or a private provider such as the American Arbitration Association or the CPR Institute for Dispute Resolution. Certification or roster membership provides evidence that the mediator satisfied some minimum training and/or experience requirement. But, membership requirements can vary considerably. Therefore, you should still agree to ask the mediator to provide detailed training and experience information. You also might ask whether the candidate subscribes to a mediator's code of ethics in order to learn about the mediator's personal standards of professional practice.[4]

You will have to probe a little to assess the quality of a candidate's mediation training. You should ask how much training she has taken and who did the training. Mediation training is typically done in small groups and intensive programs of thirty to forty hours. Quality is mostly related to the quality of the trainers because training is highly personalized with intensive hands-on exercises and individualized feedback. Information on quality of training programs can be difficult to acquire by the newcomer although the information is widely known to dispute resolution professionals. You should ask around.

You also will have to delve into the quality of a candidate's mediation experience. You should ask a candidate about the number of mediations per year she has conducted and for attorney references from those cases. Mediation is a skill that can be developed and refined only through

---

4. *See, e.g.*, American Arbitration Association, American Bar Association and Society of Professionals in Dispute Resolution, *Model Standard of Conduct for Mediators* (1995) (contains nine standards including the standard that a mediator shall recognize the principle of self-determination by the parties and the standard that the mediator shall respect parties' expectations regarding confidentiality). For a copy of the Model Standard and other standards, rules, and principles for mediators and ADR (Alternative Dispute Resolution) providers, *see* Appendix M.

experience. It is disturbing that many court-annexed programs use mediators who handle only one to two cases a year. Such a low volume of cases will not give the mediator an opportunity to develop and maintain skills. This is not to say that inexperienced mediators cannot be successful. But, inexperienced mediators will not give participants the full benefits of a problem-solving process, especially in relatively complex disputes.

Finally, you should agree to ask each candidate to describe her approaches to the mediation process in order to assess whether her mix of approaches is likely to meet your client's needs. This subject is considered in detail in the next subsection on "Mediator's Approaches."

DIFFERING VIEWS

Should Mediator Possess Substantive Expertise?

1. Not Necessary
2. Some Expertise
3. Significant Expertise

Recommendation: You are better off with a mediator who has *some* substantive understanding of the dispute. However, you should unambiguously instruct the mediator to not give any substantive opinions, unless both sides specifically request the mediator to do so.

---

ii.   Subject Matter Expertise

Should the mediator possess substantive expertise in the subject matter of the dispute? This is a much debated topic.

Some contend that a trained mediator can mediate any sort of dispute. The mediator does not need to have any substantive expertise. A person who has mastered the mediation skills, so the argument goes, can resolve any type of conflict.

Others believe that process expertise alone is insufficient. Many attorneys in various practice areas prefer a mediator with substantive expertise who can knock some sense into the *other* side. Numerous business attorneys are more confident in a mediator acquainted with the law and the customs and practices of the relevant industry. They believe that the mediator should understand the substantive context of the dispute. In trademark disputes, the mediator should be familiar with trademark law and the role of marks in building a business. In international business disputes, the mediator should understand how documentary transactions operate. This same line of reasoning has been adopted by many matrimonial attorneys who prefer mediators who understand family dynamics and are familiar with laws regulating custody, visitation, and the splitting of assets. Many negligence attorneys think mediations are much more efficient when mediators understand how much juries are likely to assess particular injuries.

However, if you prefer a problem-solving process, you should guard against selecting someone with too much substantive expertise who might slip into an evaluative mode. The more substantive expertise possessed by the mediator, the more likely the person will develop strong views of the merits and indirectly, if not directly, convey those views, thereby transforming a facilitative, problem-solving process into an evaluative, quasi-adjudicatory one.[5] As will be pointed out in the next section, if you think the mediator will offer a substantive opinion, you also are bound to modify your representation strategy. Rather than engage primarily in problem-solving, you will likely posture and make partisan arguments aimed at securing a favorable opinion. As a safeguard, you should agree to instruct the mediator to not give any evaluations unless so requested by the parties.

iii.   Neutrality and Personal Traits

The candidate should be neutral, that is the mediator should have no close connections with the parties, attorneys, or dispute. The mediator should be asked to conduct a conflicts check in order to guard against any apparent or actual conflicts of interest.

The candidate should possess certain critical personal traits. The mediator should be intelligent, articulate, and creative. The person should have a record of great personal integrity and professional credibility. And, the mediator should be known for her patience and persistency because problem-solving mediations succeed in great part due to the mediator's quiet, even-tempered perseverance.

---

5. As a mediator, I have found that my substantive knowledge of a dispute has helped me understand what was really at stake in the dispute and to more credibly communicate with the participants. However, whenever I have had considerable expertise and experience, I have been surprised by how much discipline it took to hide my opinions, especially when it was vividly clear to me who had the stronger legal claims.

b.   Mediator's Approaches

```
┌─────────────────────────────────────────────────────┐
│               ■ CRITICAL JUNCTURE ■                  │
│                                                       │
│        What Is the Optimum Mix of Approaches          │
│                  by the Mediator?                     │
│                                                       │
│   How Manage Process: Conduct a Facilitative,         │
│   Evaluative, or Transformative Process?              │
│                                                       │
│   How View Problem: Define Problem Broadly or         │
│   Narrowly?                                            │
│                                                       │
│   How Involve Clients: Participate Restrictively or Actively? │
│                                                       │
│   How Use Caucuses: Employ Caucuses Selectively,      │
│   Extensively, or Not at All?                         │
└─────────────────────────────────────────────────────┘
```

Mediators do not use a uniform approach to the mediation process even though they may be influenced by similar professional standards.[6] Mediators follow different approaches shaped by their professional philosophy, training, experiences, and personality. Mediators' approaches tend to fall within four distinct subject areas that you should consider when selecting a mediator: (1) How Manages Process: Do you prefer a mediator who emphasizes facilitating the sessions, providing evaluations, or cultivating a transformative process? (2) How Views Problem: Do you prefer a mediator who approaches the presenting problem narrowly or broadly? (3) How Involves Clients: Do you prefer a mediator who limits or encourages active client participation in the sessions? (4) How Uses Caucuses. Do you prefer a mediator who employs caucuses selectively, extensively, or not at all?

Your choices are important because they impact on what you can expect from the mediator during the sessions and how you should represent your client.[7] But, how do you determine which mix of approaches best serve your client? If you prefer a problem-solving process, you will usually want a *facilitative* mediator who views *problems broadly*, welcomes *client participation*, and either does *not use caucuses* or *uses only limited caucusing*. This ideal mix may need to be occasionally modified based on what you learned during your client interview about your client's interests, interests of the other side, and possible impediments to settlement. This section presents the reasons for this preferred mix, as well as some of the considerations that might warrant changing the mix.

---

6. *See* Chapter 2.2 where mediator's professional standards are discussed.

7. *See* Chapter 5.1(e), "Strategy: Take Advantage of Mediator's Mix of Approachs."

Selecting a mediator with your preferred mix can be difficult to accomplish in practice. Many mediators do not wear these labels on their lapel or print them in their resumes. When they do advertise their approaches, they do not always follow them strictly. They may lack the depth or commitment to stick to their advertised approaches especially when the mediation becomes arduous. Others represent with pride that they mediate with flexibility, switching from problem-solving to evaluation based on whatever the moment calls for. But the facility to switch is not the same as being flexible; it can really be a decision to give up problem-solving, possibly prematurely. Therefore, you should investigate the credentials of candidates, including talking with other attorneys who have had experience with the candidates. Unfortunately, you still are likely to find it difficult to know whether you selected the right mediator until you see the mediator at work in your case.

i.   How Manage Process: Facilitative, Evaluative, or Transformative[8]

In a problem-solving process, you should select a facilitative mediator,[9] not an evaluative one. The facilitative mediator should possess both the training and experience of a skilled and disciplined neutral who is committed to a problem-solving approach. Only then can you confidently develop a representational strategy that may realize the creative settlement potential of mediation.

The drawback of selecting a transformative mediator is that you cannot rely on the mediator to engage in initiatives to create or maintain a problem-solving process. You can only count on the mediator to support a problem-solving process structured and implemented by you, your client, and the other side.

The practices of facilitative mediators can be gleaned from the heated debate over whether mediators should facilitate, evaluate, or use a hybrid approach. Fortunately, you do not need to take sides because if you are electing a problem-solving process, there should be little debate: you ought to select a facilitative mediator. This section defines facilitation and compares it with evaluation, describes the advantages and drawbacks of each approach, and explains how to secure an evaluation

---

8. For a definition of transformative mediation, *see* Chapter 2.2 on mediators' approaches.

9. *See* Ch. 2.6, "Advancing Problem-Solving Approach in Mediations."

when you need one. It ends by warning you that because facilitation is practiced imperfectly, you need a representation strategy in which you actively ensure that your mediator follows a predominately facilitative approach.

Definition: Facilitation and Evaluation

In order to appreciate what is at stake in the debate as well as to understand what facilitative mediators do, you should first review the differences between facilitation and evaluation. The central distinguishing feature is how the neutral helps each side evaluate the merits of the legal case, the consequences of failing to settle, and any settlement proposals.

Facilitation: A facilitative mediator creates an environment in which parties work together collaboratively as problem-solvers. The mediator uses techniques that place full responsibility for resolving the dispute on the shoulders of the participants. She gives special attention to improving the rapport and communications between the parties. She assists the attorneys and parties in identifying both sides' interests, in generating options for settlement, and in shaping their own creative solutions. The mediator helps the parties conduct an evaluation, if an evaluation would be useful, using techniques consistent with the facilitative approach. The neutral poses evenhanded, probing questions to the participants such as inquiring why a settlement proposal is attractive or unappealing. She also may introduce the use of decision-tree analysis by asking participants to formulate the branches and to suggest the key data for analysis.[10] But, the neutral will *not* give her opinion regarding the merits of the legal dispute, the consequences of failing to settle, or the benefits of any particular settlement proposal.

Evaluation: The mediator assists the participants in breaking impasses by offering her views of the situation. For instance, if each side has strongly conflicting views of the legal merits, the neutral might try to break the impasse by giving her evaluation of the legal case. By predicting the likely outcome in the adjudicatory forum, the neutral gives the participants a basis against which to assess the attractiveness of emerging options for settlement. If parties seem ready to give up trying to settle, the neutral might suggest how failure would impact on the interests of each party. If each side has strongly conflicting views of the benefits of a

---

10. For a full explanation of decision trees, *see* Appendix A.

particular settlement proposal, the neutral might give her assessment of how the proposal might benefit each side. The neutral might even present her own settlement proposal (sometimes known as the "mediator's proposal.") When presenting these assessments, the mediator might do so gently as something for the participants to consider or aggressively as something that they should adopt.

As stressed in the subsection below on "Warning: Guard Against Imperfect Practices," a mediator who engages in evaluation is no longer engaging in a predominately facilitative, problem-solving approach to the mediation process. The neutral is engaging in a mixed approach or a predominately evaluative one.

Advantages and Drawbacks of Each Approach

Facilitation

The advantage of facilitation untarnished by the prospect of the mediator giving an evaluation is that it can create a collaborative, problem-solving process.

The single biggest drawback of facilitation is that you will not get an on-the-spot assessment from the mediator if you need one to break an impasse. This limitation can be a serious drawback when the need for an evaluation becomes apparent during a mediation session and you must delay the session in order to negotiate an alternative way of securing the evaluation. (See below on "Securing an Evaluation.")

Evaluation

A mediator's evaluation can be valuable for breaking impasses that are due to uncertain or clashing views of what might happen in the adjudicatory forum, the consequences of not settling, or the reasonableness of particular settlement proposals. If parties could agree on the likely adjudicatory outcome in a dispute in which legal rights are critical, they could probably settle their own dispute with little difficulty or at least avoid one daunting obstacle. If the parties could agree about the consequences of not settling or the reasonableness of a particular settlement proposal, the dispute would likely settle quickly.

When parties and/or attorneys cannot agree due to misjudgments or selective bias, these errors can be corrected by a credible evaluation. It can be especially useful for the attorney who is encountering difficulties in educating her client about the reasonableness of a proposal or the weaknesses of her case.

A mediator's evaluation offers other benefits. The process of securing the evaluation can satisfy a client's need for a "day-in-court." The psychological equivalent can be experienced by a client participating in a process of presenting arguments, discussing the case, and receiving a reasoned decision. Furthermore, the decision can lift the client's burden of sorting out what she can live with. The decision also can be used to justify settlement terms with outside parties such as supervisors and constituencies. And, these benefits can be achieved expeditiously with little additional costs when the neutral who is facilitating gives the evaluation.

The drawbacks are considerable because they will corrupt the problem-solving process and subvert your representation.

First and foremost, an evaluative process impacts on how you would represent your client. If you expect the mediator to evaluate the legal case and you consider the evaluation vital, you will be torn between two conflicting representational strategies: one appropriate for a problem-solving process and one appropriate for securing a favorable assessment. To secure a favorable assessment, you will be under pressure to resort to familiar adversarial strategies of presenting the strongest case possible without candidly admitting any material weaknesses while disparaging the other side's case. You also may be reluctant to appear open to any compromises because of your fear that the evaluative mediator might interpret any compromises as conceding a weak legal case. These conventional adversarial strategies can impair your problem-solving representation.

Second, when each side must shift into adversarial roles, the resulting advocacy strategies can restrict the participation of clients and "inhibit collaboration and creativity."[11] The focus on "winning" a favorable evaluation can enmesh the participants in strategies that re-relegate clients to passive roles in which they no longer participate directly and fully in resolving their own dispute. This preoccupation with winning can divert the participants from a process of full exploration of all issues, settlement obstacles, and settlement possibilities to a process limited to

---

11. Kovach & Love, *Mapping Mediation: The Risks of Riskin's Grid*, 3 HARV. NEG. L.R. 71, 98–101, 103–104 (1998).

assessing legal rights. This narrow focus can lead participants to miss opportunities to solve the entire dispute.[12] This focus on "winning" may leave little energy and space for participants to develop inventive options and inventive solutions.

Third, when the mediator announces an evaluation, the mediator appears to have taken sides, engendering suspicion about her continued neutrality, especially in the minds of the side that views the evaluation as unfavorable. The side harmed by the evaluation may begin doubting the good faith motives of the mediator's initiatives. That side may distrust the purpose of any hard questioning about weaknesses in the legal case and of any suggestions on how to proceed. They may become reluctant to share sensitive information or thoughts. These changes can all happen because of the concern that the mediator is no longer neutral; she now needs to bolster her negative evaluation.

Fourth, the prospect of an evaluation can stifle the bargaining process. When one side thinks it may be vindicated with an evaluation, that side may soften their commitment to negotiating a solution. They may keep negotiating, but only half-heartedly.

Fifth, the mediator selected primarily as an expert in dispute resolution may not posses the in-depth expertise to give a convincing opinion. The resulting opinion may cloud the settlement process by becoming the subject of debate instead of illuminating a pathway out of the dispute.

Securing an Evaluation

What can you do if the parties need an independent evaluation of the legal case or of particular settlement proposals? You have two options that will preserve the integrity and viability of the problem-solving process.

In the optimal option, you would not use the mediator to provide an evaluation. Instead, you would negotiate an agreement with the other side for the parties to retain an independent neutral with deep substantive expertise. This option ensures that you and the other participants receive a high quality and credible evaluation while giving you the

---

12. "Evaluation, in other words, often 'solves' the wrong problem and by doing so, obscures serious, hidden causes of impasse." D. Golann & M. Aaron, *Using Evaluation in Mediations*, DISP. RESOL. J. 26, 29 (Spring 1997).

confidence to proceed with a consistent representational plan appropriate for a facilitative process.

In a second and less optimal option, you would agree that any evaluations by the mediator would not be given until the end of the mediation and would only be given when the participants specifically consent. Any evaluation would usually be restricted to evaluating any emerging settlement proposals and only occasionally might cover the merits of the legal case.

This option for evaluating proposals can work because you would have engaged in a representation strategy in the mediation that was *mostly* consistent with a process that also results in the mediator evaluating proposals. You would have made representation decisions suitable for a facilitated discussion of which settlement proposals best meet your client's interests. But, you would not have made all the representation decisions appropriate for an evaluation because you would not have been advocating for a favorable evaluation of the emerging proposals.

In contrast, your representation decisions would have been inconsistent with a process that produces a legal evaluation. You would have purposely avoided advocating assertively and fully your client's legal positions. The process would not have developed a "full record" on which the mediator could base a convincing evaluation.

Nevertheless, even under these unfavorable circumstances, there still may be tolerable occasions when you would want to consent to an evaluation of the legal case.[13] You may sometimes feel that you have amply presented your legal points and gained enough confidence in the mediator to permit the mediator to offer a reputable legal evaluation at a propitious, final moment to spur an "end-of-the-day" settlement.

Warning: Guard Against Imperfect Practices

The pure form of facilitation is easily corrupted in practice. Many mediators experience difficulties trying to maintain a pristine facilitative approach. And, this unstable practice can subvert your representation strategy.

---

13. *See* Kovach, *supra* note 11, at 109; Golann, *supra* note 12, at 33.

The facilitative approach can evolve over a continuum of five practices that starts with predominately facilitative and moves toward the sixth practice of evaluation. (See chart.)[14]

Facilitative

1. Predominantly Facilitative (with essential evaluation)

↓

2. Slippage

↓

3. Inconsistent Practices

↓

4. Flexible Practices

↓

5. Request Evaluation (switch roles)

↓

6. Predominantly Evaluative

Evaluative

---

14. *See* L. Riskin, *Understanding Mediators' Orientations, Strategies, and Techniques: A Grid for the Perplexed*, 1 Harv. Neg. L.R. 7, 23–24 (1996) (introduces a grid to map two basic mediators' orientations: facilitative-evaluative continuum and continuum based on a broad-narrow view of problem).

In 2003, Professor Riskin modified his renowned grid, renamed it his "New Old Grid," and replaced the facilitative-evaluative continuum with a directive/elicitive continuum. He views directive mediators as ones that tend to direct parties toward something or away from it. In contrast, elicitive mediators tend to draw out information, the direction of the mediation, etc, from the parties.

Professor Riskin also created a new grid that he calls his "New New Grid" in which he shifts the focus away from mediators' approaches to a focus on how mediators and lawyers along with their clients influence the way the mediation process will work. For example, the point where the mediator will operate along the directive-elicitive continuum results from a sort of struggle or negotiation between the mediator and the attorneys/clients. The New New Grid captures one of the key premises of this book—that attorneys and their clients can influence how the mediation process will work. This book coaches attorneys and parties on how to select a suitable mediator and to advocate in a way that fosters the kind of mediation process they want. In the Riskin scheme, this book suggests how attorneys and clients can be sophisticated and knowledgeable influencers of how the mediation process will work. *See* Riskin, *Decision-Making in Mediation: The New Old Grid and the New New Grid System*, __Notre Dame L.R.__ (2003) and *Who Decides What? Rethinking the Grid of Mediator Orientations, Disp. Resol. Mag. 22* (Winter 2003).

This continuum prevails for six reasons.

1. Predominately Facilitative [with essential evaluation]

It is extremely difficult for a mediator to maintain a purely facilitative approach because even a dedicated facilitative mediator will likely engage in some essential "evaluative" activities.[15] This happens because the mediator must continuously evaluate what is happening in the unfolding mediation and make numerous judgments regarding how to move the mediation forward. These evaluative activities might include:

Reframing components of the conversation so that parties can hear them without reacting defensively; structuring the bargaining agenda to maximize the opportunity for successful collaboration between the parties; probing assessments and positions to ensure that a party properly understands and considers counterassessments and positions; challenging proposals that might derail the negotiation or that seem unrealistic or suboptimal; urging parties to obtain additional resources and information; and sometimes making suggestions about possibilities for resolution in order to stimulate the parties to generate options.[16]

Therefore, many facilitative mediators can be more accurately described as "predominately facilitative."[17]

2. Slippage

The predominately facilitative mediator may *slip* into a classically evaluative mode in the heat of the mediation when trying to bring the mediation to closure. For instance, when the monetary difference is small, the mediator might suggest splitting the difference—a move that entails evaluating the situation and recommending a solution. Or, the mediator might prod a party to accept an emerging settlement by stressing the less favorable outcome of returning to court. Depending on your vantage point, these evaluative moves may be welcomed or objectionable. If you agree with the mediator's assessment, the evaluation appears brilliant! It may be the decisive move that brings the mediation to closure. If you disagree, you are likely to think that the mediator breached your agreement to not evaluate. You will be disadvantaged because your client will

---

15. *See* Kovach, *supra* note 11, at 103–104 (Some evaluative activities are "essential parts of a mediator's *facilitative* role").

16. *Id.* at 79–80.

17. *See* Riskin, *supra* note 14, at 24–26, 35–36.

be burdened with an assessment that was formed without the benefit of your zealous arguments and your strategically advanced anchoring.

3. Inconsistent Practices

Many mediators in practice may not conform to their advertised predominate orientation. They may not have had sufficient training and experience to know how to perform swiftly and consistently in response to the myriad of things that can happen in fast-moving sessions. They may hastily resort to an ad hoc mixture of facilitative and evaluative techniques.[18]

4. Flexible Practices

Some mediators may go one step further and avoid labels. Instead, they present themselves as flexible mediators. They will use whatever techniques they see as necessary to resolve the dispute.[19]

5. Request Evaluation [switch roles]

Some mediators may be asked by the participants to give an evaluation. The evaluation may be requested to overcome an impasse that arose as the mediation unfolded. Because the mediator is already present and familiar with the dispute, the mediator becomes a convenient candidate to give the evaluation. The mediator may have been selected with the prospect of an evaluation or the participants may spontaneously decide to request the neutral to switch roles and give an evaluation.

6. Predominately Evaluative

Some mediators are predominately evaluative.[20] That is, the mediators structure a process in which the participants present their case to the mediator and the mediator evaluates the legal case or settlement proposals. The mediator might even present her own detailed settlement proposal, known as a "mediator's proposal." This predominately evaluative approach has been more accurately described as "neutral evaluation" instead of mediation.

---

18. *Id.* at 35–38.

19. *Id.* at 36.

20. K. Feinberg, *Mediation—A Preferred Method of Dispute Resolution*, 16 Pepperdine L.R. S5, S12–S20 (1989) (Feinberg mediates by first hearing all sides, then preparing a written settlement recommendation for adoption, and finally shuttling between the parties in order "to convince the parties to minimize their differences with respect to it [the mediator's recommendations]").

The imperfect practices reflected in the second through fifth points on the continuum present a dilemma for you when planning an effective and coherent representation strategy. They mean you may not be able to count on your mediator maintaining a relatively stable approach throughout the sessions.

If the mediator's approach shifts during the sessions and crosses the "great divide"[21] from primarily facilitation to primarily evaluation, the settlement process would cross the divide from a process of problem-solving to a process that resembles nonbinding arbitration. If you expect the mediator's approach might change, you may want to adjust your representation strategy. But, adjusting your representation strategy can subvert your problem-solving goal. It is very difficult to maintain a consistent problem-solving approach while anticipating the risk of your mediator crossing the great divide. If you try to blend representation strategies, you are likely to jeopardize your problem-solving approach by pitching partisan legal arguments and withholding information in anticipation of the mediator switching roles to evaluate.

To guard against the risk of imperfect practices, you should conscientiously select a predominately facilitative mediator. Be sure to avoid picking one who presents herself as flexible or predominately evaluative. Then, you should be prepared to interrupt the mediator if you see her slipping or acting inconsistently, and proactively intervene to dissuade your mediator from changing roles.

ii.   How View Problem: Narrowly or Broadly

Whether you want to select a mediator who approaches the problem narrowly or broadly depends on the needs of your client.

A mediator may approach a dispute at one or more of four "levels" of problem definition according to Professor Leonard Riskin.[22] At Level I-Litigation Issues, the neutral focuses narrowly on the legal case, its strengths and weaknesses, and what would likely happen in the adjudicatory forum. At Level II-"Business" Interests, the neutral broadens the focus to consider interests that an adjudicatory resolution could not satisfy but are important to the participants. A resolution that involves restructuring a business relationship is the classic example.

---

21. *See* Kovach, *supra* note 11, at 106–108.

22. *See* Riskin, *supra* note 14, at 18–23.

At Level III-Personal/Professional/Relational Issues, the neutral invites parties to consider more personal issues and interests. As Professor Riskin points out, "mediation participants often must address the relational and emotional aspects of their interactions in order to pave the way for settlement of the narrower economic issues."[23] At Level IV-Community Interests, the neutral reaches for a broad "array of interests, including those of communities or entities that are not parties to the immediate dispute."

If you take a broad problem-solving approach, then you will want a mediator who has the skills to bring to the surface more than the presenting legal claims. You should choose a mediator who can assist your client in uncovering Level II business interests and Level III personal, professional, and relational interests. However, if you prefer that the mediation be limited to resolving the legal claim because the conflict is indisputably limited to money between parties who have no previous relationship and no interest in a future one, such as a personal injury suit between a driver and a pedestrian, then you should select a neutral who knows how to approach the problem narrowly as a Level I litigation issue.

iii. How Involve Clients: Restrictively or Actively

You usually will want to select a mediator who encourages not limits, client participation in the mediation sessions.

In chapter 5, I not only recommend that clients be present but that they also participate actively in a problem-solving process.[24] You will want to select a mediator who knows how to constructively and actively involve your client and the other client in the mediation sessions while respecting your attorney-client relationship. If you are convinced that your client should not participate or should participate only restrictively, then you should select a neutral who knows how to conduct mediations through attorneys.

---

23. *Id.* at 20 (Addressing these personal and relational problems can be useful regardless whether the dispute is resolved. This can be useful in order to promote moral growth and "transformation" as suggested by Professors Bush and Folger in their widely read book THE PROMISE OF MEDIATION: RESPONDING TO CONFLICT THROUGH EMPOWERMENT AND RECOGNITION (1994)).

24. The reasons are developed in Chapter 5.5(b) on "Should the Client be Present and Active?" ; Chapter 5.6 on "Splitting Responsibilities Between Attorney and Client," and Chapter 5.10 on "Begin to Prepare Opening Statements."

iv.   How to Use Caucuses: Primarily, Selectively, or Not at All

You usually will prefer to select a mediator who uses caucuses selectively or not at all.

A caucus is simply a private, confidential meeting between the mediator and one side. It provides an opportunity for you and your client to discuss matters with the mediator in the absence of the other side. The three approaches to caucusing are explored later.[25] For a problem-solving process, caucuses should be limited to specific purposes that cannot be accomplished in a joint session. You might even consider mediating without any caucusing. By limiting or avoiding caucusing, you will maximize the interaction and opportunity for collaboration between the parties. But, if you think that the hostility between the parties is so intense that you do not dare put them in the same room, then you may prefer a mediator who uses caucuses extensively.

c.   Single or Co-Mediators

Should you agree to select a single mediator or two mediators to co-mediate? While you will usually select a single mediator because it is less costly and easier, you may find it beneficial to choose two mediators in complex cases, multi-party cases, and cases involving ethnic, gender, or cross-cultural differences. In these types of cases, you may find it advantageous to select two mediators with complementary expertise or experiences who can work together as a team. For example, you may find it helpful to select one mediator with deep process expertise and another with deep substantive expertise. The downsides of co-mediation, however, are several: You may have difficulties agreeing on a second mediator; you face the risk that they cannot work together smoothly; the cost of the mediation is obviously higher when you retain a second mediator; and scheduling sessions can be more difficult when you have to work around the schedule of a second mediator.

d.   Paying the Mediator

You should resolve the arrangement for paying the mediator. Although usual practice is splitting the costs evenly among the parties, this practice should not and is not blindly followed. Sometimes it is fairer for the party with obviously greater resources to pay a greater percentage

---

25. *See* Chapter 5 .11, "Consider When to Caucus."

of the costs. Or, the person requesting the mediation may offer to pay a greater percentage in response to the cost objections of the other side. But, the mediator should not be advised of the allocation formula in order to avoid compromising her appearance of impartiality.

e.   Procedure for Selecting the Mediator

You should be especially clear about the procedures for selecting the mediator. You can choose from a number of procedural options. Each side could nominate several mediators and then negotiate over which one to select. Both sides could choose from a roster maintained by a highly reputable organization. The rules of a dispute resolution organization could be adopted. In one such procedure, each side ranks the top five candidates from one to five and then the candidate with the lowest total is selected. The court could assign the mediator, subject to veto for cause by either side. Regardless of the option selected, you may want to include a provision that if the parties fail to select a mediator within a certain timetable, the mediator will be selected by a named dispute resolution organization.

A number of mediation-seasoned attorneys, who are savvy, favor asking the other side to recommend a highly credentialed mediator whom the other side respects and trusts. Then, they readily agree to that person unless there is some glaring reason for vetoing the choice such as a lack of solid mediation training or blatant bias. This procedure increases the likelihood of a successful mediation because the other side will feel more bound to the process and consequently be more likely to participate diligently. Seasoned attorneys can feel secure deferring because they are experienced in mediation advocacy and realize that they can always walk away from this nonbinding process.

3.   Negotiating Agreement to Mediate—Other Provisions

a.   Appropriate Client Representatives[26]

You should be sure that the other attorney agrees to bring to the mediation session her key clients, the ones with substantial and flexible settlement authority as well as meaningful knowledge of the underlying dispute.

---

26. For a fuller discussion, *see* Ch. 5.5, "Resolve Who Should Attend the Mediation Sessions."

b. Sufficient Discovery[27]

You should discuss what discovery, if any, must be completed before the parties can participate productively in the mediation session.

c. Adequate Confidentiality[28]

You should routinely include a confidentiality provision in which the participants agree that whatever happens in the mediation sessions will be held in confidence and not be admissible in any adjudicatory proceedings. In a court-referred mediation, the court rules may provide for some confidentiality protection

d. Standstill Agreement

You should consider whether you need a standstill agreement for any pending proceedings for the period you are in mediation.

e. Location and Language

You may want to resolve where the mediation sessions will be held, especially in a dispute where parties are located at great distance from each other. In a court-annexed mediation, the courthouse can be a convenient, neutral option. In a mediation in which multiple sessions are expected, the site could be alternated between the offices of each attorney or party.

If the parties do not have in common the same first language, you will want to select the language in which the mediation will be conducted and decide whether interpreters may be necessary and who will pay for them.

f. Default Rules and Administering the Mediation[29]

You should consider incorporating by reference a set of mediation rules designed and tested by a reputable dispute resolution organization. The tested rules can be invaluable for filling in any gaps that you and

---

27. For a fuller discussion, *see* Ch 5.12, "Consider Need for Discovery and Motions."

28. For a fuller discussion, *see* Ch. 5.13, "Consider Level of Confidentiality that You Need."

29. *See* Appendix H and I for the mediation rules offered by the American Arbitration Association and the CPR Institute of Dispute Resolution; Appendix F for selected list of administering organizations and other dispute resolution rules; and Appendix G for sample clauses that incorporate private mediation rules.

the other side fail to address when negotiating the mediation agreement or fail to resolve when drafting the agreement or implementing it at the time of the dispute. For instance, if you and the other attorney omit inserting a confidentiality provision or are unable to agree on a mediator, the default rules will rescue both sides by furnishing a confidentiality rule or mandating a mediator selection method.

You also might consider whether to select the mediator or an experienced ADR provider to administer the mediation. While the administration of mediations is simpler than for arbitrations, there are a number of details that are unavoidable, details that multiply as the number of parties in the dispute increases.

You will need someone to handle such administrative details as scheduling the sessions (time and date), sending out notices, billing for mediation services, and arranging a location, preferably a neutral one, for the mediation session. These sorts of details can be handled by the attorneys, the mediator, or an experienced ADR administering organization.

You also need someone to handle the process of selecting the mediator, a process that includes giving you both access to a roster of trained mediators and help in selecting a mediator suitable for your client's dispute, plus someone to manage the process of selecting, challenging, and replacing the mediator. This mediation appointment process can be handled between the attorneys or by an experienced ADR provider who may either administer the entire mediation or serve as an appointing authority limited to administering the mediator selection.[30]

When deciding whether to rely on the attorneys and the mediator or to pay a separate fee to a professional organization, you should weigh the possible savings against the convenience of one-stop service. Attorneys who participate routinely in mediations or are first-time users can find it expedient and efficient to pay a trusted organization to handle the mediation administration. First-time users can especially welcome a guide through the somewhat unfamiliar territory of setting up a mediation and selecting a mediator. If you conclude that you prefer relying on an ADR provider to administer the entire mediation or just the mediator appointment process, you will want to resolve with the other side what specific provider to name in the agreement to mediate.

---

30. For example, the CPR Institute of Dispute Resolution serves only as an appointing authority and does not fully administer mediations.

4. Selecting the Mediator

After the agreement to mediate has been signed, you will next follow the agreed-upon procedures for selecting a mediator. When selecting the mediator, you will need to investigate each candidate's credentials, mix of approaches, references, and potential conflicts of interests to be sure that you select a suitably qualified mediator.

5. Checklist: Negotiating Agreement to Mediate

Procure Agreement to Mediate: Options
☐ 1. Activate mediation agreements and pledges.

☐ 2. Use third parties to procure agreement.

☐ 3. Persuade other side.

Negotiate Agreement to Mediate[31]
Checklist of provisions
    1. Selecting a mediator.
        a. Credentials.
            ☐ Training.
            ☐ Experience.
            ☐ Subject Matter Expertise.
            ☐ Conflicts Check.
            ☐ Personal Traits.

        b. Mediator's approaches.
            ☐ Predominately facilitative mediator.
            ☐ Need an evaluation.
            ☐ Broad or narrow view of problem.
            ☐ Active or limited client participation.
            ☐ Caucuses—none, selective, primarily.

---

31. *See*, Sample Agreements to Mediate, that incorporate the suggestions in this chapter, in Appendix G.

❐　c.　Single or co-mediators.

❐　d.　Arrangement for paying the mediator.

❐　e.　Procedure for selecting the mediator.

2.　Other provisions.

❐　a.　Best client representatives.

❐　b.　Discovery before first session.

❐　c.　Adequate confidentiality.

❐　d.　Need standstill agreement.

❐　e.　Location of sessions.

❐　f.　Language of sessions.

❐　g.　Default rules.

❐　h.　Administering organization.

❐ 3. Select a mediator, in accordance with agreed upon procedures.

CHAPTER FIVE
PREPARING YOUR CASE FOR MEDIATION

Topics in this chapter include:

1. Prepare a Mediation Representation Plan
2. Prepare a Representation Plan for a Cross-Cultural Mediation
3. Select the Mediator and Study the Mediation Rules
4. Prepare for Pre-Mediation Contacts with the Mediator
5. Resolve Who Should Attend the Mediation Sessions
6. Divide Responsibilities between Attorney and Client
7. Select Your Primary Audience in the Mediation
8. Research Legal Case—the Public BATNA
9. Prepare Presentation of Your Legal Case
10. Prepare Preliminarily the Opening Statements
11. Consider When to Caucus
12. Consider Need to Gather Information and File Motions
13. Consider Level of Confidentiality that You Need
14. Consider How to Abide by Conduct Rules
15. Consider What to Bring to the Mediation Session
16. Checklist for Preparing Case and Mediation Representation Plan

Success in mediation is inextricably dependent on devoting the time and effort necessary to prepare properly and thoroughly for the mediation session. This chapter canvasses what needs to be done. (And, much needs to be done which is why this chapter is the longest one in the book.) Before meeting with your client, you should develop a full-fledged representation plan, gather essential information, and prepare to discuss several vital matters with your client. The subjects of this chapter are intertwined with the subjects of the next chapter on preparing your client for the first mediation session.

The consequences of inadequate preparation are clear and inevitable: You will prolong the mediation and increase the risk of failure. At a minimum, you will compel the mediator to spend considerable time "educating" you and your client on how to participate productively. For instance, if your client arrives wedded to the extreme positions in his pleadings and is unrealistically optimistic about his success in court, the mediator will have much work to do. The mediator will spend time shifting the discussion from your client's positions to his interests and helping your client more accurately assess the benefits and risks of going to court. If your client arrives without considering why the case has not yet settled, the mediator will spend time assisting your client in diagnosing the obstacles to settlement and ways to overcome them. This "education" may require multiple sessions. And the education may not fully succeed, resulting in the mediation failing to achieve its potential.

CRITICAL JUNCTURE

Formulate Mediation Representation Plan

1. Negotiation Approach: Creative Problem-Solving
2. Goals: Meet Parties' Interests and Overcome Impediments
3. Strategy: Take Advantage of Mediator's Presence (The Mediator's Mix of Approaches, Specialized Techniques, and Process Control)
4. Where Implement: At Each Key Juncture in the Mediation Process

---

1. Prepare a Mediation Representation Plan

Your single most important representational task is to craft a reasoned, tailored plan. Your mediation representation plan will govern what you and your client will do throughout the mediation process. It addresses the type of mediator you will need and what information you should put in your briefing paper. It includes what you will want to accomplish in the pre-mediation conference, what you and your client will say in opening statements, and how you and your client will participate in joint sessions and caucuses.

Your representation plan should be developed with your client, as explained in the next chapter on preparing your client.

You should try to prepare the representation plan in writing although you may not always find it practical to do so, especially for modest cases. At a minimum, you should use the checklist at the end of this chapter as a handy guide to help you think through your plan for mediation representation. The checklist also can serve as the outline for a written plan and the relevant sections of the plan can serve as the outline for preparing any pre-mediation submissions and opening statements.

a.   Overview of Plan

Your representation plan, based on the mediation representation for-mula,[1] consists of your plan for negotiating, using the *creative problem-solving approach*, to meet the *interests* of your client and to overcome any *impediments* by taking advantage of the *ways the mediator might contrib-ute to resolving the dispute* at *key junctures* in the mediation process.

b.   Negotiation Approach: Creative Problem-Solving

Your representation plan is propelled by the way you and your client negotiate. Remember, mediation is simply a continuation of the nego-tiation process.

Under the *Getting to Yes*[2] division of the world into adversarial (po-sitional) and problem-solving (principled) approaches to negotiations, each approach will produce a different representation plan. The two basic approaches were amplified in detail in chapter 1. Each approach points to a different way for developing settlement proposals and reach-ing an agreement.

In the classically adversarial (positional) approach, you commence the opening offer strategy and negotiation dance by taking firm, extreme positions in the briefing paper and focusing your opening statements on justifying your positions as the just and correct result. You know full well that your initial positions are unrealistic, presented only as an opening gambit. In the briefing paper, opening statements, joint sessions, and caucuses, you "spin" the mediator, hide the bottom line, use threats and a few tricks, and relentlessly delay any major concessions or compromises until the rapidly approaching "at the end of the day" deadline.

In a variation of the classic adversarial approach, you view the media-tion session as an opportunity to frighten the other party into settling.[4] The mediation session is not seen as an opportunity for collaboration or even compromise. Instead of offering an olive branch, you offer a well-orchestrated adversarial presentation of the merits of the case and

---

1. *See* Section 2 of the Introduction Chapter.

2. ROGER FISHER ET AL., GETTING TO YES (2d ed. 1991).

3. *See* Chapter 2, which examines in detail the differences between the adversarial and problem-solving approaches.

4. For a discussion of various competitive games, *see* CHARLES B. CRAVER, EFFECTIVE LEGAL NEGOTIATION AND SETTLEMENT 181–224 (3d ed. 1997).

a dramatic preview of what will happen to the other party if he dares to show up in court. You focus your entire participation, starting with the briefing paper and opening statements, on trying to demonstrate that you will win in court and that this mediation offers a less costly and painful way out of this misery.

In stark contrast, this book presents the problem-solving prescription. You will recall the general definition of creative problem-solving in the introductory chapter.

As a problem-solver that is creative, you do more than just try to settle the dispute. You creatively search for solutions that go beyond the traditional ones based on rights, obligations, and precedent. Rather than settling for win-lose outcomes, you search for solutions that can benefit both sides. To creatively problem-solve in mediation, you develop a collaborative relationship with the other side and the mediator, and participate throughout the mediation process in a way that is likely to result in solutions that are enduring as well as inventive. Solutions are likely to be enduring because both sides work together to fashion nuanced solutions that each side fully understands, can live with, and knows how to implement. Solutions are likely to be inventive because you advocate your client's interests instead of legal positions; use suitable techniques for overcoming impediments; search expansively for multiple options; and evaluate and package options imaginatively to meet the various interests of all parties. And solutions are likely to be found because you advocated as a creative problem-solver.

The problem-solving approach can be translated into a mediation representation plan by first selecting a mediator who knows how to conduct a problem-solving process. Then, you use the pre-mediation conference and the briefing paper to introduce a discussion of both parties' interests, prospects for creating more value (expanding the pie), and settlement ideas that are not limited to what a court might do. These topics are further expanded in opening statements and given primary attention in joint sessions. You come prepared to suggest fair standards or neutral procedures for resolving any distributive conflicts, including objective criteria for sharing any expanded value.[5] Throughout the process, you work with the other side, trying to preserve a continuing

---

5. For example, a conflict that arises over the value of real property can be resolved by using objective criteria. The parties could jointly agree to hire two real estate appraisers to appraise the property and then agree to use an average of the two appraisals.

relationship. Out of this interest-based discussion, you, your client, and the other side collaborate to develop creative and sensible settlement proposals and solutions.

c.   Goal: Meet Parties' Interests

You want to be sure that your representation plan specifically advances your client's interests while responding to the other side's interests.[6] If your client wants to develop a creative, global resolution, for instance, you should advance this goal throughout the mediation process. You should select a mediator who is skilled in searching for inventive, broad solutions, begin inviting these types of solutions in your briefing paper, raise this interest in the pre-mediation conference, and follow through in opening statements, joint sessions, and caucuses. A detailed example of how to prepare a representation plan that advances interests is offered in subsection (i).

d.   Goal: Overcome Impediments

Your representation plan should confront the reasons that the dispute is not settling. If there was no impediment, then presumably there would be no dispute. Under the Moore approach,[7] you identify the cause, classify the impediment, and develop a suitable intervention plan that takes advantage of the presence of a mediator.

In legal disputes, you are likely to encounter three types of obstacles. You may be hampered by a *relationship conflict* in which the parties are unable to communicate effectively with each other. You may be impeded by a *data conflict* in which each side is wedded to clashing views of what might happen in court, the public BATNA. Or, you may be hindered by a *structural conflict* in which the interests of a client and his attorney conflict, known as the principal-agent problem.

Several examples of representation plans to overcome impediments are supplied in subsection (h).

---

6. For a full discussion of role of interests and ways to identify them, *see* Chapter 1.3(a)(ii), "Critical Juncture (Box) -Identify Interests" ; Chapter 3.2, "Client Interviewing Techniques" ; and Chapter 3.3, "Disputes Suitable for Mediation."

7. The Moore method for diagnosing impediments was examined in detail in Chapter 3.2 on "Client Interviewing Techniques." For additional intervention techniques, *see* Chapter 8, "Breaking Impasses with Alternatives to Mediation (ATM)."

e.   Strategy: Take Advantage of Mediator's Mix of Approaches

Your representation plan should take advantage of your mediator's mix of approaches. You will recall that a mediator's approaches are influenced by the mediator's professional standards and vary within four subject areas:[8] how he manages the process (facilitative, evaluative, or transformative); how he defines the problem (narrowly or broadly); how he involves clients (limited or actively); and how he uses caucuses (extensively, limited, or not at all). At this point in your mediation representation, presumably you have either picked a mediator who follows your preferred mix of problem-solving approaches or have researched the approaches of the assigned mediator.

This section will show generally how your mediator's mix of approaches influences your representation plan. For an example of a comprehensive plan, see subsection (i).

i.   Facilitative, Evaluative, or Transformative

Whether your neutral is predominately facilitative or predominately evaluative will impact on your representation plan.[9] If your neutral will predominately facilitate settlements, you should feel confident engaging in a collaborative, problem-solving representation strategy. If your neutral will predominately evaluate, however, you may prefer a more conventional adversarial strategy that is more suited to securing a favorable assessment. If your neutral's approach will be a mix of facilitation and evaluation, your representational strategy will likely become a fragile hybrid in which you will make compromises that risk diluting the full benefits of the mediation process. For example, you may be inclined to withhold information that could be useful in a facilitative mediation in order to increase the likelihood of the neutral rendering a favorable evaluation.

If the mediator in your case is trained in transformative mediation,[10] you will need to adjust your representation plan to account for this different approach to mediation. Instead of promoting settlement for the parties, the transformative mediator will support the parties' own

---

8. *See* Chapter 4.2(b), "Mediator's Approaches."

9. *Id.*

10. For definitions and sources, *see* Chapter 2.2, "Mediators and Their Approaches."

opportunities for perspective-taking, deliberation, and decision-making regarding matters the parties themselves choose to explore. This may or may not include settlement. As a result, you and your client will have the flexibility and responsibility to shape a problem-solving process for yourselves. Although the mediator will not shape the process for you, the mediator will support opportunities for positive interactions between you and the other party in mediation. For example, instead of developing a representation plan that relies on the mediator to initiate impasse-breaking strategies, you and your client can introduce these strategies yourselves. The mediator will facilitate your communication with the other side in ways that help both sides more clearly understand the impasse and the initiatives you are taking to overcome it.

ii.   Narrow or Broad View of Problem

Your representation plan will be effected by how narrowly or broadly your mediator approaches the problem in the dispute.[11] If the mediator will focus on Level I litigation issues, you should come prepared to engage primarily in a realistic assessment of the legal issues and to creatively solve the presenting legal problem. If the mediator will consider a broader definition of the dispute, as is typically done in classic problem-solving mediations, you should be prepared to explore creative ways to satisfy Level II business interests and Level III personal, professional, and relational interests.

iii.   Limited or Active Client Participation

Your mediator's approach to client participation[12] will impact on how you should represent your client. If your mediator invites wide client participation, you should prepare your client to talk about the dispute, to explain his interests, and to answer the type of questions that are likely to be posed by the mediator, the other attorney, and the other client. If your mediator plans to restrict your client's participation, you still need to prepare your client for the level of participation that you anticipate. Regardless of your mediator's preferences, you should consider how you want to involve your client. Usually, the more ways you engage your client in a problem-solving endeavor, the more likely your client

---

11. *See* Chapter 4.2(b)(i), "Mediator's Approaches."

12. For a full discussion of role of clients in mediations, *see* Chapter 5.5(b) on "Should Clients be Present and Active?"; Chapter 5.6 on "Divide Responsibilities between You and Your Client"; and Chapter 5.10 on "Prepare Preliminarily the Opening Statements."

will uncover creative solutions. Remember that your client brings to the sessions his intimate knowledge of the problem as well as an insider's view of possible solutions that might work for him.

iv.   Primarily, Selective, or No Caucuses

Your representational plan will be influenced by your mediator's approach to caucusing.[13] If your mediator follows a no caucus approach, you and your client should develop a strategy appropriate for a process in which all communications will take place in the presence of the other side. There will be no opportunity to share information privately with the mediator. If your mediator follows a mostly caucus approach, you and your client should develop a strategy for a process that offers little opportunity to communicate directly with the other side and much opportunity to communicate through a neutral third party who can filter information, convey messages, and serve as a sounding board for proposals. If your mediator follows the preferred approach in this book, a selective caucus one, you and your client should develop a strategy for a process that will give you and your client ample opportunity to communicate directly with the other side as well as ample opportunity to caucus with the mediator to share sensitive information, test risky proposals, or guard against reactive devaluations.[14]

f.   Strategy: Take Advantage of Mediator's Specialized Techniques and Process Control

You should figure out ways to take advantage of your mediator's techniques[15] and control over the mediation process.[16] Mediator's techniques cover the skills for which he received specialized training. They include techniques for improving communications, managing emotions, and assessing the court case. Process control entails the power of the mediator to use the stages of mediation as a tool to guide the parties toward resolution. Although the line between techniques and process control is not always sharp, the two facilities do offer different opportunities that you can plan to enlist.

---

13. For a detailed discussion of caucusing options and how to benefit from the selective approach, *see* Chapter 5.11, "Consider When to Caucus."

14. Reactive devaluation describes the tendency of a party to devalue any proposal presented by the other party.

15. *See* Chapter 2.4 on techniques of mediators.

16. *See* Chapter 2.3 on stages of mediation process.

Here are a few examples of how you might gain access to your mediator's techniques and process control.

You may plan to overcome a relationship conflict by selecting a mediator who welcomes active client participation and knows how to use the early stages of mediation (opening statements and early joint sessions) for venting and mending relationships. Then, you can rely on the mediator's techniques of reframing and active listening to improve communications.

If you are having difficulty getting your client's non-legal issues on the table in the pre-mediation negotiations, you can try again in mediation by using the mediator's control over the stage of formulating an agenda as an opportunity to be sure that your client's issues are included.

You may plan to overcome a data conflict by asking the mediator to allocate time to evaluate the court option, a recognized stage in the mediation process, and then invite the mediator to use his skills to help both sides evaluate the court case.

If you think the impediment is that the other side does not know how to problem-solve, you can enlist the mediator to help convert them.[17]

g.   Implement: At Each Key Junction in Mediation Process

You should implement your plan consistently throughout the mediation process. Your plan should be tailored to take advantage of the opportunities presented at each of six critical junctures in the process. These junctures arise when you are:

1.   selecting your mediator,[18]

2.   preparing your pre-mediation submissions (briefing paper),[19]

3.   participating in a pre-mediation conference,[20]

4.   presenting opening statements,[21]

---

17. *See* Chapter 1.6 on "Advancing Problem-Solving in Mediation," and Chapter 2.4 on "Facilitating the Negotiation of a Problem-Solving Process" in mediations.

18. *See* Chapters 2.3(a), and 4.2.

19. *See* Chapters 2.3(b), and 5.4.

20. *See* Chapters 2.3(c), and 5.4.

21. *See* Chapters 2.3(d), 5.9, and 5.10.

5. participating in joint sessions with the other side and the media-tor,[22]

6. participating in a private caucus with the mediator.[23]

h. Examples—Representation Plans to Overcome Impediments

When developing a representation plan to overcome impediments, you and your client should search for ways to take advantage of your access to a mediator at each of the six key junctions. Each junction offers these generic opportunities:

1. Selecting the Mediator. At this early point in the mediation pro-cess, you can select a suitable mediator with the credibility and skills to deal with the specific obstacles to settlement.

2. Preparing the Briefing Paper. You can alert the mediator of pos-sible reasons for the impasse, the reasons that brought you and your client to mediation.

3. Participating in a Pre-Mediation Conference. Under the guid-ance of the mediator, you can begin discussing possible obstacles with the other attorney.

4. Presenting Opening Statements. At the beginning of the first me-diation session, your side's view of the obstacles can be introduced in the opening statements of either you or your client.

5. Participating in Joint Sessions. Under the guidance of the media-tor, you and your client can engage the other side in a full discus-sion of possible obstacles and ways to overcome them.

6. Meeting in a Caucus with the Mediator. In a private meeting, you and your client can engage in a frank discussion of the obstacles with the mediator without fear of inflaming the other party and escalating the conflict.

---

22. *See* Chapters 2.3(d) and 5.11.

23. *Id.*

It is virtually impossible to catalogue in detail how you should handle each possible obstacle.[24] Each situation presents its own nuances that any cataloguing would miss and, as a result, would mislead. Instead, through the use of three examples, this subsection demonstrates the basic methodology. These problem-solving examples are simple and short, designed to reveal the skeleton of the methodology. With this methodology in mind, you should be able to flesh out the details in your actual cases.

Impediment: Relationship conflict. Your client is very upset with the other party.

1. *Selecting the Mediator.* You select a mediator who is comfortable with and skilled in dealing with emotionally charged cases in which parties cannot communicate with each other and need to discharge built-up anger. Not all mediators know how to manage cases with intense relationship conflicts.

2. *Briefing Paper.* You alert the mediator to any emotional obstacles to settling the case. You might even give your client a chance to begin venting constructively by asking him to draft a section that expresses his feelings about what happened in the dispute.

3. *Pre-Mediation Conference.* You verify with the mediator that your client will have an opportunity to present an opening statement and to talk directly with the other party in the session. You also confirm with the mediator that he is ready to cope with any emotional outbursts and relationship difficulties.

4. *Opening Statements.* When assisting your client in preparing his opening statement, you encourage him to express his feelings directly, without making personal attacks, to the other party.

---

24. In an instructive, partial cataloguing, Galton selects particular settlement obstacles and then suggests possible "mediation advocacy decisions" for dealing with them. *See* ERIC GALTON, REPRESENTING CLIENTS IN MEDIATION 85–97 (1994).

In another cataloguing of strategies, Sternlight demonstrates how an attorney and client can divide up responsibilities in the mediation sessions by taking into account how the attorney or client can each contribute to overcoming the particular barrier to settlement. *See* Jean R. Sternlight, *Lawyers' Representation of Clients in Mediation: Using Economics and Psychology to Structure Advocacy in a Nonadversarial Setting*, 14 OHIO St. J. ON DISP. RES. 269, 357–365 (1999).

5. *Joint Sessions.* You encourage your client to talk directly to the other party, under the guidance of the mediator who will help the parties hear each other and guard against the interaction escalating out of control. You also caution your client to not overreact to any personal attacks that might be made by the other side.

6. *Caucus.* You use the private meeting with the mediator as an opportunity for your client to further vent and to be heard by an empathetic neutral. Your client also can share any inflammatory views and explosive information in the absence of the other party so as to avoid further stressing their relationship.

Impediment: Data conflict. You have a substantially different view of the likely outcome of the legal case than the other attorney.

1. *Selecting the Mediator.* You select a mediator who knows how to facilitate a rigorous evaluation of the legal case. You may want one who has experience using a decision-tree methodology. You should avoid a mediator who gives his own evaluation.

2. *Briefing Paper.* You alert the mediator to the difficulties of settling the case because each side holds such different views of the likely judicial outcome. Then, you succinctly and briefly explain the strengths of your client's case while acknowledging its weaknesses.

3. *Pre-Mediation Conference.* For the first time in the mediation process, you raise this obstacle to settlement with the other attorney in the presence of the mediator who can begin facilitating an evaluation of the court option.

4. *Opening Statements.* You present to the other side a cogent, reasoned, and realistic analysis of the case's merits. If the other side is listening (not a foregone conclusion, by any means), then the other side may begin to understand your perspective. You also should listen attentively to the other side's legal analysis in order to isolate the areas where you disagree.

5. *Joint sessions.* You engage in a specific, reasoned, and realistic discussion of the merits of the case with the other attorney, under the guidance of the mediator who might facilitate the discussion through the use of a decision-tree methodology. Both sides should try to understand the basis for their different assessments

and to narrow their differences in an effort to gain a shared understanding of the merits of the legal case.

6. *Caucus.* You explore in greater detail any weaknesses of your court case for the benefit of your client to be sure that he has a realistic understanding of how attractive it is to return to court.

Impediment: Structural conflict. The other side cannot settle because of a conflict within its organization.

1. *Selecting the Mediator.* You select a mediator with experience dealing with institutional parties.

2. *Briefing Paper.* You alert the mediator to the possibility that the other side may be unable to settle due to a conflict between two departments within its organization. For example, in a trademark infringement lawsuit, the defendant may be unable to settle due to a conflict between the marketing and legal departments. The marketing department may prefer a vague settlement in order to maintain marketing flexibility. The legal department may prefer a specific settlement to guard against any more lawsuits claiming infringement.

3. *Pre-Mediation Conference.* You ask the other attorney whether his client representatives in the mediation session will adequately represent all the interests in the corporation. You indicate that you want to be sure that all organizational constituencies that must approve a settlement are adequately represented in the session.

4. *Opening Statements.* You or your client asks whether the client representative from the other side might be hampered in the mediation by conflicting interests within its organization. And, if this is a risk, you or your client asks what can be done to prevent it from derailing the mediation.

5. *Joint Sessions.* You and your client discuss directly with the other side whether it can ensure that any absent people will not veto the emerging agreement.

6. *Caucus.* You enlist the mediator to mediate any possible internal conflicts within the organization of the other party. It may be less disruptive to the mediation process for you to make this request in a private session in which the other side will not be put on the spot and then possibly react defensively.

i.   Example—Comprehensive Representation Plan

Let me suggest one way to develop a representation plan in a gender discrimination case in which you represent the plaintiff-employee, Ms. Earnest. She claims that the defendant-employer, Cutting Edge Computers, failed to give her a higher pay increase because the company pays women less than men for comparable work and experience.

Ms. Earnest has been working for four years as a computer programmer for Cutting Edge Computers. She claims she has worked long hours, enthusiastically embraced all assignments, and met every deadline. Yet, for the fourth year in a row, she received a smaller pay increase than her three male co-workers in the same department. This year, she only received a 2 percent increase when each of her male co-workers received an 8 percent increase. She claims her co-workers received the higher pay increases because they are men. She said she overheard her supervisor comment that she prefers to give higher pay increases to married men who must support their families than married women who do not need the money. Her co-workers are married with large families while Ms. Earnest is married with no children.

Ms. Earnest has complained a number of times about this unequal treatment to her supervisor who has belittled her complaints, claiming her problems are in her head, not in the way she has been treated. After her fourth year review, she could no longer tolerate this unjust treatment. Even though she enjoys the work, Ms. Earnest submitted her resignation and retained you to sue for damages. In the lawsuit, you are asking for $50,000 to compensate her for lost salary increases and emotional pain and suffering. Cutting Edge's attorney responded by denying any discrimination, claiming that Ms. Earnest is simply not as productive as her co-workers.

After interviewing Ms. Earnest, you learned that she wants to be fairly compensated for her hard work and feels her supervisor did not appreciate her valuable contributions. You also found out that even though your client is reluctant about returning to her old job, she has not said never. You have surmised that Cutting Edge Computers' interests are to avoid bad publicity and to encourage productive employees. You have tentatively concluded that at least two obstacles are impeding a settlement—a relationship conflict between Ms. Earnest and her supervisor and a data conflict about the credentials of the other employees and the basis for pay increases over the last four years.

After doing your legal research, you identified what discovery you need before you can realistically assess the strength of Ms. Earnest's public BATNA. Ms. Earnest also mentioned one private cost of turning to her public BATNA. She cannot afford to wait too long for a judicial resolution because she needs the money now for a down payment on a new home. Therefore, she would be willing to accept significantly less money than her likely outcome in court.

You might prepare the following representation plan, using the checklist at the end of this chapter, to advance your client's interest and overcome impediments at each juncture. Note how the representation plan is driven by problem-solving moves that take advantage of the mediator's approaches, techniques, and process control. The plan assumes that you have completed part 1 of the checklist, "Preparation Before Preparing Representation Plan."

Mediation Representation Plan for Plaintiff, Ms. Earnest
Part 2

Analysis of the Dispute (not legal case)

1. **Goal: Interests to Meet**
    Ms. Earnest
        Fair Compensation
        Recognition for Her Work

    Goal: Interests to Accommodate
    Cutting Edge Computers
        Avoid Bad Publicity
        Encourage Productive Employees

2. **Goal: Impediments to Overcome**
    Relationship Conflict
        Between Ms. Earnest and her Supervisor

    Data Conflicts
        Credentials of Other Employees
        Basis for Each Employee's Pay Increases

3. **Identify Mediator's Possible Contributions to Resolving the Dispute**
    Approaches to Dispute
        Facilitative
        Broad View of Problem
        Active Client Involvement
        Selective Use of Caucuses

    Useful Techniques
        Promoting Communications
        Managing Emotions
        Overcoming Impediments
        Inventing Options

    Control over Mediation Stages
        Venting Stage
        Agenda Formulation Stage
        Overcoming Impediments Stage
        Generating Options Stage

Part 3

The Representation Plan for Six Junctures

(1) **Selecting your Mediator.** You plan to select a mediator with a suitable mix of approaches for helping both sides meet their interests and overcome impediments.

For a problem-solving process, you want a mediator who will *facilitate* an interest-based, value-creating negotiation and view the *problem broadly* as one about employee relations instead of one about a narrow legal dispute. You think this mix of approaches will increase the likelihood of the parties discovering inventive solutions that address your client's interests in fair compensation and recognition in a way that respects Cutting Edge Computer's interest in designing a compensation scheme that motivates employees to be productive. You want a mediator who welcomes *participation by clients* because your client is an articulate person who can sympathetically tell her story. Your client also has expertise to contribute; she knows best what options are possible and best for her. You prefer a mediator that *limits the use of caucuses* because you think that the parties are more likely to overcome the relationship conflict in joint sessions where they would talk directly with each other.

You also want to be sure that the mediator has the skills to help the parties overcome the relationship conflict. Ms. Earnest obviously distrusts her supervisor, blames her for her small pay increases, and is quite angry and upset. You want a mediator who can productively handle such a highly emotional dispute.

(2) **Briefing Paper.** You plan to use the briefing paper to introduce a broad view of the problem as one about how Cutting Edge Computers treats and evaluates its employees. The discrimination claim is the legal basis for getting the company's attention. You will focus on how Ms. Earnest was unfairly treated. Despite her loyalty and dedication, her work was never recognized and appreciated. You will suggest that the dispute over the pay increase is one manifestation of the broader problem of how Ms. Earnest has been treated in regard to a number of matters. As compared with the men in her department, she has been given less challenging assignments, less current software, and less opportunity to earn overtime. You plan to emphasize your client's interests in receiving recognition and fair compensation for her valuable work despite the

fact that she was not given an equal opportunity to demonstrate what she could contribute.

You will probably omit discussing whether she is interested in returning to work at Computer Edge Computers because she is unsure of what she wants to do for now.

You plan to flag for the mediator how his techniques and control of the process might be helpful to the parties. You will request that when he reaches the agenda formulation stage that he ensures that the agenda includes the issue whether the company appreciates Ms. Earnest's contributions. You will invite the mediator to employ his training in helping disputants overcome impediments to help the parties get past a possible relationship conflict between your client and her supervisor and to resolve a data conflict over the pattern of pay increases over four years. You will ask the mediator to use his control of the process to be sure these two potential obstacles are dealt with before moving to the stage of fashioning solutions.

You also will present your client as someone open to creative solutions so that the mediator knows to create a process in which parties brainstorm and search for solutions outside of the legal box.

You want your client, Ms. Earnest, to help draft the section on what happened as a way to help her organize her thoughts, to engage her early in the process, and to begin meeting her needs to vent about what happened. (Do not underestimate the value of engaging an angry client early and productively.)

(3) **Pre-mediation Conference.** You plan a number of ways to take advantage of this first opportunity to meet and discuss the case with the other attorney and the mediator.

You will verify with the mediator that he plans to use your preferred mix of approaches in the mediation session. You want to confirm that he will be facilitative, not evaluative, will approach the problem broadly, will actively involve your client (including welcoming her opening statement), and will conduct most of the mediation in joint sessions.

You especially want to pin down who will be the client representative for Cutting Edge Computers. You want to be sure that a person with sufficient and flexible settlement authority will be present. Before this conference, you will discuss with Ms. Earnest whether she wants her former supervisor present. You will inquire whether she needs a face-to-face exchange with her supervisor before she can move on. But, you realize that the supervisor's presence could be too provocative, making this a difficult and risky judgment call.

You plan to inquire whether the other attorney and mediator are open to viewing the problem broader than a narrow discrimination dispute and whether the other side is receptive to searching for inventive solutions.

You want to emphasize the interests highlighted in your briefing paper as well as raise for preliminary discussion the two possible impediments. In view of the data conflict, you will outline the specific objective information that you want from the personnel files of each person who currently works in the department or did for the past five years. You want to know each person's gender, age, academic credentials, record of prior employment, number of years working in the department, starting salary, annual pay increases, and annual evaluations.

By making this data request in the conference, you intend to involve the mediator in helping you secure this essential data before the first session, data that you need before you can intelligently evaluate the strength of your client's public BATNA.

(4) **Opening Statements.** You plan to invite your client to present an opening statement and to discuss ways to divide what you and your client will say.

You plan to assist your client in preparing a productive opening statement suitable for a problem-solving process. She can tell her story of what happened and how she was treated. She should tell her story sincerely and judiciously so that her statement can be heard by the other side and contribute to airing differences and mending the relationship. She should avoid personally attacking her supervisor although she should share some of the specifics about what she thought happened and how she was treated. For example, she should mention that each time she asked her supervisor for her software to be updated to the same version as her co-workers, she was told it would happen soon but it never did, and, as a result, reduced her level of productivity.

She should indicate what she wants out of the mediation. She seems to want the company to properly recognize her hard work and to fairly compensate her for what she has contributed as a computer programmer.

In your opening statement, you plan to re-acquaint the other side with your views of the legal case and ask that a more in-depth discussion be deferred to later in the session.[25] You will avoid making the traditional partisan legal arguments because you are not looking for an evaluation from the mediator and do not want the legal arguments to trump all else in the mediation.

You will encourage your client to present her opening statement first.

(5) Joint Sessions. You plan to focus your representation on advancing your clients' interests in recognition and fair compensation. You think any settlement, regardless of how elegant or creative it might be, must ultimately pass these two interest tests.

Acutely aware of the stages of mediation, you will support, if not encourage, the mediator to use his control of the mediation stages to be sure that all issues are put on the table during the agenda formulation stage and to be sure the impediments are dealt with before moving toward discussing solutions. You want to ensure that the parties have begun repairing their relationship and that the data you need has been provided and discussed before your client moves into the stage of developing options and fashioning solutions.

In regard to the data issue, you plan to discuss with the other side the information in the personnel files that you requested and were provided by the company. You want to use this data as a basis for discussing whether Ms. Earnest was fairly compensated.

You also will vigilantly guard against the mediator giving any evaluations without your prior approval.

You will encourage your client to participate actively in the joint discussions in which she first tells her story, asks and answers questions, and then contributes to the brainstorming, value creation, and the assessment of options. You plan to ask your client to think in advance about possible solutions that go beyond reinstatement and immediate payment of money to her.

---

25. *See* Section 9 on presenting the legal case and Subsection 10(b) on the tone and content of the opening statements.

(6) Caucus. You plan to do most of the work in joint sessions, limiting any caucuses to specific and narrow purposes.

You might want to request a caucus so that Ms. Earnest can advise the mediator that she is not ready to disclose to the other side whether she wants to return to Cutting Edge Computers—whether to her old position or a new one. She wants to see what happens in the joint sessions before deciding. You prefer sharing this information in caucus because the mediator, who has been trained to handle sensitive issues and confidential information, can provide a safe place for discussing why Ms. Earnest is undecided about returning.

You think Ms. Earnest may be concerned that it will be impossible to continue working under the same supervisor. The mediator might explore with Ms. Earnest whether it is possible to restore a working relationship with the supervisor or whether she would be open to moving to another department under a new supervisor. By sorting through these questions in caucus, you and Ms. Earnest can resolve whether she has an interest in returning to Cutting Edge Computers and how to present the outcome of this essential discussion in the joint session.

You also may want to use a caucus as a safe place for ensuring that Ms. Earnest understands any weaknesses in her legal case. You are concerned that such a discussion in the presence of the other side might embolden them. Your client, assuming she has not been persuaded by your legal advice, may find your answers to the mediator's probing questions more convincing.

2. Prepare a Representation Plan for a Cross-Cultural Mediation[26]

You should consider how your representation plan can anticipate and guard against cross-cultural obstacles. Such obstacles can arise in disputes between parties from different countries or between parties from within the same country but who come from different regions, recently immigrated parties, or different religious, ethnic, or professional groups.

---

26. This section is based on my chapter: *International Dispute Resolution: Cross-Cultural Dimensions and Structuring Appropriate Processes, in* RAU ET AL., PROCESSES OF DISPUTE RESOLUTION: THE ROLE OF LAWYERS Ch. VI (3d ed. 2002). This material is used by permission of Foundation Press.

Cultural obstacles can be handled in the same way as you would deal with any impediment to settlement. Under the Moore approach,[27] you would classify the impediment, and then develop a suitable intervention for overcoming it. Many cultural obstacles can be classified as interest conflicts that arise due to the parties' different cultural upbringings, upbringings that can foster conflicting wants and approaches to the negotiation.

This section defines cultural behavior and offers one specific approach for tracking and bridging cultural gaps. How to incorporate this approach into a representation plan is illustrated at the end of this section.

a. What is Cultural Behavior?

Before developing a strategy for overcoming cultural differences, you should first consider what it means to say that behavior is derived from culture. Cultural differences can be obscure and, as a result, difficult to identify. Professor Geert Hofstede, a Dutch social psychologist and author of renowned studies on culture, offers this definition:[28]

> In social anthropology, 'culture' is a catchword for all those patterns of thinking, feeling, and acting…. Not only those activities supposed to refine the mind are included …, but also the ordinary and menial things in life: greeting, eating, showing or not showing feelings, keeping a certain physical distance from others, making love, or maintaining body hygiene….
>
> Culture… is always a collective phenomenon, because it is at least partly shared with people who live or lived within the same social environment, which is where it was learned. It is the collective programming of the mind which distinguishes the members of one group or category of people from another.
>
> Culture is learned, not inherited. It derives from one's social environment, not from one's genes. Culture should be distinguished from human nature on one side, and from

---

27. The Moore approach to classifying and overcoming impasses are explained in Chs. 3.2(b) and 5.1(d).

28. *See* GEERT HOFSTEDE, CULTURES AND ORGANIZATIONS 4–6 (1997).

an individual's personality on the other, although exactly where the borders lie between human nature and culture, and between culture and personality, is a matter of discussion among social scientists.

Human nature is what all human beings, from the Russian professor to the Australian aborigine, have in common: it represents the universal level in one's mental software. It is inherited with one's genes; within the computer analogy it is the 'operating system' which determines one's physical and basic psychological functioning. The human ability to feel fear, anger, love, joy, sadness, the need to associate with others, to play and exercise oneself, the facility to observe the environment and to talk about it with other humans all belong to this level of mental programming. However, what one does with these feelings, how one expresses fear, joy, observations, and so on, is modified by culture....

The *personality* of an individual, on the other hand, is her/his unique personal set of mental programs which (s)he does not share with any other human being. It is based upon traits which are partly inherited with the individual's unique set of genes and partly learned. 'Learned' means: modified by the influence of collective programming (culture) *as well as* unique personal experiences.

b.   How to Bridge Cultural Gaps?

This section suggests one approach to identifying cultural behavior and differences in negotiations and to bridging any resulting cultural gaps.

Consider this five-step approach. In the first three steps of preparing for a cross-cultural negotiation, you master a cultural conceptual framework, learn about your own cultural upbringing, and investigate the culture(s) of the other side. The next two steps guide you in the negotiation sessions. You view the negotiating behavior of others with an open mind and then develop an intervention strategy for navigating around any obstacles.

These five steps will be demonstrated through the use of a hypothetical. Consider how you, as a U.S. attorney, would react if you were told that the other party, an institutional client, will not be represented by someone with substantial settlement authority. Instead, the other party will be represented by a team of people who will make decisions by consensus. Furthermore, all the team members will not be present in the mediation session. Under these circumstances, you are likely to suspect that the other party is acting in bad faith. The other party appears to be replacing a client with real settlement authority with an unwieldy team of people. How might you proceed?

You might approach the negotiation as follows:

First, you should become familiar with a *conceptual framework* in which cultural behavior can be identified, understood, and examined. The framework can only be grasped when you comprehend the meaning of cultural behavior and how it is different from universal human behavior. Cultural studies have recast cultural behavior into various discrete generic characteristics, including characteristics relevant to conflict resolution.[29]

---

29. *See, e.g.,* GEERT HOFSTEDE, CULTURE'S CONSEQUENCES (Abridged, 1980, 1984); GEERT HOFSTEDE, CULTURES AND ORGANIZATIONS—SOFTWARE OF THE MIND (1997); DEAN ALLEN FOSTER, BARGAINING ACROSS BORDERS—HOW TO NEGOTIATE BUSINESS SUCCESSFULLY ANYWHERE IN THE WORLD 264–272, 273–293 (1992, 1995)(shows how Hofstede's work relates to international negotiations); GLEN FISHER, INTERNATIONAL NEGOTIATION (1980) (the author served as Dean of the Department of State's Foreign Service Institute's School of Area Studies); GLEN FISHER, MINDSETS—THE ROLE OF CULTURE AND PERCEPTION IN INTERNATIONAL RELATIONS (2d ed. 1997); DONALD W. HENDON ET AL., CROSS-CULTURAL BUSINESS NEGOTIATIONS(1996); GARY P. FERRARO, THE CULTURAL DIMENSION OF INTERNATIONAL BUSINESS (2d ed. 1994); DAVID W. AUGSBURGER, CONFLICT MEDIATION ACROSS CULTURES 8–10, 26–28 (1992); and TERENCE BRAKE ET AL., DOING BUSINESS INTERNATIONALLY—THE GUIDE TO CROSS-CULTURAL SUCCESS 36–37,44–74 (1995).

For articles on the relationship of culture to mediation, *see* Raymond Cohen, *Cultural Aspects of International Mediation,* in RESOLVING INTERNATIONAL CONFLICTS—THE THEORY AND PRACTICE OF MEDIATION, Ch. 5, 107-128 (Jacob Bercovitch ed., 1996) (The author identifies three cross-cultural roles of mediators: the interpreter who bridges intercultural communication gap, a buffer who protects the face of adversaries, and the coordinator who synchronizes dissonant negotiating conventions.); Cynthia A. Savage, *Culture and Mediation: A Red Herring,* 5 AM. U.J.GENDER & LAW 269 (1996) (The author recommends that instead of approaching differences in terms of racial, ethnic, or other single identifying characteristic, negotiators should recognize differences in terms of various value orientations that also can account for individual differences and effects of multiple cultures.); SELMA MYERS & BARBARA FILNER, MEDIATION ACROSS CULTURES 23 (1994) (The author identified five cultural issues that most significantly affect the mediation process: language, assumptions, expectations that others will conform to us, biases against unfamiliar, and values in conflict.); and Paul B. Pederson & Fred E. Jandt, *Culturally Contextual Models for Creative Conflict Management,* and *The Cultural Context of Mediation and Constructive Conflict Management,* in CONSTRUCTIVE CONFLICT MANAGEMENT—ASIA-PACIFIC CASES 3–26, 249–275 (Fred E. Jandt & Paul B. Pederson eds., 1996)(This is an analysis of over 100 case studies of cultural components of mediations in various Asian cultures and substantive settings, including the testing of two models of constructive conflict resolution, one based on high or low context cultures and another based on separating culturally learned expectations of behavior from actual behavior.)

In one widely cited study, the author identified ten cultural character-istics that could affect negotiations, although he recognized that some of them also could be influenced by personality.[30] Each of these cul-tural characteristics presents the potential for an interest conflict under the Moore classification system. As the following list suggests, due to cultural differences, one party may want something that conflicts with what the other party wants, or one party may approach the negotiation in a way that conflicts with the other party's approach:

(1) The negotiating goal of one party may be a contract while the other party's goal may be a relationship. (2) The negotiating attitude of one party may be to look for win/win possibilities while the other party's attitude may be to seek win/lose solutions. (3) One party may prefer a formal personal style of interaction while the other one may prefer an informal style. (4) One party may communicate directly while the other one may communicate indirectly. (5) One party may be highly sensitive to time (e.g. time is money) while the other one may not be (e.g. lax about punctuality). (6) One party may be from a culture that tends to be highly emotional while the other one may be from a culture that tends to be emotionally passive. (7) One party may prefer a general agreement while the other one may want a specific one. (8) One party may approach building an agreement from bottom up while the other party may prefer building an agreement from top to bottom. (9) One party may be from a culture where the authority of a negotiating team resides in a leader while the other one may be from a culture where the negotiating team arrives at decisions by consensus. (10) One party may be a risk taker while the other party may be a risk avoider (differences that can be complementary as well as conflicting).

In the hypothetical, the ninth characteristic on decision-making is implicated: Does the other side's settlement authority reside with a leader or with a team that makes decisions based on consensus? This question can be investigated for the purpose of assessing whether con-flicting approaches to decision-making may present an impediment.

This generic characteristic, as with virtually all cultural characteristics, encompasses a continuum bound at each end with a value-based pole. At one extreme, societies can be found that are hierarchical in which decisions are made by leaders. At the other extreme, societies can be

---

30. Jeswald W. Salacuse, Making Global Deals 58–70 (1991).

found that are collective in which decisions are made by consensus. The actual cultural practice, rarely one extreme or the other, usually leans heavily toward one of the extremities. As practiced in U.S. businesses, for example, decision-making is predominately hierarchical, placing the practice near the leader pole but not at the pole because input and collaboration also are valued.

Second, you should fill in this conceptual framework with a deep understanding of your *own culture or cultures*.[31] You may not be cognizant of the degree to which your own behavior is universal or culturally bound. Yet, it is through this personal lens that you observe and assesses the negotiating behavior of others. Your cultural lens can distort your view of others' behavior. To reduce these cultural distortions, you should learn about your own cultural upbringing so that you can appreciate the extent to which your view of behavior may not necessarily reflect universally practiced behavior. In the hypothetical, you, as a U.S. attorney, should be aware that your view that organizations tend to be hierarchical in which decision-making is centralized in "leaders" is not universal organizational behavior.

Third, you can strengthen your conceptual framework with an understanding of the *culture or cultures of the other negotiator(s)*. You can identify and research the culture(s) of your client, the other attorney, and the other party. Furthermore, you can learn as much as possible about the other negotiators as individuals, about their personalities and ways their negotiating behavior may vary from practices of their culture(s). In the hypothetical, your research might reveal that the other side is from a society in which organizations typically make decisions based on consensus, but the research may reveal little about their individual personalities.

These first three preparatory steps in which you identify potential impediments are relatively easy to complete because they entail collecting mostly accessible information on cultural characteristics and practices. The next two steps, however, are much more challenging because they require you to suspend instinctive judgments and develop

---

31. For studies of American culture, see GARY ALTHEN, AMERICAN WAYS xiii, 4, 8, 9–10, 14, 17, 24–25, 136–137 (1988); EDWARD C. STEWART & MILTON J. BENNETT, AMERICAN CULTURAL PATTERNS—A CROSS-CULTURAL PERSPECTIVE (1991); ALISON R. LANIER, LIVING IN THE U.S.A., Part I (Charles William Gay rev., 5th ed. 1996); DEAN ENGEL, PASSPORT USA (1997); and Foster, supra note 29, at Chs.3–6.

intervention strategies during intense, dynamic, and fast moving negotiation sessions.

Fourth, you should suspend judging key negotiating behavior of the other attorney or party and instead view it with an *open mind*. This requires considerable discipline. It is too easy for an attorney who routinely judges negotiating behavior to prematurely judge it in a cross-cultural negotiation. In the hypothetical, you would withhold judging the other side's decision-making process as evidence of good or bad faith. Instead you would recognize it as key negotiating behavior that could conflict with your preferred approach and produce an impediment.

Fifth and finally, you may need a strategy to *bridge a cultural gap*. In view of your understanding of your own cultural upbringing (step 2) and the upbringing of the other side (step 3),[32] you should be able to recognize a potential interest conflict that you need to overcome.

Interest conflicts can be overcome by negotiating or deferring to the other side's practice. You could negotiate a solution through an interest-based approach, where the interests behind the practices are respected. You also might negotiate a compromise. As an alternative to negotiating over closure of the gap, you may defer to the other side's practice, especially when the other practice is not a deal-breaker or does not implicate core personal values. For instance, you may defer to the other side's formal practices of carefully using titles and avoiding personal questions about family. The gap, however, can be difficult to bridge when the conflicting practices reflect ingrained strategic practices, such as a conflict between problem-solving and haggling.

In the hypothetical, instead of viewing as bad faith the other side's claim that they cannot agree to anything without a consensus among a large number of team members, you might focus on how to respect their need for consensus while still meeting your need for clients with substantial settlement authority. You could negotiate an arrangement in which the other side brings to the negotiation sessions all the people who must concur or at least ensures that the absent people are available by telephone. Then, in the sessions, the consensus approach could be

---

32. When researching the other person's cultural upbringing, you should *not* assume that just because a person was brought up in a clearly identifiable culture, that that person will act in accordance with its cultural norms. You should test possible assumptions under step 5 when trying to bridge any gaps.

respected by giving members of the negotiating team ample time to meet privately as the negotiation progresses.

c. Examples—Mediation Representation Plan to Bridge Cultural Gaps

Example 1: In a successful mediation, you, as a typical U.S. lawyer, might insist on a signed agreement that covers many details and contingencies. However, the other side, a Japanese party and lawyer, may resist elaborating such details, creating an obstacle to drafting the settlement agreement. You, as a culturally sensitive lawyer, might view this difference as one that could be due to conflicting cultural interests. In investigating the impasse, you might realize that your own preference for reducing everything to writing may be due to your own cultural upbringing (step 2). The drafting of comprehensive contracts is taught in U.S. law schools and reinforced in law practice. A Japanese lawyer may have been brought up differently (step 3). Instead of being concerned about the details of the written agreement, the Japanese lawyer may be concerned about the business relationship, leaving for the written agreement a general statement about the relationship.

When developing a strategy for overcoming this impasse in the mediation, you should avoid the instinctive reaction that the other side is trying to evade resolving key issues. Instead, you should view the other side's behavior with an open mind (step 4). From a Japanese cultural perspective, they may not be hesitating; they just may not be interested in the details of the written agreement.

This interest conflict might be investigated in a joint session by each party explaining why the party prefers or is disinclined to put details in writing. You might be able to overcome this obstacle by discussing and respecting the reasons for the different practices and then negotiating a compromise. The clients might seek to cultivate a relationship of trust and enter into a written settlement that covers key obligations but not every conceivable contingency (step 5).

Example 2: Your mediation representation plan would be shaped by your analysis of any potential cultural obstacles uncovered under steps 1–3 on bridging cultural gaps. For example, when preparing for the mediation, you may have learned that in addition to valuing personal relationships over contract details, the other side recognizes and respects hierarchy and rank, and communicates subtlety and indirectly instead of forthrightly and unambiguously.

Under step 5 on bridging cultural gaps (overcoming cultural impasses), this information would influence what you and your client do throughout the mediation process. First, you would want to select a mediator who is sensitive to and capable of mediating disputes between parties with different cultural upbringings. Assuming you decided to bridge any cultural gaps by respecting the differences, you and your client would behave in a culturally sensitive manner in each contact with the other side: when participating in the pre-mediation conference, when presenting opening statements, and when participating in joint sessions. For instance, you and your client would communicate graciously and not brutally bluntly, would be respectful of the ranks and formalities to which the other side is accustomed, and would support cultivating a genuine working relationship. You and your client would interpret the other side's communications though their cultural lens of subtle and indirect methods of communicating. Instead of expecting the other side to flatly say "no" to a proposal, for example, you would look for other clues such as the way the other side delays giving an answer. In a caucus with the mediator, you may enlist his advice and assistance in presenting proposals to the other side in a way that is less likely to be misinterpreted due to their different cultural filter.

3. Select the Mediator and Study the Mediation Rules

If your case was referred by a judge into a court-annexed mediation program, you should examine the court's procedure for selecting mediators. Procedures vary among programs. Under one approach, the administrator may give you access to a mediation roster and invite the two sides to select a mediator. Under another approach, the administrator may assign a mediator and permit you to investigate his credentials and veto the selection for cause such as an interest conflict or unsuitable qualifications. You may then be permitted to replace the mediator with one from the court's roster or possibly a private one whom both sides can agree on. The previous chapter gave you guidance on investigating a mediator's credentials and approaches to mediating.[33]

---

33. *See* Chapter 4.2(a) and (b) on credentials and approaches of mediators.

If you and the other side had decided to use mediation on your own, you would have investigated the credentials of the mediator when you negotiated the mediation agreement and selected the mediator.

Under either selection scenario, you and the other attorney should contact the mediator about two matters. You should inquire whether to submit a pre-mediation submission as discussed in the next subsection and whether a pre-mediation conference will be held to discuss the matters enumerated in the subsection on pre-mediation conferences.

Finally, you should read any applicable state statutes and court rules, giving special attention to any confidentiality rules and rules that might authorize the mediator to report anything to the court.[34]

4. Prepare for Pre-Mediation Contacts with the Mediator

CRITICAL JUNCTURE

*Prepare Pre-Mediation Submissions
and Prepare for Pre-Mediation Conference*

You have two valuable opportunities to launch a productive problem-solving process even before you appear in the first mediation session. You should consider how to use the two pre-session junctures for submitting a briefing paper and participating in a pre-mediation conference for advancing your client's interests and overcoming any impediments. These two pre-session junctures are surprisingly underutilized.

---

a. Prepare Briefing Paper (Pre-Mediation Submissions) (See Sample Briefing Paper in Appendix D.)

The pre-mediation submissions, sometimes known as briefing papers, offer you your first opportunity to begin cultivating a working relationship with your mediator and educating him about your client's interests and what impediments may be impeding the case's resolution.

Before preparing a briefing paper, you should ask the mediator whether he wants one and, if so, what information to include, the maximum number of pages, and whether the briefing paper will be held in confidence or should be sent to the other attorney(s). Practices vary among

---

34. *See* Section 13 on confidentiality.

mediators. Do not prepare any pre-mediation submissions before getting the answers. If you submit a briefing paper without inquiring what the mediator wants, you may end up wasting time preparing two briefing papers—the one you thought the mediator would want and the one the mediator does want.[35]

The type of information that the mediator requests reveals how the mediator plans to use the pre-mediation submissions. Purposes can vary among mediators. When the mediator asks you to summarize legal positions, factual issues, and demands, and requests that you submit copies of pleadings, the mediator probably wants to only become acquainted with the legal case and its status. When the mediator requests you to amplify the legal arguments and submit copies of legal briefs, the mediator may be preparing to evaluate the merits of the legal case. When the mediator inquires about your efforts to settle, why the matter has not settled, and what your client wants that might go beyond conventional judicial solutions, the mediator not only wants to broaden his understanding of the dispute but also may be trying to reorient both sides into a problem-solving mode.

If your mediator does not require a briefing paper, you should inquire whether you can submit one because of the opportunities it offers to launch the problem-solving process. If the mediator does not advise you what to include or does not restrict what you can include, you might consider covering the following information using the following format with the phrases in quotations serving as headings:

"Description of Dispute and Legal Case"

1. "Factual Summary," including a chronology of events, statement of key factual issues in dispute, and your client's view on each issue;

2. "Critical Legal Issues" in dispute, including your client's view on each issue and key cites;

3. "Relief" sought, including a particularized itemization of all damages claimed;

---

35. I have had several cases in which an attorney sends a briefing paper before asking what it should contain. Then, after the attorney receives my letter requesting specific information, the attorney unenthusiastically prepares a second, more suitable briefing paper.

4. "Motions" filed and their status;

5. "Discovery Status," including what still needs to be done to be ready for trial;

"Settlement Analysis"

6. "Interests of Your Client" that you want met in mediation;

7. "Settlement Discussions" including any offers or counteroffers previously made;

8. "Why Not Settled" covers your views on the obstacles to settling this dispute and ways to overcome them;

9. "What Want Out of the Mediation" especially what you want the mediator to do and what inventive settlement concepts that you would like the other side to consider;

"Other Information"

10. "Who Will Attend" the mediation sessions and the title of any client representatives;

11. Attach critical documentary evidence.

In the briefing paper, you should present a balanced view of the facts and legal case, and attach essential documentary evidence. But, do not send every piece of discovery that has been collected in the case unless the mediator so requests. You should limit your attachments to critical evidence such as key contracts and revealing excerpts of depositions and documentary evidence, the sort of information that you will want to present in the mediation to give the other side an understanding of the strengths of your legal case. But, the briefing paper is not similar to a trial brief in which you would present a comprehensive partisan case. Such a strategy would be a waste of time and money because the mediator will not decide the case.

You should keep in mind that when you prepare your briefing paper, you also are preparing for the mediation session. Most of what you do will be recycled. Much of what you include in the briefing paper may be suitable for presenting in your opening statements. The questions that the mediator asks you to answer in the briefing paper are likely to be the same questions that the mediator will pose in the session. When the mediator asks you to briefly summarize your legal position in the briefing paper, for instance, you are being asked to prepare the points that you may want to cover in your opening statements and in your responses to questions about the legal case during the session.

You should prepare the briefing paper with your client. By involving your client, you ensure that your client's specific interests are reflected in the briefing paper, and you convey the message early to your client that he will perform an active, vital role in the mediation process.

b.   Prepare for Pre-Mediation Conference

You should consider what you want to accomplish in a pre-mediation conference. You can use this juncture to advance the problem-solving process. The pre-mediation conference is usually held, if at all, shortly before the first mediation session in a telephone conference call with only the attorneys and mediator. You should consider requesting a conference if the mediator fails to do so.

At the conference, you should determine whether the mediator plans to use a mix of approaches that will foster a problem-solving process and whether the other side knows how to participate in such a process or needs to be educated by the mediator. You also should be sure that the parties or client representatives with sufficient knowledge and flexible settlement authority will be participating in the sessions. In addition, you can confirm the scheduling details. If held early enough, the conference can be used to clarify what the mediator wants included in any pre-session submissions and to resolve what information you need from the other side before the session.

For a fuller discussion of what to do in a pre-mediation conference, read chapter 7.1.

5.   Resolve Who Should Attend the Mediation Sessions

You should not approach lightly the question who should attend the mediation session. The wrong people at the table can derail a mediation. Unfortunately, it is not always obvious who the right people are.

a.   Should Attorneys Be Present?

Attorney practices vary depending on the subject area of the dispute.

Generally, in commercial mediations and mediations involving governmental parties, attorneys should and do participate with their clients in the mediation session. When weighing with your client whether you should participate, you and your client should consider such factors as the complexity of the case, the nature of the factual and legal issues, ability and bargaining power of your client, amount at stake, and attorney costs. In simple cases in which relatively little money is at stake, you and your client may be comfortable with your client appearing alone and limiting your involvement to preparing your client for the session and reviewing any mediated settlement before it is finalized and signed.

In matrimonial cases, clients are strongly encouraged to be represented by attorneys but attorneys usually do not participate in the session, especially if the session is limited to custody and visitation matters.[36]

In community disputes, in contrast, clients are rarely represented by attorneys because the disputes tend to be interpersonal with negligible legal issues. Many community dispute resolution programs even discourage participation by attorneys because of the fear that they will convert an informal, disputant-centered process focused on finding fair solutions into a formal, legalistic one focused on proving legal rights.

CRITICAL JUNCTURE

Client Participation

1. Clients should usually participate actively (subsection 5(b)).
2. The best client representative for an institutional client should be selected (subsection 5(c)).
3. A plan for splitting responsibilities between you and your client in the session should be formulated (subsection 6).

---

b. Should Clients Be Present and Active?[37]

Parties with firsthand knowledge of the dispute and broad flexible settlement authority should participate in any mediation session that

---

36. For a study of the benefits of attorneys participating in sessions, *see* Craig McEwen & Nancy Roger, *Bring the Lawyers into Divorce Mediation*, Disp. Resol. Mag. 8–10 (1994) (In a study of mandated mediation in contested divorce cases, the authors found that in Maine attorneys along with their clients participated actively in the sessions and that the attorneys contributed constructively.)

37. Dwight Golann, Mediating Legal Disputes—Effective Strategies for Lawyers and Mediators § 5.1.3 (1996).

claims to promote problem-solving. Parties should be both present as well as active contributors.

i.   Changing the Traditional Arrangement

There is a widely followed deal between attorneys and their clients. Clients unload their legal problems on their attorneys so that clients can return to do what they do best as businesspeople or whatever they do. Attorneys like this arrangement because then they can do what they do best—deal with legal problems. This division of responsibilities has become a comfortable and tidy arrangement. As a result, clients rarely become deeply involved in the primary forums of resolving disputes. Clients seldom show up in settlement conferences with judges. When they do show up in court, they are limited to serving as a witness or observer.

This long-standing arrangement is a fragile one. Even though clients prefer attorneys to take care of their legal problems, the legal problems still belong to the clients who must live with any negotiated solutions. Even though attorneys prefer to be left alone, attorneys cannot settle cases or make any other significant legal moves without securing approval from their clients. Each partner contributes something different and vital to the resolution of legal disputes: attorneys contribute as experts of the legal process, law, and ways to resolve legal problems; clients contribute as experts on the underlying substantive problem. In contrast with court and judicial settlement conferences, mediation takes full advantage of the different expert abilities of attorneys and their clients by inviting both to participate actively throughout the process.

ii   Benefits of Client Participation

Your client might benefit greatly from the initiatives of the mediator who progressively involves your client in the resolution of his dispute.

The mediator structures a process in which clients interact with each other so that they personally hear each other's views and perspectives. Communication errors are reduced that might otherwise arise when communications travel through multiple people, for example, from your client to you, from you to the other attorney, from the other attorney to the other client. Among other initiatives, the mediator helps your client and the other party clarify each of their goals and interests, and exploits their expert understanding of the underlying problem. The mediator also can expose your client and the other party to a methodical discussion by you and the other attorney of the strengths and weaknesses of the legal case.

By hearing what is being said and participating in the discussions, clients can develop a better understanding of their dispute and, as a result, become acutely appreciative of the possibilities for trade-offs and deeply involved in shaping the settlement terms. By being heard and hearing others, clients can experience the psychological equivalent of a day in court, a form of "hearing" that may be just what they need before they can move forward to resolving their dispute.

c. Who Should Attend on Behalf of an Institutional Client?

i. Ideal Client Representative

You are likely to have trouble identifying the best institutional representative in a large organization because the ideal person might be buried in the bureaucracy and must be capable of doing so much. The person should possess broad settlement authority and a broad understanding of the institution's interests. He should possess knowledge of the dispute but not such intimate involvement that he is unable to be objective. The person should project integrity and respectability and be level-headed and not too emotional. He should possess superior communication skills and come off as a good witness. And, this ideal person should be available to prepare for and participate in one or more days of mediation sessions.[38] For you to find this person, you will need a sophisticated understanding of the internal bureaucratic organization and decision-making process of your corporate or government client.

ii. Key Credential—Settlement Authority

Your client representative must possess broad and flexible settlement authority. The person who partakes in the mediation experience should be the person who decides what settlement terms are acceptable. Otherwise, your client is unlikely to realize the full benefits of mediation. A client representative with inadequate authority will be relegated to the arduous task of summarizing and conveying to the person with settlement authority a full appreciation and nuanced understanding of how the settlement proposal incrementally came together. Hearing a

---

38. In large corporations, the higher the representative is in the corporate ladder, the greater the settlement authority, with the board of directors possessing the broadest authority. For governmental parties, the same principle applies with the governor, president, or even a legislative body possessing the broadest settlement authority. The higher the person is in the hierarchy, the more difficult it usually is to convince the person to attend the mediation sessions.

summary of what happened cannot substitute fully for being there. It is too easy for the absent person to reject the proposed settlement and say try harder.

You should convey clearly to your institutional client the type of settlement authority the client representative should possess. In a case with multiple issues, different issues may call for different types of settlement authority. For example, a damage claim requires money authority while a claim for a trademark infringement calls for someone who can decide acceptable uses of the mark. It is not always clear at the outset what will be the likely settlement terms, making it perilous to determine in advance the necessary settlement authority.

You should carefully verify the settlement authority of your client representative. Unfortunately, your representative may not always candidly admit his limited authority. If your client's lack of authority derails the mediation, your credibility could be impaired for the remainder of your representation in the dispute.

iii.   Next Best Client Representative

Your ideal client representative may not be available. If the ideal representative exists, the person may have too many other responsibilities and commitments and be unwilling to spend time preparing for, traveling to, and participating in the mediation session. In corporations and government, the ideal person may be a group that may be too unwieldy or unwilling to participate in the session. In corporations, the person may consist of the board of directors or a committee within a department or across departments. In government, the person may consist of a legislative body, a committee within the client agency, an intra-agency committee, or two separate government agencies—the agency directly involved with the dispute and the agency responsible for overseeing all governmental expenditures such as the budgetary agency or the comptroller.

Under these circumstances, you need to find the next best client representative. Sometimes, that representative may be a team of two or three key representatives.

The next best client representative must possess unquestionable credibility with the person or group who has the ultimate settlement authority. The next best representative should agree in advance that he will put his personal prestige and integrity behind his endorsement of a settlement agreement when he tries selling it to the person or group with ultimate settlement authority. The person or a delegated representative of the group with ultimate settlement authority should be available by telephone.

iv.   Role of In-house Counsel

Your client representative should usually *not* be an attorney in your client's in-house counsel office. An in-house counsel is likely to contribute more like an attorney than a client. Your client representative should be a person who can bring a client perspective and see the dispute, not as a legal problem, but as a business or policy problem. You may want to weigh making an exception for an in-house counsel who knows the business or government agency well and has considerable experience functioning more like a client than an attorney at the institution.

v.   Convincing Client Representative to Participate

Your ideal or next best client representative may resist participating because the person is consumed by other pressing institutional matters. You should try to convince this reluctant representative of the enormous benefits of personally participating, using the points covered in the previous subsection, 5(b), on why clients should be present and active in the mediation session.

If you cannot get the commitment of even the next best client representative, you should consider whether or not the mediation may be worthwhile and discuss this with your institutional client.

d.   Should Other People Be Present?

It may be essential that your client bring his "advisors" to the mediation session. These advisors can be one or more key people that your client relies on for input. These advisors might offer hard information (fact or expert witnesses), provide psychological and emotional support, or possess unofficial settlement authority. For instance, in a patent case, a party might be unable to assess the strength of an infringement claim without input from a technical advisor during the session. In a discrimination case, a party might be unable to settle without hearing the reactions and suggestions of his spouse and getting her approval. In a case in which a claim is covered by insurance, a party may be unable to agree on the amount of money to pay without approval of the person with the checkbook, a carrier representative. (Because of insurance carrier's focus on money, the representative also may not be interested in the creative solutions that mediation tries to foster.) If one of these key "advisors" is left out of the session, the advisor may derail the settlement by giving advice or even vetoing a settlement based on considerations that are not informed by what happened in the session. Furthermore, the discussions in the session would not have been informed by valuable input from the advisor.

6. Divide Responsibilities Between You and Your Client

You and your client should resolve how to share responsibilities in the mediation session. Four basic arrangements[39] are possible.

a. Options

In the first two options, your client performs the dominant role. This approach is more likely to be practiced in family or community disputes. In the first option, you, as the attorney, would be a "non-participant," limiting your counseling and representation to before and after the session. In the second option, you would participate in the session as a "silent advisor," known at the "potted plant," intervening only when necessary to protect your client's interests.

In the third and fourth options, you, as the attorney, perform an active role. In the third option, the one commonly practiced in business disputes and disputes with government parties, you serve as a "co-participant" with your client. You and your client divide up the responsibilities in the session. In the fourth option, you perform as the "primary or sole participant."

b. Recommendations

Especially in a problem-solving process, you and your client should consider an allocation arrangement in which your client participates actively.[40] To engage your client early in the mediation session, you should consider inviting your client to share in presenting an opening statement.[41] Then, you should look for other opportunities for your client to

---

39. *See* John Murray et al., Processes of Dispute Resolution 370–371 (1996).

40. *See* Chapter 5.5(c) and 5.10(c) and (d) on who should attend the mediation sessions and the role of the client in presenting opening statement.

41. Precisely how responsibilities should be split can vary depending on the particular case. *See*, e.g., Sternlight, supra note 24, at 274, 345–48, 365–66 (suggests that the reasons for the impasse in the negotiations can guide how to split up responsibilities between attorney and client).

contribute throughout the session. You, as the attorney, have other responsibilities in the session: You prepare and protect your client, ensure that any legal matters are intelligently considered, assist your client in assessing settlement options, and help draft a legally sound and enforceable settlement agreement.

In some cases, you or your client may be reluctant about your client participating actively. Your client may not be a skilled speaker. Your client may not speak fluently the language used in the mediation. Your client may be too shy, upset, or angry. Your client may have been emotionally or physically harassed or abused by the other party. Or, your client may be less educated, feel less worldly, or have less bargaining power. Nevertheless, your client should still try to say something in a guarded effort to overcome some of these participation barriers. Your client will still be protected by you who will prepare him for the session and should be sitting next to him during the session.

Consider this advice for how to suitably share responsibilities between you and your client:

> The extent to which mediation can prove useful in bridging economic, psychological, and strategic gaps between attorneys and their own clients is crucially dependent on the roles played by the attorney and client in the mediation. No single lawyer's role is always best in mediation. Rather, the attorney's appropriate role in mediation should vary depending on which barriers seem to be impeding the appropriate settlement of a particular dispute. That is, while the attorney should remain an advocate for his client at all times, he should adjust the manner in which he attempts to further his client's interest depending upon which barriers are preventing the fair settlement of the dispute. For example, given many of the barriers, the attorney should frequently stop himself from dominating the mediation, instead allowing the client to play an active role in the process. In other situations, however, the attorney must be active and assertive to ensure that his client is not coerced by the opposing party or client. The attorney should not himself determine these relative roles, but rather should in most circumstances consult with the client regarding this issue.[42]

---

42. *See id.* at 274.

7. Select Your Primary Audience in the Mediation

> **DIFFERING VIEWS**
>
> *Who is Your Primary Audience?*
>
> 1.   Other Party
> 2.   Other Side
> 3.   Mediator
> 4.   Mediator and Other Side
>
> Recommendations: *Your primary audience should
> be the other party.*

Your primary target in a problem-solving process is clear: It is the other party.[43] The other party has ultimate settlement responsibility, not the other attorney whose role is limited to counseling the other party or the mediator whose role is limited to facilitating the mediation process, not evaluating or deciding the case. The other party will ultimately decide whether to settle and on what specific terms.

You and your client should conscientiously and productively use this unique opportunity to speak personally with the other party. Through face-to-face interactions, you and your client can exchange information more reliably with the other side. You can circumvent the other attorney who may have over-sold the case to his client and would otherwise filter any communications. You can avoid the other attorney failing to accurately convey the nuances of what your client wants his client to hear and the nuances of what his client wants your client to hear.

But, this opportunity can be easily squandered if you do not consider how to communicate in a way that will be heard by a suspicious if not hostile other party. Conventional adversarial presentations and arguments are likely to be counterproductive for an audience that is not a neutral third party who is unaccustomed to hearing partisan presentations and who is not dedicated to listening with an open mind. You and your client must craft presentations for an audience who may not be in the mood for listening.

Some attorneys maintain that the primary audience should be the mediator. The mediator performs the primary role of structuring and

---

43. *See, e.g.*, Stephen P. Younger, *Effective Representation of Corporate Clients in Mediation*, 59 ALB.L.R 951, 958 (1996).

facilitating the process. You want to get the mediator on your side and then enlist him to use his power over the process to prod the other side to move in a direction favorable to your client. Even though the mediator is a professional committed to neutrality, the mediator still can subtly steer the direction of the settlement discussions. For example, if your client seems reasonable while the other side appears stubborn and blinded to the weaknesses in their court case, you can try to nudge the mediator to engage in reality-testing strategies with the other side to be sure that the other side understands and factors in the weaknesses. While the mediator may have this power over the process, he still should be your secondary audience as compared with the other party who has the indisputable authority to accept or reject any emerging settlement agreement.

At least one commentator recommends that clients face the mediator when speaking in order to prevent the clients' interactions escalating the conflict. If your client talks directly to the other party, your client's comments might seem accusatory or demeaning which may arouse and inflame the other party. [44] However, this very real risk can be guarded against by preparing your client to speak and not react and the mediator sensitively managing the exchange between parties.

In addition to the mediator, the other attorney can be an important secondary audience. The other attorney will be counseling the other party so you want to be sure that that advice is informed by your side's presentations. In some cases, you may need to influence the other attorney because he may be the obstacle to settlement. For example, he may prefer litigating the dispute even though his client prefers settling.

8.   Research Legal Case—the Public BATNA

There is nothing unusual about how you research your legal case for mediation. This undertaking is a familiar one for attorneys. You should identify key legal issues and research relevant law. What you learn will obviously impact on what discovery you need to do for gaining a meaningful understanding of your client's legal case.[45]

How you use your research in mediation can be less familiar. The distinctively different way becomes evident when you compare it with the

---

44. *See* JOHN W. COOLEY, MEDIATION ADVOCACY 91–92 (1996).

45. For a fuller discussion of discovery in mediations, *see* Section 12 of this chapter.

way research is used in court and settlement conferences with judges. In court and settlement conferences, you use the research to "win" arguments. In court, you present your strongest, partisan arguments in an effort to convince the judge that your client is legally right and the other side is legally wrong. In settlement conferences, you may either make the same partisan arguments or temper them to maintain credibility in an effort to convince the settlement judge to signal his views of the case. You want the judge to either signal that your side has the stronger case or signal enough uncertainty to motivate both sides to compromise and settle.

In mediation, you use your research differently. Instead of using the research to justify your strongest partisan arguments to a neutral third party, you use the research as the basis for methodically discussing the public BATNA with the other side, the mediator, or both. You use the research to inform your discussion of the strengths and weaknesses of the case, the likely judicial outcome, the probability of it happening, and the legal costs of getting there. The mediator wants to ensure that both sides have a clear understanding of the merits and uncertainties of going to court so that each client can assess accurately when going to court may be less attractive than staying in the mediation.

9.   Prepare the Presentation of Your Legal Case

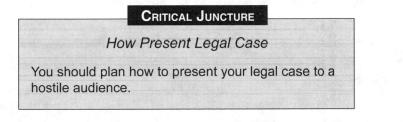

CRITICAL JUNCTURE

How Present Legal Case

You should plan how to present your legal case to a hostile audience.

You should consider *how* and *when* to present your legal case, the public BATNA, in a process that is not an adversarial one.

a.   How to Present It

When you present your legal case in a problem-solving process, you should adopt a different approach than what you customarily do in court or a settlement conference. You should modify the tone, language, content, and emphasis. You need a different approach because you are not trying to convince a neutral audience—a judge; you are trying to influence an averse audience—the other side. A conventional approach can derail the mediation. It might antagonize the other side who would then feel compelled to respond in kind, leading you into a contentious legal debate.

You should give great care to how you present your client's legal case in order to take full advantage of this opportunity to talk directly with the other attorney and his client, under the guidance of a trained neutral. Your case should be presented in a way that it can be heard by a lawyer who thinks he knows more about the legal case than you do and a client who is probably distrustful and antagonistic. Your tone should be humble, sincere, and civil. Your language should be plain, devoid of legal jargon, and understandable to lay people. Your content should be succinct and substantive and should emphasize a realistic and thoughtful assessment of the legal case.

b.   When to Present It

You will have an opportunity to present your legal case in four different settings during the mediation session.

1. You may set forth your legal case when presenting your opening statement. In the next section on opening statements, two approaches are considered—a limited summary or a fuller presentation.

2. You will have an opportunity to discuss the legal case when the mediator poses questions about its strengths and weaknesses. The mediator may explore the case in joint sessions or caucuses.

3. You are likely to feel compelled to present your legal case whenever the other attorney vigorously and pugnaciously argues his client's legal case. You should resist copying the other attorney's tactic. Instead of responding with an equally combative stance, you should respond calmly and confidently (if warranted) about your client's case and ask the mediator whether this is the occasion for a full discussion of the legal case. The mediator will either defer the topic and shift the discussion to another subject or elect to structure an orderly analysis of the legal issues. Your tact should avoid a contentious legal debate while returning management of the process to the mediator.

4. You may want to re-visit the legal case whenever the other side appears too entrenched in their negotiation positions because they are overly confident in securing a judicial victory. You may even

ask the mediator to assist everyone in engaging in an in-depth assessment of the legal case.

10. Prepare Preliminarily the Opening Statements (See Sample Opening Statements in Appendix E.)

> **CRITICAL JUNCTURE**
>
> *Opening Statements*
>
> 1. You should carefully determine the tone and content of the opening statements.
>
> 2. You should figure out how much of an opening statement can be productively presented by your client.

a.   The Challenge

The opening statements of attorneys and clients set the tone for the mediation. Excellent statements can propel the settlement process forward by establishing a positive, problem-solving environment for settlement negotiations. Poor opening statements can set back the settlement process by creating a hostile and distrustful environment. Opening statements must be crafted for an audience that is likely to be not only antagonistic but also personally knowledgeable and protective of its view of the facts and law. If you have little mediation experience, you should aim for the modest goal of doing no harm! As you gain more experience, you should be able to do some good.

Consider the following warnings and advice:

> Permit me to be blunt. With your opening statement, you can do tremendous good for your client, or you can do so much damage that you destroy any chance for a favorable resolution. I have observed exceptional opening statements that have created unbelievable results for the clients. And I have heard opening statements that were so inappropriate and unfortunate that chances for resolution were obliterated with the uttering of those words. In those cases, I have had to spend countless hours in private caucus helping parties get beyond their rage at the words said by opposing counsel. Sometimes, and sadly, it is an impossible task.

* * *

[P]reliminarily, you must analyze how your opening statement at mediation is different from your opening at trial
and understand what your goals in a mediation opening
statement happen to be.

***

What do people who neither like nor trust you do when
you speak to them? The answer is simple—*they do not listen.*
And you need the other party to listen. More than with a
jury who will forgive you (because it is not their dispute),
the other party will seize on any word or phrase you say to
confirm their pre-existing distrust and dislike for you. And
if your words evoke such feelings, you will not persuade
them or even get them to listen.

As a litigator, you do everything possible to get *neutral*
people to like you, listen to you, and be persuaded by you.
Isn't it the ultimate challenge, as the mediation advocate, to
get the other party at least to listen if not be persuaded?[46]

You should keep in mind that opening statements provide you your
first opportunity to set the tone for the mediation session as well as your
only opportunity to present a comprehensive, coherent, and compelling
summary of what is important. There is no opportunity to give closing
statements because as the mediation progresses, the focus moves forward toward clarifying issues and interests, narrowing areas of dispute,
and developing possible solutions. The mediation ends, not with closing statements, but with an impasse or a resolution.

b.   Tone[47]

You should give considerable attention to creating the right tone in
the opening statements. You want to establish a rapport with the other
party, attorney, and mediator, and cultivate a problem-solving atmosphere for resolving the dispute. The statements should be presented
in a way that they can be heard by the other party who is likely to be
sensitive, suspicious, and even hostile. The tone should be different than
what you are accustomed to conveying in an opening statement presented in court or arbitration.

---

46. ERIC GALTON, REPRESENTING CLIENTS IN MEDIATION 75–76 (1994).

47. *See* Cooley, *supra* note 44, at 104–107; Galton, *supra* note 24, at 28–30, 75–80.

The opening statements should convey the commitment of you and your client to be reasonable, to listen, and to keep an open mind in search of a solution that meets the interests of everyone. And, that the two of you are prepared for the mediation and acting in good faith.

You and your client should sincerely thank the other attorney and client for participating in the mediation sessions. The opening statements should be presented with respect and compassion and acknowledge the other party's perspectives. The statements should not sound righteous or vindictive and avoid exaggeration, threats, and personal attacks (especially attacks to the integrity of the other party or attorney). The wording should be in plain language with minimal use of legal jargon. You should find ways to specifically invite the other side to collaborate in devising sensible and inventive solutions. Any highly delicate issues should either be deferred or presented in carefully crafted, non-provocative language.

The opening statements can be made more captivating by presenting key documentary evidence and creatively using audio or visual aids.[48]

c.   Content—the Story, BATNA, and What Want[49]

Based on your representation plan that is designed to advance parties' interests and to overcome impediments, you should begin outlining the opening statements. The content and emphasis in mediations are somewhat different than opening statements in arbitration or court. The content can cover four subjects: the story, the legal case and any other BATNAs, what your client wants out of the mediation, and what you would like the mediator to do.

i.   The Story

The opening statements should cover the story, that is what led up to the dispute. The statements should approach the story broadly, although sometimes a narrow version might be warranted if you prefer to approach the problem narrowly. The statements should present a sympathetic story (the "facts") and if relevant, acknowledge any mistakes and even offer an apology. Although the details need not be constrained by rules of evidence, the credibility of the story will be affected by what can be proven in court.

---

48. *See* Section 15 on what to bring to the mediation session.

49. *See id.*

ii.   The Public and Personal BATNAs

The opening statements should cover the legal case. They also might cover some of your client's personal benefits and costs of litigating and any other attractive personal alternatives to settlement that you want to educate the other side about.

Public BATNA. You may want to say something about the legal case in the opening statement. You may need to recognize this alternative to settlement, the one that provides the context for the mediation. If you skip the legal case all together, the other side might think that your client lacks faith in his court option and as a result has no other viable options but to capitulate to an unfavorable settlement.

Presenting the legal case is by far the most treacherous part of the opening statements. If you make a conventional, trial-oriented opening statement in which legal positions, supporting evidence, and precedent are ardently advocated, you are likely to antagonize the other participants, escalate the dispute, and derail any problem-solving efforts. Therefore, you need to tailor a different, more suitable approach to covering the legal case. Here are two possible options:[50]

In one approach, you treat the legal case as a small part of your opening statement. You summarize briefly your legal positions. In order to avoid the impression that you lack faith in your case, you might explain that "Because we are committed to working together to try to creatively settle this case, we are deferring our detailed discussion of the legal case. Of course, we are ready for that discussion whenever you want to have it." By adopting this approach, the legal arguments are less likely to preempt the discussion of other more productive subjects.

In another approach, you give your legal case greater prominence because you think it has a convincingly high probability of success and therefore should substantially influence the settlement terms. Your client also may need to hear his personal outrage expressed in your vigorous presentation of the legal positions. Even you may need to present the legal case because you have become so vested in your legal work. Only after experiencing this "psychological hearing" can your client (and sometimes even you) move on.

---

50. Obviously, if participants are engaging in positional negotiations, they will use the opening statement to present forcefully their legal case and legal positions.

But, this approach poses the risk that the legal arguments will initially dominate the mediation session, preempting discussion of other ways to resolve the dispute. You should work hard to temper your legal presentation. You might even begin it with a warning that "what my client and I have to say may be provocative to you but it is important for us to air the legal issues that we believe are germane to this case. But, we do not want our discussion of the legal case to prevent us from exploring other creative ways for resolving this dispute."

As part of the legal presentation, you may want to request from the other attorney any additional information that you may need to assess the legal case. For example, you could ask what key cases or what specific language in a statute that the other attorney is relying on.

You also should say something that demonstrates that you are prepared to listen to the other attorney's legal points or that you heard and understood the other attorney's legal position, even though you may not agree with everything said.

Personal BATNA. You or your client might note some of the personal benefits or even costs of litigating that are individual to your client. For example, if your client finds going to court attractive because it may create a precedent that will discourage other plaintiffs from suing, you may want to mention this personal benefit. If you think that the other side also would like to preserve a continuing relationship, you might mention that going to court poses the drawback (personal costs) of possibly destroying the relationship between the parties who seem interested in working together in the future. But, it may be premature or counterproductive to discuss all your client's personal benefits and costs of litigation. You probably do not want to include in the opening statements, for instance, that your client has little tolerance for the personal cost of suffering through the litigation process and risk getting nothing.

Occasionally, your client may have a viable BATNA other than going to court. If so, you should figure out a gentle and tactful way to educate the other side about this other option. You or your client should not be too forceful so that the explanation is not construed as a threat that may drive the other side away. If, for example, the defendant is in dire financial condition, the defendant's alternative to settlement might be filing for bankruptcy. The defendant might raise this alternative to settlement along with some credible supporting evidence. But, if presented so bluntly that it comes across as a threat, the other side may walk out.

iii.   What Your Client Wants Out of the Mediation

The opening statements should express generally what your client wants out of the mediation. This is the moment to set forth your client's interests that might go beyond dealing with the legal issues that your client would like met as well as the moment to sincerely recognize that the other party has legitimate interests that need to be met. Your client also might suggest possible impediments that your client hopes will be overcome in the mediation. But, you and your client should usually avoid presenting any detailed settlement proposals.

You may find it surprising that you should avoid presenting specific proposals, an approach to opening statements that can be frustrating to the other side. The other side may be anxiously waiting for a serious proposal and may be deeply disappointed when none is forthcoming. At this stage, however, references to proposals, especially monetary ones, can be inherently provocative and may trump everything else that is being said and derail efforts to stimulate out-of-the-legal-box thinking in the mediation. Nevertheless, you and your client should come prepared to discuss during the session the damages claimed and how they were computed.

You and your client also might start priming the pump for value-creating ideas, although you should guard against prematurely going into detail. In an employment discrimination case, you might indicate that your employee-client is open to options unavailable in court by suggesting a few possibilities such as promotions and good references, and emphasize that these specific examples should not be viewed as positions or proposals. Then, you might invite a fuller discussion of these and other options in the mediation.

iv.   What You Would Like the Mediator to Do

In your opening statement, you might want to suggest which approaches and techniques of the mediator could be helpful and how he could use his control of the mediation stages to advance the settlement efforts. The mediator might welcome your analysis of how he could be helpful and welcome your flagging these opportunities early in the session. When making these suggestions, you do not want to appear to be telling the mediator how to do his job. For example, if you think that a data conflict is impeding the settlement, you might invite the mediator to help the participants gather the information that they need. If you think the parties are stuck and obstinate, you might inquire whether the mediator could design a process for creative brainstorming. If you think the other side has not fully analyzed the legal case, you might ask the mediator to spend time in the session facilitating a discussion of the legal case. Of course, these suggestions could be deferred until a later opportune moment in the session when the need for these actions arises.

d.   Should Your Client Present an Opening Statement?

When you and your client plan to both participate in the session, you need to resolve whether your client will present an opening statement. In a problem-solving process, your client should usually present an opening statement for the same reasons that your client should appear in the mediation sessions.[51] Presenting an opening statement is the first step to engaging the person with ultimate settlement authority, your client, in the mediation session. When preparing an opening statement, your client begins shifting his role early in the mediation process from a passive one that is customarily encountered in other settlement processes and litigation to a much more participatory one. An opening statement by your client can aid in giving your client the experience of a psychological day in court. This early client involvement should help him become comfortable with the process quicker and therefore ready to resolve the dispute quicker.

An opening statement by your client also can be effective in moving others. Your client is in the best position to talk authoritatively, sincerely, and therefore persuasively about his circumstances. Your client may be able to empathetically connect with the other party due to their shared experience with the dispute.

You or your client may be reluctant about your client presenting an opening statement for the same reasons you may be reluctant about your client participating actively throughout the sessions.[52] Nevertheless,

---

51. *See* Chapter 5(b) on "Should be Client Be Present and Active?"

52. As indicated in Chapter 5.6, you may be reluctant about your client participating for a number of reasons: "Your client may not be a skilled speaker. Your client may not speak fluently the language spoken in the mediation. Your client may be too shy, upset, or angry. Your client may have been emotionally or physically abused or harassed. Or, your client may be intimidated by the other party because your client is less educated, feels less worldly, or has less bargaining power."

your client should still say something even if it is as little as simply introducing himself and briefly indicating his interest in resolving the dispute. Your client's opening statement provides a way to engage your client early in the process. Your client will still be protected by you who will help him prepare his statement and will be sitting next to him in the session.

e. How Should You Divide Opening Statements Between You and Your Client?

Generally, you should encourage your client to cover as much as he is comfortable doing. He can usually tell his story—what happened and how it impacted on him, as well as explain what he wants out of the mediation. As already indicated, your client is in the best position to talk about his own circumstances and needs, and to empathetically recognize the other party's needs. He can even suggest what some of the impediments might be; he could be in a credible position to indicate potential sources of the conflict (e.g., data or relationship conflict). He can say things to prime the pump for creating value and generating new settlement ideas. He may be capable of talking about personal alternatives to a negotiated settlement. However, your client should not cover subjects which he is ill-equipped to discuss such as the law, strength of the legal case, and what is happening in the legal process. You may need to adjust this split based on how secure your client is about speaking and his facility in explaining things.

f. Should You or Your Client Speak First?

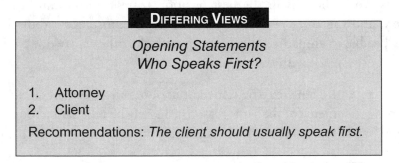

You need to resolve whether you or your client will speak first when you and your client will be presenting opening statements.

Your client should speak first for the same reasons that your client should present an opening statement.[53] This arrangement clearly and further engages your client early in a process that cannot result in settlement without his approval. If your client speaks first, you also are less likely to inadvertently preempt your client's prepared statement, leaving little for your client to say of substance. However, this arrangement increases the risks of your client setting the wrong tone and saying the wrong things at the beginning of the first session. You can reduce these risks by properly preparing your client and guiding him during the opening statements.

Some attorneys still firmly believe that you should speak first and do most of the speaking because your client hired you to speak on his behalf. You are the expert orator who is comfortable with the forum and knows how to sympathetically and skillfully present a case. This circumscribed role for your client increases your control over the tone and content of what is said in the session. But, it runs the risk of chilling your client's early involvement in the session because he may see you as the primary participant instead of a partner in the session.

As a compromise that still keeps your client deeply involved, you might start with a brief statement in which you introduce your client, indicate that your client is participating in good faith, and provide some procedural background that puts your client's presentation in context. Your client then gives his story and describes what he wants out of the mediation. You finish the opening statements by presenting the legal case, suggesting how the mediator can be helpful, and adding any concluding comments.

11. Consider When to Caucus

In preparing for the mediation sessions, you should consider when it will be advantageous to move from a joint session to a caucus and what you want to accomplish in the caucus.[54]

---

53. In a case that I mediated a few years ago, the attorney preferred to speak first because his client was not very confident speaking in English. As a compromise, I encouraged the attorney to help his client prepare a brief written opening statement. The attorney thought it was an idea worth trying. At the mediation, his client read a very brief statement and then his attorney took over. However, after the opening statements, the client got deeply involved in the discussions and the case resolved after a short but critical private meeting between the clients. Whether the case would have resolved without the client speaking, we will never know. But, it clearly did not hurt and probably did help.

54. Joint sessions are when the mediator meets with all the parties and attorneys. Caucuses are when the mediator meets privately with one side.

```
┌─────────────────────────────────────────────────┐
│              ██ DIFFERING VIEWS ██                │
│                                                   │
│                 When to Caucus                    │
│                                                   │
│  Options:                                         │
│                                                   │
│  1.  Not At All                                   │
│  2.  Most of the Time                             │
│  3.  Selectively                                  │
│                                                   │
│  Recommendations: In a problem-solving process,   │
│  you should limit the use of caucuses to serve    │
│  specific, limited purposes.                      │
│                                                   │
└─────────────────────────────────────────────────┘
```

a. Options for Caucusing

Caucusing is a controversial subject that is hotly debated in the field of mediation. Different mediators and advocates are guided in the use of caucusing by different philosophies on how to manage information, maintain neutrality, and move disputing parties.

Some mediators and advocates prefer a *no caucus approach* because they believe the mediator should work with the parties in joint sessions in which the parties share information directly with each other.[55] They mistrust caucuses because of how private meetings with the mediator can taint the neutrality of the mediator. Caucusing also can undermine the opportunity for parties to work together to resolve their own problems because caucusing cuts off vital direct communications and creates undue reliance on the mediator, who is the only person with a full view, for transmitting reactions and information between sides and for fashioning a solution.

At the other extreme, some mediators as well as advocates prefer a *mostly caucus approach* in which the sides meet jointly only at the beginning of the mediation and then again at the end when signing the settlement agreement. You and your client have little opportunity to interact directly with the other side. By primarily using caucuses, the mediator insulates hostile parties from each other and as a result limits the opportunity for the dispute to escalate. The mediator carefully screens and tightly manages the flow of information and the way proposals are framed and presented.

---

55. *See* GARY J. FRIEDMAN, A GUIDE TO DIVORCE MEDIATION, 281–282 (1993).

Two of the leading proponents and practitioners of the no-caucus approach are Jack Himmelstein and Gary Friedman at the Center for Mediation in Law at www.mediationinlaw.org.

Other mediators and advocates prefer a *selective caucus approach* in which most meetings are held in joint sessions in order to promote communications between the parties and preserve the mediator's neutrality. These mediators and advocates limit caucusing to narrow and laser-sharp purposes that they believe can be accomplished only in private meetings. Under this approach, you and your client are able to communicate directly with the other side as well as to meet in caucus with the mediator to share sensitive information, test risky proposals, or guard against reactive devaluation,[56] among other purposes.

b. Recommendations

In a problem-solving process that is designed to promote collaboration, out-of-the-box legal thinking, and creative solutions, you should avoid using the caucus as a crutch. When unsure what to do next, you should not react reflexively with a request to caucus with the mediator. Instead, you should either avoid caucusing or limit caucusing to selective, narrow purposes. Even if you are requested by the mediator to go into a caucus, you should consider whether the mediator is using the caucus as a crutch. If you doubt the value of caucusing at that moment, you should raise this question for discussion with the mediator.

You should limit the use of caucuses to serving specific purposes that cannot be accomplished in a joint session. Here are some purposes that might be best accomplished in a caucus:

1. You or your client may need to *vent privately or share confidential, inflammatory, or damaging information.*

    Extreme venting that might escalate tensions in joint sessions can usually be safely expressed in a caucus. You or your client may need to discharge much built-up anger. Only after experiencing the release from the extreme venting, you or your client may be capable of moving forward in the joint session.

    Confidential, inflammatory, or damaging information may need to be disclosed to the mediator if you want to ensure that he has the information necessary for helping the parties resolve the dispute. If you have a document damaging to your client, for example, you may avoid the risk of the other side exploiting this information by disclosing it only in a caucus. By doing this,

---

56. Reactive devaluation describes the tendency of parties to devalue any proposal presented by the other party.

the mediator will be able to facilitate your assessing whether and when to disclose the information and how to factor it into the negotiations. If you have evidence damaging to the other side, you may want to disclose the evidence to the mediator so the mediator has a full picture of the case. But, you may want to delay disclosing the information to the other side until it is likely to be heard and productively used such as when the parties are exploring their BATNAs in joint sessions.

2.   You may want the mediator to help *clarify your client's interests.*

As the mediation advances and new information and perspectives spew to the surface, your client may become overwhelmed and less sure of what he wants to accomplish in the mediation. You and your client may need to re-visit and clarify the interests that your client wants met in the mediation. You may be more comfortable first clarifying your client's interests in a private meeting with the mediator before sharing a more nuanced understanding of your client's interests with the other side.

3.   You may need a safe place to give a *candid assessment of the legal case.*

In a caucus, you may be more willing to openly explore the strengths and weaknesses of the legal case, the public BATNA, with the mediator and respond more frankly to the mediator's reality-testing questions or questions about quantifying the inputs for a decision-tree analysis.[57] With the absence of the other side, you will be under less pressure to posture as an advocate.

Hearing a candid discussion of the legal case can help your client understand more fully whether or not the court option is more attractive than any emerging settlement proposals. Furthermore, by demonstrating a realistic assessment of the case, including its weaknesses, you protect your client from the mediator suggesting that the in-caucus assessment should be a basis for adjusting any sensible offers already made by your client.

4.   You may welcome *advice from the mediator* on how to package or react to a proposal.

The mediator can counsel you and your client about proposals because the mediator brings to the session his experience as a

---

57. *See* Appendix A on Decision-Tree Plus Analysis.

dispute resolution expert and can acquire during the session an objective feel for what is possible to do in the mediation based on what he learns in joint sessions and caucuses about each side's attitudes, interests, priorities, and bottom line. Therefore, instead of risking derailing the mediation in a joint session, you might first test a daring proposal with the mediator. The mediator may offer his reactions and give advice on how to shape and present the proposal so that it is likely to be heard and even accepted by the other side. You also may want to solicit the mediator's private advice on how to constructively react to a proposal presented by the other side.

5. You may want to present a *serious proposal for the mediator to present hypothetically to the other party* ("What if" proposals—"What would you do if the other side proposed X?").

    You may prefer transmitting proposals through the mediator for two reasons. First, you may want to protect your client from being trapped into bargaining against himself. Your client may be ready to present a bottom line proposal that includes his final concessions so long as it will result in an agreement. By the mediator presenting your client's proposal hypothetically to the other side, the mediator can guard against the other side simultaneously rejecting it and then insisting that your client up the ante with another significant concession. Second, you and your client may want to guard against wasting the final concession by the other party's reactive devaluation of it. Reactive devaluation describes the tendency of a party to devalue any proposal presented by the other side.[58] "If they are willing to present it, then there must be something wrong with it."

6. You may want to convey private suggestions to the mediator when formulating a *mediator's proposal*.

    If the parties request the mediator to present a final settlement proposal, you should try to provide some personal input before the mediator fully formulates and proffers the proposal to each side. A mediator's proposal works briefly as follows: If both sides confidentially accept the proposal, then the proposal is adopted.

---

58. *See* Golaan, *supra* note 37, at Ch.7.2.2; Robert H. Mnookin, *Why Negotiations Fail: An Exploration of Barriers to the Resolution of Conflict*, 8 Ohio St. J. on Disp. Resol. 235, 246–47 (1993).

If one or both sides reject the proposal, then the decisions are not revealed so that if one side did accept the terms, the other side would not know it.[59]

12. Consider Need to Gather Information and File Motions[60]

You need to assess how much of the case should be cleaned up and illuminated before your client can participate meaningfully in the mediation. Your client may not be ready until you clarified or narrowed the dispute by assembling essential information or by asking a judge to decide a focused motion.

a. Information Gathering[61]

i. Assembling Essential Information

You should consider whether any information needs to be collected either informally or through discovery before you and your client are ready to engage in productive negotiations. In mediations, as in any negotiations, you must confront the prospect of settling a case without full information. This prospect runs counter to your U.S. legal training and practice of exhaustive discovery. You need to make an informed but inherently uncertain judgment call: What critical information must you know before you can help your client settle? You need sufficient information to elucidate dispositive facts and to adequately but not necessarily thoroughly evaluate the merits of the legal case. You may be able to gain this information informally from public sources such as the internet or from the other side. Otherwise, you may have to secure this information through formal discovery.

ii. Reducing Discovery Costs

Your client may ask you how to reduce the discovery costs and the time it takes because he wants to minimize his dispute resolution costs and extricate himself quickly from the conflict. First, you should be

---

59. *See* Chapters 2.4 and 7.2(d) where the mediator's proposal is described in detail including the process, opportunities, and risks.

60. *See, e.g.*, Edward F. Sherman, *The Impact of Litigation Strategy of Integrating Alternative Dispute Resolution into the Pretrial Process*, 15 REV. LITIG. 503 (1996)(considers how discovery and motion practice are impacted by the use of ADR processes, including mediation).

61. *See* Cooley, *supra* note 44, at 24–29.

sure that your client understands the benefits and risks of settling before completing discovery.[62] Then, you should consider ways to reduce discovery costs by taking advantage of the opportunities in the mediation process for inexpensively and informally gaining information. As the session progresses, you can ask questions, request data, and gain an in-depth view of the case. When the credibility of the parties weighs heavily in the court outcome, you and the other attorney can observe each other's client in the session instead of testing them in costly depositions. Attorneys with mediation experience commonly declare that they can "learn more in one day of mediation than in six to twelve months of expensive, formal discovery."

You also should consider ways to cost-effectively use formal discovery. You can reduce the costs by agreeing with the other side what documents to exchange, the form and number of discovery devices, deadlines for completing discovery, and the number of specific issues or witnesses that will be subject to discovery. If you and the other attorney are unable to negotiate a truncated and efficient discovery schedule or resolve any disputes over compelling discovery, you can avoid contested motions or ad hoc conferences with the judge by folding these issues into the mediation process. Then, the mediator can help you resolve the issues in a pre-mediation conference or the session.

iii.   Avoiding Discovery Abuses

Some attorneys react to this less costly access to information with alarm, contending that attorneys abuse the mediation process by using it in bad faith as a cheap, easy, and one-sided way to gain discovery for trial instead of using mediation to try settling the dispute. When you consider that it is usually only a matter of time and more expense before the other side gains the discovery, you should be willing to take a chance in the mediation under the guidance of a third-party expert in settling cases, an expert who can foster a reciprocal and fair exchange of information. By providing the discovery in the mediation, you also are likely to increase the chances of settling the case. If it works, your client will be happy or at least relieved. If it does not, then some of the discovery would have been accomplished at less cost to your client.

---

62. For a discussion of the costs and benefits, *see* Chapter 6.4, "Review Needs for Discovery and Risks of Incomplete Discovery,"

b.   Motions

Sometimes, you may consider filing a motion or welcome the other side doing so in order to clean up the case for the mediation. A motion to dismiss or a summary judgment motion can eliminate extraneous aspects of the case such as causes of action that you consider frivolous. Motions also can solidify strong claims that you do not want to compromise or that you want to use as leverage when negotiating in the mediation. Any resulting judicial decisions may guide both sides in assessing the strengths and weaknesses of the most contentious legal issues.

13.   Consider Level of Confidentiality that You Need

Before the first session, you should review the sources of confidentiality that cover the mediation process. You, your client, and the other side may each need assurances that what is said in the mediation will be held in confidence as a condition for participating openly in the mediation session. You want to be sure that these sources will sufficiently protect your client from being haunted outside the mediation by what happens in the mediation.

You ought to give attention to the level of confidentiality because a party may challenge it after the mediation. This might happen if the mediation fails to settle all the issues or a party wants to dispute the mediated settlement agreement or the interpretation of a key provision. The contesting party is usually motivated by the prospect of using advantageous information disclosed in the mediation in the litigation over any unsettled issues or the enforcement of the mediated agreement.

a.   Sources

The typical sources of confidentiality include rules of evidence that protect settlement discussions, statutory or common law mediation privileges, court rules, private mediation rules,[63] and confidentiality agreements.[64] The law on protecting confidentiality in mediations has been developing intermittently and erratically and can vary among the

---

63. *See e.g.,* AAA and CPR Mediation Procedures in Appendices H and I.

64. *See* Golaan, *supra* note 37, at Ch.13.14; NANCY ROGERS & CRAIG A. MCEWEN, MEDIATION—LAW, POLICY, PRACTICE, Ch. 9 (2d ed. 1994).

states and even among the federal courts.[65] Therefore, all these confidentiality sources should be researched to determine the level of protection that you can expect in the jurisdiction of the mediation session as well as the jurisdictions of the likely place of trial and enforcement.

Confidentiality law may gain new vigor and vision from the recent approval of the Uniform Mediation Act (UMA) by the National Conference of Commissioners on Uniform State Laws and the American Bar Association. The publication of the UMA is expected to spur many states into action and shape the content of a new generation of state mediation privilege laws.[66]

Until the law on protecting confidentiality is more fully developed and stable, you will want to sign a private confidentiality agreement. The proposed agreement may incorporate a confidentiality rule found in the private mediation rules of a dispute resolution organization.[67] Remember that the confidentiality agreement is simply a private contract, subject to the traditional legal requirements and defenses as to formation and enforceability of any contract. Typically, the proposed confidentiality agreement is offered by the administering organization, court sponsor, or mediator. The proposed agreement should be studied to be sure it gives your client sufficient protection.

A thorough confidentiality agreement[68] would apply to all discussions done under the auspices of the mediation, all documents produced in the mediation process that are not otherwise independently discoverable, and all observations and notes of the mediator and other participants. The agreement would prohibit using this information as evidence or for

---

65. *See* Weston, *Confidentiality's Constitutionality: The Incursion on Judicial Powers to Regulate Party Conduct in Court-Connected Mediation*, 8 HARV. NEG. L.REV. 29 (2003)(explores the inherent judicial power to monitor, regulate, and sanction participants in court-connected mediation even where participants are protected by a broad statutory privilege); Deason, *Predictable Mediation Confidentiality in the U.S. Federal System*, 17 OHIO ST. J. ON DISP. RESOL. 239 (2002)(concludes that no counsel can predict with confidence the level of confidentiality in mediation that will be upheld by the courts); and Litt, *Note: No Confidence: The Problem of Confidentiality by Local Rule in the ADR Act of 1998*, 78 TEX. L. REV. 1015 (2000).

66. *See* Uniform Mediation Act in Appendix O. For a copy of the Uniform Mediation Act that includes an extensive Prefatory Note and detailed Reporter's Notes and to learn whether your state is considering or has adopted the UMA, *see* www.nccusl.org.

67. *See* Appendices F, H, and I for cites to and examples of private mediation rules.

68. *See* Appendix C—Sample Confidentiality Agreement.

impeachment in pending or future proceedings including judicial, arbitration, and administrative agency proceedings. The agreement might even include provisions to aid enforcement. For instance, the agreement might obligate each signatory to notify other signatories of any effort by a third party to secure the confidential information. It also might provide for liquidated damages to be paid by the breaching party to cover any harm caused to the other party.

b.   No Airtight Protections

A confidentiality agreement does not provide airtight protections. As in any contract, it is only binding on signatories, not other third parties that may try to obtain and use the information. You can reduce this third-person risk by securing the signatures of known, key nonparties—although it can be difficult to convince people who are not participating in the mediation to sign on. Furthermore, courts may not enforce a confidentiality agreement when the need for confidentiality clashes with the need for public disclosure such as the need to report activities that may harm third persons. When a party is a governmental entity, information exchanged may be subject to disclosure under a state or federal freedom of information law. Even if your client has a clear legal protection, enforcement can be problematic. By the time the breach is discovered, it may be too late for an injunction to be helpful and proving damages can be difficult and not always cost-justified. Finally, because confidentiality agreements have been rarely tested in court, judicial attitudes toward enforcing them have not been fully formed.

Even though confidentiality cannot be guaranteed, a confidentiality agreement in mediation will usually be broader than the confidentiality protections secured in alternative settlement forums such as conventional negotiations between attorneys. In conventional negotiations, you can normally only count on the usual rules of evidence that bar admitting information from settlement discussions in any pending court case, and these protective rules contain their own exceptions and minefields.[69]

---

69. For example, Federal Rule of Evidence 408 bars introducing evidence from settlement discussions unless, among other exceptions, the evidence will be used to impeach a witness or might be otherwise discoverable. *See* Appendix O—Federal Rule of Evidence 408. For a discussion of the risks posed by Rule 408 and how to negotiate around them, *see* Michaels, *Rule 408: A Litigation Mine Field*, 19 Litig. 34 (Fall 1992).

Ultimately, you must assess whether the relatively small risk of disclosure to third parties or the likely harm due to disclosure is outweighed by the distinctive opportunities for settlement in mediation.

c. Withholding Information Despite Confidentiality

Regardless of confidentiality protections, you ought to consider whether your client should withhold disclosing any specific information from joint sessions or caucuses. Any information that you hide from the mediation process should be scrupulously selected and narrowly confined because withholding information can diminish the potential benefits of mediation. Nevertheless, you may want your client to withhold some types of information. For instance, you may want to instruct your client to not disclose particular trade secrets, financial projections, propriety business data, damaging evidence, or private conversations between you and your client about the negotiation strategy. You should state clearly to your client what specific information to withhold from the mediation process.

You might consider whether any of this withheld information could be disclosed to the mediator in a caucus. Disclosure would enable the mediator to discuss with you and your client whether the information may be of some help in settling the case and how to use the information while preserving any necessary confidentiality. For instance, you may want to disclose to the mediator evidence damaging to your client's case that is unknown to the other side when your client is resisting a settlement proposal that you think fairly reflects his vulnerability in court. You may want to caucus with the mediator and your client so that the mediator and you can help your client craft a settlement proposal that factors in the litigation risk.

14. Consider How to Abide by Conduct Rules

You should check the local rules in your own jurisdiction to learn the specific professional conduct rules that govern your behavior as a lawyer that would apply to your behavior in mediation. The American Bar Association's latest thinking on how to approach a range of representation issues can be found in the ABA Model Rules of Professional Conduct.[70] The rules prescribe your duty to prepare, to be diligent, and to consult with your client about the means for accomplishing objec-

---

70. Selected ABA rules relevant to mediation representation can be located in Appendix N.

tives. The rules obligate you to maintain client's confidences, to not make false statements of material fact or law, to further meritorious, not frivolous claims and contentions, and to avoid means designed to embarrass, delay, or burden a third person. The rules also regulate how to communicate with represented clients, ways to deal with conflicts of interest, and when you can appear in mediations in another jurisdiction. There is no separate professional code for attorney-advocates in mediation although a lively discussion of those obligations, including suggestions for tailor-made ones, is unfolding and someday may produce model conduct rules for mediation advocates.[71]

One separate legal obligation that impacts directly on the way you and your client conduct yourselves has begun to take hold, an obligation that participants participate in "good faith" throughout the mediation process. Good-faith participation is required by a substantial number of state statutes as well as the rules of a number of state courts and federal district courts although most of these mandates fail to define good faith.[72] You should determine whether a good-faith requirement applies in your jurisdiction and how the requirement has been interpreted. The good-faith obligation has triggered a handful of reported cases[73] in which parties alleged bad faith when the other party failed to attend the session, bring a representative with sufficient settlement authority, submit a pre-mediation memorandum, bring experts, participate substantively, provide requested documents, and sign a mediated agreement.

There is much debate about what good-faith behavior is and whether a good-faith standard is efficacious or could be made efficacious.[74] At

---

71. *See e.g.,* Symposium, *Focus on Ethics in Representation in Mediation,* 4 DISP. RES. MAG. (Winter 1997).

72. *See* Lande, *Using Dispute System Design Methods to Promote Good-Faith Participation in Court-Connected Mediation Programs,* 50 UCLA L. REV. 69, 78–81(2002)(reported on requirements in twenty-two states, territory of Guam, twenty-one federal district courts, and seventeen state courts.)

73. Id. at 82–83 (analyzed twenty-seven reported cases).

74. *See e.g.,* Id at 87–108; Weston, *Checks on Participant Conduct in Compulsory ADR: Reconciling the Tension in the Need for Good-Faith Participation, Autonomy, and Confidentiality,* 76 IND. L.J. 591 (2001); Kovach, *Good Faith in Mediation—Requested, Recommended, or Required? A New Ethic,* 38 S.TEX. L. REV. 575 (1997); Brazil, *Continuing the Conversation About the Current Status and the Future of ADR: A View from the Courts,* 2000 J. DISP. RESOL. 11, 30–33; Sherman, *Court-Mandated Alternative Dispute Resolution: What Form of Participation Should Be Required,* 46 SMU L. REV. 2079, 2089–94 (1993).

least one critical observer recommends relegating the good-faith standard to a last resort option and instead trying a system designs approach for inducing good-faith participation.[75] As more litigated cases surface, this ongoing debate is likely to produce specific rules or incentives to guide you and your client's participation in the mediation.

15. Consider What to Bring to the Mediation Sessions

You should bring to the mediations sessions the case file including pleadings, depositions, critical documentary evidence, and any court orders or decisions in the case. You also should bring your legal research including copies of key statutes and court cases. This information may be essential if you expect to evaluate the merits of the legal case. Some of this information may be used as part of your opening statements; other information may become relevant as the mediation progresses.

You also should think creatively about how to present visually important information in a way that effectively engages the other side. The information could be presented on pasteboards, large newsprint pads, overheads, or computer-generated PowerPoint® presentations. For instance, key documents might be enlarged; chronologies might be presented on pasteboards; or key depositions, schematics, and contracts might be shown in a PowerPoint presentation. But, do not get too creative. You want to guard against your visual aids being more engaging than the substantive points that you want to communicate. PowerPoint presentations, for instance, can be so dazzling that the other side can become more absorbed by your technological prowess than your substantive presentation.

---

75. *See* Lande, *Using Dispute System Design Methods to Promote Good-Faith Participation in Court-Connected Mediation Programs,* 50 UCLA L. Rev. 69, (2002)(sharply criticizes the effectiveness of a good-faith participation standard and recommends, as an alternative, the use of dispute system design principles and system design policies.).

16. Checklist: Preparing Case and Mediation Representation Plan

This checklist consists of three parts: Parts 1 and 2 cover the homework you should do before you prepare your representation plan. Part 3 covers what to include in your representation plan when implementing it at six junctures in the mediation process.

Part 1
Preparation Before Preparing Representation Plan

❐ 1. Analyze dispute (not legal case). (See part 2.)

❐ 2. Research legal case (public BATNA).

❐ 3. Develop with your client your client's personal alternatives to settlement (personal BATNA.)

4. Consider whether you need to gather any information or file any motions before the session.
   - ❐ a. What information do you need?
   - ❐ b. How can you keep the costs of collecting information down?
   - ❐ c. Should you file any motions?

5. Decide who should attend the mediation session.
   - ❐ a. Should you attend?
   - ❐ b. Should your client attend?
   - c. How do you involve an institutional client?
     - ❐ Who should participate on behalf of an institutional client?
     - ❐ Does the person have sufficient and flexible settlement authority?

       ❐   How can you convince the client representative to participate?

       ❐   What should be the role of an in-house counsel?

   d. Should any other people participate (advisors)?

       ❐   Expert Witnesses?

       ❐   Fact Witnesses?

       ❐   Personal Advisors or Supporters (family member or friend)?

       ❐   Other?

❐ 6. Resolve who your audience is in the session.

   7. Prepare presentation of the legal case.

     ❐ a. How can you productively present the legal case?

     ❐ b. When do you want to present it—in opening statements or later?

   8. Consider level of confidentiality that you need.

     ❐ a. What are the sources? Look at mediation contract, any binding private mediation rules, and local laws.

     ❐ b. Are they adequate?

     ❐ c. Do you want to withhold any information despite confidentiality?

   9. Consider how to abide by conduct rules.

     ❐ a. Check local professional conduct rules relevant to mediation representation.

     ❐ b. Check whether a local obligation to participate in good faith applies and how it is interpreted.

10. Contact mediator.
   - ☐ a. Inquire whether the mediator plans to hold a pre-mediation conference.
   - ☐ b. If not planning one, request one if you determine that it would be useful.
   - ☐ c. Inquire whether the mediator wants a pre-mediation submission. If yes,
        - ☐ Determine what the mediator wants included.
        - ☐ Determine whether the mediator will share any information in the submission with the other side.
        - ☐ Determine that if the mediator plans to share any information, whether the mediator wants you to send the entire submission or a portion to the other side.
   - ☐ d. If mediator does not want one, request one if you determine that it would be useful.

11. Consider what to bring to the mediation session.
   - ☐ a. What will you bring to the session?
   - ☐ b. How will you visually present key information?

Part 2
Analysis of the Dispute
(not legal case)

Identify three components of the mediation representation formula: interests, impediments, and ways the mediator might contribute to resolving the dispute.

1. **Goal: Identify Interests to Meet**
   ❐ Your Client's

   Goal: Identify Interests to Accommodate
   ❐ Other Side's

2. **Goal: Identify Impediments to Overcome**
   ❐ Relationship

   ❐ Data

   ❐ Value

   ❐ Interests

   ❐ Structural

3. **Identify Mediator's Possible Contributions to Resolving the Dispute**

   Approaches to Dispute. You want the mediator to use the following mediator's approaches:
   - ☐ a. Manage the process by primarily facilitating, primarily evaluating, or following a transformative approach.
   - ☐ b. View the problem broadly or narrowly.
   - ☐ c. Involve clients actively or restrictively.
   - ☐ d. Use caucuses extensively, selectively, or not at all.

   Useful Techniques. You want the mediator to use his or her techniques to:
   - ☐ a. Facilitate the negotiation of a problem-solving process.
   - ☐ b. Promote communications through questioning and listening techniques.
   - ☐ c. Deal with the emotional dimensions of the dispute.
   - ☐ d. Clarify statements and issues through framing and reframing.
   - ☐ e. Generate options for settlement (e.g. brainstorming).
   - ☐ f. Separate process of inventing settlement options from selecting them.
   - ☐ g. Deal with power inequalities.
   - ☐ h. Overcome the impediments to settlement.
   - ☐ i. Overcome the chronic impediment of clashing views of the court outcome (public BATNA).
   - ☐ j. Close any final gaps (consider your preferred methods for closing gaps).
   - ☐ k. Deal with _____

Control over Mediation Stages. You want the mediator to use his or her control over the mediation process to:

❏ a.   Use the mediator's opening statement to set up a problem-solving process.

❏ b.   Use the information gathering stage for venting and securing information for the specific purposes of understanding issues, interests, and impediments. (Opening Statements of Participants, First Joint Session, and First Caucus)

❏ c.   Use the stage of identifying issues, interests, and impediments to ensure that key information is clearly identified.

❏ d.   Use the agenda formulation stage to ensure key issues and impediments will be addressed.

❏ e.   Use the overcoming impediments stage to overcome known impediments.

❏ f.   Use the generating options stage to ensure creative ideas are developed. (Inventing stage)

❏ g.   Use the assessing and selecting options stage to ensure that your client's interests are met. (Deciding stage)

❏ h.   Use the concluding stage to ensure that any written settlement meets your client's interests or if no settlement, a suitable exit plan is formulated.

Part 3
Mediation Representation Plan for Six Junctures

Develop a representation plan based on the mediation representation formula: *Plan to negotiate using a creative problem-solving approach to meet interests and overcome impediments in a way that takes advantage of how the mediator can contribute to resolving the dispute at six key junctures in the mediation process.*

Plan for Each Key Juncture (Use the information you collected and the choices you made when doing your homework in Parts 1 and 2.)

1. **Select Mediator**
    - ❐ a. Select person who is facilitative, evaluative, or transformative.
    - ❐ b. Select person who views problem broadly or narrowly.
    - ❐ c. Select person who involves clients actively or restrictively.
    - ❐ d. Select person who uses caucuses extensively, selectively, or not at all.

2. **Pre-Mediation Submission (Assuming you plan to submit one.)**
    Consider whether you want to cover the following points in the submission:

    "Description of Dispute and Legal Case"
    - ❐ a. "Factual Summary," including a chronology of events, statement of key factual issues in dispute, and your client's view on each issue;
    - ❐ b. "Critical Legal Issues" in dispute, including your client's view on each issue and key cites;
    - ❐ c. "Relief" sought including a particularized itemization of all damages claimed;
    - ❐ d. "Motions" filed and their status;
    - ❐ e. "Discovery Status," including what still needs to be done to be ready for trial;

"Settlement Analysis"

☐ f.   "Interests of Your Client" that you want met in mediation;

☐ g.   "Settlement Discussions" including any offers or counteroffers previously made;

☐ h.   "Why Not Settled" covers your views on the obstacles to settling this dispute and ways to overcome them;

☐ i.   "What Want Out of the Mediation" especially what you might want the mediator to do and any inventive settlement concepts that might not be available in court;

"Other Information"

☐ j.   "Who Will Attend" the mediation session and the title of any client representatives;

☐ k.   Attach critical documentary evidence.

3. **Pre-Mediation Conference—Agenda**

☐ a.   Verify mediator's mix of approaches to the mediation.

☐ b.   Verify other side's approaches to the mediation.

☐ c.   Verify attendance by the other side's best client representatives with sufficient and flexible settlement authority.

☐ d.   Verify date, time, place, and length of session.

☐ e.   Resolve what information you need from the other side before or by the session.

☐ f.   Resolve whether the mediator plans to have any ex parte conversations with each side before the session.

☐ g.   Consider signalling the likely interests of your client.

☐ h.   Consider broaching a discussion of possible impediments.

☐ i.   Ask about the pre-mediation submission, if questions still unresolved.

    ☐ Determine whether the mediator wants you to submit any pre-mediation materials.

    ☐ Determine what the mediator wants included in the pre-mediation submission.

❐ Determine whether the mediator will share any information in the submission with the other side.

❐ Determine that if the mediator plans to share any information, whether the mediator wants you to send the entire submission or a portion to the other side.

❐ j.   Identify any other issues that need to be resolved in the pre-mediation conference.

4. **Opening Statements**
    ❐ a.   Tone.
       b.   Content.
             ❐ Tell story.
             ❐ Cover BATNAs—public and personal.
             ❐ Suggest what your client wants out of the mediation (no specific proposals yet).
             ❐ Suggest how the mediator might help the parties resolve the dispute.
    ❐ c.   Should your client present an opening statement?
    ❐ d.   How should you divide the opening statements between you and your client?
             ❐ Story.
             ❐ Legal Case—public BATNA.
             ❐ Other BATNAs—personal and other.
             ❐ What want out of the mediation.
             ❐ How want the mediator to contribute to resolving the dispute.
    ❐ e.   Should you or your client speak first?

5. **Joint Sessions**
    ❐ Determine how to advance interests and overcome impediments at each mediation stage:
    ❐ a.   When venting and gathering information.

    ❐ b.   When identifying issues, interests, and impediments.

❏ c.   When formulating agenda.

❏ d.   When overcoming impediments.

❏ e.   When generating options.

❏ f.   When assessing and selecting options for settlement.

❏ Determine ways to enlist assistance of the mediator.

❏ Resolve how to split responsibilities between you and your
   client.

6. Caucus
   ❏ Select purposes that you want to accomplish in any caucuses.

Chapter Six

Preparing Your Client for Mediation

Topics in this chapter include:

1. Explain the Mediation Process and Your Client's Role
2. Explain How Your Role is Different than in Court
3. Re-Interview Your Client about Interests, Impediments, and Options
4. Review Needs for Information and Risks of Incomplete Discovery
5. Review Strengths and Weaknesses of Legal Case (Public BATNA)
6. Probe for Your Client's Personal Benefits and Costs of Litigating (Personal BATNA)
7. Finalize Mediation Representation Plan
8. Prepare Your Client to Answer Likely Questions
9. Finalize Opening Statements
10. Checklist

The better you prepare your client for the first mediation session,[1] the more comfortable your client will be in the session and the more confident she will be to make the inevitably difficult settlement decisions. You should prepare your client as suggested in this chapter regardless of the role that you expect to perform in the session. Most of this preparation will be useful whether you serve as a co-participant, silent advisor, dominant participant, or non-participant.

1. Explain the Mediation Process and Your Client's Role

You may want to demystify the mediation process for your client. Your client may need a feel for the mediation setting and welcome a vivid account of what to expect.

---

1. *See* Jacqueline M. Nolan-Haley, Lawyers, Clients, and Mediation, 73 Notre Dame L. Rev. 1369 (1998) (develops an approach to mediation client-counseling based on a deliberative process.)

You should emphasize that mediation is a continuation of the negotiation process. Your client should understand that she will retain full control of what happens in the mediation. The mediator has no decision-making power; the mediator serves as a neutral to facilitate the process. No resolution can happen without your client's approval. Moreover, no resolution can happen without the other party's approval, which is why the other party is the primary audience, not the mediator.[2]

Your client should understand that mediation is not an adversarial process. Instead, both sides will be collaborative, engaging in a problem-solving search for sensible and inventive solutions. The tone is not accusatory. Your client should be advised to be respectful, listen attentively, and show empathy. Your client may consider offering a sincere apology, if warranted. Your client should understand that the goal is not to "win"; it is to resolve the dispute.

Your client should be educated about the credentials of the mediator and what will likely happen in the first session. The session will consist of different stages from openings, information gathering, and so forth toward conclusion.[3] Your client should know the difference between joint sessions and caucuses, including the distinctive opportunities offered by caucusing.[4] Your client should be aware of the typical techniques used by mediators such as the way mediators can act as a devil's advocate, engage in reality testing, carry offers and counteroffers back and forth, and so forth.[5] Your client is likely to appreciate seeing a videotape that demonstrates the key features of the process.

Your client should understand the extent to which what is said in the mediation session will be held in confidence.[6] You should emphasize the degree to which anything said in the mediation session cannot be used later against your client in a legal proceeding. Be sure that your client is aware of the confidentiality limits. Your client should be told whether any information (if any) will be transmitted to the court. You also should carefully review with your client whether any particular information ought to be withheld or only disclosed in a caucus with the

---

2. *See* Chapter 5.7 on "Select Your Primary Audience in the Mediation."

3. *See* Chapter 2.3 on stages of mediation.

4. *See* Chapter 5.11 on "Consider When to Caucus."

5. *See* Chapter 2.4 on mediators' techniques.

6. *See* Chapter 5.13 on confidentiality.

mediator. Your client should be advised that if she is unsure what to disclose, she should consult you privately.

Finally, your client should be reminded to be patient and open-minded. Your client should come prepared to reach impasses and to participate in lengthy and multiple sessions. Your client should be aware that even if the entire dispute is not resolved, mediation is still likely to result in settling some issues and narrowing the remaining areas of dispute.

2. Explain How Your Role Is Different Than in Court

You should explain to your client that you will perform a collaborative, problem-solving role in the mediation session instead of the familiar adversarial one typically observed in litigation. You might consider reviewing the distinctive differences covered in chapter 1 on negotiating. Otherwise, your client might lose confidence in you for not performing in the anticipated role of zealous adversarial advocate. Then, you may feel pressured to perform as your client expects even though that approach may not be the most effective one in the mediation session.

CRITICAL JUNCTURE

Re-Interview Your Client

1. Solidify substantive and process interests of your client.
2. Explore possible interests of other party.
3. Clarify likely impediments.
4. Prod your client to think about creative settlement options.

---

3. Re-Interview Your Client about Interests, Impediments, and Options

You should re-interview your client because a significant amount of time has probably elapsed between your initial interview and the upcoming first mediation session. New information may have surfaced. The personal circumstances of your client may have changed. Your client has had time to mull over what she wants. And, your client is now sharply focused and presumably ready to make hard decisions about how to handle the upcoming session.

In both the initial interview and the re-interview, the goals and techniques for interviewing are the same.[7] You should re-interview your client to help her solidify her understanding of her interests as well as sort out the impediments that are likely to arise in the mediation session. You also should prod your client to envision creative monetary and non-monetary options for resolving the dispute. But, you should discourage your client from developing a firm bottom line.[8] It is premature. Your client should go to the mediation session with an open mind.

a. Clarifying Interests and Impediments

When re-interviewing your client, you should assertively inquire about your client's substantive interests—what your client really wants at the end of day.[9] What your client says she wants may not be what she really wants. Applying the frequently cited Fisher-Ury dichotomy of "positions" versus "interests,"[10] clients usually voice their "positions." This common and narrow view of needs can miss what your client really wants to achieve in the mediation. Your client probably wants to satisfy her broader "interests"; the stated positions simply express one way to satisfy those interests.

Your client may not have thought carefully or clearly about her underlying interests. By pursuing this threshold inquiry, you are giving your client an opportunity to think more thoroughly about the interests that she wants advanced in the mediation session. It gives you an opportunity to ensure that you understand your client's needs. Be sure to review how to interview your client about interests in chapter 3.2.

You also should explore with your client what might be the interests of the other party. Remember, the case cannot settle without the consent of the other party. If you learn about all the parties' interests, you and your client will be better equipped to develop, assess, and propose solutions that might be acceptable to everyone at the table.

---

7. *See* Chapter 3 on the initial client interview.

8. *See* Chapter 7.2(d)(iii) on how to handle your client's bottom line in the session.

9. *See, e.g.*, John W. Cooley, Mediation Advocacy Ch. 3.4 (1996); Dwight Golann, Mediating Legal Disputes—Effective Strategies for Lawyers and Mediators Ch. 3.2 (1996).

10. Roger Fisher Et Al., Getting to Yes—Negotiating Agreement Without Giving In Ch. 3 (2d ed. 1991).

Finally, you should re-visit what your client thinks might be the obstacles to settlement. This is your last chance before the mediation session to be sure that you have a grasp of the likely impediments. You should inquire whether the impediments might be due to data, relationship, value, structural, or interest conflicts. Be sure to review how to interview your client about impediments in chapter 3.2.

b.   Prodding Creative Solutions

During the re-interview, you also should prod your client to begin exploring options for settling the dispute. This is the occasion for you and your client to begin thinking outside the "legal box"; this is the occasion to be imaginative and inventive.[11] Your discussion should not be limited to monetary solutions despite the fact that your client's positions and legal claims may have been framed in monetary terms. Payment of money from one party to the other is not always the best or exclusive solution. You may be surprised by what you learn when you persist in exploring fresh ways to satisfy your client's interests.[12]

Your understanding of your client's interests can be the launching pad for discovering more value and non-monetary solutions. Your client should be asked about sources of value, objective criteria, and non-monetary options, especially possibilities that a court cannot or is unlikely to order but could be included in a settlement agreement.[13] In a surprisingly large number of cases, mediators have found that parties want more than money or something other than money. For instance, in an employment dispute, an employee's interests in new challenges and dignity may be met by the employer changing the employee's job responsibilities, providing her good references, or even offering an informal or published apology. If critical interests can be met with inventive, non-monetary solutions, the parties may become more flexible in resolving any remaining monetary issues.

---

11. *See* Chapter 1[3] on preparing for a problem-solving negotiation. Techniques are suggested for stimulating outside-of-the-legal-box thinking.

12. Fisher, *supra* note 10, at 42.

13. *See* Chapter 1.3 on preparing for a problem-solving negotiation. Techniques are suggested for identifying sources of objective criteria and value.

4. Review Needs for Information and Risks of Incomplete Discovery

You should review with your client the information that she needs before she is ready to engage seriously in the mediation session. Your client will have to make some difficult, if not painful judgments, about what information she requires short of full discovery. She needs to contemplate settling the dispute without a complete understanding of everything that happened in the case.

You should discuss with your client the risks and benefits of settling before completing full discovery. Your client must weigh the distressing possibility that more discovery might have unearthed more valuable information that might have resulted in a more favorable settlement. This risk shrinks as discovery increases. Of course, more discovery increases the risk of the other party unearthing information damaging to your client. Other benefits of less discovery and early settlement include saving time and money, reducing the acrimony and angst inherent in the adversarial discovery process, and increasing the likelihood of salvaging the personal or professional relationship between the parties.

5. Review Strengths and Weaknesses of Legal Case (Public BATNA)[14]

You should engage your client in a brutally frank discussion about the strengths and weaknesses of her legal case. Your discussion should be thorough and include a candid assessment of the probability of success in the adjudicatory forum, the likely outcome, and the cost of getting there. This decision-tree-type analysis[15] will give your client a rational reference point against which to judge whether settling may be more or less attractive than adjudicating. Such an analysis will avoid the common and frustrating obstacle that arises when your client thinks going to court is more attractive than it really is.

---

14. Fisher, *supra* note 10, at ch. 6 (The BATNA is the Best Alternative to a Negotiated Agreement. The BATNA is the best alternative to settling the dispute or what happens to the party if the party does not settle the dispute. In legal cases, the BATNA is usually what would happen in court.).

15. For a full discussion of the use of decision trees, see Appendix A.

This discussion will not only prepare your client to answer potential questions in the mediation session, it also will prepare your client to hear your likely answers to questions about the legal case, answers that might otherwise surprise and upset your client if heard for the first time in the session.

6. Probe for Your Client's Personal Benefits and Costs of Litigating (Personal BATNA)

You should help your client identify her personal BATNA—the benefits and costs of litigating that are personal to her and that she is uniquely qualified to identify and appraise. By combining the value of your client's personal BATNA with the value of the public BATNA, your client will learn how attractive going to court really is as compared to any settlement offer.

For example, only your client would be able to figure out how much she would be willing to give up to settle and salvage a continuing relationship with the other side. Only your client would be in a position to estimate, for instance, that she would be willing to accept $10,000 less than the value of her public BATNA (the benefit of going to court) if she could settle the case and save the relationship. Her personal cost of litigating, the cost of her personal BATNA, would be $10,000. Therefore, a settlement offer that is $10,000 less than the likely outcome in court would be attractive.

Only your client would be able to assess how much she would be willing to give up to go to court in an effort to establish a precedent or to be vindicated. Only she would be able to estimate that she would be willing to achieve in court $15,000 less than the value of her likely public BATNA if she could secure the personal benefit of being vindicated, for instance. To gain her personal benefit of litigating, which is the value of her personal BATNA, she would be willing to sacrifice $15,000 in court. Therefore, a settlement offer that is $15,000 more than the likely judicial outcome would be attractive.

How to probe for your client's specific personal benefits and costs is explained in the decision-tree plus appendix.[16]

---

16. *See* Appendix A on Decision-Tree Plus Analysis, Section 3.

7. Finalize Mediation Representation Plan

You should finish developing your representation plan with your client. The plan consists of a strategy for advancing the parties' interests and overcoming any impediments.[17] Your plan may need to be refined after you re-interview your client about interests, impediments, opportunities for expanding value, objective criteria for resolving distributive issues, and creative possibilities for settlement. As already discussed,[18] your plan will shape the tone and content of your briefing paper, opening statements, what is said during the joint sessions and caucuses, and the direction of any settlement discussions. However, your plan should not rigidly precondition what you and your client do. The plan should be flexible enough to accommodate new information, challenges to key assumptions, and spontaneous, creative new possibilities for resolution. In other words, you and your client should implement the plan with an open mind.

8. Prepare Your Client to Answer Likely Questions

You should review with your client the questions that she is likely to be asked by the mediator, other party, or other attorney.[19] This preview gives your client an opportunity to prepare productive answers that comport with a problem-solving approach as well as an opportunity to guard against any surprising answers.

Possible questions that your client should be ready to answer:

[The story]

What happened?

What documents do you have to support your conclusions?

What witnesses will support your conclusions?

[Interest analysis and stimulate out-of-the box legal thinking]

What are your interests/goals/needs?

What do you think are the interests of the other party?

---

17. *See* Chapter 5.1 on preparing a representation plan.

18. *See* Chapter 5.1 on preparing your case for the mediation session.

19. For a sampling of questions, *see* Tom Arnold, *"Advocacy in Mediation"* in *Alternative Dispute Resolution: How to Use It to Your Advantage,* CA13 ALI-ABA 535, 563–564 (1996); Dina R. Jansenson, *Representing Your Clients Successfully in Mediation: Guidelines For Litigators,* THE NY LITIGATOR, Nov. 1995, at 15, 20.

What do you want out of the mediation?

Do you have any new ideas for possible solutions?

[Evaluation of BATNA]

Are you familiar with any weaknesses in your legal case?

What do you think is the probability of your succeeding in court?

What do you think is the likely court outcome?

How much more time will it take to prepare your case for trial?

How long do you expect the trial to run?

What are the remaining approximate costs of getting ready for trial and the trial?

What are your options if there is no settlement?

[Diagnosing the impasses]

Why do you think you have been unable to settle the dispute?

What efforts have you already made to settle and why have they failed?

[Status of negotiations]

Do you have any offers still on the table? If so, what are they?

What is your bottom line?

9. Finalize Opening Statements

You should finish preparing the opening statements. You should resolve whether your client will present an opening statement, who will speak first, and how to divide the presentation of the story, BATNA, what your client wants, and what help you want from the mediator. You need to work through the tone and content of these statements and be sure that your client understands how they are different than opening statements in court.[20]

You should advise your client that if she omits any important information in her opening statement, she will have a chance to supply the information later. You will elicit the information directly from her by posing follow-up questions. Because you want to keep your client engaged actively, you should resist the temptation to fill in missing facts yourself.

---

20. *See* Chapter 5.10 on preparing opening statements, and Appendix E, "Sample Opening Statements."

10. Checklist: Preparing Client

1. Explain mediation process to your client.
   - ❐ a. Remind your client that mediation is a continuation of the negotiation process.
   - ❐ b. Explain that it is a problem-solving process.
   - ❐ c. Review stages of the mediation.
   - ❐ d. Review techniques of mediators.
   - ❐ e. Show a videotape of an actual mediation.
   - ❐ f. Review the level of confidentiality.
   - ❐ g. Determine whether any information should be withheld from the joint sessions or mediator.
   - ❐ h. Advise your client to be patient and open-minded.

❐ 2. Explain your different role in the mediation session.

3. Re-Interview your client.
   - ❐ a. Clarify Interests
   - ❐ b. Clarify Impediments
   - ❐ c. Prod for Creative Solutions

❐ 4. Review what essential information your client needs before the mediation session and the risks of incomplete discovery.

❐ 5. Review strengths and weaknesses of the legal case (public BATNA).

❏   6.   Probe for your client's personal benefits and costs of litigating (personal BATNA).

❏   7.   Finish developing your mediation representation plan.

❏   8.   Prepare your client to answer likely questions.

❏   9.   Finalize the opening statements.
       ❏   a.   Will your client present a statement?
       ❏   b.   How will you divide the presentation of the story, public and personal BATNAs, what your client wants, and what you want the mediator to do? (*See* Mediation Representation Plan, part 3.4.)
       ❏   c.   Will your client speak first?

CHAPTER SEVEN

APPEARING IN THE MEDIATION: PRE-MEDIATION CONFERENCE, MEDIATION SESSION, AND POST-SESSION

> Topics in this chapter include:
>
> 1. Pre-Mediation Conferences
> 2. Mediation Session
> 3. Post-Session
> 4. Checklist

1. Pre-Mediation Conference

The mediator may convene a pre-mediation conference. Only the attorneys and the mediator usually participate in this conference scheduled one to thirty days before the first session. The conference is typically conducted over the telephone, although in unusually complex cases, it may be conducted in person. Not all mediators insist on a pre-mediation conference. If your mediator does not, you should consider requesting one because of the opportunities it can provide for furthering the problem-solving process.

The pre-mediation conference offers you a chance to determine whether the mediator will be fostering a problem-solving approach to the mediation. When you selected the mediator, you presumably would have learned about his mix of approaches.[1] Now you can verify them. If you had not sorted out the approaches beforehand, this is your last opportunity to do so before the first mediation session. If you do not think that the mediator's particular mix would be the most efficacious,

---

1. The four primary classifications including which variations are likely to promote a problem-solving process were discussed in Chapter 4.2(b). The four classifications are: (1) How Manage Process: Will the mediator primarily facilitate, primarily evaluate, or engage in a transformative approach? (2) How Define Problem: Will the mediator approach the dispute narrowly or broadly? (3) How Involve Clients: Will the mediator limit or actively involve clients? (4) How Use Caucuses: Will the mediator employ caucuses extensively, selectively, or not at all?

then you should negotiate specific modifications with the other attorney and mediator. For example, if the mediator does not normally welcome opening statements by clients and you think clients should present such statements, you should raise this issue for discussion in the pre-mediation conference.

This discussion of the mediator's approaches can provide you an opening to advance your primary goals in the mediation. You can signal the interests that your client hopes will be met in the mediation and inquire what obstacles the other attorney thinks may be impeding settlement. Your initiatives may trigger a discussion that could point the way for both sides and the mediator to productively prepare for the session.

If you are concerned that the other side might resist or be inexperienced in problem-solving, you can diplomatically invite the mediator to "educate" you and the other side on how he thinks participants can productively participate in the mediation sessions. By posing questions about the role of clients, what should be discussed in opening statements, methods for assessing the legal case, and ways to develop creative solutions, you are giving the mediator an opportunity to educate and even coach the other side on how to productively represent his client in the sessions.

The pre-mediation conference also offers you your last opportunity to be sure that the right people will be participating in the mediation session. This is an indisputably crucial item to resolve. You want to be sure that the other attorney brings his best client representative, the person with the necessary information and flexible settlement authority as well as any valuable "advisors." The same considerations that you weighed when ensuring that you selected your best or next best client representative apply when you are verifying whether the other party, especially an institutional one, is bringing the right people to the session.[2] If the other party is a government one, you also want to be sure that the other attorney is the right government attorney, one with sufficient authority and telephone access to his supervisor.[3]

---

2. *See* Chapter 5.5(b), (c), and (d) on client participation.

3. When discussing who will be representing a government party, you not only should be familiar with the internal decision-making process of the government agency, you also should be familiar with the internal decision-making process of the government's attorney's office. Especially for the federal government and large states, the internal decision-making process can be elaborate. You want to be sure that both the right client representative and the right attorney will be participating.

There are few mistakes that can more quickly destroy the settlement atmosphere, if not the entire effort, than your client discovering that his counterpart did not bother showing up after your client went to the trouble of clearing his hectic calendar for the day. Even if your client is willing to plow ahead, the opportunity to settle would have been crippled due to the absence of a party with sufficient knowledge and settlement authority. This threshold issue is customarily given careful attention by mediators.

Finally, you should verify with the mediator that sufficient time for an intensive, problem-solving process has been scheduled and that everyone knows how much time to clear for the session. If you and your client, who cleared the day, learn early in the morning that one of the other parties or even the mediator plans to leave in the early afternoon, the settlement opportunity could be stifled if not destroyed.

If the pre-mediation conference is scheduled sufficiently in advance of the first session, the conference can offer you two additional benefits. You can clarify what the mediator wants included in any pre-session submissions.[4] You also can try to resolve any discovery issues in time for the production of critical documents before the first session or at the session.[5]

2. Mediation Session

Consistent with your representation plan to advance interests and overcome impediments, you should be prepared to make the large number of legal and strategic judgments that were considered in chapter 5 on preparing your case and chapter 6 on preparing your client.

Throughout the session, you should perform three particular anticipatory measures. As an agreement begins to emerge, you should keep verifying the settlement authority of any client representatives at the table including your own client's authority. You want to be sure that the agreement is not unexpectedly derailed by a client representative who lacks the authority to sign off and needs approval from someone who did not participate in the session.[6] You should listen attentively for any inadvertent clues from the mediator about the other side's strategy or

---

4. *See* Chapter 5.4(a).

5. *See* Chapter 5.12(a).

6. *See* Chapter 5.5(b),(c), and (d) on client participation.

bottom line. Remember that the mediator might have picked up valuable confidential information from the other side.[7] And, you should show off your client as a good witness to the other side who will be assessing your client's credibility and persuasiveness in court when weighing the risks of not settling and going to court.

You should give close attention to the following representation opportunities as they arise during the mediation session.

a. Use Proactively the Presence of the Mediator

You should use the distinctive opportunities for representation in the mediation session that are not usually or easily available in other forums. These opportunities arise because a mediator is present who brings to the settlement process a mix of approaches, specialized techniques, and control over the process. You should be attentive to spotting ways for enlisting assistance from the mediator in the heat of the session. Presumably, you have already developed some ideas of how to do this when you prepared your representation plan.[8]

One opportunity that you may not have considered can arise during the session when the mediator either fails to make a problem-solving move or slips into a non-problem-solving mode. You should be prepared to proactively coax an aberrant mediator back into a problem-solving mode. You should try to influence your mediator to use his approaches, techniques, and process control to convert adversarial negotiators into problem-solvers and to help participants maintain a problem-solving approach for advancing interests and overcoming impediments.

Your coaxing strategy depends on the particular needs of the moment. For example, if you think the mediator is failing to help the parties overcome a relationship conflict due to severe communication difficulties, you can tactfully invite the mediator to use his control over the early stages of the mediation to create an opportunity for the parties to talk directly and constructively with each other. You might specifically ask

---

7. *See* John W. Cooley, Mediation Advocacy 118–119 (1996).

8. For a full discussion of ways to take advantage of the mediator's presence, *see* Chapter 5 [1] on developing a representation plan; Chapter 4.2(a) and (b) on credentials of mediators and their approaches; Chapter 3.2 on interviewing clients about interests and impediments; Chapter 1.5 on "Converting Adversarial Negotiations into Problem-Solving"; 1.6 on "Advancing Problem-Solving in Mediations"; Chapter 2.4 on mediators "Facilitating the Negotiation of a Problem-Solving Process."

the mediator whether the participants might be able to spend more time in the session gathering information (early stage) before moving forward to agenda formulation and generating options (later stages). Then, you can rely on the mediator's skills to help the parties communicate with each other and productively interact. If you are at an impasse due to an interest conflict caused by entrenched positions that are impeding developing creative alternatives, you may ask your mediator for help in clarifying parties' interests and generating more options for resolving the dispute, and then benefit from your mediator's skills in identifying interests and conducting brainstorming sessions in which parties invent multiple options.

b. Answer Predictable Questions

You and your client will likely be asked a number of standard questions by the mediator and the other side during the mediation session. The questions that your client should be ready to answer were considered in chapter 6.7 on preparing your client.

You also should be prepared to answer a number of legal questions. At the beginning of the first session, you may be asked to advise your client whether to sign a confidentiality agreement.[9] As the session progresses, you may be asked a number of legal questions about the court case. You may be questioned about what still needs to be done to prepare for trial, how much time you need, the likely number of trial days, and the costs of completing discovery and trying the case. You may be asked how you will prove key factual claims. And, you may be invited to evaluate the strengths and weaknesses of the legal case including employing a decision-tree analysis[10] in which you predict the probability of success and the likely judicial outcome.

You and your client may be asked to suggest creative settlement options and to assess which ones best meet the interests of both sides. And, your client may be asked what his "bottom line" is, the subject of subsection (d).

You and your client should avoid terse, positional answers in a problem-solving process. You should give full answers with principled

---

9. *See* Chapter 5.13 on what should be covered in a confidentiality agreement and its limitations.

10. For a discussion on how to prepare decision trees, *see* Appendix A.

explanations. Your answers ought to project a rational, reasonable posture that might encourage others to respond in kind, resulting in a focused and intelligent discussion of issues, interests, and obstacles. This reasoned approach also makes it feasible for you to modify answers based on a face-saving substantive analysis instead of a face-losing capitulation. Therefore, instead of responding that you want full payment of all the damages listed in the pleadings, you might respond by explaining that you are seeking full payment of all the damages that can be reasonably documented by credible medical reports. This answer would naturally move the discussion toward how to credibly document the damages, leaving you space to adjust your damages up or down based on the cumulating objective evidence.

c. Take Advantage of Caucusing Opportunities

During the course of the mediation session, you should consider whether, when, and how to use each of these three caucusing opportunities.

i. Mediator Caucus with Attorney and Client[11]

As discussed previously, mediator caucuses are controversial and should be used selectively in a problem-solving process. You should limit their use to serve goals that cannot be accomplished in a joint session.[12] Your possible occasions for using caucuses should have been considered when preparing your representation plan.

At the end of each caucus, it behooves you to reaffirm with the mediator exactly what will be held in confidence. Mediators will usually remind you and your client that what happened in the caucus is confidential and that either everything will be held in confidence unless otherwise agreed or that nothing will be held in confidence unless otherwise agreed. You and your client should make your own independent judgment regarding your preferred scope of confidentiality.

Confidentiality Options: You and your client have four primary options: (1) Both of you may conclude that nothing was said that should be kept confidential. Then, you can authorize the mediator

---

11. *See* John W. Cooley, Mediation Advocacy Ch. 5.4 (1996); Dwight Golann, Mediating Legal Disputes—Effective Strategies for Lawyers and Mediators Sec. 3.2 (1996).

12. For a discussion of when to use caucuses, *see* Chapter 5.11.

to convey to the other side any information that the mediator thinks would be useful. (2) Both of you may decide that everything should be kept confidential. (3) Both of you may resolve that everything should be kept confidential except what the two of you specifically authorize for disclosure. (4) Or, both of you may realize that everything can be disclosed except what the two of you specifically want held in confidence.

Recommendations: If particularly sensitive information was revealed, such as limits of settlement authority or the bottom line, you should specifically and carefully reaffirm the information that should be held in strict confidence. You want to minimize the risk of inadvertent disclosures. If you want anything specifically disclosed, you should review with the mediator exactly what to disclose. If the details are considerable or intricate, such as an elaborate settlement proposal, you may want to reduce the proposal to writing in order to avoid any risks of miscommunications.

ii.   Mediator Caucus with Attorneys[13]

Occasionally, you or all the attorneys might request a caucus with the mediator without the clients. An attorney caucus may provide the attorneys an opportunity for a deeper discussion of legal issues without any pressure to impress clients. A caucus with just you and the mediator can provide you an opportunity to discuss any problems that you may be experiencing with your client. For instance, you may want to meet separately with the mediator to privately recognize that your client has an exaggerated view of the legal case and to request the mediator to structure a discussion of the case in a caucus with you and your client. However, attorney caucuses should be rarely used because they can undermine the mediation process by removing clients from this client-centered process and generating client paranoia about what their attorneys are saying behind their backs.

iii.   Attorney-Client Caucus

At any time during the mediation session, you or your client should feel comfortable requesting a caucus with each other. This type of caucus can provide a valuable opportunity for you and your client to re-group and discuss suitable responses to such questions like how to react to any pending proposals, whether to present any new proposals, and what information to disclose to the mediator or the other side.

---

13. *See* Eric Galton, Representing Clients in Mediation 50–51(1994).

The attorney-client caucus also can be used for simply taking a breather from the rapidly moving mediation session.

d. Disclosing Information Prudently (Advantageous Evidence, Harmful Information, and Bottom Lines)

Three especially vexing issues loom large in the mediation session: Should you disclose to the other side evidence that might sacrifice an advantage at trial? Should you acknowledge information to the other side that might be harmful to your client? And, should you reveal to the mediator your client's bottom line?

i. Disclosing Advantageous Evidence

Advantageous evidence that you may want to conceal until trial may need to be disclosed in the mediation. You may be inclined to withhold evidence that can bolster your case or hurt the other party's case until the optimum striking moment in the trial, assuming that you can shield the evidence from broad discovery rules. But, saving the evidence for trial, an event that is statistically unlikely to happen, may hinder settling the dispute. The evidence may be useful in the mediation to persuade the other side of the strength of your case and the benefits of settling over litigating.

Remember that the earlier that you and the other side have full information, the earlier that both sides can move toward meaningful option building and resolving the dispute. The longer you delay disclosure, the greater the likelihood of your losing credibility with the other side, in addition to the other side over-estimating their BATNA and the mediation missing creative settlement opportunities.

The negotiation chapter on problem-solving[15] considered the benefits of sharing information when trying to expand value as well as how to do it in a way that can reduce the harm to your client when the time arrives for claiming value (splitting up the pie). In mediation, you should consider sharing the beneficial information with the mediator in an early caucus. By doing this, you can develop a trusting relationship with the mediator who might view you more as an earnest problem-solver than a crafty adversarial negotiator. Also, you give the mediator a fuller picture of the dispute early so that he can assist you in productively using the information in the mediation session.

---

15. *See* Chapter 1.3(a)(ii) on how to productively share information.

Some attorneys suggest holding back advantageous evidence until later in the mediation when it can be used to extract one last major concession for closing the final gap. This familiar strategy assumes an adversarial, not problem-solving approach.

In one documented mediation,[16] for example, the defendant's attorney wanted to withhold maintenance records that would have vividly demonstrated that the defendant's antifreeze that allegedly damaged the plaintiff's trucks was not in a few of the damaged trucks. The defendant's attorney informed the mediator that he wanted to save the evidence for trial. Presumably if the other side did not discover the evidence before trial, the evidence at trial would leave a powerfully negative impression on the jury that more than a few damaged trucks did not have the antifreeze. Late in the mediation session, the defendant's attorney realized that this harmful evidence could be used to his client's advantage in the mediation. He decided to authorize the mediator to reveal the evidence to the plaintiff when it could be used to clinch the settlement deal. He did not want to "waste the information." In a problem-solving process, disclosure serves a different purpose. Instead of strategically timing disclosure until late in an effort to extract a final concession, he should have considered disclosing the information early. Early disclosure would have given the plaintiff the information that he needed to accurately assess whether to diligently try settling or risk litigating.

ii.　Acknowledging Harmful Evidence and Legal Weaknesses

You should be prepared to respond intelligently and honestly to any evidence and law harmful to your client's case that may be known to the other side. If you ignore or deny this damaging truth, you will lose credibility with the other side and the mediator, credibility that you will need when negotiating creative solutions or engaging in hard bargaining at the end of the day. A caucus with the mediator can provide you a safe place to recognize any weaknesses and to explore ways for factoring in the harmful information and for acknowledging the information with the other side.

---

16. *See* Dwight Golann, *Representing Clients in Mediation: How Advocates Can Share a Mediator's Powers*, A.B.A. Study Guide, 46–47 (2000).

iii.   Moving Toward the Bottom Line

CRITICAL JUNCTURE

Should You Disclose Your Client's Bottom Line to the Other Side or the Mediator?

1.   Consider the risks.
2.   Select disclosure method that minimizes the risks.

At some point in the mediation, you may need to disclose your client's bottom line. Your instinct to hide the bottom line could result in hiding the possibility of settlement. You want to avoid the unforgivable blunder of failing to settle because of failing to reveal the information that would have shown that the parties were within a settlement range.

At this critical moment in the mediation, you and the other party need a safe way to move toward bottom lines. This subsection first defines a bottom line, suggests when to formulate it, examines the risks of disclosing it, and considers whether your client should hold back a final concession when formulating his bottom line. Then, this subsection canvasses and evaluates mediators' methods for inducing each party to move safely toward his bottom line.

What is a bottom line?[17]

The bottom line is what your client is convinced that he must minimally secure in the mediation before he will sign anything. If your client is the plaintiff, his minimum is the smallest benefit that he will accept to settle. If your client is the defendant, his minimum is the most that he will tolerate giving up to settle. The bottom line includes your client's final concession to the other side.

Formulating a bottom line is a quintessential client decision. Your client usually arrives at his bottom line by factoring in what would happen if the dispute does not settle, known as his best alternative to a settlement (BATNA). The value of your client's BATNA is influenced by a multitude of objective and subjective factors. In legal cases, its value usually comprises the value of going to court, the public BATNA, and

---

17. For a technically more precise definition of bottom line, also known as reservation value, and its relationship to the BATNA, *see* chapter 1.2(a)(ii) on how to establish a client's bottom line in an adversarial negotiation. The subsection includes examples involving the use of decision-tree-type calculations.

the value of your client's private benefits and costs of litigation, your client's personal BATNA. In mathematical terms, your client's total BATNA (TB) is calculated by adding together the values of his public BATNA (PubB) and his personal BATNA (PersB).[18]

At this point in the mediation, the bottom line would usually have been whittled down to mostly money, although your client may have earlier expressed a non-monetary demand that sounded like a bottom line. The non-monetary demand might have been an interest that your client did not want to disclose because of the fear that the other side would exploit the information. At this point, you should know whether this interest will likely be met in the mediation and how much your client would be willing to pay or receive in the mediation to satisfy the interest, an estimate necessary for calculating the value of your client's personal BATNA (PersB).[19]

Unless your client comes to terms with the likely value of his total BATNA, your client will probably fail to fix an accurate bottom line. This mistake can result from inadequately educating your client about the value of his public BATNA. If your uninformed client, a plaintiff, establishes a bottom line of securing $350,000 when his realistic BATNA is $100,000 to $150,000, your client's bottom line will fall unambiguously outside the settlement range of an educated opponent and will produce a deadlock. In order to avoid this mistake, you, as the attorney, serve a vital role in educating your client as he formulates an intelligent bottom line.

---

18. For fuller definitions of public and personal BATNAs and a full explanation of how to calculate your client's total BATNA, *see* Appendix A entitled "Decision-Tree Plus Analysis."

19. For example, your client may have wanted a continuing relationship, but feared that if disclosed, the other side would try to extract a substantial concession such as a much lower payment of damages. Yet, a continuing relationship may be something your client wants to achieve in the mediation. This demand may sound like a bottom line but it may really be an interest that your client wants met in the mediation.

At this late point in the mediation, you should know whether this interest might be met. When calculating the value of your client's personal BATNA, you may ask your client how much more he would want in court in order to give up a continuing relationship with the other party. In other words, how much would he sacrifice in the mediation in order to maintain a continuing relationship? If your client estimates $10,000, then that amount would be deducted from the value of your client's public BATNA in order to calculate the value of his total BATNA, a bottom-line value that if unmet in mediation, will trigger your client returning to court.

When should your client formulate a bottom line?

At some point in the mediation, your client may need to formulate a bottom line. You should keep this pivotal moment in context. In a problem-solving process, the moment is not early in the mediation session. Your client should not start with a firm bottom line. Instead, your client should arrive to the mediation familiar with but not wedded to a particular BATNA. Based on what you know before the first session, you would have advised your client about the likely value of his public BATNA—the likely court outcome and the likelihood of success. Your client would have thought about the components of his private BATNA. And, your client should start the session with an open mind, ready to learn more about the dispute and perspectives of others, about interests and options, and about his own BATNA and the BATNA of the other side.

Not having an early bottom line averts two often-posed dilemmas—whether you should disclose your client's bottom line early and how to overcome your client's resistance to modifying a prematurely announced bottom line in the face of new information.

The moment for fixing the bottom line is usually a momentous and intense event at the end of the day when the dispute has reached an intractable distributive juncture. All possibilities for creating and splitting value would have been exhausted, and an issue, usually about money, is blocking the pathway home. It is time for the final crunch when decisions that are inherently difficult and painful can no longer be deferred. At this moment, you must give your best, most considered prediction of the value of your client's public BATNA. Your client must settle upon a value for his personal one. It is time for your client to make any final concessions and formulate his final, final, bottom line.

What are the risks of disclosing the bottom line?

Should you disclose your client's bottom line to the other side or the mediator?

First, a caveat about bottom lines that are disclosed by clients: Despite the use of rigorous decision-tree analysis, clients' bottom lines can be notoriously undependable.[20] Clients can act strategically with you. They may give you aspirational bottom lines, ones that are better than their real ones. They may do this because they want to harness your creative energies to advocate for their higher goals while reserving a concession in case you need one to bridge a final gap. Clients may change their bottom lines, as they ought to, when they learn new information in the mediation. You would expect their bottom lines to vary with the ebb and flow of information. And, clients' firm bottom lines can collapse as the prospect of settling becomes imminent and their appetite for closure take over.

If the unreliability of a client's bottom line does not stop you from disclosing it, the risk of disclosing it to the other side might. The other side may misconstrue your client's final offer as simply the next counteroffer in the negotiation dance, a response that would effectively negate the benefit of making this final concession to settle the dispute. Unless you can convince the other side that this is your client's last concession, you risk losing the concession for closing a final gap.

But, should you be willing to disclose your client's bottom line to the mediator? You should be more inclined and confident sharing your client's bottom line with the mediator who can then learn the other side's bottom line and, as a result, can determine whether settlement is feasible. A mediator trained in problem-solving should know how to handle this determinative and sensitive information responsibly and productively.

Yet, you still may not want to disclose your client's bottom line if you plan to use the strategy of enlisting the mediator to do your bidding for an advantageous result. Under this non-problem-solving tactic, you view the mediator as an additional party in the mediation, a party that you must persuade and strategically negotiate with. You want to convince the mediator that your client's bottom line is higher or lower than it actually is and then rely on the mediator to prod the other side to settle for an advantageous result while you keep a concession in reserve.

---

20. I mediated a case where a seasoned and highly regarded litigator that I personally knew told me in a caucus that he will reveal his client's "real" bottom line only because he knew me personally and trusted me. He rarely does this, so he told me. The case settled when his client paid much more than his real bottom line! The attorney told me later that he was shocked how much his client ultimately agreed to pay.

If you are not contemplating using this questionable tactic, you should consider disclosing your client's bottom line to the mediator. But, disclosing to a mediator still poses its own risks that you need to guard against:[21]

The mediator may be unconvinced that the bottom line disclosed by your client is his real one. Like the other side, the mediator might treat your client's bottom line as the number that your client must now negotiate against, in effect treating your client's bottom line as his "next to last" number.[22] Your client might tell the mediator that he will pay no more than an additional $25,000 for a total of $125,000 and that number is his final, last, end-of-the-day offer that if the other side rejects, he will abandon the mediation and return to court. Thinking that the other side will reject the offer, the mediator might push your client to pay more to bridge the final gap, in effect trying to induce your client to bargain against himself. The mediator may goad your client by exhorting that "for another 10 percent or $12,500 everyone can go home and get on with their lives. You will incur at least that much additional cost to try the case and even then face the risk of the court ordering you to pay more than the total of $137,500."

The mediator may carelessly disclose to the other side that your client has not reached his bottom line. He might do this by inadvertently signaling to the other side that your client will pay more, a piece of information that could embolden the other side to seek more from your client. The mediator might do this in a caucus by inartfully saying to the other party, the plaintiff: "You should consider accepting an additional $5,000 for a total of $50,000 to resolve this. While the other side has not formally authorized me to tell you that they will pay more, they are reasonable and practical people."

The mediator may misuse your client's bottom line. Your client may want the mediator to guide parties toward a settlement within the boundary of his bottom line, not to use the bottom line as the goal. If your client, the plaintiff, says he is willing to accept as little as $125,000, the mediator may latch onto that number as the one to encourage the other side to offer.

---

21. *See* Cooley, *supra* note 7, at 117–118 (discusses some of the risks when disclosing the bottom line too early) (1996).

22. *See* Golann, *supra* note 11, at 16.

Disclosing your client's bottom line might box in your client. Once disclosed, your client may resist changing it even when he wants to because of the need to save face and preserve credibility. If your client says to the mediator that "this is my final, final, final bottom line of $125,000," then he may have difficulty finding a way to give a little more money at the end just to get out of the dispute.

Finally, your client's candor with the mediator can be exploited strategically by the other party disclosing a bottom line that is higher or lower than his real one. By doing this, the other party can create a favorable settlement range in anticipation of the mediator pressuring the parties to split the difference. The other party, the defendant, might convey a false bottom line of paying $100,000 instead of his real one of paying $120,000, while your client, the plaintiff, discloses his real bottom line of wanting $120,000. If the mediator suggests splitting the difference, your client will either walk away or be pressured to accept $110,000 even though the other party was prepared to pay your client's bottom line of $120,000.

Should you hold back a final concession?

In view of these various risks, your instinct may be to advise your client to withhold a final concession when he is formulating his bottom line. This instinct seems sound when you consider the disclosure risks described in the previous section. You may want your client to hold back one last, modest concession in case your client needs it to bridge a final gap. But, a strategy of less than candor in mediation can be hazardous. The full potential of mediation can be best realized when parties frankly and prudently exchange information. The candor disincentive posed by the disclosure risks can be substantially reduced, if not eliminated, by using one of the disclosure methods described in the next section.

What creative methods are available for reducing disclosure risks?

DIFFERING VIEWS

Disclosing Bottom Lines
Which Methods Are Best for Reducing the
Disclosure Risks?

Options:
1.   Binding Final-Offer Arbitration
2.   Mediator's Proposal
3.   Hypothetical Testing
4.   Confidential Disclosure of Bottom Lines
5.   Confidential Disclosure of Settlement Numbers
6.   Safety Deposit Box

Recommendations: The two options that most reduce the disclosure risks are: "final-offer arbitration" in which bottom lines are likely to be used and the "confidential disclosure of settlement numbers" where bottom lines are not requested. The least attractive options are: "confidential disclosure of bottom lines" and the widely used "mediator's proposal."

This subsection examines specific methods that are designed to induce parties to use or move toward their real bottom lines.[23] These methods take advantage of the presence of a mediator.

Binding Final-Offer Arbitration (FOA)[24]

If you think that your client's bottom line is likely to be more reasonable than the other party's, you can suggest that each side present their bottom line to the mediator and then authorize him to select the most reasonable one. Under this scheme, your client (and the other side) is motivated to develop a rational bottom line—one that can be justified or else assume the risk that the other side's bottom line will be selected. Because final-offer arbitration results in a final binding resolution, both sides can fashion bottom lines without needing to withhold any concessions for later use.

The drawback of final-offer arbitration in a problem-solving process is that the mediator must change his role from a neutral facilitator to

---

23. A general approach to sharing information was considered in Chapter 1 on how to negotiate distributive issues. *See* Chapter 1.3(a)(iii).

24. For a fuller explanation of final-offer arbitration, *see* Chapter 8.2(a)(3).

the role of an adjudicator who must now formulate views on the reasonableness of each side's proposal. Switching roles is problematic. The neutral must meld the two distinctively different roles of mediator and adjudicator, which might result in the mediator undercutting the problem-solving process and your commingling incompatible representation strategies to serve this blended process. Therefore, you are safest using this method after both sides have carefully considered its pros and cons, when both sides still retain confidence in the mediator's neutrality, and when the binding feature will bring closure so that no need will arise for the mediator-turned-adjudicator to switch back to mediate.

Mediator's Proposal[25]

The mediator puts together a proposal that each side either accepts or rejects. The proposal may be based on the mediator's view of the likely judicial outcome or what might be barely acceptable to both sides. Your client must decide whether the proposal falls within the boundary of his bottom line. Under this scheme, your client's decision to accept the proposal is kept confidential unless the other side also accepts the proposal. Therefore, the other party cannot learn that your client was willing to go as far as the terms in the mediator's proposal unless the other party also was willing to go that far. Your client can safely reject the proposal without the other side learning that those terms exceeded your client's bottom line. You can influence the terms in the proposal by trying to persuade the mediator that your client's views are reasonable enough to incorporate in the proposal.

This clever scheme is popular for a number of reasons. Parties like its efficiency. They do not need to select a new neutral. The mediator with whom the parties have been working formulates the proposal and implements the scheme. By the time parties must decide whether to use it, typically toward the end of the session, they usually know enough about the mediator to assess whether they trust the mediator to fairly execute the method.

The mediator's proposal also lifts a number of burdens from the parties. They can avoid making several difficult decisions. They do not need to formulate their own proposals. They avoid weighing whether to withhold a concession. They do not need to come to terms with their own

---

25. For a fuller explanation of how the mediator's proposal works, *see* Chapter 2.4(j).

bottom line. And, if they do have a bottom line, they do not need to consider whether to risk disclosing it to the mediator or the other side.

The method offers a few enticing benefits. A party can make a concession to the other side in the form of accepting the mediator's proposal without the other side learning of the concession unless the other side also accepts the proposal. Parties can have some input into the formulation of the proposal, either in a joint session or caucus. And, most importantly, if a party does not like the mediator's proposal, the party is not bound by it. The party can always reject it.

However, the mediator's proposal requires the mediator, when formulating an acceptable settlement proposal, to shift roles from a neutral facilitator to a quasi-adjudicator, as occurs with binding final-offer arbitration. Switching roles can result in the mediator commingling two incompatible roles of facilitator and adjudicator, and the attorneys responding by commingling two incompatible representation strategies—problem-solving for the mediation and adversarial for securing a favorable proposal—a response that can undermine the coherency and consistency of their approach to mediation representation. The non-binding feature of the scheme makes it riskier to use than final-offer arbitration because once the mediator has formulated a proposal, the mediator may subtly or blatantly lobby for his own proposal, and then if unsuccessful, shift back to mediating, now possibly compromised and no longer imbued with the essential trait of neutrality. It is for these various reasons that the mediator's proposal can diminish the problem-solving potential of the mediation process.

Hypothetical Testing

You disclose confidentially your bottom line number to the mediator without the other side knowing that you have done so. Then, the mediator asks the other side whether they would accept that number if it could be secured from your client. This commonly used "what if" device gives your client the opportunity to find out whether the two sides are within a settlement range without your client sacrificing his last concession unless it will close the final gap. But, this method does not prevent the other side from speculating that your client has approved the hypothetical number and then bargaining for more, a reaction that leaves your bottom line unprotected. At least with this method, the other side cannot manipulate their bottom line to create a favorable bargaining range because the other side is not asked to submit a bottom line.

Unfortunately, this scheme fails to eliminate the various risks that arise when you disclose your client's bottom line to the mediator. To reduce these risks, you first should figure out whether you can trust the mediator to not carelessly disclose or misuse the information. To prevent the mediator from pressuring your client to bargain against his own bottom line, you need to make it convincingly clear to the mediator that the disclosed bottom line is absolutely the final one. Then, you might take a chance of disclosing your client's real bottom line to the mediator, although as a safeguard, you might still want to withhold a modest final concession.

Confidential Disclosure of Bottom Lines

Each side discloses confidentially their bottom lines to the mediator. Then, the mediator tells both sides whether the numbers overlap—which means the dispute can be easily resolved; whether the numbers are close enough to bridge—which means that with a little more work, the dispute can be resolved; or whether the numbers are just too far apart to try. When the numbers overlap or fall within a small range, the mediator might suggest splitting the difference. When the numbers fall within a wide range that does not seem insurmountable, the mediator might suggest that the parties consider revealing the numbers to each other, revisiting the assessment of their BATNAs, or using one of the alternative dispute resolution processes described in chapter 8.

This method is the least attractive option in this section because it fails to specifically eliminate any of the risks that arise when disclosing your client's bottom line, including the two risks that can readily negate any benefits from this method—the risk that the mediator does not believe that your client disclosed his real bottom line and the risk that the other side did not submit his real bottom line but instead presented a strategic number. Unfortunately, this method is often used by less experienced mediators (including me early in my mediation career) because of its appealing simplicity. If the mediator can convince the parties to honestly disclose their bottom lines, then the mediator can learn what the parties want to know but cannot safely learn on their own—whether the parties are within a settlement range.

It is probably prudent to avoid using this method, although there are a few ways to try reducing the risks of using it. First, you can assess whether you can trust the mediator to not carelessly disclose or misuse the bottom line number. Then, you can try to convince the mediator that the bottom line that your client disclosed is his final one. But, you still face the risk of the other party or attorney giving the mediator a strategic bottom line number that is designed to create a favorable settlement range for when the mediator suggests splitting the difference. You could eliminate this risk by approving this method only if both sides would agree that the difference would not be split, thus eliminating the incentive to submit a false bottom line number. But, such an agreement would fail to eliminate the inherent pressure to split the difference at the end of the day. More importantly, the agreement would eliminate the very formula that might make sense to use if both sides had submitted their real bottom lines. Despite these difficulties, if you decide to use this method, you should consider formulating a bottom line in which a final concession is withheld.

Confidential Disclosure of Settlement Numbers

Instead of asking each side to disclose their real bottom lines to the mediator, a request that is unlikely to be honestly honored, your client and the other party are requested to each submit a new, confidential settlement proposal.[26] The mediator might ask: "What are you really ready to do to settle this?" "What do you think would actually be a fair solution?" Or, "What would you offer if the other side was reasonable?" If the settlement numbers are within a close range, the mediator may ask you and your client to allow him to disclose your side's settlement proposal, provided that the other side does likewise. The parties might then split the difference. Even if the numbers are not very close, your client and the other party may still choose to mutually disclose the confidential proposals in order to cut through the posturing and learn how far apart they are. The parties might surprise each other, which can stimulate further movement, as they work with the mediator to bridge the remaining gap.

This approach eliminates the two primary risks of the previous method on disclosing the bottom line because no one is expected to submit

---

26. This method was suggested to me by Professor Dwight Golann of Suffolk University School of Law, who has found this method effective in a variety of commercial cases.

a real bottom line. You no longer have to worry about whether you can successfully convince the mediator that your client's bottom line is final. You also no longer have to wonder whether the other side will submit a strategic number in order to gain a favorable settlement range; they probably will. Although this method is unlikely to motivate parties to use their bottom lines, it can move parties closer to their bottom lines. It also can be a handy way to jump-start stuck parties, especially parties who are about to give up.

Safety Deposit Box

A hybrid scheme designed to temper the weaknesses of the "confidential disclosure of bottom lines" method and to strengthen the "mediator's proposal" method has been called the "safety deposit box."[27] Under this scheme, parties first disclose to the mediator their confidential bottom line numbers and then if the case does not settle, the mediator uses the confidential numbers to develop a mediator's proposal. Knowing that the bottom lines disclosed in the first stage might be used to fashion a mediator's proposal in the second stage, parties might be motivated to honestly disclose their bottom lines to the mediator. According to Peter Contuzzi, here is how the scheme works:

> While they have the virtue of simplicity [hypothetical testing and confidential disclosure of bottom lines], these common techniques lack both sufficient incentives for candor and protections against manipulation. They may also leave unclear what will happen next if they do not produce an agreement. For example, the parties may be wary of winding up with an unwanted value opinion or a settlement proposal from the mediator that they suspect may be nothing more than a splitting of the difference between their confidential bottom line numbers. Given these risks and uncertainties, how candid can they afford to be?

> To address these shortcomings,.... I ask them to think of me as a Safety Deposit Box and explain that numbers go into the box but not out—they remain locked in the box. My explanation continues with words similar to the following:

---

27. *See* Peter Contuzzi, *Should Parties Tell Mediators Their Bottom Line?*, 6 Disp. Resol. Mag. 3, Spring 2000, 30, 31–32.

[Confidential Disclosure of Bottom Lines]

I will separate you one last time in a few minutes and ask you to put your final bottom line number into the Safety Deposit Box. Please give careful thought to your number, because it will be used by me in several ways.

These numbers will not be disclosed unless, as happens occasionally, they are the same. If they are the same, I will bring you together to sign a settlement agreement. A few times in the past, these numbers have overlapped, i.e., the plaintiff's final number was lower than the defendant's. That is the one and only situation in which the midpoint between your final numbers will arbitrarily become the settlement amount.

If there is a gap of any significance between your final numbers, I will inform each party that a gap exists, without disclosing either number or the size of the gap. You may then choose among three options: (1) to keep your number confidential; (2) to disclose your number to the other side; or (3) to condition your disclosure on the other party's agreeing to disclose its number to you.

[Mediator's Proposal]

If this step does not lead to an agreement, the mediation will conclude with a brief joint meeting during which you will have an opportunity to decide if you wish to move on to the optional last stage of the process—a joint request for a final settlement proposal from the mediator. If you jointly request a settlement proposal from me, I will use the final numbers you put in the Safety Deposit Box in the following way:

Sometimes, I believe the final number of one party is significantly more fair than the other. Then I adopt that same number as my own number in my proposal. In fact, my preference is to do this in order to provide an extra incentive for you to be as candid as possible when putting your number in the Safety Deposit Box. I obviously do not indicate if my number is an adopted one, although if you have already chosen to disclose your final number, the other side will know that.

Sometimes, however, I develop my own number. It is my strong policy not to propose the midpoint between your two numbers. My proposed number will always be closer to whichever of your numbers I consider more fair.

You will have some time to consider the proposal and then respond confidentially to me with a simple "yes" or "no." If you say "yes," you are entitled to hear the other party's response, but your "yes" is not communicated by me to the other party unless it also said "yes." If you say "no," you are not entitled to hear the other party's response. The case either settles for the proposed terms or else nobody's position changes.

* * *

The limitations of this procedure should also be noted. It does not guarantee protection against all forms of manipulation, and there is no way to know if the parties are placing their actual bottom line numbers in the Safety Deposit Box...[28]

e.   Resolve Any Remaining Distributive Issues

As the session moves rapidly toward closure, a difficult distributive issue can finally crystallize and block the way home. This last issue may be resolved only in a way that benefits one party at the expense of the other. Negotiators traditionally turn to a combative strategy consisting of severe opening offers and counteroffers that produce a brash dance toward a strained compromise. You should temper these familiar strategies in a problem-solving process. One set of modified strategies was examined in the negotiation chapter and is summarized here.[29]

---

28. Peter Contuzzi, *Should Parties Tell Mediators Their Bottom Line?*, 6 DISP.RESOL. MAG. 3 (Spring 2000). © American Bar Association. Reprinted by Permission.

29. For a full discussion on how to approach easy and difficult distributive disputes, see Chapter 1.3(a)(iii), "Manage Remaining Distributive Conflicts."

Instead of selecting a combative dance, you may engage in a more collaborative one that commences with a modulated opening-offer strategy consisting of offers, counteroffers, and compromises. In such an approach, you would eliminate such harsh and aggressive moves as a pugnacious tone, clever tricks, belligerent threats, and deviously and purposefully misleading disclosure of information. Each offer, counteroffer, compromise, or concession would be justified with reasoned explanations and principled justifications. You would add or emphasize such problem-solving moves as cultivating a relationship with the other side, promoting effective communications, learning the other sides' interests and perspective, and sharing information in a way that reduces the risk of exploitation. You might even acknowledge the moment as one where both sides are claiming value at the expense of the other. And, you would use your client's BATNA as a guide for the negotiation dance, and consistent with a problem-solving approach, you would avoid theatrical posturing and threats and instead try to assess realistically both sides' BATNAs.

You also might select one of the mediators' methods examined in the previous section for inducing parties to move toward their bottom lines. These methods can be particularly effective for resolving difficult distributive conflicts. When parties are stuck over how much money one party should pay another and are reluctant to disclose their bottom lines to each other, parties may welcome these mediators' methods as a safe, less adversarial way to find out whether their bottom lines put them within a settlement range.

f.   Use Other Dispute Resolution Processes for Breaking Impasses

If the mediation process reaches an impasse, you, the other side, or the mediator may want to propose an alternative process for breaking the impasse and resolving the dispute. The process would still be conducted under the auspice of the mediation. For instance, if the mediation stalls because of a good-faith difference of opinion regarding a dispositive legal question, the mediator might propose bringing in a neutral legal expert to render a binding legal opinion. Or, if the case reaches an impasse because of conflicting views of reasonable damages, the mediator might propose the use of final-offer arbitration.[30] You should avoid a

---

30. Final-offer arbitration is when each party submits to an arbitrator his final offer for settlement. Then the arbitrator must select one offer or the other. *See* Chapter 8.2(a)(iii).

knee-jerk rejection of an unfamiliar process. Instead, carefully weigh the advantages and risks of each alternative route out of the conflict.[31]

g.   Wrap-Up

i.   Draft a Settlement Agreement

If the mediation results in a settlement, you should not leave the mediation session without a signed agreement. In the rush at the end of the day, you may lack the patience or time to execute a final and comprehensive agreement. But, do not leave without signing something. At a minimum, the participants should draft and sign a handwritten agreement that contains the agreed-upon essential terms. You can agree to fill in the details later. You may consider including a clause in which the parties commit to negotiate in good faith a formal, detailed agreement that is not inconsistent with the agreed-upon essential terms.

The mediator will usually set up a timetable for finalizing the written agreement. The mediator might offer to either mediate the drafting of the agreement or to be available in case any drafting disputes arise. The mediator, for example, might establish a deadline for finalizing the settlement agreement by scheduling a telephone conference call with the attorneys to resolve any issues that are not resolved by the conference call date.

ii.   Formulate an Exit Plan If No Settlement

If the mediation fails to fully resolve the dispute, do not pack up and leave yet. Instead, you should first clarify what progress, if any, was made. You might be able to sign a partial agreement that resolves some of the issues as well as what discovery still needs to be done before trial. You also may be able to agree which keys facts are uncontested and which key ones are still contested. You might even decide to try resolving the dispute in another dispute resolution process.[32] You might find appealing another non-binding process, one that is administered outside of the mediation, such as a minitrial or early neutral evaluation. Or you might prefer a new binding process to replace going to court, such as an expedited arbitration process.

---

31. For a full discussion of these process options, See Chapter 8.2, Breaking Impasses with Alternatives to Mediation (ATM).

32. *Ibid.*

3. Post-Session

Your responsibilities usually do not end with the conclusion of the mediation session. You will likely need to perform a number of post-session tasks.

a.   If You Represented Your Client in a Successful Session

In a successful mediation, you may not have time to draft the settlement agreement before the end of the last session. You may have to defer finalizing the agreement until afterwards.

Drafting settlement agreements is a familiar and demanding task. Even though the most contentious issues may have been resolved, you know the importance of giving careful attention to drafting the details. You will need to be patient and persistent. You should be sure that the agreement accurately reflects the settlement terms and satisfies your client's interests. It should contain the usual releases and set forth the details vital for smooth implementation, including details that may not have been considered in the session. You also should consider adding a dispute resolution clause so that a process is in place in case something goes wrong during implementation. Even mediated agreements are occasionally breached, leaving for you the task of seeking compliance, either through negotiations, mediation, or legal action. The steps for enforcement should be set forth in the dispute resolution clause of the settlement agreement. Finally, you should deal with any technical matters such as the proper filing of the agreement with the court.

You should consider who will draft the agreement and the role of the mediator in finalizing it. You presumably are already familiar with the advantages and disadvantages of your controlling the drafting or letting the other attorney do the drafting. In mediations, you have the third option of the mediator helping with the drafting.

Mediators typically follow one of two basic approaches to drafting settlement agreements. You should consider which approach you prefer. Some mediators offer to draft the settlement agreement because a mediator's draft is likely to be viewed as neutral and balanced. By removing the drafting from the attorneys, you and the other attorney are less likely to return to legal posturing and risk unraveling the agreement. Other mediators encourage the attorneys to draft the settlement agreement because drafting entails quintessential lawyering work. You know how to draft settlement agreements; you presumably do this routinely. This approach fortifies your integral involvement in the mediation process. However, you may still enlist the mediator to help resolve any prickly issues. This help can be delivered in a telephone conference call that either a far-sighted mediator scheduled at the end of the last session or one of the attorneys initiated by calling the mediator for assistance.

After the mediated agreement is signed, it must be implemented. You should be involved in monitoring and even managing the implementation such as the handing over of property or payments. Mediated agreements experience a high rate of compliance because of the way mediators involve the participants in shaping the agreement, help them craft the implementation details, and instill in them a commitment to follow through.

b.   If You Represented Your Client But Did Not Participate in the Successful Session

If you represented your client in the mediation process but did not appear with your client in the session, you must perform all the responsibilities described above in subsection a in the face of a new obstacle. You must ensure that the agreement reflects what happened in a session that you did not participate in. You will have to rely on your client's recollections and a draft prepared during the session.

c.   If You Represented Your Client in a Session That Was Not Fully Successful

If the mediation session is not completely successful, you might represent your client in the next effort to resolve the dispute. The next effort may turn out to be a continuation of the negotiations! This can happen because the mediation session will have usually cleaned up the dispute, leaving both sides with a clearer view of what needs to be done to finally resolve the dispute. For this reason, a large number of mediated cases that do not settle fully do settle shortly after the last mediation session. After a little time for participants to cogitate about the case, both sides may return to the negotiations to finish settling the dispute. The parties may even enlist the mediator to help out.

If you are unable to settle the case in the negotiations, you will likely return to court where you will continue representing your client. Or, your next effort may be in a new forum selected by both sides at the end of the mediation session or soon after the last session.[33] Fortunately, much of the preparation for the mediation can be recycled for use in other forums.

d.   If You Were Retained after the Session to Approve a Proposed Settlement

When a client shows up in your office after a successful mediation in which you did not represent the client, the client presents you with your most challenging role. The client is asking you whether he should sign an agreement that you have had no involvement in negotiating. For many attorneys, this is an unfamiliar role but it is an important one for supporting the use of mediation.

In the following excerpt,[34] Gary Friedman and Jack Himmelstein succinctly express the dilemma you face and suggest a number of ways that you might ensure that your client's interests are met in the mediated agreement.

> A client walks into your office, pulls out a document, thrusts it onto your desk and says: "I have just finished mediating a dispute that has been a source of great aggravation to me, and this is our agreement. I just want you to look this over before I sign it. What do you think?"
>
> You glance quickly at the document, and ask your client a few questions. Your first impression is that your client has made a deal that leaves her considerably worse off than if she were to go to court or to have left the negotiation in your hands.
>
> What are you to do? "Simple," you think to yourself: "I should just help my client recognize that she's getting screwed in this mediation. If she leaves this matter in the hands of a competent professional, someone like you who is an expert negotiator, she is much more likely to end up with a better deal."

---

33. *Ibid.*

34. Gary Friedman and Jack Himmelstein, *Deal Killer or Deal Saver: The Consulting Lawyer's Dilemma*, 4 Disp. Resol. Mag. 7 (Winter 1997). ©1997 American Bar Association. Reprinted by Permission.

That's the problem with mediation, you have long suspected. Would your client consider piloting an airplane without sufficient training? This is really no different, and you know it. Important decisions are being made and they require more than a cursory glance at an agreement. They require professional negotiation. That is what you as a lawyer do for a living, and you decide to give her your best legal advice: Bag the deal.

Or maybe you are a lawyer with a different attitude, have taken a mediation training and even meditated with the monks in Marin. After all, you certainly have had enough experience as a litigator to know that not all clients are satisfied with the litigation results, or even negotiation results, that you have been able to obtain for them. And, being honest with yourself, you also know that lawyers on the other side tend to see the likely result as much from what is in their clients' interests as you do from yours, and both of you can't be right at the same time.

While it is true that your client has agreed to a deal that leaves her worse off than what you think you could have gotten, she seems to be pretty satisfied, and she is the one who will have to live with the consequences. Besides, you don't like continually being cast as part of the Evil Empire, the "deal killer." You would like to support the mediation process and are ready, after gulping hard, to soft-pedal your concern about the poor result your client obtained on her own.

Tough Problem, Basic Principles

. . . The job of the consulting lawyer, as we view it, is not to yield to the temptation of either killing the deal because it is different than what you would have recommended, or blindly supporting the mediation process by rubber-stamping the result.

This dilemma is very real, and worthy of much more consideration than is possible here. Still, a few basic principles help begin pointing the way out.

First, you need to have a clear understanding about your role as a consulting lawyer. That role, as we see it, is to be a resource for your client: providing the perspective of an advocate without assuming the role of an advocate.

Second, and this is critical, you need to communicate that understanding to your client and come to a decision together about the parameters of your role. Mediation, correctly done, empowers clients. Supporting mediation as a consulting attorney can do likewise. In litigation, lawyers and clients generally take the lawyer's role for granted. In mediation, it is best that the lawyer's role be the result of explicit agreement. Rather than make assumptions about what your client wants from you, explore directly which responsibilities you can offer and which the client wants you to perform.

Third, you need to carry out those responsibilities in a manner that supports your client's responsibility in the mediation process and for the decisions that she is making. Your responsibilities can include:

- Informing your client of the applicable law, the principles underlying the law, and the likely outcomes in court. Your client is entitled to all of the knowledge of what you think would likely happen in court—and of the risks and costs associated with that strategy. But she is also entitled to your respect and support for her choice to participate in mediation, and to your assessment of how much weight to give to the legal perspective. The law is part of the picture, not the whole picture.

- Assisting your client (to the extent needed) in understanding the practical and legal consequences of what is considered in the mediation, and "reality testing" a proposed agreement to make sure that it will work over time.

- Assisting your client in developing an understanding of what is centrally important to her in the resolution of the dispute, and clarifying the priorities that need to be met for a successful outcome.

- Supporting your client in assuming the responsibility she chooses to take for participation in mediation and the decisions reached there, including advising the client about the negotiation process.

- Ensuring that the written agreement coincides with her understanding of what she thought she agreed to in the mediation.

* * *

If after that, your client concludes that the agreement really does fail to meet what she intended or what she values, then explore with her how she might, with your support, bring her concerns into the mediation. That must be done with sensitivity to the other party's likely concern that your client could be seen as reneging on the agreement, with you as the deal killer cheering her on.

4. Checklist: Mediation Appearances

1. Pre-Mediation Conference Agenda (from chapter 5)

❏ a. Verify mediator's mix of approaches to the mediation.

❏ b. Verify other side's approaches to the mediation.

❏ c. Verify attendance by best client representatives with sufficient and flexible settlement authority.

❏ d. Verify date, time, place, and length of session.

❏ e. Ask about the pre-mediation submission.

  ❏ Determine whether the mediator wants you to submit a pre-mediation submission.

  ❏ Determine what the mediator wants included in the pre-mediation submission.

  ❏ Determine whether the mediator will share any information in the submission with the other side.

  ❏ Determine that if the mediator plans to share any information, whether the mediator wants you to send the entire submission or a portion to the other side.

❏ f. Resolve what information you need from the other side before or by the session.

❏ g. Resolve whether the mediator plans to have any *ex parte* conversations with each side before the session.

❏ h. Signal likely interests of your client.

❏ i. Broach discussion of possible impediments.

❏ j. Identify any other issues that need to be resolved in the pre-mediation conference.

2. Formal Mediation Sessions

❏ a. Proactive uses of mediator's approaches, techniques, and process control.

❏ b. Anticipate questions that you and your client may be asked.

❏   c. Plan use of caucuses.
        ❏ Mediator caucuses with you and your client.
        ❏ Mediator caucuses with one or more attorneys.
        ❏ Caucuses with you and your client.

❏   d. Plan disclosure.
        ❏ Advantageous evidence to your side.
        ❏ Harmful information to your side.
        ❏ Bottom line.
            ❏ Formulate as mediation progresses.
            ❏ Consider disclosure risks and methods for reducing them.

❏   e. Resolve any remaining distributive issues.

❏   f. Plan use of other dispute resolution processes for breaking impasses.

❏   g. Wrap-up.
        ❏ Sign agreement with essential terms.
        ❏ Formulate exit plan, if no settlement.

3. **Post-Session**
❏   a. Successful mediation session.
        ❏ Resolve who will draft the final agreement.
        ❏ Ensure agreement includes key substantive provisions.
        ❏ Ensure agreement satisfies your client's interests.
        ❏ Ensure agreement covers vital implementation details.
        ❏ Ensure agreement includes any necessary releases.
        ❏ Ensure agreement includes suitable dispute resolution clause.
        ❏ Determine what you need to do to ensure implementation.

❐   b.   Attorney represented client but did not participate in successful session.
- ❐   Resolve who will draft the final agreement.
- ❐   Ensure agreement includes key substantive provisions.
- ❐   Ensure agreement reflects what your client thinks happened in the session.
- ❐   Ensure agreement covers vital implementation details.
- ❐   Ensure agreement includes any necessary releases.
- ❐   Ensure agreement includes suitable dispute resolution clause.
- ❐   Determine what you need to do to ensure implementation.

❐   c.   Attorney represented client in session that was not fully successful.
- ❐   Continue negotiations.
- ❐   Return to adjudication.
- ❐   Select new process.

❐   d.   Attorney retained after mediation session to approve proposed settlement.
- ❐   Advise your client on your limited role.
- ❐   Help your client make an informed judgment.

CHAPTER EIGHT

BREAKING IMPASSES WITH ALTERNATIVES TO MEDIATION (ATM)

Topics in this chapter include:

1. Causes of Impasses: Needs Unmet in the Mediation
2. Alternatives to Mediation (ATM)—A Glossary

This chapter examines impasses that can be overcome by using processes of dispute resolution other than mediation.

During the mediation session or toward its end, the dispute may reach an impasse that cannot be surmounted in the mediation session. The mediator's mix of approaches, techniques, and process control are just not enough to help the parties get past the impasse. To overcome this structural obstacle, you should consider resorting to an alternative process. Alternative processes may be suggested by the mediator who has expertise in impasse analysis and ways to overcome impasses. Even you or the other side might realize the benefits of an alternative process and propose it. You should be prepared to assess the advantages and drawbacks of various process options and hone your skills in selecting the most suitable one to try next.

This chapter considers first some of the process needs that may be unmet in mediation. Then, it examines alternative process solutions.

1. Causes of Impasses: Needs Unmet in the Mediation

This section canvasses a list of process needs that may not be met in mediation. (See Table 1.) A number of these needs, also known as interests, are the same ones that you considered when you initially interviewed your client for the purpose of selecting a suitable dispute resolution process.[1] At this late point in the mediation, it may have become evident that mediation cannot meet one or more of these process needs.

---

1. *See* Chapter 3.2, 3.3, and 3.4 on interviewing clients.

The descriptions of the unmet needs in this section include suggested process solutions along with a few examples of how you might go about selecting the most suitable process. However, this section does not identify the best dispute resolution method for meeting each need for the obvious reason that the answer depends on the particulars of the dispute. For you to determine which one makes best sense in your client's particular case, you should examine the glossary in section 2 where the distinctive features of each process are highlighted and then assess which mix of features that make up each process best serve your client's unmet needs.

TABLE 1

Unmet Process Needs

Your client needs a process that will provide:
a.   Realistic Assessment of Facts
b.   Realistic Interpretation of Law
c.   Realistic Assessment of Likely Court Outcome
d.   Realistic Assessment of Amount of Damages
e.   Vindication
f.   Protection of a Principle or Value
g.   Precedent or Deterrence to Future Litigation
h.   Efficient Alternative to Court
i.   Opportunity to Go for a Jackpot
j.   Incentive to the Other Party to Secure Adequate
      Representation
k.   Participation by a Critical Party
l.   Good Faith Participation by the Other Side

Each possible unmet process need is classified in brackets in accordance with Moore's impasse breaking scheme.

a.   Realistic Assessment of Facts [data conflict]

The parties may reach an impasse because of conflicting views of critical facts. The dispute could be due to conflicting views of eyewitnesses, conflicting or ambiguous documentary evidence, or conflicting expert opinions. Because the resolution of the factual dispute may impact vitally on the likely adjudicatory outcome, one or all the parties cannot move forward in the mediation. This data conflict can be addressed in a facilitative mediation by the mediator helping the parties identify and assemble the critical data and then structuring a discussion that tries to resolve the factual dispute. If these initiatives do not overcome the data conflict, the parties' need for a realistic assessment of disputed facts may be met in a different process.

Initially, the parties will have to resolve whether the results of a non-binding process will carry enough weight to help them overcome the factual conflict. The parties can gain a realistic assessment of the facts in a non-binding or binding *fact-finding process* or *expert evaluation,* or in a non-binding *summary jury trial* or *mini-trial,* as well as in *court.*

Example
Selecting Process to Break Impasse

In a suit for breach of a construction contract, parties dispute their oral understandings of several key contractual terms and disagree over whether the construction work complied with the engineering specifications in the contract. These factual disputes are holding up a settlement. If the parties will likely respect the outcome of a non-binding process, the parties have a number of options to consider. If one party is confident about a favorable and generous reaction from a jury, the party may want to try to demonstrate this in a *summary jury trial.* If a party thinks that it would be helpful to involve senior business executives in resolving the dispute, the party may want to engage the senior executives in a *mini-trial.* If the dispute over the oral understandings is preventing a settlement, the parties may want to enlist a non-binding *neutral fact-finder.* If the engineering issues are blocking a settlement, the parties could jointly retain an engineering expert to give her non-binding *expert evaluation.*

b.   Realistic Interpretation of Law [data conflict]

The parties may be at an impasse because of conflicting views of a dispositive legal question. Even though they may agree on the relevant facts, you and the other attorney may disagree over whether a particular statute or legal precedent applies or how to interpret a determinative statute or court case. Parties, for instance, may be in agreement that the buyer e-mailed an offer and the seller e-mailed an acceptance, but you and the other attorney may disagree as to whether the exchange of e-mails satisfied the writing and signature requirements of the statute of frauds. This data conflict can be addressed in a facilitative mediation by the mediator helping you and the other attorney participate in a focused discussion in which specific difference are either reconciled or isolated, and each attorney articulates the likelihood of being right or wrong. If these initiatives do not overcome the data conflict, your client's interest in a realistic interpretation of the law may be met in a different process, a process that produces a persuasive or binding interpretation of law. As an alternative to *court,* the legal interpretation could be obtained efficiently from a *neutral legal evaluator.* It also could be obtained from the neutral chair in a *mini-trial.*

c. Realistic Assessment of Likely Court Outcome [data conflict]

The parties may be at an impasse because of conflicting views of what would happen if the case were litigated to the end—to a bench judgment or jury verdict. In contrast with the previous two interests where a few narrow factual or legal disputes could be isolated and assessed, the parties here face numerous contested facts and disputed legal issues. The parties may hold vigorously conflicting opinions regarding what will be the likely court outcome and therefore need a more judicial-like process. This data conflict can be addressed in a facilitative mediation by the mediator helping the attorneys and parties identify their differences through the use of a decision-tree analysis. If this initiative does not succeed, the need for a realistic assessment of the court outcome may be met in a different process.

Initially, the parties will have to decide whether a non-binding process will carry sufficient weight. Processes that can help predict what a court might do include a non-binding *summary jury trial,* non-binding *mini-trial,* or non-binding *legal neutral evaluation.* Processes that could replace the *court* in deciding the outcome include binding *conventional arbitration,* binding *high-low arbitration,* binding *final-offer arbitration,* binding *legal neutral evaluation,* and binding *private judging.*

Example
Selecting Process to Break Impasse

In a complicated licensing agreement in which parties are disputing the interpretation of the contract, how the licensee used the trademark, and the applicable federal and state trademark law, the parties need a process that will either *predict* what a court will do or will *decide* the case. Assuming the parties conclude that a non-binding predictive process will not be sufficiently respected to move the negotiations toward a resolution, the parties could adopt a binding process that would replace the court in deciding the outcome. If the parties are looking for a more expeditious and economical process than court, they should consider conventional arbitration. If they fear that any monetary award could be oppressively extreme, they may want to bracket the award in a high-low arbitration. If parties cannot tolerate giving up such procedural rights as full discovery and rights to appeal in arbitration, they may prefer private judging, if available under local law. Although the process of legal neutral evaluation could be expanded to provide for a binding judicial-like process, to do so would be to convert the legal expert into a sole arbitrator and to transform the process into a conventional arbitration.

d.   Realistic Assessment of Amount of Damages [data conflict]

The parties may be at an impasse because they are unable to agree how much damages the defendant owes. They may have resolved other issues including the question of liability and may even have designed some creative features for the settlement package. But, they cannot resolve the remaining money issue. They agree the defendant must pay something; they just cannot agree on the amount. The parties are facing a distributive dispute in which one party gains at the expense of the other one. An increased payment to the plaintiff comes out of the pocket of the defendant or a decreased payment to the plaintiff means more for the defendant. For example, in a breach of contract suit for delivery of computers, the parties may have agreed that the defendant breached the contract, that the defendant will continue to provide computers for the next two years, and that the defendant owes something for damages due to the late deliveries. But, they cannot agree on the amount of damages.

This data conflict can be addressed in a facilitative mediation by the mediator helping both sides collect data, agree on the components of the damages, and calculate the total damages. If these initiatives do not work because the sides just cannot agree on the numbers and are unable to compromise, the need to calculate damages may be met in a different process. The distributive conflict can be creatively addressed in binding *final-offer arbitration*. A dispute over damages also can be investigated in either a binding or non-binding *fact-finding process*. If the parties cannot agree to any of these options, they can go to *court* for a judicial decision.

e.   Vindication [interest or structural conflict]

The parties may be at an impasse because one of them needs some form of vindication. A party may need to be exonerated, to find another person at fault, or to satisfy people not at the table.

Exoneration: A party's need to be exonerated may conflict with the other party's need to be exonerated or to avoid clarifying who is responsible. For example, a manager accused of breaching a contract may need an authoritative decision that will clear her with her superiors back at the home office while the other party may want to avoid resolving who is responsible for what went wrong. A party can be exonerated in any process that declares who is at fault. This need can be addressed in a facilitative mediation by the mediator helping the parties come to an understanding of who was at fault without the parties ever reaching a level of decisive clarity. But, this may not be enough.

Find Another Person at Fault: A party may need to clear her name by pinning blame on the other party who is not willing to take responsibility. For example, an architectural firm accused of designing a defective roof for an auditorium may need a determination that the roof collapsed due to the failure of someone else such as the construction firm. This interest conflict can be addressed in a facilitative mediation by the mediator constructing a process for the exchange of data and discussion that could help the parties come to an understanding of who was at fault. But, this may not be sufficient.

Satisfy People Not at Table: The parties may be at an impasse because one of them is having difficulty satisfying constituencies that are not at the table. This impasse can arise when a party represents an institution or group such as a corporation or a union or when a party is accountable to someone not at the table such as a spouse or supervisor. For example, a manager in a large corporation may have trouble shaping a credible settlement with her superiors back at corporate headquarters. In order to protect herself from suspicion or criticism, the party may need an authoritative decision from an independent third party. This structural conflict can be overcome in a facilitative mediation by the mediator helping the parties either identify who else should be at the table or formulate an agreement that may satisfy people not there.

If the various initiatives in mediation are unsuccessful, the need for some form of vindication may be met in a different process. The party seeking vindication will have to decide whether a non-binding decision would be sufficient. Non-binding and binding decisions can be secured from *conventional arbitration, a fact-finding process, legal neutral evaluation, expert evaluation, or a mini-trial.* A non-binding decision can be procured from a *summary jury trial.* A binding decision can be obtained in *private judging* or *court.*

Example
Selecting Process to Break Impasse

A party accused of racial discrimination may need to be exonerated in order to clear her name. If the party concludes that a non-binding decision would not provide sufficient vindication, the party could select a suitable binding process that will efficiently produce a credible determination. If the dispute is over critical facts, the party may need only a credible *fact-finding process.* If the facts are mostly undisputed, the party may need only a *legal neutral evaluation.* If both facts and the application of law are heatedly contested, the party may need a more judicial-like process like *conventional arbitration* or a *summary judicial trial* or a full judicial process like *private judging.*

f.   Protection of a Principle or Value [value conflict]

The parties may be at an impasse because one of them is wedded to a principle or value that the party will not "compromise." For example, in a divorce action, the mother may never agree to share custody with the father because the mother's parenting values on how to bring up their children conflict with the father's. She can avoid compromising herself by participating in an adjudicatory process in which she can protect her parenting values by seeking custody. If she loses, she did not choose to compromise herself although she may be compelled to comply with a compromising decision.

Value conflicts can be avoided in a facilitative mediation by the mediator helping the party move toward a resolution that does not require compromising her principles or values. Instead of focusing on sharing custody, the mediator might suggest re-framing the issue to whether the mother might consider sharing parenting time with the father. If this initiative fails, this value conflict may be overcome in a different process.

The party should consider whether voluntarily complying with a negative non-binding decision allows her to preserve her principle or values. If not, she will need to select a suitable binding process such as binding *conventional arbitration, fact-finding process, legal neutral evaluation,* or *expert evaluation.* A binding decision also can be obtained in *private judging* or *court.*

g. Establish Precedent or Deterrence to Future Litigation [interest conflict]

A party may need a process that establishes a precedent that will be binding on future similar disputes as well as will help the party establish a reputation that she will not cave in to threats of baseless litigation. The other party might hold a conflicting interest in avoiding a precedent or a conflicting interest in settling.

A company suing a former employee for breaching a covenant not to compete may need a precedent upholding the terms of the provision in order to discourage other departing employees from ignoring it. The employee may not care about the precedent, only whether she can work in a new position. This interest conflict might be overcome in a facilitative mediation by the mediator helping the parties negotiate an agreement that permits the former employee to work again after paying some damages for the breach. The agreement might give the employer the opportunity to publicize the mediated agreement so that it can serve as a precedent that may deter future litigation. If this effort fails to meet the needs of the parties, the interest conflict may be overcome by a different process.

A binding precedent can be secured from a *private judging* process when the local law authorizes the resulting private judgment to be entered as a judicial judgment. Other alternative dispute resolution processes may produce decisions that are not binding legal precedents, but they can provide persuasive authority and discourage conduct that varies from them. These non-precedental, persuasive decisions can be obtained from a *conventional arbitration, legal neutral evaluator, expert evaluator,* or even a *summary jury trial.* If the parties cannot agree to use any of these options, they can go to *court* for a judicial decision.

h. Efficient Alternative to Court [structural conflict]

After exhausting all possibilities for settling the case in mediation, parties may not want to return to court. They may prefer a less costly and less adversarial adjudicatory option. For example, when parties end the mediation of a contract breach case in which key terms are still disputed, the parties may want to avoid returning to court for a final adjudication. They may prefer an alternative to court.

This structural conflict can be overcome by the mediator helping the parties select and design an alternative adjudicatory process. Alternative processes that could provide a binding resolution include *conventional arbitration, high-low arbitration, Med-Arb,* and *private judging.*

i. Opportunity to Go for a Jackpot [structural conflict]. The parties may be at an impasse because one of them may be tempted by the possibility of a big win before a jury, judge, or arbitrator. Even though a mediator can conduct a reality-checking session, the prospect of a big jackpot can sometimes be just too enticing. This structural conflict can be overcome by the parties agreeing to use an alternative that will give the prospect of a jackpot a test run or a final test.

Initially, the party will have to decide whether a non-binding decision that predicts whether she will get the jackpot will provide her sufficient leverage in negotiating favorable terms. Non-binding and binding decisions can be secured in a *conventional arbitration, fact-finding process, legal neutral evaluation, expert evaluation,* or *mini-trial.* A non-binding decision can be procured from a *summary jury trial.* A binding decision can be obtained in *private judging* and of course *court.*

Other Unmet Needs

j. Incentive to Other Party to Secure Adequate Representation [structural conflict]. Parties may be at an impasse because the other party cannot effectively represent her interests in the mediation and is not represented by counsel.

k. Participation by Critical Party [structural conflict]. Parties may be at an impasse because an essential party is not participating in the mediation.

l. Good Faith Participation by Other Side [structural conflict]. The parties may be at an impasse because the other party has a history of acting in bad faith including engaging in delay strategies.

You may try to convince the other side to use an alternative process that will motivate the other side to secure representation, involve a critical party, or act in good faith or else risk getting stuck with an unfavorable result imposed by the alternative process. If the other side would agree to use any of the variations of *arbitration*, for instance, the other side would then have the incentive to do what is necessary to be successful or else be burdened with an adverse binding or non-binding result. However, these other processes can be activated only with the consent of the other side, which you may have difficulty securing. Therefore, your most viable option may be the only one with compulsory jurisdiction, the option of going to *court*.

2. Alternatives to Mediation (ATM): A Glossary

In this section, a number of alternatives to mediation (ATM) are described. Each description emphasizes the distinguishing features that define the process. By canvassing these features, you should be able to gain an overall understanding of each process and what distinguishes it from the other processes. But, these features are not proffered as rigid requirements that must be strictly observed every time the process is employed. You can vary and refine the specific details of each process to meet the needs of each particular situation.

The court option has been added at the end in order to highlight the ways its familiar features distinguishes it from less familiar alternatives. The court option has been included as a reminder that your goal is not to select an alternative to court but to select the *appropriate* dispute resolution option for breaking the impasse.[2] Sometimes, that option may be going to court.

The distinguishing features of each process have been highlighted by answering the following generic process questions for each process.

Generic Process Questions

(i) **What Types of Disputes Are Suitable for the Process?** Is the process suitable for disputes that involve contested questions of fact or law or both? Does the process provide an opportunity for assessing the credibility of key fact or expert witnesses? Is the process appropriate for complex disputes?

---

2. This list of dispute resolution options has been called ADR. I prefer using the now more accurate translation of ADR as "Appropriate Dispute Resolution" instead of the more popular nomenclature of "Alternative Dispute Resolution." The "appropriate" label reminds us that ADR is not about searching for "alternatives" to court. It is about searching for the most appropriate dispute resolution option which sometimes might be the option of going to court.

(ii) Is It a Process of Negotiation or Adjudication? Whether the underlying process fosters negotiations or delivers adjudication depends on whether the results are non-binding or binding. The type of process is not determined by whether the method of presentation and participation is the familiar adversarial one used in adjudicatory forums. If any resulting decision is non-binding, thereby making the decision advisory, the underlying process promotes negotiations. By the third party neutral supplying the parties new and credible input about the merits of the dispute, the parties can gain valuable input into the negotiations that they can choose to be guided by or to ignore. Parties would be foolish to ignore the input because of the insight it can provide into what might happen in court. This insight can help parties assess during the negotiations whether going to court is more or less attractive than any emerging negotiated settlement.

If the results of the dispute resolution process are binding, the underlying process is one of adjudication: A third party neutral renders a decision in which winners and losers are announced and remedies imposed. Parties may elect a binding process in order to decisively resolve the contested issues.

(iii) What Is the Structure of the Process? The structure for producing a result can vary from the familiar adversarial procedures to creative variations of participation, presentation, and third-party neutral involvement.

(iv) Who Is the Neutral Third Party? Each of these alternatives has in common one key feature: Each one introduces a third party into the process of resolving the dispute. The third party is usually neutral and selected by the parties. The credentials of the third party can range the full gamut from extensive judicial experience to substantial legal or technical expertise in relevant fields to specialized training in dispute resolution.

(v) What Is the Role of the Third Party? The third party can engage in a range of roles from the traditional, umpiring role of a judge to an active force in shaping a settlement to a less directive facilitator.

(vi) What Is the Role of the Clients? The clients' roles can range from the traditional, passive one performed in the courtroom to an active partnership with the lawyer.

(vii) What Are the Outcome/Remedies? Outcomes/Remedies can vary greatly. They can consist of court-like decisions that declare winners and traditional judicial remedies. Or, they could be limited to findings of fact or law. Or, they can entail expansive, creative, tailored remedies.

This section describes ten ATMs plus the familiar court option.[3] (See Table 2.)

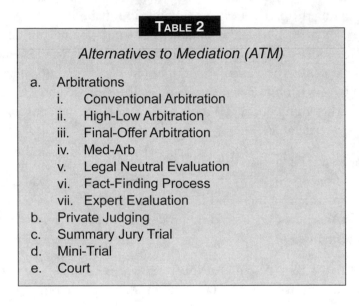

TABLE 2
Alternatives to Mediation (ATM)

a. Arbitrations
    i.   Conventional Arbitration
    ii. High-Low Arbitration
    iii. Final-Offer Arbitration
    iv. Med-Arb
    v.   Legal Neutral Evaluation
    vi. Fact-Finding Process
    vii. Expert Evaluation
b. Private Judging
c. Summary Jury Trial
d. Mini-Trial
e. Court

a.   Arbitrations

Arbitration commonly consists of four distinguishing features:

- Parties selecting

- A neutral third party (or panel),

- Who hears the dispute and renders a decision,

- In a flexible and relatively expeditious process that can be tailored to the needs of the parties and dispute.

In addition to "Conventional Arbitration," there are a number of creative variations that could be the right process for an unmet need. These variations are: High-Low Arbitration, Final-Offer Arbitration,

---

3. *See* Appendix F for a selected list of Web sites for locating private rules suitable for a range of dispute resolution processes including variations of arbitration.

Med-Arb, Legal Neutral Evaluation, Fact-Finding Process, and Expert Evaluation.

i.   Conventional Arbitrations

What Types of Disputes Are Suitable for the Process? Conventional arbitrations are suitable for any dispute that involves questions of fact, especially ones that implicate the credibility of fact or expert witnesses. Although arbitrations can resolve contested questions of law, arbitrators are not bound by the principle of *stare decisis* and usually do not feel obliged to make decisions based on strict interpretations of law. Even though arbitrations do not traditionally permit the sort of extensive discovery common in judicial proceedings, arbitrations are nevertheless suited to handle complex disputes due to their flexible procedures and hand-picked arbitrators with substantive expertise in the subject matter of the dispute.

Is It a Process of Negotiation or of Adjudication? If the parties choose to be bound by the results, then the process is clearly one of adjudication. But, if the parties agree that they are not obliged to comply, then the process is one of negotiation in which the advisory opinion can influence what the parties do in the related negotiations.

What Is the Structure of the Process? Arbitration is conducted in accordance with a classically adjudicatory format in which the third party decides the dispute. The arbitration process is organized like a court hearing, with opening and closing arguments, presentation and cross-examination of witnesses, opportunity for presenting rebuttal, and filing of briefs (sometimes). But, the full rules of evidence do not apply and the arbitrator's decision usually omits any explanation and is subject to severely limited judicial review.

Who Is the Neutral Third Party? The third party is usually a person or panel of three with substantive expertise in the subject matter of the dispute. The parties ordinarily select the third party or panel; they usually select someone other than the mediator.

What Is the Role of the Neutral Third Party? The third party hears the case and decides who wins and who loses.

What Is the Role of the Clients? The clients serve in the limited role of witnesses and sources of information for the attorneys.

What Are the Outcome/Remedies? Remedies closely resemble the sort of remedies available in court—based on legal rights but tempered by a sense of fairness.

ii.   High-Low Arbitration

High-low arbitration is conventional arbitration with one major modification.

What Types of Disputes Are Suitable for the Process? The remaining contested issue is primarily about money. The parties want to reduce the risk of an extremely high or low money award by agreeing to an upper and lower amount for any award.

Is It a Process of Negotiation or Adjudication? Parties usually agree that the results of high-low arbitration will be binding, making the process adjudicatory. Because the high-low feature gives parties the protection they need from extreme results, the parties are more receptive to a binding process. Parties, however, are not likely to select this method to promote negotiation because parties do not learn much for the negotiation from a non-binding arbitration award bounded by party-imposed bracketed amounts.

What Is the Structure of the Process? The parties negotiate maximum and minimum dollar amounts of any award. Those amounts could consist of the last settlement offers made by each side. The mediator can assist the parties in negotiating a range within which they can live. The parties should be motivated to negotiate a reasonable range because the plaintiff wants the security of a high minimum award and the defendant wants the protection of a low maximum award. If the range is too wide, the parties do not gain an advantage over conventional arbitration. The arbitrator is not informed of the bracketed range. In all other ways, the arbitration operates like a conventional arbitration.

Who Is the Neutral Third Party? The third party is usually the same one(s) selected in a conventional arbitration.

What Is the Role of the Neutral Third Party? The arbitrator functions in exactly the same way as the arbitrator in a conventional arbitration; but she is not informed of the bracketed range for recovery until she issues the award.

What Is the Role of the Clients? The clients serve the same limited role as they do in conventional arbitration.

What Are the Outcome/Remedies? The arbitrator's decision is binding if it falls within the bracketed range. If the decision falls outside the range, the award is adjusted to the maximum or minimum recovery, whichever one is closest to the arbitrator's award.

iii.   Final-Offer Arbitration (FOA)[4] (See FOA Rules in Appendix J.)

What Types of Disputes Are Suitable for the Process? Disputes where the remaining contested issue is primarily about money. The parties might be reluctant to use conventional arbitration or high-low arbitration because of the fear that the arbitrator will split the difference between what each party wants instead of making a hard decision on the merits. Under final-offer arbitration, the arbitrator must select the final offer of one of the parties.

Is It a Process of Negotiation or Adjudication? Parties usually agree that the results of the final-offer arbitration will be binding, thereby making the process adjudicatory. But, this binding feature can transform the adjudication into a negotiation. The binding feature can motivate each party to prepare a final offer that is reasonable because the failure to do so could result in the arbitrator selecting the other party's offer. As parties focus on preparing their final offers, their differences can narrow to the point that they can negotiate a settlement. Therefore, it is not unusual for parties to agree to use final-offer arbitration and then settle the case.

Final-offer arbitration can be an especially effective way to encourage negotiated settlements when one or both parties are wedded to going to court. By replacing going to court with going to FOA, the parties replace the court option with an adjudicatory option that is consistent with settlement efforts. Instead of participants posturing about who will win in court, they posture about who will present the more reasonable final offer. Instead of settlement offers consisting of painful compromises of positions taken in court papers, settlement offers consist of proposals that harmonize with the final offers that will be submitted to the arbitrator. As a result, parties shift from a litigation and compromise mind-set to a reasonable settlement mind-set.

---

4. Final-offer arbitration is popularly known as baseball arbitration because of its use in settling salary disputes of professional baseball players.

What Is the Structure of the Process? The hearing might consist of a conventional arbitration hearing, a paper hearing based on written submissions by each side, the mediation sessions, and any pre-mediation submissions, or a hybrid of these options. After the hearing, each party submits a "final offer" to the arbitrator. The arbitrator must adopt one of the offers. As the parties prepare their final offers, the parties may try settling the dispute or welcome the mediator's assistance in settling.

Who Is the Neutral Third Party? The final-offer arbitrator is usually a person with substantive expertise in the subject matter of the dispute. It is better practice to select someone other than the mediator in order to maintain the integrity of the two different processes of arbitration and mediation (This is discussed in detail in the next section on Med-Arb under "Who is the Neutral Third Party?") However, in FOA parties may consider making an exception. If the mediator will not mediate after the final-offer arbitration, parties may want to select the mediator to serve as the final-offer arbitrator, assuming the parties have confidence in the mediator-turned-arbitrator despite what the parties know that the mediator learned during the mediation. This arrangement has a number of advantages. Parties can save time and money by avoiding the need to select a new neutral. Presentations and hearings can be greatly reduced because the mediator already knows much about the dispute. As the parties prepare their final offers, the mediator can help the parties settle the dispute. Finally, knowing that the arbitrator is immediately available and ready to arbitrate, the parties face a courthouse-type deadline.

What Is the Role of the Neutral Third Party? The arbitrator must select one of the offers. The arbitrator cannot split the difference or make any modifications to either offer. As the parties prepare their final offers, the parties might welcome the mediator's assistance in helping them settle the dispute.

What Is the Role of the Clients? Clients participate actively in preparing the final offer and in any settlement efforts. If an arbitration hearing is held, clients serve the familiar and prescribed roles of parties.

What Are the Outcome/Remedies? If the final-offer arbitration process is completed, the outcome will be the one prepared by the winning party. But, because the process of FOA can encourage parties to negotiate a settlement, the parties could end up negotiating a tailored resolution.

iv.   Med-Arb (Mediation-Arbitration)

This subsection focuses on how Med-Arb is different from conventional arbitration.

What Types of Disputes Are Suitable for the Process? During the course of the mediation, parties may want to replace the court option with arbitration, if the parties think the dispute is suitable for arbitration. Then, if the mediation reaches an impasse, the more expeditious and less expensive arbitration option will be in place and can be quickly activated in order to bring closure to the dispute.

Is It a Process of Negotiation or of Adjudication? In Med-Arb, the arbitration component typically produces binding results, making the arbitration adjudicatory. But, the immediate availability of arbitration can motivate parties to negotiate a resolution on their own terms rather than risk an imposed outcome by an arbitrator.

What Is the Structure of the Process? Med-Arb is simply a process that combines two familiar methods of dispute resolution into one back-to-back process in which arbitration becomes immediately available if the mediation does not succeed.

Who Is the Neutral Third Party? Parties should select two different neutrals: a mediator and an arbitrator. By doing this, the parties can ensure that the integrity of each process will be preserved and the full process benefits of each will be realized. If the same neutral serves both roles, each process might be compromised.

> The primary risk is that one neutral may not be able to perform effectively the two distinctively different roles of arbitrator and settler (mediator) in the same case. In order to preserve the integrity of each process, the neutral must simultaneously maintain her *impartiality* as arbitrator and her *flexibility* as settler (mediator).
>
> The neutral must figure out how to preserve her impartiality when trying to settle a case. Settlers [mediators], for instance, may solicit confidential information for purposes of settlement, hold ex parte meetings (caucuses), engage in "reality testing," and even assess merits of claims (evaluations). These initiatives may benefit the settlement process but may expose the arbitration process to legal attack. A party

may challenge the arbitrator or the award on the grounds that the arbitrator was influenced by information learned during settlement efforts. A party also may claim that the arbitrator prejudged the case during settlement efforts when she offered an evaluation of the merits of the case. A party might even complain that the arbitrator retaliated against the party in the arbitration proceeding for not heeding her advice during settlement discussions. Therefore, arbitrators face the daunting risk of engaging in settlement initiatives that may disqualify them as arbitrators. In trying to reduce this risk, arbitrators may feel compelled to limit their use of some basic techniques that can make settlement efforts effective.

Other problems arise when the same neutral serves two processes. For settlement efforts to be successful, parties must talk candidly with the neutral. Parties may be reluctant to talk candidly for strategic reasons when they realize that the neutral may later serve as the arbitrator.[5]

Nevertheless, parties may still want to take these risks and arrange for the same neutral to serve both roles in order to save the time and money that would otherwise be expended for selecting, educating, and compensating a second neutral. Also, as in settlement conferences with judges, some parties may want the third party to have the power of the ultimate decision-maker. Then, by hinting what the third party might do as the arbitrator, the third party can induce parties to settle.

What Is the Role of the Neutral Third Party? The role of the neutral third party depends on whether the same neutral serves as both mediator and arbitrator. If different neutrals serve each role, then the neutral as mediator performs as any mediator and the neutral as arbitrator performs as any arbitrator. But, if the same neutral serves both roles, how the neutral will act becomes less clear. Ideally, no differences should exist. But in practice, as just described, it can be difficult for the neutral to keep the roles separate and difficult for the parties to trust that the neutral will keep the roles separate.

What Is the Role of the Clients? When in mediation, clients perform the active role elaborated in the mediation representation chapters. When

---

5. Abramson, *Protocols for International Arbitrators Who Dare to Settle Cases*, THE AM. REV. OF INTL. ARB. 1, 3–4 (1999).

in arbitration, clients perform the more limited role described under conventional arbitration.

What Are the Outcome/Remedies? The outcome could be a creative, tailored solution if the dispute resolves in mediation or a legal rights-based solution if the case ends in arbitration.

v.   Legal Neutral Evaluation

What Types of Disputes Are Suitable for the Process? A legal neutral evaluation can be helpful when the parties need the opinion of a recognized legal expert in the subject matter of the substantive dispute. The neutral evaluator can give her independent legal opinion when each side holds different interpretations of dispositive statutes or case law or different views of the likely court outcome. The neutral evaluator also can help parties isolate areas of agreement and disagreement, develop an efficient and orderly discovery schedule for settlement, or negotiate the settlement of the dispute. This process is frequently called early neutral evaluation (ENE) because of the recognized benefits of bringing in a neutral expert early in the litigation before a lot of money and time has been expended and before positions become too entrenched. But, neutral evaluation can also be valuable toward the end of a mediation as a method of breaking an impasse involving legal issues.

Is It a Process of Negotiation or Adjudication? Neutral evaluation is usually non-binding, making it an advisory process that produces new information for the parties to use in the negotiations. While the expert evaluator may prod the parties to settle, the parties still retain the power to walk away. However, the parties could agree to be bound by the evaluator's legal opinion. Their agreement would then create a binding arbitration process for resolving selected issues.

What Is the Structure of the Process? The process follows a series of distinct stages. First, each side presents their view of the case, in conventional adversarial presentations. There usually are no witnesses and no formal cross-examination. Then, the evaluator may assist the parties in isolating areas of agreement and disagreement, drafting stipulations, and developing an efficient discovery plan. Next, the evaluator may offer her opinion regarding the strengths and weaknesses of the case and how a court might resolve key legal issues. Finally, the evaluator may help the parties settle the dispute. The entire process can be relatively short—from a couple hours to a half day.

Who Is the Neutral Third Party? Parties select a recognized and highly respected legal expert in the subject matter of the dispute. In contrast with selecting a mediator who should possess considerable expertise in the process of resolving disputes, the legal evaluator is selected for her substantive expertise and credibility.

What Is the Role of the Neutral Third Party? In performing the different tasks described under the "Structure of the Process," the neutral may behave like many settlement judges who progressively pressure the parties to settle at each stage of the discussions or behave like a mediator who facilitates the different stages of the discussion.

What Is the Role of the Clients? Clients usually attend in order to hear the evaluation but they do not participate actively because the discussion is mostly about legal matters. However, the clients may become more actively involved during the settlement stage.

What Are the Outcome/Remedies? The outcomes are likely to include a clearer and more focused understanding of differences, a contained and orderly discovery schedule, predictions of how a court might interpret the law or how a court might decide the case, and possibly a settlement shaped by the likely judicial outcome.

vi.   Fact-Finding Process[6]

What Types of Disputes Are Suitable for the Process? When the critical facts in the case are either highly contested or very unclear, parties may want to use an alternative fact-finding process. Instead of using the conventional approach of discovery, adversarial testing of witnesses and documents, and determinations by a judge or jury, parties may want to appoint a neutral fact-finder to investigate the facts and issue a fact-finding report. This process could be a quicker, less costly, and less acrimonious way of establishing facts. If the factual disputes involve highly technical matters, the parties may want to use the process discussed in the next section called "Expert Evaluation."

Is It a Process of Negotiation or Adjudication? A fact-finding process is usually non-binding, making it an advisory process that fosters negotiations. The new information in the fact-finding report can prod the parties toward settlement. However, the parties could agree to be bound by

---

6. *See* JOHN W. COOLEY, MEDIATION ADVOCACY 163–164 (1996).

the report, an agreement that would create a binding arbitration process for resolving selected factual disputes.

What Is the Structure of the Process? The parties request the fact-finder to investigate the facts of the case. The fact-finder interviews witnesses, assembles relevant written documents, and assesses the collected information. The fact-finder might give the parties an opportunity to comment on a draft report before finalizing it. The final report is given to the parties and possibly the mediator.

Who Is the Neutral Third Party? The parties select a fact-finder who has the skills to collect, digest, and assess factual information. The neutral should know how to interview witnesses, judge their credibility, and handle sensitive information, including maintaining its confidentiality. It can be helpful for the fact-finder to possess expertise in the subject matter of the dispute.

What Is the Role of the Neutral Third Party? The third party investigates the facts and issues a fact-finding report.

What Is the Role of the Clients? The clients are key witnesses who provide written information, compile lists of other witnesses, and are interviewed by the fact-finder.

What Are the Outcome/Remedies? The outcome will be a credible report that sets forth the neutral's conclusions regarding key facts. The neutral also may clarify contested facts for which the fact-finder could not draw any firm opinions. The report typically does not contain any conclusions of law or suggested remedies.

vii.   Expert Evaluation

What Types of Disputes Are Suitable for the Process? When a technical, non-legal issue is dividing the parties, they may want to consult a mutually agreed upon specialist. For instance, if the parties cannot agree on the reasons for an airplane engine failure, they may want to hire an engineering expert to study the failed engine and submit her written findings. The use of a mutually agreed upon technical expert provides an alternative to the traditional "battle of the experts" where each party hires her own expert whose partisan findings are tested in an adversarial process of presentation, cross-examination, and rebuttal.

Is It a Process of Negotiation or Adjudication? Expert evaluation is usually non-binding, making it an advisory process that produces new information that the parties can use in the negotiations. The expert's opinion should carry considerable weight in the negotiations. However, the parties could agree to be bound by the expert's opinion, an agreement that would transform the process into binding arbitration for resolving the selected technical issues.

What Is the Structure of the Process? Each party furnishes the expert with the information she requests and with whatever other information the party wants to submit. The expert may need access to internal reports, witnesses, parties' experts, physical evidence, and the subject of the technical investigation. Over a relatively short period of time (possibly several months), the expert compiles the information, interviews people, studies what has been collected, and prepares a draft report. After giving each side an opportunity to comment, the expert issues her final report of findings in which the expert explores and explicates different approaches and tests different assumptions.

Who Is the Neutral Third Party? The technical expert or panel of experts brings superb professional credentials and experience in the subject matter of the dispute. The expert(s) is selected by the parties, but they may find it difficult to select someone jointly. When trying to select an expert, the parties should maintain a clear view of the goal to use a different process. Instead of each party selecting respected partisan experts for testing in a conventional adversarial process, the parties are trying to select an expert that both sides respect. If the parties fail to reach an agreement, each party may select an expert and then ask them to work together to prepare a joint report.

What Is the Role of the Neutral Third Party? As described above in "What is the Structure of the Process," the third party expert investigates the contested technical aspects of the dispute and issues a findings report.

What Is the Role of the Clients? Clients are likely to work closely with the expert by providing her vital information.

What Are the Outcome/Remedies? The outcome is a credible report of reasoned findings that resolves highly contested technical issues.

b.   Private Judging

What Types of Disputes Are Suitable for the Process? Private judging can be an effective option for resolving any dispute suitable for a non-jury judicial proceeding. Using conventional judicial procedures, private judges can assess the credibility of witnesses and decide contested facts, disputed law, and complex cases.

Is It a Process of Negotiation or Adjudication? Private judging is classically an adjudicatory process that uses adversarial procedures that result in a binding decision.

What Is the Structure of the Process? Private judging is structured like a formal, non-jury trial conducted in accordance with traditional rules of evidence. It provides parties with full rights of discovery and an opportunity to present opening arguments and witnesses, cross-examine adverse witnesses, present closing arguments, and submit briefs. The private judge issues a written decision that is filed as a court judgment, subject to appeal on the same basis as any court judgment. Two particular features can make private judging advantageous over a conventional judicial trial: parties can choose the trial judge as well as control the scheduling of the trial. Private judging must be authorized under the laws of the state in which the private judging takes place. This option is widely used in California[7] and available in New York.[8]

Who Is the Neutral Third Party? The parties select the third party who is likely to be a retired judge with substantial experience conducting trials.

What Is the Role of the Neutral Third Party? The third party hears the case and decides who is right and wrong.

What Is the Role of the Clients? The clients serve in the limited role of witnesses and sources of information for the attorneys.

What Are the Outcome/Remedies? The outcome consists of conventional judicial remedies.

---

7. Cal. R. Civ. P. 638(1) (West Supp. 1996).

8. *See* NY C.P.L.R. Art. 43 (Trial By A Referee); Shapiro, *Private Judging in the State of New York: A Critical Introduction*, 23 Col. J. of L. & Soc. Prob. 275 (1990).

c.   Summary Jury Trial[9]

What Types of Disputes Are Suitable for the Process? When parties have widely divergent views of how a jury might weigh the evidence and assess the credibility of witnesses, they may want to secure a relatively quick and inexpensive preview of what a jury might do by using a summary jury trial.

Is It a Process of Negotiation or Adjudication? The results of a summary jury trial are typically non-binding, making it an advisory process that is intended to foster negotiations. The advisory jury verdict can carry considerable weight in the negotiations despite the truncated trial procedures because of the insights the results can offer into what might happen at trial. The parties can convert a summary jury trial into a binding arbitration process by agreeing to be bound by the summary jury verdict.

What Is the Structure of the Process? A summary jury trial proceeds in stages. First, the judge, at a pretrial conference, disposes of any necessary motions and resolves any essential discovery disputes. The judge also sets the date for the summary jury trial and establishes time limits for opening statements, presentation of case, rebuttal, and closing arguments. The judge may request short trial briefs with proposed jury instructions. On the day of the summary jury trial, attorneys select a jury of the sort that would likely be impaneled at a full trial and then each attorney presents a summary of her case. The attorneys are usually limited to presenting testimony in a narrative form and introducing key physical evidence and exhibits. They may present a few live witnesses or videotapes of a couple critical witnesses. While the trial may take place in one day instead of two to four weeks, the format, evidentiary rules, and presentations must be close enough to what might happen at a full trial in order for the results to be sufficiently credible to motivate parties to settle.

Following the advisory verdict, the jurors are debriefed by the judge and attorneys. The debriefing provides a valuable opportunity for each side to learn how the jurors reacted to the case. With these fresh insights into the strengths and weaknesses of the case, the parties try to settle the dispute.

---

9. *See* Cooley, *supra* note 6, at 165–167.

Who Is the Neutral Third Party? The neutral third party usually consists of a sitting judge and a jury selected from an actual jury pool.

What Is the Role of the Neutral Third Party? The judge assists the sides in getting ready for the summary jury trial, conducts the trial, and supervises debriefing and settlement efforts. The jury hears the case, renders an advisory verdict, and participates in a debriefing.

What Is the Role of the Clients? The clients hear the summary case of both sides and the jury's reactions. They might testify.

What Are the Outcome/Remedies? The outcome resembles what might happen if the dispute went to a jury trial.

d.   Mini-Trial (See AAA and CPR Mini-Trial Procedures in Appendices K and L.)

What Types of Disputes Are Suitable for the Process? Mini-trials are suitable for substantial, complex disputes between large corporations. Suitable disputes include ones fueled by radically different views of the facts or law such as claims for breach of complex business or construction contracts, for infringement of patents, and for product liability.

Is It a Process of Negotiation or Adjudication? A mini-trial is designed to foster negotiations by engaging in the settlement effort the key senior business executives. The senior executives first educate themselves about the dispute by listening to and participating in a mini-adversarial presentation of key information and legal issues. Then they try to negotiate a resolution. A mini-trial is different from the other alternatives to mediation described in this section. It is not designed to produce a decision on the merits, although the neutral chair might predict what a court is likely to do.

The parties could introduce an adjudicatory feature into the mini-trial by agreeing that if they are unable to negotiate a resolution, they would be bound by a determination of the panel's neutral member.

What Is the Structure of the Process? The mini-trial is a flexible process that can be tailored to the preferences of the parties. In a mini-trial agreement, the attorneys negotiate the details of a two-part structure for exchanging information and participating in settlement negotiations. The agreement provides for the selection of a panel, confidentiality of the process, and opportunities for discovery before the information exchange.[10] The agreement may carefully limit discovery to a fixed number of documents and short depositions that must be completed within a tight timetable. Before the information exchange, parties may agree to exchange short briefs, lists of a limited number of witnesses, and documents that will be presented. The agreement also provides for the details of how to conduct the information exchange, also known as a mini-hearing, and sets forth the stages of post-hearing negotiations.

At the mini-hearing, each side presents its partisan case and rebuttal through opening and closing arguments and presentation and cross-examination of a few essential witnesses. Rules of evidence are not followed, and the hearing may last only a day. After the hearing, the panel engages in several stages of negotiations that may last a couple weeks, as described in the section below on "What is the Role of the Neutral Third Party?"

Who Is the Neutral Third Party? The third party consist of a three person panel composed of a less-than-neutral senior business executive from each company involved in the dispute and a neutral chair who might be a practicing attorney, academic, or retired judge with substantive or dispute resolution expertise. The senior executives must have full authority to negotiate a settlement. They also should not be the people who were directly and deeply involved in the underlying dispute so that they are able to view the dispute dispassionately as a business problem. The panel may need access to technical advisors from each company.

What Is the Role of the Neutral Third Party? The panel functions in different ways as the mini-trial process progresses. During the information exchange, the neutral chair manages the process and may ask questions and comment on what is said. Then, when the process turns to the settlement negotiations, the two senior executives meet in one or more sessions to negotiate. They may meet alone, without the participation of their attorneys. The neutral chair may not initially participate, except to provide advice or clarification. If the senior executives reach an impasse, they may invite the neutral chair to mediate. If still stuck at an impasse, the neutral chair might give her prediction of what a court is likely to do. In view of this new information, the senior executives try again to negotiate a resolution. If they still cannot settle, the parties

---

10. *See* AMERICAN ARBITRATION ASSOCIATION, THE AAA MINI-TRIAL PROCEDURES (Appendix)(1994); CPR INSTITUTE FOR DISPUTE RESOLUTION, CPR MINITRIAL PROCEDURE (Rev. 1989).

usually wait for a "cool-down" period before returning to court. The cool-down period provides one last opening for the parties to try settling the dispute.

What Is the Role of the Clients? There are really two clients for each side participating in the mini-trial. One client is a senior business executive who serves on the panel as described above and participates in negotiating a resolution. Another client assists the attorney in the adversarial presentation of the case to the panel.

What Are the Outcome/Remedies? The parties are not limited to the remedies available in court; they can negotiate a creative, tailor-made solution.

e. Court

What Types of Disputes Are Suitable for the Process? Courts can be effective for concluding any dispute in which parties need a third party to assess the credibility of witnesses and resolve contested facts, disputed law, and complex cases.

Is It a Process of Negotiation or Adjudication? Courts offer the classic adjudicatory process that imposes a binding decision on the parties. It is the only adjudicatory process that is compulsory in that a party can be compelled to participate.

What Is the Structure of the Process? The trial process is a highly structured proceeding conducted in accordance with detailed rules of procedure and evidence. It provides parties with full rights of discovery and an opportunity to present opening arguments and witnesses, cross-examine adverse witnesses, present closing arguments, and submit initial and reply briefs. The result, a judge's decision and jury verdict, is subject to appeal to a higher court.

Who Is the Neutral Third Party? The case is typically assigned by the court to a judge who is usually experienced in conducting trials. If the case qualifies, parties can elect to present it to a jury.

What Is the Role of the Neutral Third Party? The judge and jury hear the case and decide who is right and wrong. The judge resolves legal questions and factual ones if no jury has been impaneled. Otherwise, the jury finds the facts.

What Is the Role of the Clients? The clients serve in the limited role of witnesses and sources of information for the attorneys.

What Are the Outcome/Remedies? The outcome consists of traditional judicial remedies.

APPENDIX A
DECISION-TREE PLUS ANALYSIS[1]

Topics in this appendix include:

1. Introduction to Decision-Tree Plus Analysis
2. Calculating the Value of the Public BATNA
3. Calculating the Value of the Personal BATNA
4. Testing the Sensitivity of the Results
5. Illustrating the Calculating of the Total BATNA

How to Calculate the Total Value of the Going-to-Court Option

Too many lawyers and clients fail to thoroughly and objectively analyze all the benefits, costs, and risks of pursuing the judicial remedy. This common failure produces poor legal advice to clients, unrealistically attractive alternatives to settlement (BATNAs),[2] and impasses in negotiations and mediations. As a mediator, I have seen many cases where opposing attorneys were equally optimistic about the judicial outcome. One of them will be proven wrong. Inflated assessments can lead clients astray because they will overestimate the benefits of returning to court and, as a result, may mistakenly reject what might otherwise be acceptable settlement proposals.

You can reduce the risk of this client error by using the decision-tree plus techniques suggested in this appendix for calculating the value of your client's total BATNA. Using these techniques can improve the quality of your case analysis and help your client pinpoint her personal benefits and costs of litigating, crucial yardsticks when your client is weighing whether to settle. Familiarizing your client with these techniques also will prepare yourself and your client for the possibility that

---

1. This appendix collects together in one place materials scattered throughout the book and further develops this important subject. This appendix is designed to be self-contained and comprehensive.

2. The term BATNA(Best Alternative To a Negotiated Agreement) was coined by Roger Fisher and William Ury in FISHER ET AL., GETTING TO YES 100 (2d ed.1991). The BATNA is your client's best option if the negotiation fails.

the mediator might ask you to use this methodology in the mediation session.

This appendix explains the decision-tree plus approach for calculating the value of your client's total BATNA. Then it illustrates how to do the calculations in a hypothetical legal case.

1. Introduction to Decision-Tree Plus Analysis

Your client's BATNA in legal mediations can be divided into two distinct components: public and personal.

The *public BATNA* covers the portion that you are uniquely qualified to calculate. You, as the attorney, have the expertise to predict the likely judicial outcome, the probability of that outcome occurring, and the legal fees and court costs the client will incur. You frequently make these predictions in your law practice. Based on discovery, legal research, and experience, information that is mostly available to both sides, you routinely estimate the key inputs for calculating the value of the public BATNA.

The other component, the *personal BATNA*, addresses the portion that your client is uniquely qualified to calculate. It is the component idiosyncratic to your client. For example, your client can best assess the added value of going to court to establish a judicial precedent or to be vindicated. Your client can best approximate the added cost of possibly destroying a continuing relationship with the other party by going to court. Your client is the expert. Only your client can ponder and quantify his or her own subjective views of these additional litigation benefits and costs.

The value of your client's total BATNA is simply the sum of the values of the public and personal BATNAs. It can be expressed using the formula:

TB=PubB + PersB

TB is the total BATNA

PubB is the public BATNA

PersB is the personal BATNA

For calculating the value of the public BATNA, the conventional decision-tree analysis presented in the next section can be used. For calculating the value of the personal BATNA, a client interview can be used with the "plus" questioning techniques described in section 3.

2. Calculating the Value of the Public BATNA

What is a decision-tree analysis?

Decision-tree analysis can be valuable when you face a situation where you lack control over the outcome. You are contemplating taking a chance. You are thinking of gambling. You need a way to intelligently play the odds. We all intuitively engage in decision-tree-type analysis in our daily lives whenever we face a risky situation. When deciding whether to take a chance, we in effect predict the likely outcome and the probability of it happening.

When crossing the street, we subconsciously estimate the potential harm if hit by a car and the chances of getting hit. We may guess that when the light is green, the likely harm will be modest and the risk of it happening will be very low, say less than 2 percent, and as a result, we elect to cross the street. When the light is red, we tend to estimate a much higher possible harm and risk, and usually elect not to cross the street. When in a rush, we might take a few precautions to reduce the risk of getting hit by a car and take the chance of crossing against a red light.

I recall only too well the day that I learned firsthand the risks of relying on decision-tree analysis. At the time, I was in graduate school taking courses on decision-making methodologies. I was rushing home and decided to cross a busy street in the middle of the block. I figured a very high probability of success. I was still hit by a car! As I bounced off the car's hood and landed on the hard pavement, the abstruse subject of probabilities became painfully and vividly clear. When estimating the very high 95 percent probability of crossing the street safely, I also assumed a low percent chance of getting hit. I got hit and suffered the consequences.

We engage in the same sort of decision-tree analysis when choosing how to finance the purchase of a home. When choosing between a fixed rate or a variable rate, we are guessing whether interest rates will go up in the future, making a fixed rate more attractive, or whether interest rates will decline, making a variable rate more attractive.

As lawyers, we routinely use a crude decision-tree analysis when counseling our clients whether to litigate or settle. We investigate the facts, study the relevant law, and become familiar with the strengths and weaknesses of the case. We then predict the likely judicial outcome and the odds of it happening. We make educated guesses. Decision-tree analysis offers a methodology that can improve the quality of these vitally important guesses when calculating the value of a client's public BATNA (PubB).

How do you prepare a decision tree?

The central purpose of decision-tree analysis is to calculate the *expected value*.[3] The expected value calculation quantifies the value of your client's public BATNA—the value of the litigated outcome. In essence, this methodology quantifies playing the odds in court. The underlying concept of expected value may not be intuitive for those who are mathematically challenged. Here is one definition expressed in lay terms that may be more accessible to the innumerate:

> In simple terms, the expected value of a course of action is the average value of taking that course of action many times. If one were to try the identical case 100 times, and there is a 60 percent likelihood of a plaintiff's verdict, approximately 60 trials would result in a plaintiff's verdict while 40 would result in a defense verdict. The average recovery would be 60 victories multiplied by $100,000 per victory or $6,000,000, plus 40 losses multiplied by $0 per loss, divided by 100 cases for an average recovery of $60,000. Thus, the expected value associated with the litigation node is $60,000.[4]

The expected value is calculated by using a decision tree that maps chronologically the entire litigation option along a main branch and a series of subbranches. As you move from left to right along the branches, you will cross three key junctions, known as nodes:

---

3. *See* JOHN MURRAY ET AL., PROCESSES OF DISPUTE RESOLUTION 192–218 (2d ed. 1996); Aaron & Hoffer, *Decision Analysis as a Method of Evaluating the Trial Alternative, in* MEDIATING LEGAL DISPUTES 307–334 (Dwight Golaan ed., 1996); and Hoffer, *Decision Analysis as a Mediator's Tool*, 1 HARV. NEG. L.R.113 (1996).

4. *See* Aaron & Hoffer, *Decision Analysis as a Method of Evaluating the Trial Alternative,* in MEDIATING LEGAL DISPUTES 314 (Dwight Golaan ed., 1996).

You will first face a *decision node,* the point in the analysis when your client has a choice to make. In legal disputes, the choice is usually whether to settle or to litigate. A decision node is represented by a square [■].

You will next reach a *chance node*, the point in the litigation when your client cannot control the outcome. Instead of making a decision to accept or reject, your client takes a chance in the litigation process. Your client may take a chance by seeking more discovery, filing a motion, going to trial, taking an appeal, etc. Your client does not know for sure what will be the outcome of each of these actions.

To assist your client, you need to study each key chancy event in the litigation process and make two critical predictions: What is the likely outcome of each chancy event? And, what is the probability of each event happening? These predictions are quintessential lawyering judgments that you commonly make in practice. In constructing a tree, you will frequently identify a series of chance points along a fully mapped branch. Your client might first take a chance on more discovery, then with a summary judgment motion, and then at a jury trial. Each chance node is represented by a circle [●].

And finally, you will end each branch or subbranch of analysis with a *terminal node*, the end point in the mapping of the branch. Each terminal node is represented by a triangle pointing to the left [◀].

After you map all the key chance points in the litigation process, you calculate the expected value of the litigation branch by starting with each terminal node and moving backwards toward the first chance node. The mathematical calculations will be illustrated in an example at the end of this appendix.

Should you adjust the expected value to a present value?

It depends. You want to be sure that you do NOT compare an expected value due at the end of a trial, say in three years, with a settlement offer to pay or receive something today. The dollar amounts are not comparable. You may need to adjust the expected value in the future to a present value. You may need to calculate how much money in the future would be worth today.

To do this, you discount the expected value that you would expect to pay or receive in the future and translate it into a present value that can be compared to the present settlement offer. For example, in a negligence case, the plaintiff should compare a $65,000 settlement offer with the discounted litigated expected value of $75,000 (60 percent probability of recovering times $125,000 at trial). Assuming three years until conclusion of the trial and an opportunity to earn an average interest rate of 6 percent per year over the three years, the $75,000 received in three years would be worth $62,971 today.[5] In other words, if the plaintiff received $62,971 today and invested it and earned an average of 6 percent interest per year over the next three years, the plaintiff would have $75,000 in three years. Therefore, the $65,000 offer today is better than waiting three years for an amount that would be worth $62,971 today.

Discounting may be unnecessary, however, when the local law permits collecting prejudgment interest at the same rate as the interest rate used for discounting. Prejudgment interest may be collectable from the date of the filing of the suit until payment of the judgment. Thus, your predicted amount at the end of trial is functionally a discounted value. The present value adjustment is offset by the prejudgment interest. But, if the discounted interest rate is greater than the prejudgment interest rate, you should discount the expected value for the difference.

Prejudgment interest may be available[6] in contract cases and occasionally in wrongful death, personal injury, and property damage cases, although non-compensatory damages such as pain and suffering may be excluded. Check your local law to determine whether prejudgment interest is collectable, for what time period, and at what rate.

3. Calculating the Value of the Personal BATNA

How do you calculate a client's personal benefits and costs of litigating? The Plus Analysis

Decision trees can fail to analyze your client's personal benefits and costs of litigating.[7] The value of your client's personal BATNA (PersB) needs to be approximated by your client. This will not be easy for your

---

5. *See* Present Value Charts in Appendix B, for 6 percent discounted over three years: .839619 x EV of $75,000 = $62,971.

6. JOHN MURRAY ET AL., PROCESSES OF DISPUTE RESOLUTION 212 (2d ed. 1996).

7. *See id.* at 205.

client to do. Instead of inviting your client to use a formal decision tree,[8] you can take the simpler but still demanding approach of asking your client some probing and formidable questions. This supplement to decision trees is the plus analysis. For example, you might press your client, say a plaintiff, to come to terms with how much less money she would be willing to accept to settle now and not suffer the risks of waiting out the litigation or the risks of destroying a relationship in the litigation. In other words, how much money would your client be willing to sacrifice for settling now? Not an easy question to answer.

How do you probe your client's specific personal benefits and costs?

This subsection illustrates how you might probe two common personal factors: your client's tolerance for risk and the need to scare off future plaintiffs.

1. You may want to ask your client whether the PubB value should be adjusted to reflect her subjective comfort with taking risks.[9] Each chance node in the decision tree includes a probability estimate that reflects the risk of taking the next step in the litigation. At each chance node, your client risks winning or losing something.

Let's assume that you are representing the plaintiff in the just mentioned negligence case in which the expected value of litigating is $75,000 (60 percent probability of recovering $125,000 at trial).

You might begin by helping your client reflect on her propensity to take risks by asking her to consider the following question: "In a hypothetical case, would you prefer receiving $80,000 today or an 80 percent chance of recovering $100,000 at an immediate trial?" If she answers that she does not care, that she can live with either option, she seems to be risk neutral. If she prefers the $80,000 today, she apparently does not want to take the risk of getting nothing at trial, and can be

---

8. It is possible to construct a decision tree that accounts for the chance that the litigation choice could produce some personal benefits or costs. You could develop branches for each chancy personal benefit or cost. For example, your client might estimate a 30 percent chance of preserving a continuing relationship after litigation and value preserving the relationship at $10,000. Then, your client could construct an expected value of maintaining the relationship after the litigation. The expected value would be $3,000 [($10,000 x 30%) + ($0 x 70%) = $3,000].

9. *See* Murray, *supra* note 6, at 216–218 (Authors discuss factors that influence a person's attitudes toward risk taking.).

characterized as risk-averse. If she prefers taking the chance of recovering $100,000 at trial, she seems inclined to take risks, making her risk prone.

After sensitizing your client to her own sense of risk taking, you might then ask some questions about the settlement options. You could ask: "Are you willing to settle the case for the expected value of $75,000? Would you be willing to accept less in order to settle the case? Or, do you want to take a chance at trial of recovering $125,000?" After working through these three options, your client may prefer taking a chance at trial. Then you might ask: "Would you settle for an offer that is less than the predicted court outcome of $125,000 but more than the expected value of $75,000?"

If your client is risk neutral, she will be comfortable accepting the straightforward expected value of $75,000. The value of her PersB would be zero.

If your client is risk averse, a propensity among one-time plaintiffs, she will be willing to accept a settlement offer that is less than $75,000 in order to avoid the risks of litigating. Then, her PersB Value would be a negative amount. She might value it as a negative $10,000. In other words, she might reduce the expected value of going to court by $10,000 to reflect her aversion to litigating. Then her TB would be $65,000 (PubB $75,000 – PersB ($10,000) = TB $65,000). She would accept any offer that is $65,000 or more.

If your client is risk prone, a propensity among plaintiffs who have little to lose or repeat-player defendants who are accustomed to playing the odds, she will want to go to trial for the possibility of a greater payoff. If plaintiff is willing to accept something less than the likely payoff in a trial, she has a limit on her risk taking. If she is willing to settle for $100,000, she will risk litigation for up to $25,000 above the expected value of $75,000, at which point she would rather take the money than risk getting nothing at trial. Therefore, her TB would be PubB $75,000 + PersB $25,000, for a total of $100,000. She would accept any offer that is $100,000 or more.

2. You may ask your client, a repeat-player defendant, whether she wants to litigate for the purpose of scaring off future plaintiffs. You may ask your client to weigh the benefits of sending a message and to estimate its value. Say that your defendant client thinks she is willing to

pay $10,000 more in court to make his point. If you estimate the PubB of litigating to be an expected loss of $40,000, you would deduct the value of the PersB, a $10,000 benefit, to arrive at the defendant's TB of a negative $30,000. The defendant would be willing to settle by paying up to $30,000. Otherwise, the defendant would turn to her PubB and take the chance in court of paying an expected average loss of $40,000.

4.   Testing the Sensitivity of the Results

The reliability of decision-tree plus analysis is dependent on the reliability of the predictions used. It is the old story: garbage in, garbage out. Needless to say, predicting is always fraught with the risk of inputting garbage. That risk can be reduced by using sensitivity analysis. When you are less confident of particular predictions, you can use a range of predictions, instead of single ones. For instance, when predicting the likelihood of winning a favorable jury verdict, you may feel shaky predicting a 65 percent chance of winning, but more confident predicting 60 percent to 70 percent chance. How to incorporate sensitivity analysis into the decision-tree plus methodology is demonstrated in the next section.

5.   Illustrating the Calculating of the Total BATNA

Calculating the value of the total BATNA will be demonstrated using the employment dispute that was presented in chapter 1. The facts are repeated here:

Stephen Saleson founded, owns, and runs a small company called *Shirts for You*. The company sells several major brand name shirts to retail outlets and is staffed by two support people and one other salesperson, Philip Upton. When Stephen hired Philip several years ago, Philip signed an employment contract in which he agreed that if he left his position, he would not compete against *Shirts for You* within the city of Buffalo for three years.

During the first year of employment, Stephen spent considerable time teaching Philip the "secrets" of good salesmanship. Under Stephen's tutelage, Philip quickly learned the job and did superlative work solidifying and maintaining existing customers in Buffalo. Unfortunately, the personal relationship between Philip and Stephen soured during their third year together. Philip felt that Stephen was stifling Philip's professional development by preventing him from developing new customers. Stephen reserved those opportunities for himself. So, even though Philip continued to admire Stephen's sales skills and welcomed his mentoring, he quit the sales position and went into his own business selling a different brand of shirts. Because Philip had become such an excellent salesman, he was able to secure a group of retail customers in Buffalo that Stephen had never solicited for sales.

Stephen, who was very upset that his protégé had abandoned him, sued Philip for breach of the covenant not to compete and sought an injunction and damages in the amount of $100,000 for lost sales. Philip responded by claiming that he was not violating the non-compete clause because he was selling a different brand of shirts to a different group of retail customers in Buffalo.

How do you prepare a simple decision-tree plus analysis?

Plaintiff Stephen would ask his attorney to research thoroughly the strengths and weaknesses of the court case and then predict the likely court outcome and the probability of winning.[10] For the winning branch of the tree, his attorney may predict a likely favorable jury verdict of $80,000 and then deduct his estimated attorney fees and other litigation costs of $20,000, for a net benefit of $60,000. Stephen's attorney would then multiply the net benefit of $60,000 by his predicted 60 percent chance of winning, to arrive at a positive $36,000.

For the losing branch of the tree, Stephen's attorney realizes that Stephen would still have to pay attorney fees and other litigation costs of $20,000. Stephen's attorney would multiply the $20,000 times his predicted 40 percent chance of losing to arrive at a negative $8000. By subtracting the negative $8000 from the positive $36,000, Steven's attorney would arrive at the litigated expected value of Stephen's public BATNA (PubB) in the amount of $28,000.

---

10. Stephen faces a risk of losing the court case because it is not clear whether Philip has breached the covenant to not compete when Philip is selling a different brand of shirts to a different group of customers in Buffalo.

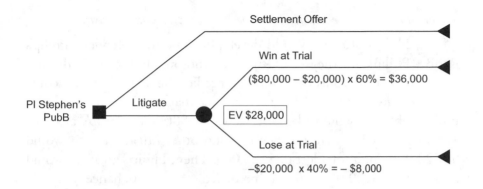

Stephen's EV of PubB: $36,000–$8000 = $28,000[11]

Assuming that the prejudgment interest would be equal to the discount rate, Stephen's attorney would not need to discount the expected value of litigation, the PubB, for the estimated three years of litigation.[12]

Plaintiff Stephen's PubB may need to be adjusted for a number of personal benefits and costs. The difficult-to-quantify costs might include spending time preparing for the case, suffering the emotional angst of being consumed by litigation, and living with the 40 percent chance of losing. Stephen needs to make a rough and subjective estimate of what he is willing to give up to avoid suffering these costs. He may decide that he is willing to sacrifice up to $10,000. By deducting the $10,000 from his PubB Value of $28,000, Stephen would calculate the value of his total BATNA (TB) to be $18,000. (Stephen's TB: PubB $28,000 – PersB $10,000 = $18,000.)

Thus, if Stephen cannot secure at least $18,000 at the negotiation table, a settlement that avoids incurring the personal costs of litigating, Stephen should leave the table to take a chance of securing his public BATNA benefit, the likely litigated net outcome of $28,000.

---

11. If Stephen's attorney thinks that his prediction of a 60 percent chance of winning is a bit shaky, she might want to develop a safe range of predictions. He might be more confident that the chance of success is somewhere between 60 percent and 70 percent. Then he may re-do the numbers assuming a 70 percent chance of winning.

Win: $60,000 x 70% = $42,000.

Lose: $20,000 x 30% = -$6000.

PubB: $42,000 - $6000 = $36,000.

Stephen would then use a range for the PubB of $28,000 to $36,000.

12. If no prejudgment interest applied and assuming that the end of the trial is three years away and the interest rate is 6percent, the $28,000 would be discounted to $23,509.

How do you test the sensitivity of the decision-tree plus analysis?

First, Philip's attorney would develop a value for defendant Philip's PubB. Philip's attorney would research thoroughly the strengths and weaknesses of the court case and then predict the likely court outcome and the risks of losing.[13] He may predict that if a jury verdict holds Philip liable, he would likely be liable for $80,000. Philip's attorney also might predict that attorney fees and other litigation costs would be $20,000, for a total lost of $100,000. Then, Philip's attorney would multiply the $100,000 times his predicted 40 percent chance of losing, to arrive at a negative $40,000.

If Philip wins, he would still have to pay his attorney's fees and other litigation costs of $20,000. Philip's attorney would multiply the $20,000 times his 60 percent chance of winning to arrive at a cost of negative $12,000. By adding the negative $12,000 to the negative $40,000, Philip's attorney would arrive at the expected value of Philip's public BATNA in the amount of a negative $52,000.

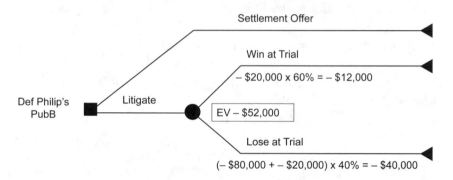

Philip's EV of PubB (60% winning chance): –$12,000 + –$40,000 = –$52,000

Next, Philip's attorney would test how much the results change due to changing one or more key predictions in the decision tree. He realizes that predictions are not guarantees and may want to do a sensitivity analysis involving ranges for the less certain predictions. He may not be confident predicting the litigation costs, the amount of the jury verdict, or the probability of winning. If he thinks that the 60 percent chance of winning is a bit shaky, he may be more confident predicting a range of

---

13. Stephen faces a risk of losing the court case because it is not clear whether Philip has breached the covenant to not compete when Philip is selling a different brand of shirts to a different group of customers in Buffalo.

somewhere between 40 percent and 60 percent. He may redo the decision tree using a second scenario with a 40 percent chance of winning. The second calculation would be (numbers in parenthesis are negative ones or losses):

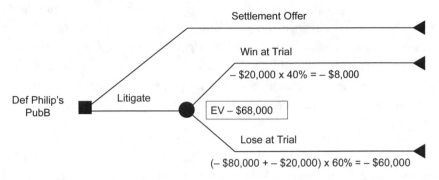

Philip's EV of PubB (40% winning chance): –$8,000 + –$60,000 = –$68,000

Therefore, when calculating the TB, defendant Philip would use a range for the value of the PubB consisting of losing from $52,000 to $68,000.

Now, defendant Philip's public BATNA needs to be more fully analyzed and adjusted to account for a number of difficult-to-quantify personal costs and benefits. By going to court, Philip may incur the costs of spending time preparing for the case and suffering the emotional stress of litigation. But these costs may be exceeded by two possible benefits of litigating. Philip may welcome the 40 to 60 percent chance of winning and paying nothing, a risk-taking propensity common among defendants as a group, and he may want to try to exonerate himself in court so he can freely pursue his lucrative business in Buffalo. Philip may estimate that the personal benefits are worth roughly $10,000 to $15,000 more than the personal costs.

Philip would deduct this $10,000 to $15,000 benefit from the PubB expected loss of $52,000 to $68,000 to arrive at a total BATNA of a low loss of $37,000 ($52,000 – $15,000) to a high loss of $58,000 ($68,000 – $10,000). Therefore, Philip's TB would range from a loss of $37,000 to $58,000.

Thus, if settlement possibilities involve Philip paying more than $37,000 to $58,000, Philip should leave the table to litigate, where he may pay nothing but his attorney fees or risk losing on average $52,000 to $68,000.

How do you prepare a more complex decision tree?

In most cases, your client will be facing more than one chance node when assessing the litigation chronological branch. Assume that Philip's attorney thinks defendant Philip has a good chance of winning a motion to dismiss. He predicts a 70 percent chance of winning. If Philip wins the motion, the case is over. If Philip loses, he would then go the next stage of trial and face the risk of winning or losing at trial.

The decision tree needs to account for the two sequential chancy events. The calculations are done from right to left. For the branch that maps losing the motion, Philip's attorney would add to the expected value of going to trial of negative $52,000, which was calculated above, a negative $5,000 of additional legal fees that would be incurred due to filing the motion to dismiss, for a total negative $57,000. Then, he would multiply the negative $57,000 by the 30 percent chance of losing the motion to produce a negative $17,100. For the branch that maps winning the motion, he would multiply the 70 percent chance of winning times a negative $5,000 of additional legal fees due to filing the motion, for a negative $3,500. Then he would add together the winning and losing branches to produces an expected value of litigation in the amount of a negative $20,600.

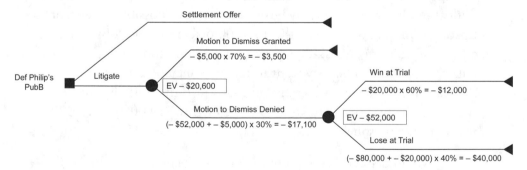

Defendant Philip's EV of PubB:

Step (1)   Trial EV: –$12,000 + –$40,000 = – $52,000

Step (2)   Factor in Motion to Dismiss Chance Node:

EV –$20,600 = 30% chance of losing x (–$52,000 + –$5,000) + 70% chance of winning x –$5,000

The difference between the expected value of trial without making the motion to dismiss and the expected value when making the motion reflects the benefit of making a motion with a 70 percent chance of winning. The benefit is the difference between paying the expected value of going to trial of $52,000 and paying the expected value of making the motion and going to trial of $20,600, or a benefit of $31,400 for making the motion. Therefore, Philip would be well advised to file the motion to dismiss before trying to settle the case. When negotiating to settle the case, Philip should find appealing a settlement proposal by plaintiff Stephen that Philip would pay $15,000—especially when that amount is compared with the expected value of litigating a motion and trial, a risk that translates into an expected value of paying $20,600.

APPENDIX B

PRESENT VALUE CHARTS

This table shows how much $1, to be paid at the end of various periods in the future, is currently worth with interest at different rates compounded annually.

To use the table, find the vertical column under your interest rate (or cost of capital). Then find the horizontal row corresponding to the number of years it will take to receive the payment. The point at which the column and the row intersect is your present value of $1.

By multiplying this value by the number of dollars you expect to receive, you calculate the present value of the amount you expect.

Present Value of $1 to Be Paid in Future

Year	3.0%	3.5%	4.0%	4.5%
1	$0.970874	$0.966184	$0.961538	$0.956938
2	$0.942596	$0.933511	$0.924556	$0.915730
3	$0.915142	$0.901943	$0.888996	$0.876297
4	$0.888487	$0.871442	$0.854804	$0.838561
5	$0.862609	$0.841973	$0.821927	$0.802451
6	$0.837484	$0.813501	$0.790315	$0.767896
7	$0.813092	$0.785991	$0.759918	$0.734828
8	$0.789409	$0.759412	$0.730690	$0.703185
9	$0.766417	$0.733731	$0.702587	$0.672904
10	$0.744094	$0.708919	$0.675564	$0.643928

Year	5.0%	5.5%	6.0%	6.5%
1	$0.952381	$0.947867	$0.943396	$0.938967
2	$0.907029	$0.898452	$0.889996	$0.881659
3	$0.863838	$0.851614	$0.839619	$0.827849
4	$0.822702	$0.807217	$0.792094	$0.777323
5	$0.783526	$0.765134	$0.747258	$0.729881
6	$0.746215	$0.725246	$0.704961	$0.685334

7	$0.710681	$0.687437	$0.665057	$0.643506
8	$0.676839	$0.651599	$0.627412	$0.604231
9	$0.644609	$0.617629	$0.591898	$0.567353
10	$0.613913	$0.585431	$0.558395	$0.532726

Year	7.0%	7.5%	8.0%	8.5%
1	$0.934579	$0.930233	$0.925926	$0.921659
2	$0.873439	$0.865333	$0.857339	$0.849455
3	$0.816298	$0.804961	$0.793832	$0.782908
4	$0.762895	$0.748801	$0.735030	$0.721574
5	$0.712986	$0.696559	$0.680583	$0.665045
6	$0.666342	$0.647962	$0.630170	$0.612945
7	$0.622750	$0.602755	$0.583490	$0.564926
8	$0.582009	$0.560702	$0.540269	$0.520669
9	$0.543934	$0.521583	$0.500249	$0.479880
10	$0.508349	$0.485194	$0.463193	$0.442285

Year	9.0%	9.5%	10.0%	10.5%
1	$0.917431	$0.913242	$0.909091	$0.904977
2	$0.841680	$0.834011	$0.826446	$0.818984
3	$0.772183	$0.761654	$0.751315	$0.741162
4	$0.708425	$0.695574	$0.683013	$0.670735
5	$0.649931	$0.635228	$0.620921	$0.607000
6	$0.596267	$0.580117	$0.564474	$0.549321
7	$0.547034	$0.529787	$0.513158	$0.497123
8	$0.501866	$0.483824	$0.466507	$0.449885
9	$0.460428	$0.441848	$0.424098	$0.407136
10	$0.422411	$0.403514	$0.385543	$0.368449

Year	11.0%	11.5%	12.0%	12.5%
1	$0.900901	$0.896861	$0.892857	$0.888889
2	$0.811622	$0.804360	$0.797194	$0.790123
3	$0.731191	$0.721399	$0.711780	$0.702332
4	$0.658731	$0.646994	$0.635518	$0.624295
5	$0.593451	$0.580264	$0.567427	$0.554929
6	$0.534641	$0.520416	$0.506631	$0.493270

7	$0.481658	$0.466741	$0.452349	$0.438462
8	$0.433926	$0.418602	$0.403883	$0.389744
9	$0.390925	$0.375428	$0.360610	$0.346439
10	$0.352184	$0.336706	$0.321973	$0.307946

Year	13.0%	13.5%	14.0%	14.5%
1	$0.884956	$0.881057	$0.877193	$0.873362
2	$0.783147	$0.776262	$0.769468	$0.762762
3	$0.693050	$0.683931	$0.674972	$0.666168
4	$0.613319	$0.602583	$0.592080	$0.581806
5	$0.542760	$0.530910	$0.519369	$0.508127
6	$0.480319	$0.467762	$0.455587	$0.443779
7	$0.425061	$0.412125	$0.399637	$0.387580
8	$0.376160	$0.363106	$0.350559	$0.338498
9	$0.332885	$0.319917	$0.307508	$0.295631
10	$0.294588	$0.281865	$0.269744	$0.258193

Year	15.0%
1	$0.869565
2	$0.756144
3	$0.657516
4	$0.571753
5	$0.497177
6	$0.432328
7	$0.375937
8	$0.326902
9	$0.284262
10	$0.247185

Appendix C

Sample

MEDIATOR RETAINER
AND
CONFIDENTIALITY AGREEMENT

Case: _____

The Parties have agreed to retain the Mediator for this Mediation. To enable the Parties to discuss all aspects of their dispute freely and to enable the Mediator to assist the Parties in reaching a voluntary resolution of their dispute, the Participants agree as follows:

A. CONFIDENTIALITY AND IMMUNITY

1. Conferences and discussions which occur in connection with mediation services provided pursuant to this Agreement shall be deemed settlement discussions, and nothing said or disclosed, nor any document produced, which is not otherwise independently discoverable, shall be offered or received as evidence or used for impeachment or for any other purpose in any current or future litigation, administrative proceeding, arbitration proceeding, or in any other dispute resolution forum, regardless of the law of the forum.

In particular, the Participants, including the Mediator will not disclose any information including offers, promises, conduct, statements, or settlement terms whether oral or written, made by any of the parties, their agents, employees, experts, and attorneys. Such information is confidential and privileged under any applicable state or federal privileges, and any state confidentiality statutes, rules, or doctrine.

2. This section covers all telephone calls and sessions with the Mediator and all telephone calls and meetings in the absence of the Mediator so long as done under the auspices of the Mediation.

3. Briefing Papers, materials, and other information submitted to the Mediator by a Party or its attorney will not be disclosed to other Parties and their attorneys without the consent of the submitting Party or its attorney.

4. The Parties agree, on behalf of themselves and their attorneys, that none of them will call or subpoena the Mediator in any proceeding of any kind to produce any notes or documents related to his mediation services or to testify concerning any such notes or documents or his thoughts or impressions. If any Party attempts to compel such testimony or production, such Party shall be liable for and shall indemnify the Mediator for any liabilities, costs, and expenses, including attorney's fees and lost professional time, which he may incur in resisting such compulsion.

5. Each Participant agrees to notify the other Participants of the receipt of any subpoenas or any request for information that is confidential under this agreement.

6. The Mediator shall not be liable to any Participant for any act or omission in connection with the mediation. The Mediator shall have the same common law immunity as judges and arbitrators from suit for damages or equitable relief and from compulsory process to testify or produce evidence based on or concerning any action, statement, or communication in or concerning the Mediation conducted pursuant to this Agreement.

B. NO ATTORNEY-CLIENT RELATIONSHIP

1. The Parties understand that there is no attorney-client relationship between the Mediator and any Participant, and each Party acknowledges that it will seek and rely on legal advice solely from its own counsel and not from the Mediator.

C. DISCLOSURE OF PRIOR RELATIONSHIPS

1. The Mediator has made a reasonable effort to learn and has disclosed to the Parties: (a) all business or professional relationships the Mediator has had with the Parties or their law firms within the past five years, including all instances in which the Mediator served as an attorney for any party or adverse to any party; (b) any financial interest the Mediator has in any party; (c) any significant social, business, or professional relationship the Mediator has had with an officer or employee of a party or with an individual representing a party in the Proceeding; and (d) any other circumstances that may create doubt regarding the Mediator's impartiality in the Mediation.

2 Each Party and its law firm have made a reasonable effort to learn and has disclosed to every other Party and the Mediator any relation-

ships of a nature described in paragraph B.1. not previously identified and disclosed by the Mediator.

3. The Parties and the Mediator are satisfied that any relationships disclosed pursuant to paragraphs B.1. and B.2. will not affect the Mediator's independence or impartiality. Notwithstanding any such relationships, the Parties wish the Mediator to serve in the Mediation and the Mediator agrees to so serve.

D. FUTURE RELATIONSHIPS

1. The Mediator shall not undertake any work for or against a Party regarding the subject matter of the Mediation.

2. The Mediator shall not personally work on any matter for or against a Party, regardless of subject matter, until twelve months after termination of his services as a Mediator.

E. COMPENSATION

The Mediator shall be compensated for time expended in connection with the Mediation at the rate of $_____ , plus reasonable travel and other out-of-pocket expenses. The Mediator's fee shall be shared equally by the Parties.

Agreement made _____ , 20 __

(1) between _____ ,
party

represented by _____ ,
counsel

(2) and _____ ,
party

represented by _____ ,
counsel

(3) and _____ ,
party

represented by _____ ,
counsel

(4) and _____ .
mediator

Appendix D

Sample

BRIEFING PAPER

For Plaintiff, Ms. Earnest

Case: Earnest v. Cutting Edge Computers, Docket #03-701

This firm, Smith and Smith, has been retained to represent the Plaintiff, Ms. Earnest.

Ms. Earnest believes that Cutting Edge Computers has not appreciated her work, dedication, and loyalty. She thinks she has been unfairly treated. This dispute over pay increases is one manifestation of the broader problem of how Ms. Earnest has been treated in regard to a number of matters that are described in this briefing paper. She wants to be properly recognized and fairly compensated for her valuable work.

Description of Dispute and Legal Case

(a) "Factual Summary," including a chronology of events, statement of key factual issues in dispute, and your client's view on each issue

Ms. Earnest believes that her employer, Cutting Edge Computers, failed to give her higher pay increases because the company pays women less than men for comparable experience and work.

Ms. Earnest has been working for four years as a computer programmer for Cutting Edge Computers. She has worked hard, enthusiastically embraced all assignments, and met every deadline. Yet, for the fourth year in a row, she received a smaller pay increase than her three male co-workers in the same department. This year, she only received a 2 percent increase when each of her male co-workers received an 8 percent increase.

Ms. Earnest overheard her supervisor comment that she prefers to give higher pay increases to married men who must support their families than married women who do not need the money. Her co-workers are married with large families while Ms. Earnest is married with no children.

Of course, Cutting Edge denies any discrimination, claiming that Ms. Earnest simply has not been as productive as her co-workers. Ms. Earnest recognizes that her level of productivity has been less than her co-workers, but that occurred because she was not given the most recent computer software. Several times, she asked her supervisor to update her software to the same version as her co-workers. She was told it would happen soon, but it never did. As compared with the men in her department, she also has been given less challenging assignments and less opportunity to earn overtime. As a result of the company not giving her an equal opportunity to demonstrate what she could contribute, Ms. Earnest believes that she was penalized.

Ms. Earnest did complain a number of times to her supervisor about this unequal treatment, but she belittled her complaints, claiming her problems were in her head, not in the way she was treated. After her fourth year review, she could no longer tolerate this unjust treatment. Even though she enjoyed the work, Ms. Earnest submitted her resignation.

(b) "Critical Legal Issues" in dispute, including your client's view on each issue and key cites

We welcome an opportunity in the session to systematically examine the merits of the legal case. But we are not looking for a legal evaluation from you.

Ms. Earnest alleges sex discrimination in the ways that her salary was established and her annual salary increases were determined, in violation of Title VII of the 1964 Civil rights Act and in violation of the Equal Pay Act of 1963. She also alleges that she has been denied opportunities for advancement in her job on the basis of sex, in violation of Title VII. Her three male co-workers performed work almost identical to the work performed by Ms. Earnest, received work performance evaluations comparable to those of Ms. Earnest, and have computer program skills, training, and prior work experience comparable to those of Ms. Earnest. Despite these facts, the males received higher salaries than Ms. Earnest, received larger annual increases in their salary, and have been given opportunities for advancement on the job, which have been denied to Ms. Earnest.

(c) "Relief" sought including a particularized itemization of all damages claimed

Ms. Earnest is seeking $50,000 to compensate her for lost salary increases and emotional pain and suffering. We estimate that if she had received the 8 percent per year increase that she deserved instead of the 2 percent per year that she received, she would have earned an additional $20,000 over the four years. Under the Equal Pay Act, she also can recover liquidated damages relating to her lost salary increases in the amount of an additional $20,000. The remaining $10,000 covers the pain and suffering that she experienced due to the years of mistreatment by her supervisor.

(d) "Motions" filed and their status

We are considering filing a summary judgment motion because the critical facts are uncontested.

(e) "Discovery Status," including what still needs to be done to be ready for trial

We are still waiting for the information that we requested from the personnel files. So far, we have received only the annual written evaluations of each employee in the department for the past five years. We still need to verify each person's age, academic credentials, record of prior employment, number of years working in the department, starting salary, and annual pay increases. We also still want to depose Ms. Earnest's supervisor.

Settlement Analysis

(f) "Interests of Your Client" that you want met in mediation

Ms. Earnest wants fair compensation for her valuable services to Cutting Edge Computers. She also wants the company to recognize her contributions in a meaningful and public way.

(g) "Settlement Discussions" including any offers or counteroffers previously made

We offered to settle the dispute for $30,000, but the offer was turned down and is no longer on the table.

(h) "Why Not Settled" covers your views on the obstacles to settling this dispute and ways to overcome them

I suspect that at least two obstacles are impeding a settlement—a relationship conflict and incomplete data.

The past four years have produced much suspicion and hostility between Ms. Earnest and her supervisor, making it difficult for them to find common ground for settling this dispute. The dispute has become personal. I hope that the mediation can create an opportunity for the parties to clear the air and mend their relationship enough so that they can move on to resolve the dispute.

We are not ready to move forward until we have in our possession some key data from the personnel files of the other employees. We need specific information about each person who currently works in the department or worked there during the past five years; the information still missing is enumerated under "Discovery Status."

(i) "What You Want Out of the Mediation," especially what you want the mediator to do and what inventive settlement concepts you would like the other side to consider

Ms. Earnest wants the company to properly recognize her hard work and to fairly compensate her for what she has contributed as a computer programmer. Any settlement, regardless of how elegant or creative it might be, must ultimately pass these two interest tests.

Ms. Earnest is open to exploring creative solutions that go beyond what a court is typically willing to do. She is approaching the mediation session with an open mind, not confined by a specific solution. She is ready to learn new things in the mediation and participate in designing a suitable and creative resolution that meets the needs of both sides.

We look forward to benefiting from your preferred mix of approaches in the mediation session. We welcome your facilitating this negotiation by approaching the dispute broadly, actively involving the parties in the discussions, and conducting most of the mediation in joint sessions. For your information, my client plans to present an opening statement.

We also look forward to benefiting from your techniques and control of the process stages. When you reach the agenda formulation stage, we want to be sure that the agenda includes the issue whether the company appreciates Ms. Earnest's contributions. Before you reach the stages of developing options and fashioning solutions, we ask that you help my client and her supervisor get past a possible relationship conflict as well as help the parties resolve a data conflict over the pattern of pay increases over the last four years. We want to use this data as a basis for discussing whether Ms. Earnest was fairly compensated. We invite a mediator to facilitate a process in which parties can brainstorm and search for solutions outside of the legal box.

Other Information

(j) "Who Will Attend" the mediation sessions and the title of any client representatives

Ms. Earnest and John Smith Esq., plan to attend.

(k) Attach critical documentary evidence

Please see the copies of the evaluations of Ms. Earnest and her co-workers. You can see that the supervisor gave each of them comparable evaluations for the assignments they were given and yet gave Ms Earnest pay increases that were less than the pay increases of her co-workers.

John Smith, Esq.
Smith and Smith

Appendix E

Sample

OPENING STATEMENTS

By Plaintiff, Ms. Earnest, and her Attorney

My name is Mr. John Smith, and I represent Ms. Earnest. We are here to try to settle this dispute in this mediation session. We want to thank Cutting Edge Computers and its attorney for participating today.

Ms. Earnest will first present an opening statement in which she will explain what happened, in her own words, and will suggest what she would like to accomplish in the mediation. Then, I will briefly comment on the legal case and suggest some ways the mediator might be helpful to us today.

Ms. Earnest's Opening Statement

[Story]

I am relieved to finally have an opportunity to talk to a senior company representative about what happened. I really appreciate your taking the time from your busy schedule to be here. I want to learn your views of what happened. I hope you will be able to understand mine.

I am very upset with the way that Cutting Edge Computers has treated me during my four years as a loyal and dedicated employee. Cutting Edge Computers has not given me the higher pay increases that I deserved. The company seems to pay women less than men for performing the same work.

I have been working for your company as a computer programmer. I have worked hard, enthusiastically embraced all assignments, and met every deadline. Yet, for the fourth year in a row, I received a smaller pay increase than my three male co-workers in the same department. This year, I only received a 2 percent increase when each of my male co-workers received an 8 percent increase.

I was not surprised because I overheard my supervisor comment a few months ago that she prefers to give higher pay increases to married men who must support their families than married women who do not need the money. My co-workers are married with large families while I am married with no children yet.

Of course, Cutting Edge has denied any discrimination, claiming that I have not been as productive as my co-workers. They do make a point. I recognize that my level of productivity has been less than my co-workers, but that happened because I was not given the same opportunities as my co-workers. Several times, I asked my supervisor to update my computer software to the same version as my co-workers. I was told it would happen soon, but it never did. My supervisor also gave me less challenging assignments and less opportunity to earn overtime.

I did not sit back quietly. I complained to my supervisor a number of times about this unequal treatment, but she belittled my complaints, claiming that my problems were in my head, not in the way I have been treated. After my fourth year review, I could no longer endure this unjust treatment. Even though I really loved my work and enjoyed working with my colleagues, I resigned.

[What Client Wants]

I am asking Cutting Edge Computers to finally recognize my hard work and to fairly compensate me for what I have contributed as a computer programmer.

I am trying to approach this mediation session with an open mind. I am ready to learn new things in the mediation and participate in designing a suitable and creative resolution that meets not only my needs but also any legitimate needs of Cutting Edge Computers.

Her Attorney's Opening Statement

[Legal Case]

We welcome the opportunity to systematically examine together the merits of the legal case. But we are not looking for a legal evaluation from the mediator. Presumably you are both quite familiar with our view of the case [talking directly to the other attorney and client]. Let me summarize it for now.

Ms. Earnest alleges that the company has discriminated against her in the way it set her salary and awarded annual salary increases. Her three male co-workers performed work almost identical to the work performed by Ms. Earnest, received work performance evaluations comparable to those of Ms. Earnest, and have computer program skills, training, and prior work experience comparable to those of Ms. Earnest. Nevertheless, her male co-workers received higher salaries, received larger annual increases in their salary, and received greater opportunities for advancement on the job. We believe that the company's actions violated Title VII of the 1964 Civil Rights Act and the Equal Pay Act of 1963. Ms. Earnest also alleges that she has been denied opportunities for advancement in her job on the basis of sex, an action that also violates Title VII.

We are surely open to a more in-depth discussion of the legal case later in the session if it would be useful. We are ready to listen attentively to your analysis of the legal case and any reactions to our view. We are prepared to examine and assess any differences in our respective legal analysis.

[What We Want the Mediator to Do]

We look forward to benefiting from your mix of approaches in the mediation session. We think you can be of great value in facilitating this negotiation by approaching the dispute broadly, involving the parties in the discussions, and conducting most of the mediation in joint sessions.

We also think that your techniques and control of the process stages can assist us in moving toward a resolution. When you reach the agenda formulation stage, we will ask that the agenda include the issue whether the company appreciated Ms. Earnest's contributions.

Before you reach the stages of developing options and fashioning solutions, we invite you to help my client and her supervisor deal with their relationship conflict that may be impeding settling this dispute. We also request that you help us compile and examine critical data from the personnel files. We need to know the name of each person who currently works in the department or worked there during the past five years, and each person's age, academic credentials, record of prior employment, number of years working in the department, starting salary, and annual pay increases. We also want to see any annual evaluations that have not yet been furnished. We initially requested this information three weeks ago. We need the data for assessing and demonstrating that Ms. Earnest was unfairly compensated.

[Conclusion]

Ms. Earnest has eloquently explained how she felt she was unfairly treated. It is apparent that the pay increase dispute is one manifestation of the broader problem of how Ms. Earnest has been treated in regard to a number of matters. As compared with the men in her department, she has been given less current software, less challenging assignments, and less opportunity to earn overtime. She should not be penalized because she was not given an equal opportunity to demonstrate what she could contribute.

In the mediation, we will be emphasizing Ms. Earnest's interests in receiving recognition and fair compensation for her valuable work. Any settlement, regardless of how elegant or creative it might be, must ultimately satisfy both of her interests.

We are ready to try settling this dispute in this mediation and are prepared to search for inventive solutions that meet everyone's needs.

Thank you.

Appendix F
National Dispute Resolution Organizations

Selected List
Web Sites

(includes sites for mediation rules and rosters)

1. ABA Section of Dispute Resolution: www.abanet.org/dispute

2. Association for Conflict Resolution: www.acresolution.org

Also offers dispute resolution rules, neutral rosters, and administrative support.

3. American Arbitration Association: www.adr.org

4. CPR Institute for Dispute Resolution: www.cpradr.org

5. JAMS: www.jamsadr.com

Add own local sites.

Appendix G

Sample
AGREEMENTS TO MEDIATE

(based on recommendations in chapter 4)

This appendix suggests two sample mediation agreements: one suitable for use *before* a dispute arises and one for use *after* a dispute arises.

Before Dispute Arises: Clause to Insert into a Contract

If a dispute arises out of or relates to this contract, and if the dispute cannot be settled through negotiation, the parties agree first to try in good faith to settle the dispute by mediation before resorting to arbitration, litigation, or some other adjudicatory procedure.

The parties further agree that the mediation will be conducted as follows:

[Cross out any provision that the parties want to defer for resolution until a dispute arises.]

1. Activate Mediation Agreement

A party activates this agreement by notifying the other party in writing that the party is initiating the mediation and is requesting recommendations for mediators.

2. Credentials of Mediator

The parties agree to select a single mediator with the mediation training and experience suitable for the dispute [or co-mediators with complementary mediation training and experience suitable for the dispute.]

3. Approaches of Mediator

The parties agree to select a mediator with the following mix of approaches selected in the section. If the parties cannot or are not ready to agree to all of the mediator approaches at this time, the parties agree that within five business days after selecting the mediator, the mediator shall convene a pre-mediation conference in which the mediator will facilitate a discussion of the mix of mediator approaches and any other issues the parties want to resolve before the mediation session. Any unresolved issues will be resolved in accordance with the rules selected in clause 10.

[Select one for each subject area]

Manages Process By:

___ *Facilitating Predominately*

___ *Evaluating Predominately*

___ *Following Transformative Approach*

___ *Resolve When Dispute Arises*

Views Problem:

___ *Broadly*

___ *Narrowly as primarily the legal disputes*

___ *Leave to Discretion of Mediator*

___*Resolve When Dispute Arises*

Involves Clients:

___ *Actively*

___ *Restrictively*

___ *Leave to Discretion of Mediator*

___ *Resolve When Dispute Arises*

Uses Caucuses:

___ *Primarily*

___ *Selectively*

___ *Not at All*

___ *Leave to Discretion of Mediator*

___ *Resolve When Dispute Arises*

Engage in Evaluation of Legal Issues or Settlement Proposals:

___ *None*

___ *Only After Parties Specifically Consent to What Is to Be Evaluated*

___ *Leave to Discretion of Mediator*

___ *Resolve When Dispute Arises*

4. Procedure for Selecting the Mediator

If the parties cannot agree on a mediator within fifteen business days after one side activates the mediation clause, the selection procedure under the rules adopted under clause 10 will apply.

5. Payment of Costs

The costs of the mediator, including reasonable travel and other out-of-pocket expenses, will be shared equally by the parties unless they agree otherwise.

6. Client Participation

Parties agree to bring to the mediation session parties with broad and flexible settlement authority.

7. Information Exchange

Each party agrees to provide any discoverable information that the other party needs to meaningfully participate in the mediation.

8. Confidentiality

Parties agree that the mediation will be subject to the level of confidentiality established in the mediation rules selected in clause 10 except as modified or supplemented as follows:

9. Location and Language of Sessions

Parties agree that the mediation sessions will be held in _____ and conducted in_____ language.

10. Mediation Rules of an ADR (Alternative Dispute Resolution) Provider

Any matters not specifically covered by this agreement or cannot be resolved within fifteen business days after one side activates the mediation agreement will be resolved

___ *by the American Arbitration Association administering the mediation under its Commercial Mediation Procedures (www.adr.org),*

___ *in accordance with the CPR Mediation Procedure (www.cpradr. org), or*

___ *by [insert any other preferred ADR Provider or mediation rules].*

Date:

Signatures:

After Dispute Arises: Agreement to Submit
Dispute to Mediation

The parties agree to submit the following dispute to mediation: [describe briefly the dispute]

The parties further agree that the mediation will be conducted as follows:

[Cross out any provision that the parties want to exclude.]

1. Activate Mediation Agreement

A party activates this agreement by notifying the other party in writing that the party is initiating the mediation and is requesting recommendations for mediators.

2. Credentials of Mediator

The parties agree to select a single mediator with the mediation training and experience suitable for the dispute [or co-mediators with complementary mediation training and experience suitable for the dispute.]

3. Approaches of Mediator

The parties agree to select a mediator with the following mix of approaches:

[Select one for each subject area]

Manages Process By:
____ Facilitating Predominately
____ Evaluating Predominately
____ Following Transformative Approach

Views Problem:
____ Broadly
____ Narrowly as Primarily the Legal Disputes
____ Leave to Discretion of Mediator

Involves Clients:

___ *Actively*

___ *Restrictively*

___ *Leave to Discretion of Mediator*

Uses Caucuses:

___ *Primarily*

___ *Selectively*

___ *Not at All*

___ *Leave to Discretion of Mediator*

Engages in Evaluation of Legal Issues or Settlement Proposals:

___ *None*

___ *Only After Parties Specifically Consent to What is to be Evaluated*

___ *Leave to Discretion of Mediator*

4. Procedure for Selecting the Mediator

If the parties cannot agree on a mediator within fifteen business days after one side activates the mediation agreement, the selection procedure under the rules adopted under clause 10 will apply.

5. Payment of Costs

The costs of the mediator, including reasonable travel and other out-of-pocket expenses, will be shared equally by the parties unless they agree otherwise.

6. Client Participation

Parties agree to bring to the mediation session parties with broad and flexible settlement authority.

7. Information Exchange

Each party agrees to provide any discoverable information that the other party needs to meaningfully participate in the mediation.

8. Confidentiality

Parties agree that the mediation will be subject to the level of confidentiality established in the mediation rules selected in clause 10 except as modified or supplemented as follows:

9. Location and Language of Sessions

Parties agree that the mediation sessions will be held in _____ and conducted in_____ language.

10. Mediation Rules of an ADR (Alternative Dispute Resolution) Provider

Any matters not specifically covered by this agreement or cannot be resolved within fifteen business days after one side activates the mediation agreement will be resolved

____ by the American Arbitration Association administering the mediation under its Commercial Mediation Procedures (www.adr.org),

____ in accordance with the CPR Mediation Procedure (www.cpradr. org), or

____ by [insert any other preferred ADR Provider or mediation rules].

Date:

Signatures:

APPENDIX H
COMMERCIAL MEDIATION PROCEDURE[1]

American Arbitration Association
(include sample agreements to mediate)

Amended and Effective July 1, 2003

M-1.   Agreement of Parties
M-2.   Initiation of Mediation
M-3.   Requests for Mediation
M-4.   Appointment of the Mediator
M-5.   Qualifications of the Mediator
M-6.   Vacancies
M-7.   Representation
M-8.   Date, Time, and Place of Mediation
M-9.   Identification of Matters in Dispute
M-10. Authority of the Mediator
M-11. Privacy
M-12. Confidentiality
M-13. No Stenographic Record
M-14. Termination of Mediation
M-15. Exclusion of Liability
M-16. Interpretation and Application of Procedures
M-17. Expenses
ADMINISTRATIVE FEES

IMPORTANT NOTICE

These rules and any amendment of them shall apply in the form in effect at the time the administrative filing requirements are met for a demand for arbitration or submission agreement received by the AAA. To ensure that you have the most current information, see our Web Site at www.adr.org.

---

1. This material is reprinted with permission by the American Arbitration Association (AAA).

Mediation

If the parties want to adopt mediation as a part of their contractual dispute settlement procedure, they can insert the following mediation clause into their contract in conjunction with a standard arbitration provision:

> *If a dispute arises out of or relates to this contract, or the breach thereof, and if the dispute cannot be settled through negotiation, the parties agree first to try in good faith to settle the dispute by mediation administered by the American Arbitration Association under its Commercial Mediation Procedures before resorting to arbitration, litigation, or some other dispute resolution procedure.*

If the parties want to use a mediator to resolve an existing dispute, they can enter into the following submission:

> *The parties hereby submit the following dispute to mediation administered by the American Arbitration Association under its Commercial Mediation Procedures. (The clause may also provide for the qualifications of the mediator(s), method of payment, locale of meetings, and any other item of concern to the parties.)*

COMMERCIAL MEDIATION PROCEDURES

M-1. Agreement of Parties

Whenever, by stipulation or in their contract, the parties have provided for mediation or conciliation of existing or future disputes under the auspices of the American Arbitration Association (AAA) or under these procedures, they shall be deemed to have made these procedures, as amended and in effect as of the date of the submission of the dispute, a part of their agreement.

M-2. Initiation of Mediation

Any party or parties to a dispute may initiate mediation by filing with the AAA a submission to mediation or a written request for mediation pursuant to these procedures, together with the $325 nonrefundable case set-up fee. Where there is no submission to mediation or contract providing for mediation, a party may request the AAA to invite another party to join in a submission to mediation. Upon receipt of such a request, the AAA will contact the other parties involved in the dispute and attempt to obtain a submission to mediation.

M-3. Requests for Mediation

A request for mediation shall contain a brief statement of the nature of the dispute and the names, addresses, and telephone numbers of all parties to the dispute and those who will represent them, if any, in the mediation. The initiating party shall simultaneously file two copies of the request with the AAA and one copy with every other party to the dispute.

M-4. Appointment of the Mediator

Upon receipt of a request for mediation, the AAA will appoint a qualified mediator to serve. Normally, a single mediator will be appointed unless the parties agree otherwise or the AAA determines otherwise. If the agreement of the parties names a mediator or specifies a method of appointing a mediator, that designation or method shall be followed.

M-5. Qualifications of the Mediator

No person shall serve as a mediator in any dispute in which that person has any financial or personal interest in the result of the mediation, except by the written consent of all parties. Prior to accepting an appointment, the prospective mediator shall disclose any circumstance likely to create a presumption of bias or prevent a prompt meeting with the parties. Upon receipt of such information, the AAA shall either replace the mediator or immediately communicate the information to the parties for their comments. In the event that the parties disagree as to whether the mediator shall serve, the AAA will appoint another mediator. The AAA is authorized to appoint another mediator if the appointed mediator is unable to serve promptly.

M-6. Vacancies

If any mediator shall become unwilling or unable to serve, the AAA will appoint another mediator, unless the parties agree otherwise.

M-7. Representation

Any party may be represented by persons of the party's choice. The names and addresses of such persons shall be communicated in writing to all parties and to the AAA.

M-8. Date, Time, and Place of Mediation

The mediator shall fix the date and the time of each mediation session. The mediation shall be held at the appropriate regional office of the AAA, or at any other convenient location agreeable to the mediator and the parties, as the mediator shall determine.

M-9. Identification of Matters in Dispute

At least ten days prior to the first scheduled mediation session, each party shall provide the mediator with a brief memorandum setting forth its position with regard to the issues that need to be resolved. At the discretion of the mediator, such memoranda may be mutually exchanged by the parties.

At the first session, the parties will be expected to produce all information reasonably required for the mediator to understand the issues presented.

The mediator may require any party to supplement such information.

M-10. Authority of the Mediator

The mediator does not have the authority to impose a settlement on the parties but will attempt to help them reach a satisfactory resolution of their dispute. The mediator is authorized to conduct joint and separate meetings with the parties and to make oral and written recommendations for settlement.

Whenever necessary, the mediator may also obtain expert advice concerning technical aspects of the dispute, provided that the parties agree and assume the expenses of obtaining such advice.

Arrangements for obtaining such advice shall be made by the mediator or the parties, as the mediator shall determine.

The mediator is authorized to end the mediation whenever, in the judgment of the mediator, further efforts at mediation would not contribute to a resolution of the dispute between the parties.

M-11. Privacy

Mediation sessions are private. The parties and their representatives may attend mediation sessions. Other persons may attend only with the permission of the parties and with the consent of the mediator.

M-12. Confidentiality

Confidential information disclosed to a mediator by the parties or by witnesses in the course of the mediation shall not be divulged by the mediator. All records, reports, or other documents received by a mediator while serving in that capacity shall be confidential.

The mediator shall not be compelled to divulge such records or to testify in regard to the mediation in any adversary proceeding or judicial forum.

The parties shall maintain the confidentiality of the mediation and shall not rely on, or introduce as evidence in any arbitral, judicial, or other proceeding:

(a)   views expressed or suggestions made by another party with respect to a possible settlement of the dispute;

(b)   admissions made by another party in the course of the mediation proceedings;

(c)   proposals made or views expressed by the mediator; or

(d)   the fact that another party had or had not indicated willingness to accept a proposal for settlement made by the mediator.

M-13. No Stenographic Record

There shall be no stenographic record of the mediation process.

M-14. Termination of Mediation

The mediation shall be terminated:

(a)   by the execution of a settlement agreement by the parties;

(b)   by a written declaration of the mediator to the effect that further efforts at mediation are no longer worthwhile; or

(c)   by a written declaration of a party or parties to the effect that the mediation proceedings are terminated.

M-15. Exclusion of Liability

Neither the AAA nor any mediator is a necessary party in judicial proceedings relating to the mediation. Neither the AAA nor any mediator shall be liable to any party for any act or omission in connection with any mediation conducted under these procedures.

M-16. Interpretation and Application of Procedures

The mediator shall interpret and apply these procedures insofar as they relate to the mediator's duties and responsibilities. All other procedures shall be interpreted and applied by the AAA.

M-17. Expenses

The expenses of witnesses for either side shall be paid by the party producing such witnesses. All other expenses of the mediation, including required traveling and other expenses of the mediator and representatives of the AAA, and the expenses of any witness and the cost of any proofs or expert advice produced at the direct request of the mediator, shall be borne equally by the parties unless they agree otherwise.

ADMINISTRATIVE FEES

The nonrefundable case set-up fee is $325 per party. In addition, the parties are responsible for compensating the mediator at his or her published rate, for conference and study time (hourly or per diem).

All expenses are generally borne equally by the parties. The parties may adjust this arrangement by agreement.

Before the commencement of the mediation, the AAA shall estimate anticipated total expenses. Each party shall pay its portion of that amount as per the agreed upon arrangement. When the mediation has terminated, the AAA shall render an accounting and return any unexpended balance to the parties.

Appendix I

The CPR Mediation Procedure[1]

(includes sample agreements to mediate)

Revised and effective as of April 1, 1998

1. Agreement to Mediate
2. Selecting the Mediator
3. Ground Rules of Proceeding
4. Exchange of Information
5. Presentation to the Mediator
6. Negotiations
7. Settlement
8. Failure to Agree
9. Confidentiality
10. Form 1: Model Agreement for Parties and Mediator

1. Agreement to Mediate

The CPR Mediation Procedure (the "Procedure") may be adopted by agreement of the parties, with or without modification, before or after a dispute has arisen. The following provisions are suggested:

A. Pre-dispute Clause

The parties shall attempt in good faith to resolve any dispute arising out of or relating to this Agreement promptly by confidential mediation under the [then current] CPR Mediation Procedure [in effect on the date of this Agreement], before resorting to arbitration or litigation.

---

1. ©2004 **CPR Institute for Dispute Resolution**, 366 Madison Avenue, New York, NY 10017-3122; (212) 949-6490, www.cpr.org. This **excerpt** from **The CPR Mediation Procedure** reprinted with permission of **CPR Institute**.

The CPR Institute is a nonprofit initiative of 500 general counsel of major corporations, leading law firms and prominent legal academics whose mission is to install alternative dispute resolution (ADR) into the mainstream of legal practice.

B. Existing Dispute Submission Agreement

We hereby agree to submit to confidential mediation under the CPR Mediation Procedure the following controversy:

(Describe briefly)

2. Selecting the Mediator

Unless the parties agree otherwise, the mediator shall be selected from the CPR Panels of Neutrals. If the parties cannot agree promptly on a mediator, they will notify CPR of their need for assistance in selecting a mediator, informing CPR of any preferences as to matters such as candidates' mediation style, subject matter expertise and geographic location. CPR will submit to the parties the names of not less than three candidates, with their resumes and hourly rates. If the parties are unable to agree on a candidate from the list within seven days following receipt of the list, each party will, within 15 days following receipt of the list, send to CPR the list of candidates ranked in descending order of preference. The candidate with the lowest combined score will be appointed as the mediator by CPR. CPR will break any tie.

Before proposing any mediator candidate, CPR will request the candidate to disclose any circumstances known to him or her that would cause reasonable doubt regarding the candidate's impartiality. If a clear conflict is disclosed, the individual will not be proposed. Other circumstances a candidate discloses to CPR will be disclosed to the parties. A party may challenge a mediator candidate if it knows of any circumstances giving rise to reasonable doubt regarding the candidate's impartiality.

The mediator's rate of compensation will be determined before appointment. Such compensation, and any other costs of the process, will be shared equally by the parties unless they otherwise agree. If a party withdraws from a multiparty mediation but the procedure continues, the withdrawing party will not be responsible for any costs incurred after it has notified the mediator and the other parties of its withdrawal.

Before appointment, the mediator will assure the parties of his or her availability to conduct the proceeding expeditiously. It is strongly advised that the parties and the mediator enter into a retention agreement. A model agreement is attached hereto as a Form.

3. Ground Rules of Proceeding

The following ground rules will apply, subject to any changes on which the parties and the mediator agree.

a. The process is non-binding.

b. Each party may withdraw at any time after attending the first session, and before execution of a written settlement agreement, by written notice to the mediator and the other party or parties.

c. The mediator shall be neutral and impartial.

d. The mediator shall control the procedural aspects of the mediation. The parties will cooperate fully with the mediator.

    i. The mediator is free to meet and communicate separately with each party.

    ii. The mediator will decide when to hold joint meetings with the parties and when to hold separate meetings. The mediator will fix the time and place of each session and its agenda in consultation with the parties. There will be no stenographic record of any meeting. Formal rules of evidence or procedure will not apply.

e. Each party will be represented at each mediation conference by a business executive authorized to negotiate a resolution of the dispute, unless excused by the mediator as to a particular conference. Each party may be represented by more than one person, e.g. a business executive and an attorney. The mediator may limit the number of persons representing each party.

f. Each party will be represented by counsel to advise it in the mediation, whether or not such counsel is present at mediation conferences.

g. The process will be conducted expeditiously. Each representative will make every effort to be available for meetings.

h. The mediator will not transmit information received in confidence from any party to any other party or any third party unless authorized to do so by the party transmitting the information, or unless ordered to do so by a court of competent jurisdiction.

i. Unless the parties agree otherwise, they will refrain from pursuing litigation or any administrative or judicial remedies during the mediation process or for a set period of time, insofar as they can do so without prejudicing their legal rights.

j. Unless all parties and the mediator otherwise agree in writing, the mediator and any persons assisting the mediator will be disqualified as a witness, consultant or expert in any pending or future investigation, action or proceeding relating to the subject matter of the mediation (including any investigation, action or proceeding which involves persons not party to this mediation).

k. If the dispute goes into arbitration, the mediator shall not serve as an arbitrator, unless the parties and the mediator otherwise agree in writing.

l. The mediator may obtain assistance and independent expert advice, with the prior agreement of and at the expense of the parties. Any person proposed as an independent expert also will be required to disclose any circumstances known to him or her that would cause reasonable doubt regarding the candidate's impartiality.

m. Neither CPR nor the mediator shall be liable for any act or omission in connection with the mediation, except for its/his/her own willful misconduct.

n. The mediator may withdraw at any time by written notice to the parties (i) for serious personal reasons, (ii) if the mediator believes that a party is not acting in good faith, or (iii) if the mediator concludes that further mediation efforts would not be useful. If the mediator withdraws pursuant to (i) or (ii), he or she need not state the reason for withdrawal.

4. Exchange of Information

If any party has a substantial need for documents or other material in the possession of another party, or for other discovery that may facilitate a settlement, the parties shall attempt to agree thereon. Should they fail to agree, either party may request a joint consultation with the mediator who shall assist the parties in reaching agreement.

The parties shall exchange with each other, with a copy to the mediator, the names and job titles of all individuals who will attend the joint mediation session.

At the conclusion of the mediation process, upon the request of a party which provided documents or other material to one or more other parties, the recipients shall return the same to the originating party without retaining copies.

5.   Presentation to the Mediator

Before dealing with the substance of the dispute, the parties and the mediator will discuss preliminary matters, such as possible modification of the procedure, place and time of meetings, and each party's need for documents or other information in the possession of the other.

At least 10 business days before the first substantive mediation conference, unless otherwise agreed, each party will submit to the mediator a written statement summarizing the background and present status of the dispute, including any settlement efforts that have occurred, and such other material and information as the mediator requests or the party deems helpful to familiarize the mediator with the dispute. It is desirable for the submission to include an analysis of the party's real interests and needs and of its litigation risks. The parties may agree to submit jointly certain records and other materials. The mediator may request any party to provide clarification and additional information.

The parties are encouraged to discuss the exchange of all or certain materials they submit to the mediator to further each party's understanding of the other party's viewpoints. The mediator may request the parties to submit a joint statement of facts. Except as the parties otherwise agree, the mediator shall keep confidential any written materials or information that are submitted to him or her. The parties and their representatives are not entitled to receive or review any materials or information submitted to the mediator by another party or representative without the concurrence of the latter. At the conclusion of the mediation process, upon request of a party, the mediator will return to that party all written materials and information which that party had provided to the mediator without retaining copies thereof or certify as to the destruction of such materials.

At the first substantive mediation conference each party will make an opening statement.

6. Negotiations

The mediator may facilitate settlement in any manner the mediator believes is appropriate. The mediator will help the parties focus on their underlying interests and concerns, explore resolution alternatives and develop settlement options. The mediator will decide when to hold joint meetings, and when to confer separately with each party.

The parties are expected to initiate and convey to the mediator proposals for settlement. Each party shall provide a rationale for any settlement terms proposed.

Finally, if the parties fail to develop mutually acceptable settlement terms, before terminating the procedure, and only with the consent of the parties, (a) the mediator may submit to the parties a final settlement proposal; and (b) if the mediator believes he/she is qualified to do so, the mediator may give the parties an evaluation (which if all parties choose, and the mediator agrees, may be in writing) of the likely outcome of the case if it were tried to final judgment, subject to any limitations under any applicable mediation statutes/rules, court rules or ethical codes. Thereupon, the mediator may suggest further discussions to explore whether the mediator's evaluation or proposal may lead to a resolution.

Efforts to reach a settlement will continue until (a) a written settlement is reached, or (b) the mediator concludes and informs the parties that further efforts would not be useful, or (c) one of the parties or the mediator withdraws from the process. However, if there are more than two parties, the remaining parties may elect to continue following the withdrawal of a party.

7. Settlement

If a settlement is reached, a preliminary memorandum of understanding or term sheet normally will be prepared and signed or initialed before the parties separate. Thereafter, unless the mediator undertakes to do so, representatives of the parties will promptly draft a written settlement document incorporating all settlement terms. This draft will be circulated, amended as necessary, and formally executed. If litigation is pending, the settlement may provide that the parties will request dismissal of the case. The parties also may request the court to enter the settlement agreement as a consent judgment.

8.   Failure to Agree

If a resolution is not reached, the mediator will discuss with the parties the possibility of their agreeing on advisory or binding arbitration, "last offer" arbitration or another form of ADR. If the parties agree in principle, the mediator may offer to assist them in structuring a procedure designed to result in a prompt, economical process. The mediator will not serve as arbitrator, unless all parties agree.

9.   Confidentiality

The entire mediation process is confidential. Unless agreed among all the parties or required to do so by law, the parties and the mediator shall not disclose to any person who is not associated with participants in the process, including any judicial officer, any information regarding the process (including pre-process exchanges and agreements), contents (including written and oral information), settlement terms or outcome of the proceeding. If litigation is pending, the participants may, however, advise the court of the schedule and overall status of the mediation for purposes of litigation management. Any written settlement agreement resulting from the mediation may be disclosed for purposes of enforcement.

Under this procedure, the entire process is a compromise negotiation subject to Federal Rule of Evidence 408 and all state counterparts, together with any applicable statute protecting the confidentiality of mediation. All offers, promises, conduct and statements, whether oral or written, made in the course of the proceeding by any of the parties, their agents, employees, experts and attorneys, and by the mediator are confidential. Such offers, promises, conduct and statements are privileged under any applicable mediation privilege and are inadmissible and not discoverable for any purpose, including impeachment, in litigation between the parties. However, evidence that is otherwise admissible or discoverable shall not be rendered inadmissible or non-discoverable solely as a result of its presentation or use during the mediation.

The exchange of any tangible material shall be without prejudice to any claim that such material is privileged or protected as work-product within the meaning of Federal Rule of Civil Procedure 26 and all state and local counterparts.

The mediator and any documents and information in the mediator's possession will not be subpoenaed in any such investigation, action or proceeding, and all parties will oppose any effort to have the mediator or documents subpoenaed. The mediator will promptly advise the parties of any attempt to compel him/her to divulge information received in mediation.

10. Form 1: Model Agreement for Parties and Mediator

CPR Model Agreement for Parties and Mediator

Agreement made (date)_____, _____

between_____

represented by _____

and _____

represented by _____

and (the Meditator) _____

A dispute has arisen between the parties (the "Dispute"). The parties have agreed to participate in a mediation proceeding (the "Proceeding") under the CPR Mediation Procedure [as modified by mutual agreement] (the "Procedure"). The parties have chosen the Mediator for the Proceeding. The parties and the Mediator agree as follows:

A. Duties and Obligations

1. Mediator and each of the parties agree to be bound by and to comply faithfully with the Procedure, including without limitation the provisions regarding confidentiality.

2. The Mediator has no previous commitments that may significantly delay the expeditious conduct of the proceeding and will not make any such commitments.

3. The Mediator, the CPR Institute for Dispute Resolution (CPR) and their employees, agents and partners shall not be liable for any act or omission in connection with the

Proceeding, other than as a result of its/his/her own willful misconduct.

B. Disclosure of Prior Relationships

1. The Mediator has made a reasonable effort to learn and has disclosed to the parties in writing (a) all business or professional relationships the Mediator and/or the Mediator's firm have had with the parties or their law firms within the past five years, including all instances in which the Mediator or the Mediator's firm served as an attorney for any party or adverse to any party; (b) any financial interest the Mediator has in any party; (c) any significant social, business or professional relationship the Mediator has had with an officer or employee of a party or with an individual representing a party in the Proceeding; and (d) any other circumstances that may create doubt regarding the Mediator's impartiality in the Proceeding.

2. Each party and its law firm has made a reasonable effort to learn and has disclosed to every other party and the Mediator in writing any relationships of a nature described in paragraph B.1. not previously identified and disclosed by the Mediator.

3. The parties and the Mediator are satisfied that any relationships disclosed pursuant to paragraphs B.1. and B.2. will not affect the Mediator's independence or impartiality. Notwithstanding such relationships or others the Mediator and the parties did not discover despite good faith efforts, the parties wish the Mediator to serve in the Proceeding, waiving any claim based on said relationships, and the Mediator agrees to so serve.

4. The disclosure obligations in paragraphs B.1. and B.2. are continuing until the Proceeding is concluded. The ability of the Mediator to continue serving in this capacity shall be explored with each such disclosure.

C. Future Relationships

1. Neither the Mediator nor the Mediator's firm shall undertake any work for or against a party regarding the Dispute.

2. Neither the Mediator nor any person assisting the Mediator with this Proceeding shall personally work on any matter for or against a party, regardless of specific subject matter, prior to six months following cessation of the Mediator's services in the Proceeding.

3. The Mediator's firm may work on matters for or against a party during the pendency of the Proceeding if such matters are unrelated to the Dispute. The Mediator shall establish appropriate safeguards to insure that other members and employees of the firm working on the Dispute do not have access to any confidential information obtained by the Mediator during the course of the Proceeding.

D. Compensation

1. The Mediator shall be compensated for time expended in connection with the Proceeding at the rate of $_____, plus reasonable travel and other out-of-pocket expenses. The Mediator's fee shall be shared equally by the parties. No part of such fee shall accrue to CPR.

2. The Mediator may utilize members and employees of the firm to assist in connection with the Proceeding and may bill the parties for the time expended by any such persons, to the extent and at a rate agreed upon in advance by the parties.

_____   _____
Party   Party

By   By

_____   _____
Party's Attorney   Party's Attorney

_____
Mediator

APPENDIX J
Final-Offer Arbitration Rules[1]

Directions: Check off ONE box for each Rule and fill in the additional details.

Dispute/Case:

1. **Selecting Arbitrator**
    - ☐ a. Procedure (specify)

    - ☐ b. Designate Particular Person

2. **Formulating Final Offer**
    - ☐ a. Total Package

    - ☐ b. Issue-by-Issue

    - ☐ c. Other

---

1. The author Harold Abramson prepared these rules for an unpublished paper on how to use final-offer arbitration in mediations.

3. **Number of Final Offers**
   ☐ a.   One Final Offer

   ☐ b.   Option for Amendments

   ☐ c.   Other

4. **"Hearing" for Presentation of Final Offers**
   ☐ a.   Mediation Session

   ☐ b.   Paper Hearing

   ☐ c.   Formal Hearing

5. **Criteria for Selection of Final Offer by Arbitrator**
   ☐ a.   Most Reasonable

   ☐ b.   Applicable Law

   ☐ c.   Contract Terms or New Multiple Criteria

   ☐ d.   Other

6. **Restrictions on Selection of Final Offer by Arbitrator**

   ☐ a.　Select One or the Other Final Offer (baseball arbitration)

   ☐ b.　Select Final Offer Closest to Arbitrator's Proposed Award (which is based on criteria selected in Rule 5) (night baseball FOA)

   ☐ c.　Other

7. **Timetable**

   ☐ a.　Hearing

   ☐ b.　Submitting Final Offers

8. **Arbitrator's Selection is Binding Upon the Parties**

9. **Any other procedural issues will be resolved in accordance with the Commercial Arbitration Rules of the American Arbitration Association. The arbitrator's selection is an award upon which a judgment may be entered in any court with jurisdiction.**

We, the undersigned parties, agree to adopt these rules for arbitrating the above referenced dispute/case.

_____   _____
Signature   Signature

_____   _____
Plaintiff or Plaintiff's Attorney   Defendant or Defendant's Attorney

_____
Date

Appendix K
Mini-Trial Procedures[1]
American Arbitration Association
(1994)

1. The mini-trial process may be initiated by the written or oral request of either party, made to any regional office of the AAA, but will not be pursued unless both parties agree to resolve their dispute by means of a mini-trial.

2. The course of the mini-trial process shall be governed by a written agreement between the parties.

3. The mini-trial shall consist of an information exchange and settlement negotiation.

4. Each party is represented throughout the mini-trial process by legal counsel whose role is to prepare and present the party's "best case" at the information exchange.

5. Each party shall have in attendance throughout the information exchange and settlement negotiation a senior executive with settlement authority.

6. A neutral advisor shall be present at the information exchange to decide questions of procedure and to render advice to the party representatives when requested by them.

7. The neutral advisor shall be selected by mutual agreement of the parties, who may consult with the AAA for recommendations. To facilitate the selection process, the AAA will make available to the parties a list of individuals to serve as neutral advisors. If the parties fail to agree upon the selection of a neutral advisor, they shall ask that the AAA appoint an advisor from the panel it has compiled for this purpose.

---

1. This material is reprinted with permission by the American Arbitration Association (AAA).

8. Discovery between the parties may take place prior to the information exchange, in accordance with the agreement between the parties.

9. Prior to the information exchange, the parties shall exchange written statements summarizing the issues in the case, and copies of all documents they intend to present at the information exchange.

10. Federal or state rules of evidence do not apply to presentations made at the information exchange. Any limitation on the scope of the evidence offered at the information exchange shall be determined by mutual agreement of the parties prior to the exchange and shall be enforced by the neutral advisor.

11. After the information exchange, the senior executives shall meet and attempt, in good faith, to formulate a voluntary settlement of the dispute.

12. If the senior executives are unable to settle the dispute, the neutral advisor shall render an advisory opinion as to the likely outcome of the case if it were litigated in a court of law. The neutral advisor's opinion shall identify the issues of law and fact which are critical to the disposition of the case and give the reasons for the opinion that is offered.

13. After the neutral advisor has rendered an advisory opinion, the senior executives shall meet for a second time in an attempt to resolve the dispute. If they are unable to reach a settlement at this time, they may either abandon the proceeding or submit to the neutral advisor written offers of settlement. If the parties elect to make such written offers, the neutral advisor shall make a recommendation for settlement based on those offers. If the parties reject the recommendation of the neutral advisor, either party may declare the mini-trial terminated and resolve the dispute by other means.

14. Mini-trial proceedings are confidential; no written or oral statement made by any participant in the proceeding may be used as evidence or in admission in any other proceeding.

15. The fees and expenses of the neutral advisor shall be borne equally by the parties, and each party is responsible for its own costs, including legal fees, incurred in connection with the mini-trial.

The parties may, however, in their written agreement alter the allocation of fees and expenses.

16. Neither the AAA nor any neutral advisor serving in a mini-trial proceeding governed by these procedures shall be liable to any party for any act or omission in connection with the mini-trial. The parties shall indemnify the AAA and the neutral advisor for any liability to third parties arising out of the mini-trial process.

Administrative Fee

Parties initiating a mini-trial under these procedures will make arrangements with the local AAA office for administrative fees and neutral-advisor compensation.

APPENDIX L
CPR MINITRIAL PROCEDURE[1]
CPR Institute for Dispute Resolution
(Rev. 1989)

1. Institution of Proceeding

The parties will commence the proceeding by entering into a written agreement (the "initiating agreement"), substantially in the form attached hereto as Appendix A. The date of the initiating agreement is called the "commencement date."

2. The Minitrial Panel

2.1. The minitrial panel shall consist of one member of management from each party (the "management representative"), who shall have authority to negotiate a settlement on behalf of the party represented, and a neutral adviser (the "Neutral Adviser").

2.2. If the management representatives are not designated in the initiating agreement, each party shall name its management representative within thirty days from the commencement date by written notice to the other party and the Neutral Adviser. Each party thereafter may designate a different management representative by written notice to the other party and the Neutral Adviser.

3. The Neutral Adviser

3.1. The Neutral Adviser, who shall be independent and impartial, will perform the functions stated in this procedure and any additional functions on which the parties may hereafter agree.

---

1. ©2004 **CPR Institute for Dispute Resolution**, 366 Madison Avenue, New York, NY 10017-3122; (212) 949-6490, www.cpr.org. This excerpt from **CPR Minitrial Procedure** reprinted with permission of **CPR Institute**.

The CPR Institute is a nonprofit initiative of 500 general counsel of major corporations, leading law firms and prominent legal academics whose mission is to install alternative dispute resolution (ADR) into the mainstream of legal practice.

3.2. If the Neutral Adviser is not named in the initiating agreement, the parties will attempt to select a Neutral Adviser by mutual agreement.

3.3. If the parties have not agreed on a Neutral Adviser within 15 days from the commencement date, either party may request CPR in writing, with copy to the other party, to assist in the selection of a Neutral Adviser. A copy of the initiating agreement shall be attached to such request.

CPR shall then proceed as follows:

a. Promptly following receipt by it of the request, CPR shall convene the parties in person or by telephone one or more times to attempt to select the Neutral Adviser by agreement of the parties.

b. If the procedure provided for in (a) does not result in the selection of the Neutral Adviser, CPR shall submit to the parties a list of not less than three candidates. Such list shall include a brief statement of each candidate's qualifications. Each party shall strike from the list any candidate it finds unacceptable, shall number the remaining candidates in order of preference, and shall deliver the list so marked to CPR. CPR shall designate as Neutral Adviser the nominee willing to serve for whom the parties collectively have indicated the highest preference and who does not have a conflict of interest (see paragraph 3.4.). If a tie should result between two candidates, CPR may designate either candidate. If this procedure for any reason should fail to result in designation of the Neutral Adviser, the parties may request CPR to repeat the procedure, proposing a list of not less than three new candidates.

3.4. Each party shall promptly disclose to the other party any circumstances known to it which would cause justifiable doubt regarding the independence or impartiality of an individual under consideration or appointed as Neutral Adviser. Any such individual shall promptly disclose any such circumstances to the parties. If any such circumstances have been disclosed, the individual shall not serve as Neutral Adviser unless all parties agree.

3.5. No party, nor anyone acting on its behalf, shall unilaterally communicate with the Neutral Adviser on any matter of substance, except as specifically provided for herein or agreed between the parties.

3.6. The parties will promptly send to the Neutral Adviser such materials as they may agree upon for the purpose of familiarizing the Neutral Adviser with the facts and issues in the dispute. The parties shall comply promptly with any requests by the Neutral Adviser for additional documents or information relevant to the dispute.

3.7. The parties may jointly seek the advice and assistance of the Neutral Adviser or CPR in interpreting this procedure and on procedural matters.

3.8. The Neutral Adviser's per diem or hourly charge will be established at the time of appointment. Unless the parties otherwise agree, (a) the fees and expenses of the Neutral Adviser, CPR's time charges, and any other expenses of the proceeding will be borne equally by the parties; and (b) each party shall bear its own costs of the proceeding.

4. Discovery

4.1. If either or both parties have a substantial need for discovery to prepare for the information exchange, the parties shall attempt in good faith to agree on a plan for strictly necessary, expeditious discovery. Should they fail to agree, either party may request a joint meeting with the Neutral Adviser, who shall assist the parties in formulating a discovery plan.

4.2. Should the minitrial not result in a settlement of the dispute, discovery taken in the proceeding may be used in any pending or future proceeding between the parties relating to the dispute unless the parties otherwise agree. Such discovery shall not restrict a party's ability to take additional discovery in any such proceeding.

5. Briefs and Exhibits

Before the information exchange, the parties shall exchange, and submit to the Neutral Adviser, briefs, as well as all documents or other exhibits on which the parties intend to rely during the information exchange. The parties shall agree upon the length of such briefs, and on the date on which such briefs, documents and other exhibits are to be exchanged.

6. The Minitrial Information Exchange

6.1. The minitrial information exchange shall be held before the minitrial panel at a place and time stated in the initiating agreement or thereafter agreed to by the parties and the Neutral Adviser.

6.2. During the information exchange each party shall make a presentation of its best case, and each party shall be entitled to a rebuttal. The order and permissible length of presentations and rebuttals shall be determined by agreement between the parties, or failing such agreement, by the Neutral Adviser.

6.3. The Neutral Adviser will moderate the information exchange.

6.4. The presentations and rebuttals of each party may be made in any form, and by any individuals, as desired by such party. Presentations by fact witnesses and expert witnesses shall be permitted.

6.5. Presentations may not be interrupted, except that during each party's presentation, and following such presentation, any member of the panel may ask clarifying questions of counsel or other persons appearing on that party's behalf. No member of the panel may limit the scope or substance of a party's presentation. No rules of evidence, including rules of relevance, will apply at the information exchange, except that the rules pertaining to privileged communications and attorney work product will apply.

6.6. Members of the panel, and if the parties so agree, each party and counsel, may ask questions of opposing counsel and witnesses during scheduled, open question and answer exchanges and during that party's rebuttal time.

6.7. The information exchange shall not be recorded by any means. However, subject to Section 8, persons attending the information exchange may take notes of the proceedings.

6.8. In addition to counsel, each management representative may have advisers in attendance at the information exchange, provided that the other party and the Neutral Adviser shall have been notified of the identity of such advisers at least five days before commencement of the information exchange.

7. Negotiations Between Management Representatives

7.1. At the conclusion of the information exchange, the management representatives shall meet one or more times, as necessary, by themselves, and shall make all reasonable efforts to agree on a resolution of the dispute. By agreement, other members of their teams may be invited to participate in the meetings.

7.2. At the request of either management representative, the Neutral Adviser will meet with the management representatives jointly or separately at his or her discretion, and will give an oral opinion as to the issues raised during the information exchange and as to the likely outcome at trial of each issue. Thereupon, the management representatives will again attempt to resolve the dispute. If either management representative requests a written opinion on such matters, the Neutral Adviser shall promptly render such an opinion. Thereupon, the management representatives will again attempt to resolve the dispute. At the request of the management representatives, the Neutral Adviser may at any time mediate the negotiations and may propose settlement terms.

7.3. The terms of any settlement are to be set out in a written agreement which is to be signed by the management representatives as soon as possible after conclusion of the negotiations and will, once signed, be legally binding on the parties.

8. Confidentiality

8.1. The entire process is a compromise negotiation. All offers, promises, conduct and statements, whether oral or written, made in the course of the proceeding by any of the parties, their agents, employees, experts and attorneys, and by the Neutral Adviser are confidential. Such offers, promises, conduct and statements are privileged under any applicable mediation privilege, and are subject to FRE 408 and any state counterpart rules or doctrine and are inadmissible and not discoverable for any purpose, including impeachment, in litigation between the parties to the minitrial or other litigation. However, evidence that is otherwise admissible or discoverable shall not be rendered inadmissible or non-discoverable as a result of its presentation or use at the minitrial. The Neutral Adviser is the parties' joint counsel, or agent if not an attorney.

8.2. The Neutral Adviser will be disqualified as a witness, consultant, or expert for any party, and as an arbitrator between the parties, and his or her oral and written opinions will be inadmissible for all purposes in this or any other dispute involving the parties hereto.

9. Court Proceedings

9.1. If on the commencement date no litigation is pending between the parties with respect to the subject matter of the minitrial, no party shall commence such litigation until the minitrial proceedings have terminated in accordance with Section 10 hereof. Execution of the initiating agreement shall toll all applicable statutes of limitation until the minitrial proceedings have terminated. The parties will take such other action, if any, required to effectuate such tolling.

9.2. If on the commencement date litigation is pending between the parties with respect to the subject matter of the minitrial, the parties may promptly (a) present a joint motion to the court to request a stay of all proceedings pending conclusion of the minitrial proceedings; and (b) request the court to enter an order protecting the confidentiality of the minitrial and barring any collateral use by the parties of any aspect of the minitrial in any pending or future litigation. The grant of such stay and protective order shall not be a condition to the continuation of the minitrial proceeding.

10. Termination of Proceeding

The proceeding shall be deemed terminated if and when (a) the parties have not executed a written settlement of their dispute on or before the thirtieth day following conclusion of the information exchange (which deadline may be extended by mutual agreement), or (b) either party serves on the other party and on the Neutral Adviser a written notice of withdrawal from the proceeding.

11. Actions Against the Neutral Adviser or CPR

Neither the Neutral Adviser nor CPR shall be liable to any party for any act or omission in connection with the minitrial proceeding.

CPR Appendix A

Initiating Agreement

Agreement to Initiate Minitrial Proceeding Between

_____ [Name]. ("Party A")

_____ [address].

_____ [Name]. ("Party B")

_____ [address].

Matter

[Title/subject matter, parties, and date of contract to which dispute relates] ("the Contract").

Dispute

[Identify briefly nature of dispute, including reference to relevant provision in the Contract.] ("the dispute")

Terms of Agreement

1. **CPR Procedure**

   By this agreement we agree to seek to resolve the dispute by adopting and using the CPR Minitrial Procedure ("the CPR Procedure") as modified by the provisions of this agreement and as attached hereto.

2. **Management Representatives**

_____

[Name of Management Representative of Party A and corporate title.]

_____

[Name of Management Representative of Party B and corporate title.]

Each of the above persons ("the Management Representatives") will represent their respective companies at the information exchange and will have full authority to negotiate a settlement of the dispute.

3.   Place and Time of Information Exchange

The information exchange will take place in the manner set out in Section 6 of the CPR Procedure at:

_____

_____ [address].

on _____ at _____ [date and time].

4.   Neutral Adviser

The Neutral Adviser will be [name]. [Delete if no Neutral Adviser is to be appointed]

[OR]

The Neutral Adviser will be selected in accordance with Section 3 of the CPR Procedure.

SIGNED: _____

_____ [name]

For and on behalf of Party A

SIGNED: _____ [name]

For and on behalf of Party B

APPENDIX M
MODEL CONDUCT STANDARDS FOR MEDIATORS AND ADR PROVIDERS

1. Model Standards of Conduct for Mediators
2. American Bar Association Model Rule of Professional Conduct
3. CPR-Georgetown Commission's Model Rule for The Lawyer as Third-Party Neutral
4. CPR-Georgetown Commission's Principles for ADR Provider Organizations

1. The Model Standards of Conduct for Mediators[1]

The Model Standards of Conduct for Mediators were prepared from 1992 through 1994 by a joint committee composed of two delegates from the American Arbitration Association, John D. Feerick, Chair, and David Botwinik, two from the American Bar Association, James Alfini and Nancy Rogers, and two from the Society of Professionals in Dispute Resolution, Susan Dearborn and Lemoine Pierce.

The Model Standards have been approved by the American Arbitration Association, the Litigation Section and the Dispute Resolution Section of the American Bar Association, and the Society of Professionals in Dispute Resolution.

The views set out in this publication have not been considered by the American Bar Association House of Delegates and do not constitute the policy of the American Bar Association.

INTRODUCTORY NOTE

The initiative for these standards came from three professional groups: The American Arbitration Association, the American Bar Association, and the Society of Professionals in Dispute Resolution.

---

1. This material is reprinted with permission by the American Arbitration Association (AAA) and the American Bar Association (ABA).

The purpose of this initiative was to develop a set of standards to serve as a general framework for the practice of mediation. The effort is a step in the development of the field and a tool to assist practitioners in it—a beginning, not an end. The model standards are intended to apply to all types of mediation. It is recognized, however, that in some cases the application of these standards may be affected by laws or contractual agreements.

PREFACE

The model standards of conduct for mediators are intended to perform three major functions: to serve as a guide for the conduct of mediators; to inform the mediating parties; and to promote public confidence in mediation as a process for resolving disputes. The standards draw on existing codes of conduct for mediators and take into account issues and problems that have surfaced in mediation practice. They are offered in the hope that they will serve an educational function and provide assistance to individuals, organizations, and institutions involved in mediation.

Mediation is a process in which an impartial third party—a mediator—facilitates the resolution of a dispute by promoting voluntary agreement (or "self-determination") by the parties to the dispute. A mediator facilitates communications, promotes understanding, focuses the parties on their interests, and seeks creative problem solving to enable the parties to reach their own agreement. These standards give meaning to this definition of mediation.

I. Self-Determination: A Mediator shall Recognize that Mediation is Based on the Principle of Self-Determination by the Parties.

Self-determination is the fundamental principle of mediation. It re quires that the mediation process rely upon the ability of the parties to reach a voluntary, uncoerced agreement. Any party may withdraw from mediation at any time.

Comments

The mediator may provide information about the process, raise issues, and help parties explore options. The primary role of the mediator is to facilitate a voluntary resolution of a dispute. Parties shall be given the opportunity to consider all proposed options. A mediator cannot personally ensure that each party has made a fully informed choice to reach a particular agreement, but it is a good practice for the mediator to make the parties aware of the importance of consulting other professionals, where appropriate, to help them make informed decisions.

II. Impartiality: A Mediator shall Conduct the Mediation in an Impartial Manner.

The concept of mediator impartiality is central to the mediation process. A mediator shall mediate only those matters in which she or he can remain impartial and evenhanded. If at any time the mediator is unable to conduct the process in an impartial manner, the mediator is obligated to withdraw.

Comments

A mediator shall avoid conduct that gives the appearance of partiality toward one of the parties. The quality of the mediation process is enhanced when the parties have confidence in the impartiality of the mediator. When mediators are appointed by a court or institution, the appointing agency shall make reasonable efforts to ensure that mediators serve impartially. A mediator should guard against partiality or prejudice based on the parties' personal characteristics, background or performance at the mediation.

III. Conflicts of Interest: A Mediator shall Disclose all Actual and Potential Conflicts of Interest Reasonably Known to the Mediator. After Disclosure, the Mediator shall Decline to Mediate unless all Parties Choose to Retain the Mediator. The Need to Protect Against Conflicts of Interest also Governs Conduct that Occurs During and After the Mediation.

A conflict of interest is a dealing or relationship that might create an impression of possible bias. The basic approach to questions of conflict of interest is consistent with the concept of self-determination. The mediator has a responsibility to disclose all actual and potential conflicts that are reasonably known to the mediator and could reasonably be seen as raising a question about impartiality. If all parties agree to mediate after being informed of conflicts, the mediator may proceed with the mediation. If, however, the conflict of interest casts serious doubt on the integrity of the process, the mediator shall decline to proceed.

A mediator must avoid the appearance of conflict of interest both during and after the mediation. Without the consent of all parties, a mediator shall not subsequently establish a professional relationship with one of the parties in a related matter, or in an unrelated matter under circumstances which would raise legitimate questions about the integrity of the mediation process.

Comments

A mediator shall avoid conflicts of interest in recommending the services of other professionals. A mediator may make reference to professional referral services or associations which maintain rosters of qualified professionals. Potential conflicts of interest may arise between administrators of mediation programs and mediators and there may be strong pressures on the mediator to settle a particular case or cases. The mediator's commitment must be to the parties and the process. Pressure from outside of the mediation process should never influence the mediator to coerce parties to settle.

IV. Competence: A Mediator shall Mediate Only When the Mediator has the Necessary Qualifications to Satisfy the Reasonable Expectations of the Parties.

Any person may be selected as a mediator, provided that the parties are satisfied with the mediator's qualifications. Training and experience in mediation, however, are often necessary for effective mediation. A person who offers herself or himself as available to serve as a mediator gives parties and the public the expectation that she or he has the competency to mediate effectively. In court-connected or other forms of mandated mediation, it is essential that mediators assigned to the parties have the requisite training and experience.

Comments

Mediators should have information available for the parties regarding their relevant training, education and experience. The requirements for appearing on a list of mediators must be made public and available to interested persons. When mediators are appointed by a court or institution, the appointing agency shall make reasonable efforts to ensure that each mediator is qualified for the particular mediation.

V. Confidentiality: A Mediator shall Maintain the Reasonable Expectations of the Parties with Regard to Confidentiality.

The reasonable expectations of the parties with regard to confidentiality shall be met by the mediator. The parties' expectations of confidentiality depend on the circumstances of the mediation and any agreements they may make. The mediator shall not disclose any matter that a party expects to be confidential unless given permission by all parties or unless required by law or other public policy.

Comments

The parties may make their own rules with respect to confidentiality, or the accepted practice of an individual mediator or institution may dictate a particular set of expectations. Since the parties' expectations regarding confidentiality are important, the mediator should discuss these expectations with the parties.

If the mediator holds private sessions with a party, the nature of these sessions with regard to confidentiality should be discussed prior to undertaking such sessions.

In order to protect the integrity of the mediation, a mediator should avoid communicating information about how the parties acted in the mediation process, the merits of the case, or settlement offers. The mediator may report, if required, whether parties appeared at a scheduled mediation.

Where the parties have agreed that all or a portion of the information disclosed during a mediation is confidential, the parties' agreement should be respected by the mediator.

Confidentiality should not be construed to limit or prohibit the effective monitoring, research, or evaluation of mediation programs by responsible persons. Under appropriate circumstances, researchers may be permitted to obtain access to statistical data and, with the permission of the parties, to individual case files, observations of live mediations, and interviews with participants.

VI. Quality of the Process: A Mediator shall Conduct the Mediation Fairly, Diligently, and in a Manner Consistent with the Principle of Self-Determination by the Parties.

A mediator shall work to ensure a quality process and to encourage mutual respect among the parties. A quality process requires a commitment by the mediator to diligence and procedural fairness. There should be adequate opportunity for each party in the mediation to participate in the discussions. The parties decide when and under what conditions they will reach an agreement or terminate a mediation.

Comments

A mediator may agree to mediate only when he or she is prepared to commit the attention essential to an effective mediation.

Mediators should only accept cases when they can satisfy the reasonable expectations of the parties concerning the timing of the process. A mediator should not allow a mediation to be unduly delayed by the parties or their representatives.

The presence or absence of persons at a mediation depends on the agreement of the parties and the mediator. The parties and mediator may agree that others may be excluded from particular sessions or from the entire mediation process.

The primary purpose of a mediator is to facilitate the parties' voluntary agreement. This role differs substantially from other professional-client relationships. Mixing the role of a mediator and the role of a professional advising a client is problematic, and mediators must strive to distinguish between the roles. A mediator should, therefore, refrain from providing professional advice. Where appropriate, a mediator should recommend that parties seek outside professional advice, or consider resolving their dispute through arbitration, counseling, neutral evaluation, or other processes. A mediator who undertakes, at the request of the parties, an additional dispute resolution role in the same matter assumes increased responsibilities and obligations that may be governed by the standards of other processes.

A mediator shall withdraw from a mediation when incapable of serving or when unable to remain impartial.

A mediator shall withdraw from a mediation or postpone a session if the mediation is being used to further illegal conduct, or if a party is unable to participate due to drug, alcohol, or other physical or mental incapacity.

Mediators should not permit their behavior in the mediation process to be guided by a desire for a high settlement rate.

VII. Advertising and Solicitation: A Mediator shall be Truthful in Advertising and Solicitation for Mediation

Advertising or any other communication with the public concerning services offered or regarding the education, training, and expertise of the mediator shall be truthful. Mediators shall refrain from promises and guarantees of results.

Comments

It is imperative that communication with the public educate and instill confidence in the process.

In an advertisement or other communication to the public, a mediator may make reference to meeting state, national, or private organization qualifications only if the entity referred to has a procedure for qualifying mediators and the mediator has been duly granted the requisite status.

VIII. Fees: A Mediator shall fully Disclose and Explain the Basis of Compensation, Fees, and Charges to the Parties.

The parties should be provided sufficient information about fees at the outset of a mediation to determine if they wish to retain the services of a mediator. If a mediator charges fees, the fees shall be reasonable, considering among other things, the mediation service, the type and complexity of the matter, the expertise of the mediator, the time required, and the rates customary in the community. The better practice in reaching an understanding about fees is to set down the arrangements in a written agreement.

Comments

A mediator who withdraws from a mediation should return any unearned fee to the parties.

A mediator should not enter into a fee agreement which is contingent upon the result of the mediation or amount of the settlement.

Co-mediators who share a fee should hold to standards of reasonableness in determining the allocation of fees.

A mediator should not accept a fee for referral of a matter to another mediator or to any other person.

IX. Obligations to the Mediation Process: Mediators have a Duty to Improve the Practice of Mediation.

Comment

Mediators are regarded as knowledgeable in the process of mediation. They have an obligation to use their knowledge to help educate the public about mediation; to make mediation accessible to those who would like to use it; to correct abuses; and to improve their professional skills and abilities.

Copies of the Model Standards of Conduct for Mediators are available from the offices of the participating organizations.

We wish to express our appreciation for a grant from the Harry De Jur Foundation.

2. American Bar Association
Model Rules of Professional Conduct[2]

RULE 2.4 LAWYER SERVING AS THIRD-PARTY NEUTRAL

(a) A lawyer serves as a third-party neutral when the lawyer assists two or more persons who are not clients of the lawyer to reach a resolution of a dispute or other matter that has arisen between them. Service as a third-party neutral may include service as an arbitrator, a mediator or in such other capacity as will enable the lawyer to assist the parties to resolve the matter.

(b) A lawyer serving as a third-party neutral shall inform unrepresented parties that the lawyer is not representing them. When the lawyer knows or reasonably should know that a party does not understand the lawyer's role in the matter, the lawyer shall explain the difference between the lawyer's role as a third-party neutral and a lawyer's role as one who represents a client.

Comment

[1] Alternative dispute resolution has become a substantial part of the civil justice system. Aside from representing clients in dispute-resolution processes, lawyers often serve as third-party neutrals. A third-party neutral is a person, such as a mediator, arbitrator, conciliator or evaluator, who assists the parties, represented or unrepresented, in the resolution of a dispute or in the arrangement of a transaction. Whether a third-party neutral serves primarily as a facilitator, evaluator or decisionmaker depends on the particular process that is either selected by the parties or mandated by a court.

[2] The role of a third-party neutral is not unique to lawyers, although, in some court-connected contexts, only lawyers are allowed to serve in this role or to handle certain types of cases. In performing this role, the lawyer may be subject to court rules or other law that apply either to

---

2. *ABA Model Rules of Professional Conduct* (2004 edition). ©2004 by the American Bar Association. All rights reserved. Reprinted by permission of the American Bar Association.

Copies of *ABA Model Rules of Professional Conduct*, 2004, are available from Service Center, American Bar Association, 750 North Lake Shore Drive, Chicago, IL 60611-4497, 1-800-285-2221.

third-party neutrals generally or to lawyers serving as third-party neutrals. Lawyer-neutrals may also be subject to various codes of ethics, such as the Code of Ethics for Arbitration in Commercial Disputes prepared by a joint committee of the American Bar Association and the American Arbitration Association or the Model Standards of Conduct for Mediators jointly prepared by the American Bar Association, the American Arbitration Association and the Society of Professionals in Dispute Resolution.

[3] Unlike nonlawyers who serve as third-party neutrals, lawyers serving in this role may experience unique problems as a result of differences between the role of a third-party neutral and a lawyer's service as a client representative. The potential for confusion is significant when the parties are unrepresented in the process. Thus, paragraph (b) requires a lawyer-neutral to inform unrepresented parties that the lawyer is not representing them. For some parties, particularly parties who frequently use dispute-resolution processes, this information will be sufficient. For others, particularly those who are using the process for the first time, more information will be required. Where appropriate, the lawyer should inform unrepresented parties of the important differences between the lawyer's role as third-party neutral and a lawyer's role as a client representative, including the inapplicability of the attorney-client evidentiary privilege. The extent of disclosure required under this paragraph will depend on the particular parties involved and the subject matter of the proceeding, as well as the particular features of the dispute-resolution process selected.

[4] A lawyer who serves as a third-party neutral subsequently may be asked to serve as a lawyer representing a client in the same matter. The conflicts of interest that arise for both the individual lawyer and the lawyer's law firm are addressed in Rule 1.12.

[5] Lawyers who represent clients in alternative dispute-resolution processes are governed by the Rules of Professional Conduct. When the dispute-resolution process takes place before a tribunal, as in binding arbitration (see Rule 1.0(m)), the lawyer's duty of candor is governed by Rule 3.3. Otherwise, the lawyer's duty of candor toward both the third-party neutral and other parties is governed by Rule 4.1.

3. CPR-Georgetown Commission's Model Rule for The Lawyer as Third-Party Neutral[3]

NOVEMBER 2002

CPR-GEORGETOWN COMMISSION ON ETHICS AND STANDARDS IN ADR

Proposed New Model Rule of Professional Conduct Rule 4.5: The Lawyer as Third-Party Neutral

Reported by Professor Carrie Menkel-Meadow, Chair, CPR-Georgetown Commission on Ethics and Standards in ADR and Elizabeth Plapinger, Staff Director, CPR-Georgetown Commission on Ethics and Standards in ADR.

[Introduction from Report]

PREFACE

The Commission on Ethics and Standards in ADR (sponsored by Georgetown University Law Center and CPR Institute for Dispute Resolution) has drafted this Model Rule for adoption into the Model Rules of Professional Conduct. We offer here a framework or architecture for consideration by the appropriate bodies of the American Bar Association and any state agency or legislature charged with drafting lawyer ethics rules.

The Model Rule addresses the ethical responsibilities of lawyers serving as third-party neutrals, in a variety of alternative dispute resolution (ADR) fora (e.g., arbitration, mediation, early neutral evaluation). As an initial jurisdictional matter, the Model Rule does not address the ethical requirements of nonlawyers performing these duties, or the ethical duties of lawyers acting in ADR proceedings as representatives or advocates.

Preamble

As client representatives, public citizens and professionals committed to justice and fair and efficient legal processes, lawyers should help clients and others with legal matters pursue the most effective resolution of legal problems. This obligation should include pursuing methods and outcomes that cause the least harm to all parties, that resolve matters amicably where possible, and that promote harmonious relations. Modern lawyers serve these values of justice, fairness, efficiency and harmony as partisan representatives and as third-party neutrals.

This Model Rule applies to the lawyer who acts as a third-party neutral to help represented or unrepresented parties resolve disputes or arrange transactions among each other. When lawyers act in neutral, non-representative capacities, they have different duties and obligations in the areas addressed by this Rule than lawyers acting in a representative capacity. The role of the lawyer as a third-party neutral differs from the representational functions addressed by the Model Rules of Professional Conduct and judicial functions governed by the Judicial Code of Conduct.

Contemporary law practice involves lawyers in a variety of new roles within the traditional boundaries of counselors, advocates and advisors in the legal system. Lawyers now commonly serve as third-party neutrals, either as facilitators to settle disputes or plan transactions, as in mediation, or as third-party decision makers, as in arbitration. Such proceedings, including mediation, arbitration and other hybrid forms of settlement or decision making, occur both as adjuncts to the litigation process (either through a court-referral or court-based program, or by agreement of the parties) and outside litigation via private agreement. These proceedings are commonly known as "ADR" processes. Some state ethics codes, statutes or court rules now require or strongly suggest that lawyers have a duty to counsel their clients regarding ADR means.

When lawyers serve as ADR neutrals they do not have partisan "clients," as contemplated in much of the Model Rules, but rather serve all of the parties. Lawyer-neutrals do not "represent" parties, but have a duty to be fair to all participants in the process and to execute different obligations and responsibilities with respect to the parties and the process. Nor do the rules which apply to judges, such as the Judicial Code of Conduct, adequately deal with many issues that confront lawyer-neutrals. For example, lawyers who act as third-party neutrals in one case may serve as representational counsel in other matters and thus confront special conflicts of interest, appearance of impropriety, and confidentiality issues as they serve in the different roles of neutral and advocate. Unlike the judge or arbitrator who remains at "arms-length" distance from the parties and who hears information usually when only both parties are present, mediators have different ethical issues to contend with because they hear private, proprietary facts and information from both sides in caucuses and *ex parte* settings.

While there continues to be some controversy about whether serving as a mediator or arbitrator is the practice of law or may be covered by the ancillary practice Model Rule 5.7, it is clear that lawyers serving as third-party neutrals need ethical guidance from the Model Rules with respect to their dual roles as partisan representatives and as neutrals. The Drafting Committee believes that it is especially important to develop clear ethical rules when the lawyer, commonly conceived of as a "partisan" representative, takes on the different role of "neutral" problem-solver, facilitator or decision maker.

Lawyers may be disciplined for any violation of the Model Rules or misconduct, regardless of whether they are formally found to be serving in lawyer-like roles. Accordingly, while other associations provide guidance within specific contexts, when lawyers serve as mediators or arbitrators their ethical duties and discipline under the Model Rules of Professional Conduct may be implicated. For these reasons, this Model Rule is submitted to provide guidance for lawyers who serve as third-party neutrals, and to advise judicial officers and state disciplinary boards who enforce lawyer ethical or disciplinary standards.

Scope

This Model Rule is drafted to govern lawyers serving in the full variety of ADR third-party neutral roles, as arbitrators, mediators, facilitators, evaluators and in other hybrid processes. (*See* Definitions, *infra*). Because the Rule addresses core ethical duties that apply to virtually all neutral roles, the Drafting Committee believes that a general rule governing lawyers serving in all third-party neutral roles is appropriate. Where different neutral roles give rise to different duties and obligations, the Model Rule so provides in text or comment. A single rule approach is also consistent with the generally transsubstantive approach of the Model Rules. However, as the Model Rules continue to recognize increasing diversity of lawyer roles, *see, e.g.,* Model Rule 3.8 (Special Responsibilities of a Prosecutor); Model Rule 2.1 (Advisor); Model Rule 1.13 (Organization as Client), separate rules for lawyers as mediators or arbitrators may be appropriate in the future.

This Model Rule applies only to lawyers serving as third-party neutrals. Many other professionals now serve as arbitrators, mediators, facilitators, evaluators or ombuds, and other bodies have promulgated transdisciplinary ethical rules relating to those services. When a lawyer serves as a third-party neutral in a capacity governed by multiple sets of ethical standards, the lawyer must note that the Model Rules of Professional Conduct govern his/her duties as a lawyer-neutral and that discipline *as a lawyer* will be governed by the Model Rules. This Model Rule does not govern lawyers in their capacity as representatives or advocates within ADR proceedings. When a lawyer serves as an advocate, representative or counselor to a party in an ADR proceeding, he or she is governed by such other Model Rules as are applicable to lawyer conduct, either before tribunals (Model Rule 3.3) or in relation to all other third parties (Model Rule 4.1).

* * *

Definitions I-IV

(Lawyers who provide neutral services as described above in Definitions I-IV shall be subject to the duties and obligations specified below:)

Rule 4.5.1: Diligence and Competence

Rule 4.5.2: Confidentiality

Rule 4.5.3: Impartiality

Rule 4.5.4: Conflicts of Interest

Rule 4.5.5: Fees

Rule 4.5.6: Fairness and Integrity of the Process

[For the full text, including extensive comments, see (Public Policy Projects, CPR-Georgetown Commission, The Model Rule)]

4. CPR-Georgetown Commission's Principles for ADR Provider Organizations[4]

May 1, 2002

[Introduction from Report]

Principles for ADR Provider Organizations

The CPR-Georgetown Commission on Ethics and Standards of Practice in ADR developed the following Principles for ADR Provider Organizations to provide guidance to entities that provide ADR services, consumers of their services, the public, and policy makers. The Commission is a joint initiative of the CPR Institute for Dispute Resolution and Georgetown University Law Center, with support from the William and Flora Hewlett Foundation. The Commission, which is chaired by Professor Carrie Menkel-Meadow of the Georgetown University Law Center, has also developed the CPR-Georgetown Proposed Model Rule of Professional Conduct for the Lawyer as Third Party Neutral (Final, 2002), and provided guidance to the ABA Ethics 2000 Commission in its reexamination of the Model Rules of Professional Conduct on ADR ethics issues.

The Principles for ADR Provider Organizations were developed by a committee of the CPR-Georgetown Commission, co-chaired by Commission member Margaret L. Shaw and former Commission staff director Elizabeth Plapinger, who also served as reporter. The Principles were released for public comment from June 1, 2000 through October 15, 2001. The final version reflects many of the substantive recommendations the Commission received during the comment period.

Preamble

As the use of ADR expands into almost every sphere of activity, the public and private organizations that provide ADR services are coming

---

3. ©2002 CPR **Institute for Dispute Resolution**, 366 Madison Avenue, New York, NY 10017-3122; (212) 949-6490, www.cpr.org. This **excerpt** from **CPR-Georgetown Commission's Principles for ADR Provider Organizations** reprinted with permission of **CPR Institute**.

The CPR Institute is a nonprofit initiative of 500 general counsel of major corporations, leading law firms and prominent legal academics whose mission is to install alternative dispute resolution (ADR) into the mainstream of legal practice.

under greater scrutiny in the marketplace, in the courts, and among regulators, commentators and policy makers. The growth and increasing importance of ADR Provider Organizations, coupled with the absence of broadly-recognized standards to guide responsible practice, propel this effort by the CPR-Georgetown Commission to develop the following Principles for ADR Provider Organizations.

The Principles build upon the significant policy directives of the past decade which recognize the central role of the ADR provider organization in the delivery of fair, impartial and quality ADR services. Several core ideas guide the Commission's effort, namely that:

- It is timely and important to establish standards of responsible practice in this rapidly growing field to provide guidance to ADR Provider Organizations and to inform consumers, policy makers and the public generally.

- The most effective architecture for maximizing the fairness, impartiality and quality of dispute resolution services is the meaningful *disclosure* of key information.

- Consumers of dispute resolution services are entitled to sufficient information about ADR Provider Organizations, their services and affiliated neutrals to make well-informed decisions about their dispute resolution options.

- ADR Provider Organizations should foster and meet the expectations of consumers, policy makers and the public generally for fair, impartial and quality dispute resolution services and processes.

In addition to establishing a benchmark for responsible practice, the CPR-Georgetown Commission hopes that the Principles will enhance understanding of the ADR field's special responsibilities, as justice providers, to provide fair, impartial and quality process. This document hopes also to contribute to the ADR field's commitment to self-regulation and high standards of practice.

Scope of Principles

The following Principles were developed to offer a framework for responsible practice by entities that provide ADR services. In framing the nine Principles that comprise this document, the drafters tried to balance the need for clear and high standards of practice against the risks of over-regulating a new, diverse and dynamic field.

The Principles are drafted to apply to the full variety of public, private and hybrid ADR provider organizations in our increasingly intertwined private and public systems of justice. A single set of standards was preferred because the Principles address core duties of responsible practice that apply to most organizations in most settings. The single set of Principles may also help alert the many kinds of entities providing ADR services of their essential, common responsibilities. Additional sector specific obligations will likely continue to develop for particular kinds of ADR provider organizations, depending on their sector, nature of services and operations, and representations to the public. The proposed Principles were developed to guide responsible practice and, like ethical rules, are not intended to create grounds for liability.

Definition
I.   Quality and Competence of Services
II.   Information Regarding Services and Operations
III.   Fairness and Impartiality
IV.   Accessibility of Services
V.   Disclosure of Organizational Conflicts of Interest
VI.   Complaint and Grievance Mechanisms
VII.   Ethical Guidelines
VIII.   False or Misleading Communications
IX.   Confidentiality
Appendix A: Taxonomy of ADR Provider Organizations

[For the full text, including extensive comments, see www.cpr.org (Public Policy Projects, CPR-Georgetown Commission, Provider Principles)]

Appendix N

Model Conduct Standards for Advocates in Mediation

Model Rules of Professional Conduct[1]

American Bar Association
(Selective, 2004)

RULE 1.0(e)	TERMINOLOGY
RULE 1.1	COMPETENCE
RULE 1.2(a), (c), and (d)	SCOPE OF REPRESENTATION AND ALLOCATION OF AUTHORITY BETWEEN CLIENT AND LAWYER
RULE 1.3	DILIGENCE
RULE 1.4	COMMUNICATION
RULE 1.6(a)	CONFIDENTIALITY OF INFORMATION
RULE 3.1	MERITORIOUS CLAIMS AND CONTENTIONS
RULE 4.1	TRUTHFULNESS IN STATEMENTS TO OTHERS
RULE 5.5(c)	UNAUTHORIZED PRACTICE OF LAW; MULTIJURISDICTIONAL PRACTICE OF LAW
RULE 8.4(c) and (d)	MISCONDUCT

Comment 5 of Rule 2.4–Lawyer Serving as Third-Party Neutral states that "Lawyers who represent clients in alternative dispute-resolution processes are governed by the Rules of Professional Conduct."

The following rules may become relevant during the course of representing clients in mediation:

---

1. *ABA Model Rules of Professional Conduct* (2004 edition). ©2004 by the American Bar Association. All rights reserved. Reprinted by permission of the American Bar Association.

Copies of *ABA Model Rules of Professional Conduct*, 2004, are available from Service Center, American Bar Association, 750 North Lake Shore Drive, Chicago, IL 60611-4497, 1-800-285-2221.

RULE 1.0 TERMINOLOGY

(e) "Informed consent" denotes the agreement by a person to a proposed course of conduct after the lawyer has communicated adequate information and explanation about the material risks of and reasonably available alternatives to the proposed course of conduct.

Comment
Informed Consent

[6] Many of the Rules of Professional Conduct require the lawyer to obtain the informed consent of a client or other person (e.g., a former client or, under certain circumstances, a prospective client) before accepting or continuing representation or pursuing a course of conduct. See, e.g., Rules 1.2(c), 1.6(a) and 1.7(b). The communication necessary to obtain such consent will vary according to the Rule involved and the circumstances giving rise to the need to obtain informed consent. The lawyer must make reasonable efforts to ensure that the client or other person possesses information reasonably adequate to make an informed decision. Ordinarily, this will require communication that includes a disclosure of the facts and circumstances giving rise to the situation, any explanation reasonably necessary to inform the client or other person of the material advantages and disadvantages of the proposed course of conduct and a discussion of the client's or other person's options and alternatives. In some circumstances it may be appropriate for a lawyer to advise a client or other person to seek the advice of other counsel. A lawyer need not inform a client or other person of facts or implications already known to the client or other person; nevertheless, a lawyer who does not personally inform the client or other person assumes the risk that the client or other person is inadequately informed and the consent is invalid. In determining whether the information and explanation provided are reasonably adequate, relevant factors include whether the client or other person is experienced in legal matters generally and in making decisions of the type involved, and whether the client or other person is independently represented by other counsel in giving the consent. Normally, such persons need less information and explanation than others, and generally a client or other person who is independently represented by other counsel in giving the consent should be assumed to have given informed consent.

[7] Obtaining informed consent will usually require an affirmative response by the client or other person. In general, a lawyer may not assume consent from a client's or other person's silence. Consent may be inferred, however, from the conduct of a client or other person who has reasonably adequate information about the matter. A number of Rules require that a person's consent be confirmed in writing. See Rules 1.7(b) and 1.9(a). For a definition of "writing" and "confirmed in writing," see paragraphs (n) and (b). Other Rules require that a client's consent be obtained in a writing signed by the client. See, e.g., Rules 1.8(a) and (g). For a definition of "signed," see paragraph (n).

RULE 1.1 COMPETENCE

A lawyer shall provide competent representation to a client. Competent representation requires the legal knowledge, skill, thoroughness and preparation reasonably necessary for the representation.

Comment
Legal Knowledge and Skill

[1] In determining whether a lawyer employs the requisite knowledge and skill in a particular matter, relevant factors include the relative complexity and specialized nature of the matter, the lawyer's general experience, the lawyer's training and experience in the field in question, the preparation and study the lawyer is able to give the matter and whether it is feasible to refer the matter to, or associate or consult with, a lawyer of established competence in the field in question. In many instances, the required proficiency is that of a general practitioner. Expertise in a particular field of law may be required in some circumstances.

[2] A lawyer need not necessarily have special training or prior experience to handle legal problems of a type with which the lawyer is unfamiliar. A newly admitted lawyer can be as competent as a practitioner with long experience. Some important legal skills, such as the analysis of precedent, the evaluation of evidence and legal drafting, are required in all legal problems. Perhaps the most fundamental legal skill consists of determining what kind of legal problems a situation may involve, a skill that necessarily transcends any particular specialized knowledge. A lawyer can provide adequate representation in a wholly novel field through necessary study. Competent representation can also be provided through the association of a lawyer of established competence in the field in question.

[3] In an emergency a lawyer may give advice or assistance in a matter in which the lawyer does not have the skill ordinarily required where referral to or consultation or association with another lawyer would be impractical. Even in an emergency, however, assistance should be limited to that reasonably necessary in the circumstances, for ill-considered action under emergency conditions can jeopardize the client's interest.

[4] A lawyer may accept representation where the requisite level of competence can be achieved by reasonable preparation. This applies as well to a lawyer who is appointed as counsel for an unrepresented person. See also Rule 6.2.

Thoroughness and Preparation

[5] Competent handling of a particular matter includes inquiry into and analysis of the factual and legal elements of the problem, and use of methods and procedures meeting the standards of competent practitioners. It also includes adequate preparation. The required attention and preparation are determined in part by what is at stake; major litigation and complex transactions ordinarily require more extensive treatment than matters of lesser complexity and consequence. An agreement between the lawyer and the client regarding the scope of the representation may limit the matters for which the lawyer is responsible. See Rule 1.2(c).

Maintaining Competence

[6] To maintain the requisite knowledge and skill, a lawyer should keep abreast of changes in the law and its practice, engage in continuing study and education and comply with all continuing legal education requirements to which the lawyer is subject.

RULE 1.2 SCOPE OF REPRESENTATION AND ALLOCATION OF AUTHORITY BETWEEN CLIENT AND LAWYER

(a) Subject to paragraphs (c) and (d), a lawyer shall abide by a client's decisions concerning the objectives of representation and, as required by Rule 1.4, shall consult with the client as to the means by which they are to be pursued. A lawyer may take such action on behalf of the client as is impliedly authorized to carry out the representation. A lawyer shall abide by a client's decision whether to settle a matter. In a criminal case, the lawyer shall abide by the client's decision, after consultation with the lawyer, as to a plea to be entered, whether to waive jury trial and whether the client will testify.

(c) A lawyer may limit the scope of the representation if the limitation is reasonable under the circumstances and the client gives informed consent.

(d) A lawyer shall not counsel a client to engage, or assist a client, in conduct that the lawyer knows is criminal or fraudulent, but a lawyer may discuss the legal consequences of any proposed course of conduct with a client and may counsel or assist a client to make a good faith effort to determine the validity, scope, meaning or application of the law.

Comment
Allocation of Authority between Client and Lawyer

[1] Paragraph (a) confers upon the client the ultimate authority to determine the purposes to be served by legal representation, within the limits imposed by law and the lawyer's professional obligations. The decisions specified in paragraph (a), such as whether to settle a civil matter, must also be made by the client. See Rule 1.4(a)(1) for the lawyer's duty to communicate with the client about such decisions. With respect to the means by which the client's objectives are to be pursued, the lawyer shall consult with the client as required by Rule 1.4(a)(2) and may take such action as is impliedly authorized to carry out the representation.

[2] On occasion, however, a lawyer and a client may disagree about the means to be used to accomplish the client's objectives. Clients normally defer to the special knowledge and skill of their lawyer with respect to the means to be used to accomplish their objectives, particularly with respect to technical, legal and tactical matters. Conversely, lawyers usually defer to the client regarding such questions as the expense to be incurred and concern for third persons who might be adversely affected. Because of the varied nature of the matters about which a lawyer and client might disagree and because the actions in question may implicate the interests of a tribunal or other persons, this Rule does not prescribe how such disagreements are to be resolved. Other law, however, may be applicable and should be consulted by the lawyer. The lawyer should also consult with the client and seek a mutually acceptable resolution of the disagreement. If such efforts are unavailing and the lawyer has a fundamental disagreement with the client, the lawyer may withdraw from

the representation. See Rule 1.16(b)(4). Conversely, the client may resolve the disagreement by discharging the lawyer. See Rule 1.16(a)(3).

[3] At the outset of a representation, the client may authorize the lawyer to take specific action on the client's behalf without further consultation. Absent a material change in circumstances and subject to Rule 1.4, a lawyer may rely on such an advance authorization. The client may, however, revoke such authority at any time.

[4] In a case in which the client appears to be suffering diminished capacity, the lawyer's duty to abide by the client's decisions is to be guided by reference to Rule 1.14.

Agreements Limiting Scope of Representation

[6] The scope of services to be provided by a lawyer may be limited by agreement with the client or by the terms under which the lawyer's services are made available to the client. When a lawyer has been retained by an insurer to represent an insured, for example, the representation may be limited to matters related to the insurance coverage. A limited representation may be appropriate because the client has limited objectives for the representation. In addition, the terms upon which representation is undertaken may exclude specific means that might otherwise be used to accomplish the client's objectives. Such limitations may exclude actions that the client thinks are too costly or that the lawyer regards as repugnant or imprudent.

[7] Although this Rule affords the lawyer and client substantial latitude to limit the representation, the limitation must be reasonable under the circumstances. If, for example, a client's objective is limited to securing general information about the law the client needs in order to handle a common and typically uncomplicated legal problem, the lawyer and client may agree that the lawyer's services will be limited to a brief telephone consultation. Such a limitation, however, would not be reasonable if the time allotted was not sufficient to yield advice upon which the client could rely. Although an agreement for a limited representation does not exempt a lawyer from the duty to provide competent representation, the limitation is a factor to be considered when determining the legal knowledge, skill, thoroughness and preparation reasonably necessary for the representation. See Rule 1.1.

[8] All agreements concerning a lawyer's representation of a client must accord with the Rules of Professional Conduct and other law. See, e.g., Rules 1.1, 1.8 and 5.6.

Criminal, Fraudulent and Prohibited Transactions

[9] Paragraph (d) prohibits a lawyer from knowingly counseling or assisting a client to commit a crime or fraud. This prohibition, however, does not preclude the lawyer from giving an honest opinion about the actual consequences that appear likely to result from a client's conduct. Nor does the fact that a client uses advice in a course of action that is criminal or fraudulent of itself make a lawyer a party to the course of action. There is a critical distinction between presenting an analysis of legal aspects of questionable conduct and recommending the means by which a crime or fraud might be committed with impunity.

[10] When the client's course of action has already begun and is continuing, the lawyer's responsibility is especially delicate. The lawyer is required to avoid assisting the client, for example, by drafting or delivering documents that the lawyer knows are fraudulent or by suggesting how the wrongdoing might be concealed. A lawyer may not continue assisting a client in conduct that the lawyer originally supposed was legally proper but then discovers is criminal or fraudulent. The lawyer must, therefore, withdraw from the representation of the client in the matter. See Rule 1.16(a). In some cases, withdrawal alone might be insufficient. It may be necessary for the lawyer to give notice of the fact of withdrawal and to disaffirm any opinion, document, affirmation or the like. See Rule 4.1.

[11] Where the client is a fiduciary, the lawyer may be charged with special obligations in dealings with a beneficiary.

[12] Paragraph (d) applies whether or not the defrauded party is a party to the transaction. Hence, a lawyer must not participate in a transaction to effectuate criminal or fraudulent avoidance of tax liability. Paragraph (d) does not preclude undertaking a criminal defense incident to a general retainer for legal services to a lawful enterprise. The last clause of paragraph (d) recognizes that determining the validity or interpretation of a statute or regulation may require a course of action involving disobedience of the statute or regulation or of the interpretation placed upon it by governmental authorities.

[13] If a lawyer comes to know or reasonably should know that a client expects assistance not permitted by the Rules of Professional Conduct or other law or if the lawyer intends to act contrary to the client's instructions, the lawyer must consult with the client regarding the limitations on the lawyer's conduct. See Rule 1.4(a)(5).

RULE 1.3 DILIGENCE

A lawyer shall act with reasonable diligence and promptness in representing a client.

Comment

[1] A lawyer should pursue a matter on behalf of a client despite opposition, obstruction or personal inconvenience to the lawyer, and take whatever lawful and ethical measures are required to vindicate a client's cause or endeavor. A lawyer must also act with commitment and dedication to the interests of the client and with zeal in advocacy upon the client's behalf. A lawyer is not bound, however, to press for every advantage that might be realized for a client. For example, a lawyer may have authority to exercise professional discretion in determining the means by which a matter should be pursued. See Rule 1.2. The lawyer's duty to act with reasonable diligence does not require the use of offensive tactics or preclude the treating of all persons involved in the legal process with courtesy and respect.

[2] A lawyer's work load must be controlled so that each matter can be handled competently.

[3] Perhaps no professional shortcoming is more widely resented than procrastination. A client's interests often can be adversely affected by the passage of time or the change of conditions; in extreme instances, as when a lawyer overlooks a statute of limitations, the client's legal position may be destroyed. Even when the client's interests are not affected in substance, however, unreasonable delay can cause a client needless anxiety and undermine confidence in the lawyer's trustworthiness. A lawyer's duty to act with reasonable promptness, however, does not preclude the lawyer from agreeing to a reasonable request for a postponement that will not prejudice the lawyer's client.

[4] Unless the relationship is terminated as provided in Rule 1.16, a lawyer should carry through to conclusion all matters undertaken for a client. If a lawyer's employment is limited to a specific matter, the

relationship terminates when the matter has been resolved. If a lawyer has served a client over a substantial period in a variety of matters, the client sometimes may assume that the lawyer will continue to serve on a continuing basis unless the lawyer gives notice of withdrawal. Doubt about whether a client-lawyer relationship still exists should be clarified by the lawyer, preferably in writing, so that the client will not mistakenly suppose the lawyer is looking after the client's affairs when the lawyer has ceased to do so. For example, if a lawyer has handled a judicial or administrative proceeding that produced a result adverse to the client and the lawyer and the client have not agreed that the lawyer will handle the matter on appeal, the lawyer must consult with the client about the possibility of appeal before relinquishing responsibility for the matter. See Rule 1.4(a)(2). Whether the lawyer is obligated to prosecute the appeal for the client depends on the scope of the representation the lawyer has agreed to provide to the client. See Rule 1.2.

[5] To prevent neglect of client matters in the event of a sole practitioner's death or disability, the duty of diligence may require that each sole practitioner prepare a plan, in conformity with applicable rules, that designates another competent lawyer to review client files, notify each client of the lawyer's death or disability, and determine whether there is a need for immediate protective action. Cf. Rule 28 of the American Bar Association Model Rules for Lawyer Disciplinary Enforcement (providing for court appointment of a lawyer to inventory files and take other protective action in absence of a plan providing for another lawyer to protect the interests of the clients of a deceased or disabled lawyer).

RULE 1.4 COMMUNICATION

(a)   A lawyer shall:

(1) promptly inform the client of any decision or circumstance with respect to which the client's informed consent, as defined in Rule 1.0(e), is required by these Rules;

(2) reasonably consult with the client about the means by which the client's objectives are to be accomplished;

(3) keep the client reasonably informed about the status of the matter;

(4) promptly comply with reasonable requests for information; and

(5) consult with the client about any relevant limitation on the lawyer's conduct when the lawyer knows that the client expects assistance not permitted by the Rules of Professional Conduct or other law.

(b) A lawyer shall explain a matter to the extent reasonably necessary to permit the client to make informed decisions regarding the representation.

Comment

[1] Reasonable communication between the lawyer and the client is necessary for the client effectively to participate in the representation.

Communicating with Client

[2] If these Rules require that a particular decision about the representation be made by the client, paragraph (a)(1) requires that the lawyer promptly consult with and secure the client's consent prior to taking action unless prior discussions with the client have resolved what action the client wants the lawyer to take. For example, a lawyer who receives from opposing counsel an offer of settlement in a civil controversy or a proffered plea bargain in a criminal case must promptly inform the client of its substance unless the client has previously indicated that the proposal will be acceptable or unacceptable or has authorized the lawyer to accept or to reject the offer. See Rule 1.2(a).

[3] Paragraph (a)(2) requires the lawyer to reasonably consult with the client about the means to be used to accomplish the client's objectives. In some situations—depending on both the importance of the action under consideration and the feasibility of consulting with the client— this duty will require consultation prior to taking action. In other circumstances, such as during a trial when an immediate decision must be made, the exigency of the situation may require the lawyer to act without prior consultation. In such cases the lawyer must nonetheless act reasonably to inform the client of actions the lawyer has taken on the client's behalf. Additionally, paragraph (a)(3) requires that the lawyer keep the client reasonably informed about the status of the matter, such as significant developments affecting the timing or the substance of the representation.

[4] A lawyer's regular communication with clients will minimize the occasions on which a client will need to request information concerning

the representation. When a client makes a reasonable request for information, however, paragraph (a)(4) requires prompt compliance with the request, or if a prompt response is not feasible, that the lawyer, or a member of the lawyer's staff, acknowledge receipt of the request and advise the client when a response may be expected. Client telephone calls should be promptly returned or acknowledged.

Explaining Matters

[5] The client should have sufficient information to participate intelligently in decisions concerning the objectives of the representation and the means by which they are to be pursued, to the extent the client is willing and able to do so. Adequacy of communication depends in part on the kind of advice or assistance that is involved. For example, when there is time to explain a proposal made in a negotiation, the lawyer should review all important provisions with the client before proceeding to an agreement. In litigation a lawyer should explain the general strategy and prospects of success and ordinarily should consult the client on tactics that are likely to result in significant expense or to injure or coerce others. On the other hand, a lawyer ordinarily will not be expected to describe trial or negotiation strategy in detail. The guiding principle is that the lawyer should fulfill reasonable client expectations for information consistent with the duty to act in the client's best interests, and the client's overall requirements as to the character of representation. In certain circumstances, such as when a lawyer asks a client to consent to a representation affected by a conflict of interest, the client must give informed consent, as defined in Rule 1.0(e).

[6] Ordinarily, the information to be provided is that appropriate for a client who is a comprehending and responsible adult. However, fully informing the client according to this standard may be impracticable, for example, where the client is a child or suffers from diminished capacity. See Rule 1.14. When the client is an organization or group, it is often impossible or inappropriate to inform every one of its members about its legal affairs; ordinarily, the lawyer should address communications to the appropriate officials of the organization. See Rule 1.13. Where many routine matters are involved, a system of limited or occasional reporting may be arranged with the client.

Withholding Information

[7] In some circumstances, a lawyer may be justified in delaying transmission of information when the client would be likely to react imprudently to an immediate communication. Thus, a lawyer might withhold a psychiatric diagnosis of a client when the examining psychiatrist indicates that disclosure would harm the client. A lawyer may not withhold information to serve the lawyer's own interest or convenience or the interests or convenience of another person. Rules or court orders governing litigation may provide that information supplied to a lawyer may not be disclosed to the client. Rule 3.4(c) directs compliance with such rules or orders.

RULE 1.6 CONFIDENTIALITY OF INFORMATION

(a) A lawyer shall not reveal information relating to the representation of a client unless the client gives informed consent, the disclosure is impliedly authorized in order to carry out the representation or the disclosure is permitted by paragraph (b).

Comment

[1] This Rule governs the disclosure by a lawyer of information relating to the representation of a client during the lawyer's representation of the client. See Rule 1.18 for the lawyer's duties with respect to information provided to the lawyer by a prospective client, Rule 1.9(c)(2) for the lawyer's duty not to reveal information relating to the lawyer's prior representation of a former client and Rules 1.8(b) and 1.9(c)(1) for the lawyer's duties with respect to the use of such information to the disadvantage of clients and former clients.

[2] A fundamental principle in the client-lawyer relationship is that, in the absence of the client's informed consent, the lawyer must not reveal information relating to the representation. See Rule 1.0(e) for the definition of informed consent. This contributes to the trust that is the hallmark of the client-lawyer relationship. The client is thereby encouraged to seek legal assistance and to communicate fully and frankly with the lawyer even as to embarrassing or legally damaging subject matter. The lawyer needs this information to represent the client effectively and, if necessary, to advise the client to refrain from wrongful conduct. Almost without exception, clients come to lawyers in order to determine their rights and what is, in the complex of laws and regulations, deemed to

be legal and correct. Based upon experience, lawyers know that almost all clients follow the advice given, and the law is upheld.

[3] The principle of client-lawyer confidentiality is given effect by related bodies of law: the attorney-client privilege, the work product doctrine and the rule of confidentiality established in professional ethics. The attorney-client privilege and work product doctrine apply in judicial and other proceedings in which a lawyer may be called as a witness or otherwise required to produce evidence concerning a client. The rule of client-lawyer confidentiality applies in situations other than those where evidence is sought from the lawyer through compulsion of law. The confidentiality rule, for example, applies not only to matters communicated in confidence by the client but also to all information relating to the representation, whatever its source. A lawyer may not disclose such information except as authorized or required by the Rules of Professional Conduct or other law. See also Scope.

[4] Paragraph (a) prohibits a lawyer from revealing information relating to the representation of a client. This prohibition also applies to disclosures by a lawyer that do not in themselves reveal protected information but could reasonably lead to the discovery of such information by a third person. A lawyer's use of a hypothetical to discuss issues relating to the representation is permissible so long as there is no reasonable likelihood that the listener will be able to ascertain the identity of the client or the situation involved.

RULE 3.1 MERITORIOUS CLAIMS AND CONTENTIONS

A lawyer shall not bring or defend a proceeding, or assert or controvert an issue therein, unless there is a basis in law and fact for doing so that is not frivolous, which includes a good faith argument for an extension, modification or reversal of existing law. A lawyer for the defendant in a criminal proceeding, or the respondent in a proceeding that could result in incarceration, may nevertheless so defend the proceeding as to require that every element of the case be established.

Comment

[1] The advocate has a duty to use legal procedure for the fullest benefit of the client's cause, but also a duty not to abuse legal procedure. The law, both procedural and substantive, establishes the limits within which an advocate may proceed. However, the law is not always clear and never is static. Accordingly, in determining the proper scope of

advocacy, account must be taken of the law's ambiguities and potential for change.

[2] The filing of an action or defense or similar action taken for a client is not frivolous merely because the facts have not first been fully substantiated or because the lawyer expects to develop vital evidence only by discovery. What is required of lawyers, however, is that they inform themselves about the facts of their clients' cases and the applicable law and determine that they can make good faith arguments in support of their clients' positions. Such action is not frivolous even though the lawyer believes that the client's position ultimately will not prevail. The action is frivolous, however, if the lawyer is unable either to make a good faith argument on the merits of the action taken or to support the action taken by a good faith argument for an extension, modification or reversal of existing law.

[3] The lawyer's obligations under this Rule are subordinate to federal or state constitutional law that entitles a defendant in a criminal matter to the assistance of counsel in presenting a claim or contention that otherwise would be prohibited by this Rule.

RULE 4.1 TRUTHFULNESS IN STATEMENTS TO OTHERS

In the course of representing a client a lawyer shall not knowingly:

(a) make a false statement of material fact or law to a third person; or

(b) fail to disclose a materials fact when disclosure is necessary to avoid assisting a criminal or fraudulent act by a client, unless disclosure is prohibited by Rule 1.6.

Comment
Misrepresentation

[1] A lawyer is required to be truthful when dealing with others on a client's behalf, but generally has no affirmative duty to inform an opposing party of relevant facts. A misrepresentation can occur if the lawyer incorporates or affirms a statement of another person that the lawyer knows is false. Misrepresentations can also occur by partially true but misleading statements or omissions that are the equivalent of affirmative false statements. For dishonest conduct that does not amount to a false statement or for misrepresentations by a lawyer other than in the course of representing a client, see Rule 8.4.

Statements of Fact

[2] This Rule refers to statements of fact. Whether a particular statement should be regarded as one of fact can depend on the circumstances. Under generally accepted conventions in negotiation, certain types of statements ordinarily are not taken as statements of material fact. Estimates of price or value placed on the subject of a transaction and a party's intentions as to an acceptable settlement of a claim are ordinarily in this category, and so is the existence of an undisclosed principal except where nondisclosure of the principal would constitute fraud. Lawyers should be mindful of their obligations under applicable law to avoid criminal and tortious misrepresentation.

Crime or Fraud by Client

[3] Under Rule 1.2(d), a lawyer is prohibited from counseling or assisting a client in conduct that the lawyer knows is criminal or fraudulent. Paragraph (b) states a specific application of the principle set forth in Rule 1.2(d) and addresses the situation where a client's crime or fraud takes the form of a lie or misrepresentation. Ordinarily, a lawyer can avoid assisting a client's crime or fraud by withdrawing from the representation. Sometimes it may be necessary for the lawyer to give notice of the fact of withdrawal and to disaffirm an opinion, document, affirmation or the like. In extreme cases, substantive law may require a lawyer to disclose information relating to the representation to avoid being deemed to have assisted the client's crime or fraud. If the lawyer can avoid assisting a client's crime or fraud only by disclosing this information, then under paragraph (b) the lawyer is required to do so, unless the disclosure is prohibited by Rule 1.6.

RULE 5.5 UNAUTHORIZED PRACTICE OF LAW; MULTIJURISDICTIONAL PRACTICE OF LAW

(c) A lawyer admitted in another United States jurisdiction, and not disbarred or suspended from practice in any jurisdiction, may provide legal services on a temporary basis in this jurisdiction that:

(1) are undertaken in association with a lawyer who is admitted to practice in this jurisdiction and who actively participates in the matter;

(2) are in or reasonably related to a pending or potential proceeding before a tribunal in this or another jurisdiction, if the lawyer, or a person

the lawyer is assisting, is authorized by law or order to appear in such proceeding or reasonably expects to be so authorized;

(3) are in or reasonably related to a pending or potential arbitration, mediation, or other alternative dispute resolution proceeding in this or another jurisdiction, if the services arise out of or are reasonably related to the lawyer's practice in a jurisdiction in which the lawyer is admitted to practice and are not services for which the forum requires pro hac vice admission; or

(4) are not within paragraphs (c)(2) or (c)(3) and arise out of or are reasonably related to the lawyer's practice in a jurisdiction in which the lawyer is admitted to practice.

Comment

[5] There are occasions in which a lawyer admitted to practice in another United States jurisdiction, and not disbarred or suspended from practice in any jurisdiction, may provide legal services on a temporary basis in this jurisdiction under circumstances that do not create an unreasonable risk to the interests of their clients, the public or the courts. Paragraph (c) identifies four such circumstances. The fact that conduct is not so identified does not imply that the conduct is or is not authorized. With the exception of paragraphs (d)(1) and (d)(2), this Rule does not authorize a lawyer to establish an office or other systematic and continuous presence in this jurisdiction without being admitted to practice generally here.

RULE 8.4 MISCONDUCT

It is professional misconduct for a lawyer to:

(c) engage in conduct involving dishonesty, fraud, deceit or misrepresentation;

(d) engage in conduct that is prejudicial to the administration of justice;

Comment

[3] A lawyer who, in the course of representing a client, knowingly manifests by words or conduct, bias or prejudice based upon race, sex, religion, national origin, disability, age, sexual orientation or socioeconomic status, violates paragraph (d) when such actions are prejudicial to

the administration of justice. Legitimate advocacy respecting the foregoing factors does not violate paragraph (d). A trial judge's finding that peremptory challenges were exercised on a discriminatory basis does not alone establish a violation of this rule.

Appendix O
Federal Rules of Evidence

Rule 408
Compromise and Offers to Compromise

Evidence of (1) furnishing or offering or promising to furnish, or (2) accepting or offering or promising to accept, a valuable consideration in compromising or attempting to compromise a claim which was disputed as to either validity or amount, is not admissible to prove liability for or invalidity of the claim or its amount. Evidence of conduct or statements made in compromise negotiations is likewise not admissible. This rule does not require the exclusion of any evidence otherwise discoverable merely because it is presented in the course of compromise negotiations. This rule also does not require exclusion when the evidence is offered for another purpose, such as proving bias or prejudice of a witness, negativing a contention of undue delay, or proving an effort to obstruct a criminal investigation or prosecution.

APPENDIX P
UNIFORM MEDIATION ACT[1]

Drafted by the

NATIONAL CONFERENCE OF COMMISSIONERS ON
UNIFORM STATE LAWS

and by it

APPROVED AND RECOMMENDED FOR ENACTMENT
IN ALL THE STATES

at its

ANNUAL CONFERENCE
MEETING IN ITS ONE-HUNDRED-AND-TENTH YEAR
WHITE SULPHUR SPRINGS, WEST VIRGINIA
AUGUST 10–17, 2001

Without Comments

Approved by the American Bar Association
Philadelphia, Pennsylvania, February 4, 2002

Copyright © 2001

By

NATIONAL CONFERENCE OF COMMISSIONERS
ON UNIFORM STATE LAWS

---

1. This material is used with permission by the National Conference of Commissioners on Uniform State Laws.

Copies of this Act with Comments may be obtained from:

NATIONAL CONFERENCE OF COMMISSIONERS
ON UNIFORM STATE LAWS
211 E. Ontario Street, Suite 1300
Chicago, Illinois 60611
312/915-0195
www.nccusl.org

UNIFORM MEDIATION ACT

SECTION 1. TITLE. This [Act] may be cited as the Uniform Mediation Act.

SECTION 2. DEFINITIONS. In this [Act]:

(1) "Mediation" means a process in which a mediator facilitates communication and negotiation between parties to assist them in reaching a voluntary agreement regarding their dispute.

(2) "Mediation communication" means a statement, whether oral or in a record or verbal or nonverbal, that occurs during a mediation or is made for purposes of considering, conducting, participating in, initiating, continuing, or reconvening a mediation or retaining a mediator.

(3) "Mediator" means an individual who conducts a mediation.

(4) "Nonparty participant" means a person, other than a party or mediator, that participates in a mediation.

(5) "Mediation party" means a person that participates in a mediation and whose agreement is necessary to resolve the dispute.

(6) "Person" means an individual, corporation, business trust, estate, trust, partnership, limited liability company, association, joint venture, government; governmental subdivision, agency, or instrumentality; public corporation, or any other legal or commercial entity.

(7) "Proceeding" means:

(A) a judicial, administrative, arbitral, or other adjudicative process, including related pre-hearing and post-hearing motions, conferences, and discovery; or

(B) a legislative hearing or similar process.

(8) "Record" means information that is inscribed on a tangible medium or that is stored in an electronic or other medium and is retrievable in perceivable form.

(9) "Sign" means:

(A) to execute or adopt a tangible symbol with the present intent to authenticate a record; or

(B) to attach or logically associate an electronic symbol, sound, or process to or with a record with the present intent to authenticate a record.

SECTION 3. SCOPE.

(a) Except as otherwise provided in subsection (b) or (c), this [Act] applies to a mediation in which:

(1) the mediation parties are required to mediate by statute or court or administrative agency rule or referred to mediation by a court, administrative agency, or arbitrator;

(2) the mediation parties and the mediator agree to mediate in a record that demonstrates an expectation that mediation communications will be privileged against disclosure; or

(3) the mediation parties use as a mediator an individual who holds himself or herself out as a mediator or the mediation is provided by a person that holds itself out as providing mediation.

(b) The [Act] does not apply to a mediation:

(1) relating to the establishment, negotiation, administration, or termination of a collective bargaining relationship;

(2) relating to a dispute that is pending under or is part of the processes established by a collective bargaining agreement, except that the [Act] applies to a mediation arising out of a dispute that has been filed with an administrative agency or court;

(3) conducted by a judge who might make a ruling on the case; or

(4) conducted under the auspices of:

(A) a primary or secondary school if all the parties are students or

(B) a correctional institution for youths if all the parties are residents of that institution.

(c) If the parties agree in advance in a signed record, or a record of proceeding reflects agreement by the parties, that all or part of a mediation is not privileged, the privileges under Sections 4 through 6 do not apply to the mediation or part agreed upon. However, Sections 4 through 6 apply to a mediation communication made by a person that has not received actual notice of the agreement before the communication is made.

Legislative Note: To the extent that the Act applies to mediations conducted under the authority of a State's courts, State judiciaries should consider enacting conforming court rules.

4. PRIVILEGE AGAINST DISCLOSURE; ADMISSIBILITY; DISCOVERY.

(a) Except as otherwise provided in Section 6, a mediation communication is privileged as provided in subsection (b) and is not subject to discovery or admissible in evidence in a proceeding unless waived or precluded as provided by Section 5.

(b) In a proceeding, the following privileges apply:

(1) A mediation party may refuse to disclose, and may prevent any other person from disclosing, a mediation communication.

(2) A mediator may refuse to disclose a mediation communication, and may prevent any other person from disclosing a mediation communication of the mediator.

(3) A nonparty participant may refuse to disclose, and may prevent any other person from disclosing, a mediation communication of the nonparty participant.

(c) Evidence or information that is otherwise admissible or subject to discovery does not become inadmissible or protected from discovery solely by reason of its disclosure or use in a mediation.

Legislative Note: The Act does not supersede existing state statutes that make mediators incompetent to testify, or that provide for costs and attorney fees to mediators who are wrongfully subpoenaed. See, e.g., Cal. Evid. Code Section 703.5 (West 1994).

5.   WAIVER AND PRECLUSION OF PRIVILEGE.

(a) A privilege under Section 4 may be waived in a record or orally during a proceeding if it is expressly waived by all parties to the mediation and:

(1) in the case of the privilege of a mediator, it is expressly waived by the mediator; and

(2) in the case of the privilege of a nonparty participant, it is expressly waived by the nonparty participant.

(b) A person that discloses or makes a representation about a mediation communication which prejudices another person in a proceeding is precluded from asserting a privilege under Section 4, but only to the extent necessary for the person prejudiced to respond to the representation or disclosure.

(c) A person that intentionally uses a mediation to plan, attempt to commit or commit a crime, or to conceal an ongoing crime or ongoing criminal activity is precluded from asserting a privilege under Section 4.

6.   EXCEPTIONS TO PRIVILEGE.

(a) There is no privilege under Section 4 for a mediation communication that is:

(1) in an agreement evidenced by a record signed by all parties to the agreement;

(2) available to the public under [insert statutory reference to open records act] or made during a session of a mediation which is open, or is required by law to be open, to the public;

(3) a threat or statement of a plan to inflict bodily injury or commit a crime of violence;

(4) intentionally used to plan a crime, attempt to commit or commit a crime, or to conceal an ongoing crime or ongoing criminal activity;

(5) sought or offered to prove or disprove a claim or complaint of professional misconduct or malpractice filed against a mediator;

(6) except as otherwise provided in subsection (c), sought or offered to prove or disprove a claim or complaint of professional misconduct or malpractice filed against a mediation party, nonparty participant, or representative of a party based on conduct occurring during a mediation; or

(7) sought or offered to prove or disprove abuse, neglect, abandonment, or exploitation in a proceeding in which a child or adult protective services agency is a party, unless the

[Alternative A: [State to insert, for example, child or adult protection] case is referred by a court to mediation and a public agency participates.]

[Alternative B: public agency participates in the [State to insert, for example, child or adult protection] mediation].

(b) There is no privilege under Section 4 if a court, administrative agency, or arbitrator finds, after a hearing in camera, that the party seeking discovery or the proponent of the evidence has shown that the evidence is not otherwise available, that there is a need for the evidence that substantially outweighs the interest in protecting confidentiality, and that the mediation communication is sought or offered in:

(1)   a court proceeding involving a felony [or misdemeanor]; or

(2)   except as otherwise provided in subsection (c), a proceeding to prove a claim to rescind or reform or a defense to avoid liability on a contract arising out of the mediation.

(c) A mediator may not be compelled to provide evidence of a mediation communication referred to in subsection (a)(6) or (b)(2).

(d) If a mediation communication is not privileged under subsection (a) or (b), only the portion of the communication necessary for the application of the exception from nondisclosure may be admitted. Admission of evidence under subsection (a) or (b) does not render the evidence, or any other mediation communication, discoverable or admissible for any other purpose.

Legislative Note: If the enacting state does not have an open records act, the following language in paragraph (2) of subsection (a) needs to be deleted: "available to the public under [insert statutory reference to open records act] or".

SECTION 7. PROHIBITED MEDIATOR REPORTS.

(a) Except as required in subsection (b), a mediator may not make a report, assessment, evaluation, recommendation, finding, or other communication regarding a mediation to a court, administrative agency, or other authority that may make a ruling on the dispute that is the subject of the mediation.

(b) A mediator may disclose:

(1) whether the mediation occurred or has terminated, whether a settlement was reached, and attendance;

(2) a mediation communication as permitted under Section 6; or

(3) a mediation communication evidencing abuse, neglect, abandonment, or exploitation of an individual to a public agency responsible for protecting individuals against such mistreatment.

(c) A communication made in violation of subsection (a) may not be considered by a court, administrative agency, or arbitrator.

SECTION 8. CONFIDENTIALITY. Unless subject to the [insert statutory references to open meetings act and open records act], mediation communications are confidential to the extent agreed by the parties or provided by other law or rule of this State.

SECTION 9. MEDIATOR'S DISCLOSURE OF CONFLICTS OF INTEREST; BACKGROUND.

(a) Before accepting a mediation, an individual who is requested to serve as a mediator shall:

(1) make an inquiry that is reasonable under the circumstances to determine whether there are any known facts that a reasonable individual would consider likely to affect the impartiality of the mediator, including a financial or personal interest in the outcome of the mediation and an existing or past relationship with a mediation party or foreseeable participant in the mediation; and

(2) disclose any such known fact to the mediation parties as soon as is practical before accepting a mediation.

(b) If a mediator learns any fact described in subsection (a)(1) after accepting a mediation, the mediator shall disclose it as soon as is practicable.

(c) At the request of a mediation party, an individual who is requested to serve as a mediator shall disclose the mediator's qualifications to mediate a dispute.

(d) A person that violates subsection [(a) or (b)][(a), (b), or (g)] is precluded by the violation from asserting a privilege under Section 4.

(e) Subsections (a), (b), [and] (c), [and] [(g)] do not apply to an individual acting as a judge.

(f) This [Act] does not require that a mediator have a special qualification by background or profession.

[(g) A mediator must be impartial, unless after disclosure of the facts required in subsections (a) and (b) to be disclosed, the parties agree otherwise.]

SECTION 10. PARTICIPATION IN MEDIATION. An attorney or other individual designated by a party may accompany the party to and participate in a mediation. A waiver of participation given before the mediation may be rescinded.

SECTION 11. RELATION TO ELECTRONIC SIGNATURES IN GLOBAL AND NATIONAL COMMERCE ACT. This [Act] modifies, limits, or supersedes the federal Electronic Signatures in Global and National Commerce Act, 15 U.S.C. Section 7001 et seq., but this [Act] does not modify, limit, or supersede Section 101(c) of that Act or authorize electronic delivery of any of the notices described in Section 103(b) of that Act.

SECTION 12. UNIFORMITY OF APPLICATION AND CONSTRUCTION. In applying and construing this [Act], consideration should be given to the need to promote uniformity of the law with respect to its subject matter among States that enact it.

SECTION 13. SEVERABILITY CLAUSE. If any provision of this [Act] or its application to any person or circumstance is held invalid, the invalidity does not affect other provisions or applications of this [Act] which can be given effect without the invalid provision or application, and to this end the provisions of this [Act] are severable.

SECTION 14. EFFECTIVE DATE. This [Act] takes effect. . . .

SECTION 15. REPEALS. The following acts and parts of acts are hereby repealed:

(1)

(2)

(3)

SECTION 16. APPLICATION TO EXISTING AGREEMENTS OR REFERRALS.

(a) This [Act] governs a mediation pursuant to a referral or an agreement to mediate made on or after [the effective date of this [Act]].

(b) On or after [a delayed date], this [Act] governs an agreement to mediate whenever made.

APPENDIX Q

JUDGING CRITERIA REPRESENTATION IN MEDIATION COMPETITION[1]

2004

American Bar Association
Section of Dispute Resolution

Introduction To Judges' Score Sheet

Preface

These criteria should be interpreted to favor problem-solving strategies in the competition. Although practitioners use a diversity of representation approaches, this competition is organized on the premise that the mediators and teams will use a problem-solving approach. The criteria cumulatively enlist judges to assess whether each team consistently and competently followed a problem-solving approach throughout the mediation session. The criteria should be applied to the performance of the attorney/client team—not just the performance of the attorney. By judging the teams based on the same approach to representation, judges will be able to evaluate different teams on a comparable basis.

When these criteria refer to a problem-solving approach, the criteria refer to an approach in which negotiators learn about each other's interests and BATNAs (Best Alternative To A Negotiated Agreement), brainstorm options, and select and shape a solution that meets their interests and, where appropriate, objective standards. When there are apparently conflicting interests (distributive conflicts), teams should first try problem-solving methods before resorting to positional strategies. In contrast, the classically positional negotiator generally starts with firm, extreme and opposite positions and then makes calibrated concessions until both sides are close enough to split the difference.

---

1. Reprinted by permission of the American Bar Association (ABA).

Before the mediation begins, judges should read each side's representation plan. Each representation plan provides essential background information that will help the judges interpret what they are observing. Each plan describes briefly (1) "Responsibility Sharing"—how the team plans to share responsibilities between the attorney and the client in the mediation session; (2) "Allocation Strategy"—why the team chose the particular allocation strategy; (3) "The Team's Interests"—the interests that the team's side plans to advance in the mediation session; (4) "The Other Side's Interests"—the likely interests of the other side; and (5) "Negotiating Strategy"—the team's negotiation strategy in light of the four preceding factors.

Criteria

Please score each criterion on a scale of 1–7, with 1 as the lowest and 7 as the highest.

1= very poor
2= poor
3= somewhat poor
4= adequate
5= somewhat good
6= good
7= very good

Judges' Score Sheet

Round: _____   Team #: _____   Judge/Mediator: _____

1_____	2_____	3_____	4_____	5_____	6_____	7_____
Very Poor	Poor	Somewhat Poor	Adequate	Somewhat Good	Good	Very Good

CRITERIA	SCORE (1–7)
Presentation of Case in Opening Statements and Throughout • Presented facts and law in a way that could be heard productively by other side. • Offered proposals in a way that reflected careful planning and skillful implementation. • Accurately assessed and discussed litigation benefits and risks, as well as other consequences of failing to reach settlement (in joint session and/or caucus).	
Teamwork Between Attorney and Client (Both attorney and client will participate in session) • Effectively divided responsibilities in light of client's strengths and vulnerabilities. • Communicated effectively with each other. • Worked together as a coordinated team. • Attorney ensured that client was able to make informed choice about settlement possibilities.	
Problem-Solving Relationship Building • Established a problem-solving relationship with other side, if possible. • Recognized other side's interests and tried to satisfy them when possible given client's interests. • Took initiatives to convert other side into problem-solvers.	
Information Gathering and Communications with Other Side • Used active listening skills to promote communications. • Used appropriate questioning techniques to gather information. • Tested assumptions and collected necessary information at appropriate times.	
Generating and Selecting Creative Options • Generated range of legal and non-legal options to meet client's interests, as well as interests of other side. • Evaluated and selected options based on interests and, where appropriate, objective criteria. • Actively encouraged the development of creative ideas. • Effectively managed distributive features of dispute (effectively bridged any final gaps).	

1_____	2_____	3_____	4_____	5_____	6_____	7_____
Very Poor	Poor	Somewhat Poor	Adequate	Somewhat Good	Good	Very Good

CRITERIA	Score (1–7)
Using Opportunities in the Mediation Process • Responded appropriately to the mediator's style. • Used power of mediator over process to help break impasses and move toward resolution. • Chose intelligently whether and when to use a caucus; if caucus used, used caucus effectively. • Responded appropriately to developments that occurred during mediation, especially new information and unforeseen moves by other side.	
Advocating Client's Interests – PART A • Understood and advanced client's legal and non-legal interests throughout the mediation process.	
Advocating Client's Interests – PART B • Did not sacrifice client's interests in order to be collaborative. • Did not sacrifice client's interests in order to seek competitive advantage.	
Self-Analysis of the Team's Skills – (Mediator is not Present During Self-Analysis) Students should begin the 10-minute period of team self-analysis by answering the following questions: *(1) In reflecting upon the entire mediation, what specific problem-solving strategies did your team do well?* *(2) Also, in what areas did you experience difficulties and what would you do differently next time when facing a similar situation?* Based on this team's answer, how adequately did it learn from its experiences in this mediation exercise?	
Self-Analysis of Outcome – (Mediator is Not Present During Self-Analysis) Students should continue the 10-minute period of team self-analysis by answering the following question: *How well did the outcome advance your client's interests as presented in the written representation plan?* Students should continue the 10-minute period of team self-analysis by answering the following question: How well did the outcome advance your client's interests as presented in the written representation plan?	
RULE 10 – TIME PENALTY: Deduct up to 5 points if the team continually abused the time limits.	
RULE 14 – FAILURE TO STAY WITHIN THE RECORD PENALTY: Deduct up to 5 points if the team strayed from the record as prohibited in the Rules.	
RULE 18 – ANONYMITY PENALTY: Deduct up to 5 points if the team violated the rule prohibiting identification of school.	

CRITERIA	SCORE 1–7
GENERAL PENALTY: Deduct up to 5 points if the team violated the Rule other than 10, 14, or 18.	
Total Team Score:	
Please designate this team as Win or Lose, in accordance with Rule 11:	**Win Lose** (circle one)

INDEX